Analyzing the Relationship between Corporate Social Responsibility and Foreign Direct Investment

Marianne Ojo
North West University, South Africa

A volume in the Advances in Business Strategy and Competitive Advantage (ABSCA) Book Series

BUSINESS SCIENCE Reference
An Imprint of IGI Global

Published in the United States of America by
Business Science Reference (an imprint of IGI Global)
701 E. Chocolate Avenue
Hershey PA, USA 17033
Tel: 717-533-8845
Fax: 717-533-8661
E-mail: cust@igi-global.com
Web site: http://www.igi-global.com

Library of Congress Cataloging-in-Publication Data

Names: Ojo, Marianne, editor.
Title: Analyzing the relationship between corporate social responsibility and foreign direct investment / Marianne Ojo, editor.
Description: Hershey : Business Science Reference, 2016. | Includes bibliographical references and index.
Identifiers: LCCN 2016006119| ISBN 9781522503057 (hardcover) | ISBN 9781522503064 (ebook)
Subjects: LCSH: Social responsibility of business. | Investments, Foreign. | Investments, Foreign--Developing countries. | Banks and banking.
Classification: LCC HD60 .A4195 2016 | DDC 658.4/08--dc23 LC record available at http://lccn.loc.gov/2016006119

This book is published in the IGI Global book series Advances in Business Strategy and Competitive Advantage (ABSCA) (ISSN: 2327-3429; eISSN: 2327-3437)

British Cataloguing in Publication Data
A Cataloguing in Publication record for this book is available from the British Library.

Advances in Business Strategy and Competitive Advantage (ABSCA) Book Series

Patricia Ordóñez de Pablos
Universidad de Oviedo, Spain

ISSN: 2327-3429
EISSN: 2327-3437

Mission

Business entities are constantly seeking new ways through which to gain advantage over their competitors and strengthen their position within the business environment. With competition at an all-time high due to technological advancements allowing for competition on a global scale, firms continue to seek new ways through which to improve and strengthen their business processes, procedures, and profitability.

The **Advances in Business Strategy and Competitive Advantage (ABSCA) Book Series** is a timely series responding to the high demand for state-of-the-art research on how business strategies are created, implemented and re-designed to meet the demands of globalized competitive markets. With a focus on local and global challenges, business opportunities and the needs of society, the **ABSCA** encourages scientific discourse on doing business and managing information technologies for the creation of sustainable competitive advantage.

Coverage

- Joint Ventures
- Strategy Performance Management
- Value Chain
- Ethics and Business Strategy
- Foreign Investment Decision Process
- Small and Medium Enterprises
- Globalization
- Economies of Scale
- Cost Leadership Strategy
- Outsourcing

IGI Global is currently accepting manuscripts for publication within this series. To submit a proposal for a volume in this series, please contact our Acquisition Editors at Acquisitions@igi-global.com or visit: http://www.igi-global.com/publish/.

The Advances in Business Strategy and Competitive Advantage (ABSCA) Book Series (ISSN 2327-3429) is published by IGI Global, 701 E. Chocolate Avenue, Hershey, PA 17033-1240, USA, www.igi-global.com. This series is composed of titles available for purchase individually; each title is edited to be contextually exclusive from any other title within the series. For pricing and ordering information please visit http://www.igi-global.com/book-series/advances-business-strategy-competitive-advantage/73672. Postmaster: Send all address changes to above address.

Titles in this Series

For a list of additional titles in this series, please visit: www.igi-global.com

Handbook of Research on Driving Competitive Advantage through Sustainable, Lean, and Disruptive Innovation
Latif Al-Hakim (University of Southern Queensland, Australia) Xiaobo Wu (Zhejiang University, China) Andy Koronios (University of South Australia, Australia) and Yongyi Shou (Zhejiang University, China)
Business Science Reference • copyright 2016 • 743pp • H/C (ISBN: 9781522501350) • US $365.00 (our price)

Ethical and Social Perspectives on Global Business Interaction in Emerging Markets
Minwir Al-Shammari (University of Bahrain, Bahrain) and Hatem Masri (University of Bahrain, Bahrain)
Business Science Reference • copyright 2016 • 372pp • H/C (ISBN: 9781466698642) • US $185.00 (our price)

Strategic Approaches to Successful Crowdfunding
Djamchid Assadi (Burgundy School of Business, France)
Business Science Reference • copyright 2016 • 378pp • H/C (ISBN: 9781466696044) • US $205.00 (our price)

Handbook of Research on Entrepreneurship in the Contemporary Knowledge-Based Global Economy
Neeta Baporikar (University of Pune, India)
Business Science Reference • copyright 2016 • 607pp • H/C (ISBN: 9781466687981) • US $345.00 (our price)

Competitive Strategies for Academic Entrepreneurship Commercialization of Research-Based Products
Anna Szopa (Jagiellonian University, Poland) Waldemar Karwowski (University of Central Florida, USA) and David Barbe (University of Maryland, College Park, USA)
Business Science Reference • copyright 2015 • 317pp • H/C (ISBN: 9781466684874) • US $195.00 (our price)

Incorporating Business Models and Strategies into Social Entrepreneurship
Ziska Fields (University of KwaZulu-Natal, South Africa)
Business Science Reference • copyright 2016 • 362pp • H/C (ISBN: 9781466687486) • US $190.00 (our price)

Technological Solutions for Sustainable Business Practice in Asia
Patricia Ordóñez de Pablos (Universidad de Oviedo, Spain)
Business Science Reference • copyright 2015 • 375pp • H/C (ISBN: 9781466684621) • US $200.00 (our price)

Handbook of Research on Global Competitive Advantage through Innovation and Entrepreneurship
Luís M. Carmo Farinha (Polytechnic Institute of Castelo Branco & NECE – Research Unit, Portugal) João J. M. Ferreira (University of Beira Interior & NECE – Research Unit, Portugal) Helen Lawton Smith (Birkbeck, University of London & Oxfordshire Economic Observatory, Oxford University, UK) and Sharmistha Bagchi-Sen (State University of New York – Buffalo, Buffalo, NY, USA)
Business Science Reference • copyright 2015 • 780pp • H/C (ISBN: 9781466683488) • US $375.00 (our price)

IGI GLOBAL
DISSEMINATOR OF KNOWLEDGE
www.igi-global.com

701 E. Chocolate Ave., Hershey, PA 17033
Order online at www.igi-global.com or call 717-533-8845 x100
To place a standing order for titles released in this series, contact: cust@igi-global.com
Mon-Fri 8:00 am - 5:00 pm (est) or fax 24 hours a day 717-533-8661

Life, like any other journey, is filled with obstacles and miracles.
How we choose to embrace life's "wonders",
and how we react to such hindrances as disappointments, distractions, betrayals or set-backs,
not only demonstrates the memories or legacies we choose to leave,
but also serves as a signature and footprint that may impact other lives.

Wonders in the form of unmerited and priceless gifts of love, understanding, and reciprocal or non-reciprocal attributes which appear at various phases – all not evidently aimed at pushing us through difficult phases at the time, and whilst not even appearing to be extraordinary – and merely posing as simple acts of kindness, eventually magnifying their significance and even growing to become pivotal aspects and fundamentals which shape our paths.

This volume is particularly dedicated to life's miracles – and all those who have assisted not only in facilitating the dreams of others, but have also as a result, continued to play an enduring role in the lives of those who succeed their legacies. Angels appear in different forms – and whilst some choose to live, or remain amongst ordinary people, some have left to continue life as "real angels" - appearing, once every while in different forms – visiting or being sent through the most unimaginable means and gifts. And the most wonderful gift of love – the main essence of life and survival for many. Love appreciated and never under-estimated is twice as fulfilling – and in appreciation of all those who have supported life's endeavors and objectives through other acts of kindness and compassion – particularly those endeavors aimed at making positive contributions, my gratitude is extended to such. I would also like to thank my most enduring angel of all – my mother.

Un Ange Frappe (Encore) A La Porte…and "Florence" means so much more than just a wonderful town and a nursing role model (Florence Nightingale), whose contribution to nursing and affection continues to impact lives and future generations to come…A lesson for humanity - in nature and culture.

Editorial Advisory Board

Table of Contents

Detailed Table of Contents

As well as highlighting the importance of corporate governance mechanisms such as audits in facilitating Corporate Social Responsibility objectives and Foreign Direct Investment – where corporate social objectives are not unduly compromised, this chapter applies the political economic theory that emphasizes social relations aspects of professional activity rather than economic forces alone. In a case study format where qualitative data was gathered mainly from primary and secondary source materials, the study found that the function of auditing in the Malaysian society in most cases is devoid of any essence of mission; instead it is created, shaped and changed by the pressures which give rise to its development over time. The largely insignificant role that it serves is intertwined within the contexts in which it operates. Furthermore, chapter is aimed at highlighting the importance and role of external audits – particularly in the aftermath of the 2008/09 global Financial Crisis.

Should regulatory incentives which incorporate the lowering of environmental and labor standards, generate life threatening and environmental repercussions, as well as those resulting in moral hazard and excessive risk taking levels, be encouraged? This chapter not only investigates whether central bank independence is positively correlated with inflation, but also highlights other variables which could impact the relationship between Corporate Social Responsibility and Foreign Direct Investment. It will highlight why a continuous need for updating of data is necessary given the inability to capture data specific variables and why the introduction of complementary standards would serve to bolster measures aimed at promoting financial stability and encouraging investors – rather than incentives aimed at diluting such standards. In so doing contributes to previous and current literature on the topic – by way of reference to investigations and studies which have revealed concerns in the ability to adequately capture data – particularly in light of the recent 2008/2009 Financial Crisis.

If audits serve as formidable internal monitoring tools which facilitate corporate governance, and Corporate Social Responsibility has been proven to serve as "an extension of corporate governance", as well as a signaling device, are both tools not instrumental in promoting Foreign Direct Investment? Through an analysis and evaluation of the literature relating to audits and Corporate Social Responsibility, this chapter aims to investigate the above claim and question on how Corporate Social Responsibility, as "an extension of corporate governance", as well as a signaling mechanism, could facilitate and promote Foreign Direct Investment.

In accounting for the gaps in the literature between the period 2011 and 2016, more recent literature – particularly empirical related studies on the topic have been consulted to consolidate on the paper "Foreign Direct Investment in China: Its Sectoral and Aggregate Impact on Economic Growth". As highlighted by Wei, it is important to recognize and acknowledge that the relationship between FDI and employment is affected by many variables, such as growth of the national population, increased exports, and growth of the domestic economy. Furthermore, as illustrated by Iamsiraroj and Doucouliagos, whilst positive and negative effects may be demonstrated in relation to economic growth, in some countries, no effects can be deduced as regards the relationship between economic growth and FDI in certain other countries. This chapter also aims to accentuate the need for greater focus on environmental issues - as well as poverty alleviation - than is currently the case within the sphere and framework of Carroll's pyramid of Corporate Social Responsibility.

Corporate Social Responsibility necessitates effective engagement of stakeholders and investors – both at local and international levels. As well as demonstrating that changes in perceptions do not warrant an internship program as a means of reducing the audit expectations gap as misperceptions are still found

Foreword

There has been a rise in the volume and dispersal of Foreign Direct Investment (FDI) since the nineties. Although the largest source as well as recipient for foreign inflows continues to be the US, and FDI is concentrated in the advanced economies, the share of developing countries has gone up. This period of high FDI flows has also seen the emergence of a strong focus on Corporate Social Responsibility (CSR), and given rise to a literature on the interaction between CSR and FDI. When firms are venturing into multiple destinations, sometimes with very different cultures, CSR may be a strategy that helps business to fit into a new environment. A large amount of work on the altruistic motive in economics has also increased interest on CSR as a topic (Schmitz & Schrader, 2015). An interesting question is whether intrinsic responsibility to stakeholders drives CSR or do firms derive some pecuniary benefit from it? This timely volume is well-posed to address many important questions in this area.

This volume aims to provide better knowledge and understanding of the relationship between CSR and FDI from a multidisciplinary perspective which includes the perspectives of both developing and developed countries, although the former especially needs to be re-evaluated.

It seeks to explore models of extended corporate governance whereby those in control of the firm have fiduciary duties to all the firm's stakeholders in addition to such duties towards the owners (principals) of the firm, and how these can be fulfilled.

Responsibilities to much wider stakeholders, including all those whose lives are likely to be impacted by the firm's activities, can come from institutional, legal, social, political and environmental structures in addition to intrinsic preferences. The volume aims to explore innovation, entrepreneurship, and other means whereby CSR can become a more effective tool for promoting worthy causes, meeting obligations to the ecosystem and to wider stakeholders. The engagement of these stakeholders, could itself serve as a possible corporate governance tool mitigating asymmetric information between the principal and the agent. Contracts have to be incomplete because of the lack of predictability and uncertainties concerning who is likely to be affected as a result of a firm's actions. This gives a role for CSR to protect wider stakeholders.

This does not, however, mitigate the need for a competitive market environment with optimal regulations. By facilitating transparency and disclosure, it would help create the trust, confidence necessary to attract investors who could foster growth and development.

Goyal (2006) illustrates some major issues. CSR can work as a form of signaling for unknown firms entering new countries. Multinational firms have often contributed to local communities. This improves labor relations, and expands their customer base. Over time, it improves the quality of the resources they can draw upon, and therefore contributes directly to their competitive edge. Alliances with NGOs and with community institutions expand the resources they can command to meet their own targets. Sharing management practices improves local efficiency and spreads better standards. Active collaboration with community associations helps a firm leverage its assets and identify business opportunities. As corporates adopt villages, sponsor education and training, improve the environment and infrastructure, social capital rises and raises productivity. Domestic consumers, employees, and shareholders would reward an entering firm if it demonstrated social responsibility, which allayed fears that foreign firms intend to exploit resources and poor environmental standards, to harm the ecosystem.

Even if the majority of firms are inclined towards cooperation, there are always others who want to free ride. Similarly, countries are competing keenly to attract foreign firms, giving them attractive conditions. Even so, excessive tax or excess transfers by firms can still cause a Prisoner's Dilemma structure to the payoffs, resulting in an inefficient Nash equilibrium. The Prisoner's Dilemma is an example of a collective action failure, where purely self-interested action that attempts to maximize own returns, leads to an outcome, where all are worse off.

Although the country prefers a cooperative strategy, it opts for a non-cooperative one if that is the dominating strategy for the firm. But signalling expenditure can change the payoffs to the firm, so that cooperation becomes its dominant strategy. A cooperative firm has a longer-term commitment to a business plan, which gives it the capacity to design credible signals of its type, since it is then willing to amortize its signalling expenditure over a longer period. A lower discount rate or more weight on future payoffs contributes to this capacity. CSR allows the accommodating firm to reveal its type, making cooperation the equilibrium outcome. The game differs from standard models since signalling changes payoffs. Signalling expenditures, therefore, are productive, unlike in labor signalling models where their only contribution is to signal quality. Signalling is not a purely wasteful consequence of asymmetric information. It is not a tax imposed on foreign firms, but a voluntary contribution that improves profits.

A unique separating equilibrium can be shown to exist where only cooperative firms signal. But a pooling equilibrium, with all firms making positive signalling expenditure, becomes more likely when the proportion of cooperative firms is high, when growth is higher, and as rewards from social responsibility rise. Social capital increases with the number of contributing firms. Therefore, as more firms undertake such activities, the rewards to these activities rise.

Cooperative firms will always signal, as long as taxation is below a critical level. Others will make positive signalling expenditure only in the pooling equilibrium. A pooling equilibrium can establish CSR as a social norm. It can also be understood as changing preferences towards altruism.

The chapters in the book ably expand on these issues as they take up topics such as auditing, NGOs, regulation, innovation, stakeholders, growth, sustainable development, and inflation, all in the context of CSR and FDI.

Ashima Goyal
Indira Ghandi Institute of Development Research, India

Ashima Goyal *is the first Professor P.B. Brahmananda Memorial Research Grant Award for the year 2010-11 for a study on "History of Monetary Policy in India since Independence". She was presented with the 'Award for Excellence' in recognition of outstanding contribution in Economics, given by the FICCI Ladies Organization as part of their Silver Jubilee celebrations, 28 April 2009. She was also selected as one of four most powerful women in economics, a thought leader, by the editorial team across Business Today, in its Women's Special issue -The Most Powerful Women in Business, Oct. 19, 2008; profiled in India Today (Woman), October 20, 2008. The following also constitute some of her notable achievements: Awarded the Fulbright Senior Research Fellowship over September 2004-April 2005 at the Claremont Graduate University, USA; Second prize for* *the best research on Governance and Development, in the Global Development Network, second Annual Awards Competition, GDN2001, Rio de Janeiro; First prize for the best research on Gender and Development, in the Global Development Network, first Annual Awards Competition, GDN2000, Tokyo, Her fields of interest include Open economy macroeconomics, international finance, financial markets and regulation, institutions and development; General research agenda: Analysis of emerging markets in an institutional context; Current research: Monetary policy and markets, fiscal and monetary policies, financial stability, wages and labour markets, inflation, growth and governance, pro-growth incentive structures.*

REFERENCES

Goyal, A. (2006). Corporate social responsibility as a signaling device for FDI. *International Journal of the Economics of Business*, *13*(1), 145–163. doi:10.1080/13571510500520077

Schmitz, J., & Schrader, J. (2015). Corporate social responsibility: A microeconomic review of the literature. *Journal of Economic Surveys*, *29*(1), 27–45. doi:10.1111/joes.12043

Preface

Corporate Social Responsibility necessitates effective engagement of stakeholders and investors – both at local and international levels. Where Corporate Social Responsibilities are fulfilled, and responsibilities and goals within the sphere of Carroll's pyramid of Corporate Social Responsibility are realized, such that the engagement of stakeholders is facilitated primarily through legal and ethical responsibilities, and ultimately through economic and philanthropic responsibilities then Foreign Direct Investment is expected to yield the benefits which accrue to the economy as well those which should materialize through formidable corporate social responsibility reporting.

Whilst Corporate Social Responsibility is considered to be generally used as "an umbrella term to describe the complex and multifaceted relationships between business and society and to account for the economic, social and environmental impacts of business activity," another definition which incorporates the role of corporate governance, regards corporate social responsibility as:

- A model of extended corporate governance whereby those in control of the firm have responsibilities that range from the fulfilment of their fiduciary duties owed towards the owners (principal), to the fulfilment of analogous fiduciary duties owed towards all the firm's stakeholders (Sacconi, 2004).

In this sense, a distinction can be drawn between the traditional principal agent theory which involves a narrower range of stakeholders and the stakeholder theory which embraces, not just those stakeholders with direct stakes, but also those whose lives are likely to be impacted by the firm's activities particularly with respect to social, economic and environmental consequences. Given the uncertainty and unpredictability of such consequences, the topic of incomplete contracts and their role in the stakeholder theory model becomes apparent.

It is precisely because of the lack of predictability and uncertainties concerning who is likely to be affected as a result of the firm or enterprise's actions, particularly in unforeseen circumstances based on longer term future occurrences, that contingencies need to be provided for in such contracts.

A financial environment which operates with the optimal level of regulatory requirements, which are crucial in facilitating a business environment built on trust, confidence – such that investors are able to rely on information being generated by the management and directors of an enterprise or business, as well as an environment which facilitates transparency, disclosure, should generally constitute incentives for investors to be attracted to such an environment. Further, as rightly, indicated in OECD Guidelines, a competitive market environment, should also serve as an engine which fosters growth and development.

Why is it then the case that foreign direct investment in certain jurisdictions does not necessarily translate to propellers of growth and development in such jurisdictions – whether these are developed, emerging or developing economies?

One plausible reason can only be that certain jurisdictions have failed to consider the benefits of fully implementing or complying with regulatory, environmental or ethical standards, or are encouraging investment incentives which whilst aimed at encouraging growth and development, are not necessarily facilitating the generation of benefits which full implementation of certain regulatory and ethical standards would have facilitated.

This volume is aimed at contributing to knowledge and providing a better understanding of the relationship between corporate social responsibility and foreign direct investment, as well as variables which operate within the framework of such a relationship, from a multidisciplinary perspective as well as the perspectives of developing and developed countries.

Furthermore, the volume seeks to highlight why a redress in the focus of Corporate Social Responsibility, as regards developing countries particularly, needs to be re-evaluated. Through an incorporation of the role of corporate governance, the importance and significance of innovation and entrepreneurship, the volume aims to recommend means whereby Corporate Social Responsibility, hereinafter referred to as CSR, can serve as a more effective tool for promoting worthy causes, and ensuring that obligations to the ecosystem and wider stakeholders, are realized.

By way of reference to corporate collapses which have severely and adversely impacted the lives of many "uninsured" stakeholders, particularly in developed countries, the volume also aims to address how the fulfilment of obligations and commitments to such stakeholders, can be secured.

Objectives of this volume include the following: 1) To investigate the relationship between Corporate Social Responsibility and Foreign Direct Investment as well as the causes attributed to a focus on variables and factors such as economic, political, social and environmental considerations. 2) To incorporate an interdisciplinary based approach on the topic, one which would recommend and provide a possible model to complement present approaches to Corporate Social Responsibility. 3) To investigate the role and impact of Foreign Direct Investment on CSR in developing and developed countries. 4) To investigate means whereby the audit expectations gap can be mitigated through CSR.

Corporate Social Responsibility is not only assuming ever greater significance in corporate governance owing to the devastating impact of corporate collapses on the lives of countless uninsured and unprotected stakeholders, but also because of its potential to limit possible devastating consequences to the ecosystem.

Further, the engagement of stakeholders, and particularly, wider stakeholders, could serve as a possible corporate governance tool and avenue, not only in the mitigation of asymmetric information between the principal and agent, but in also mitigating the audit expectations gap.

Ultimately, the aim and objective of this publication is to provide an inter-disciplinary response which would not only benefit the fields of accounting, economics, law and finance, but which would also encourage and pave way for other inter and multidisciplinary approaches that would contribute immensely in generating innovative and revolutionary solutions to fields of research.

Audit and Accounting has continued to feature prominently - in the recent Financial Crisis, as well as corporate collapses. Audit quality has consequences for corporations as well as investors, since audits serve as vital signaling mechanisms which convey sensitive information to the financial markets and investors alike.

The need to give greater consideration, account for and incorporate environmental considerations and poverty alleviating objectives in the pyramid of Corporate Social Responsibility (Carroll's pyramid of CSR) is highlighted under this section – with a need for an accentuation of environmental and poverty alleviating objectives – as illustrated in this volume.

In line with the main themes of this volume, namely, the need for greater focus on poverty alleviation as a principal and core issue which should feature exclusively within the Corporate Social Responsibility model, as well as the appropriateness of encouraging regulatory incentives as a means of promoting Foreign Direct Investment, the introductory chapter kicks off by highlighting why legal objectives and ethical codes, within the framework and hierarchy accorded under the Carroll's pyramid of Corporate Social Responsibility, should command greater priority and focus, than is currently the case.

The extent to which environmental considerations are gradually influencing economic objectives is reflected under this section – as evidenced by the recent decision by the United States to reject the XL Pipeline Project.

Further the volume also seeks to illustrate the increased influence of environmental, legal, ethical and poverty alleviating considerations within the framework of Corporate Social Responsibility, the need to incorporate and account for these considerations within the CSR model – as well as highlight why such considerations, in addition to macro-economic factors and policies, also have an impact on Foreign Direct Investment.

As well as highlighting the need for greater environmental considerations, Chapter 2, "The Importance of National, Regional Laws and Globally Enforceable International Agreements: The Case of Port Talbot and the XL Pipeline Project," illustrates and consolidates on the understanding of why institutional, legal, social, political and environmental structures constitute some of the factors which may impact a firm's responsibilities to much wider stakeholders, and particularly its commitment to ensuring that its activities do not adversely impact the ecosystem in which it operates. Further, the chapter highlights the importance of value creation - as well as expands on the role of Corporate Social Responsibility in facilitating compliance with legal codes, standards and ethics, as a means of facilitating broader objectives aimed at complying and abiding by environmental standards, international agreements and obligations. Could better communication between management and stakeholders have mitigated current problems at Port Talbot? To what extent were the information asymmetries which existed between the management and stakeholders and why could it have taken so long for the extent of daily losses to be revealed?

Chapter 3, "Corporate Social Responsibility as a Tool for Poverty Reduction: Globalization, Corporate Social Responsibility, and Poverty Revisited," highlights and consolidates on why a greater focus is required in respect of the goal of poverty alleviation, than is presently represented within the framework and sphere of the Corporate Social Responsibility model. The chapter also highlights and expansiates on the limitations of the current CSR model – such limitations as identified by Jenkins as including: "firstly, the way in which CSR prioritizes the 'business case' which, is particularly difficult to make in relation to poverty reduction; the second being traced to the origins of the current CSR movement as a response to criticism of the environmental and social impacts of TNCs – which has led to a definition of CSR largely in negative terms; and thirdly, the centrality of stakeholders within CSR which also limits its usefulness in approaching poverty." The chapter recommends why and how poverty alleviation can assume greater relevance within the framework of Corporate Social Responsibility. Further, it explores why and how wider and more vulnerable stakeholders can be effectively engaged in the model of Corporate Social Responsibility.

As well as focusing on legal, accounting and ethical considerations, Chapter 4, "IFRS Harmonization and Foreign Direct Investment," also incorporates the role of audits and IFRS in fostering Corporate Social Responsibility and Foreign Direct Investment through a demonstration of the role which Corporate Social responsibility could assume as a tool of corporate governance, as well illustrating how audits serve as vital signaling mechanisms which convey sensitive information to the financial markets and investors alike.

Chapter 5, "Corporate Social Responsibility and Foreign Direct Investment: Engaging Innovation, Auditors, and Stakeholders in Corporate Social Responsibility," not only focuses on another key theme and element of this volume, namely, the significance of the engagement of stakeholders, and how this can be effectively implemented, but also highlights and recommends how corporations and multinational enterprises can be effectively engaged in entrepreneurship and innovation, as a means of fulfilling corporate social responsibility goals and objectives. Further, the chapter aims to propose means whereby auditors could fulfil corporate governance roles more effectively. Having drawn vital lessons from past corporate collapses and the devastating effects of these, in terms of unemployment – particularly for uninsured wider stakeholders, a vital goal of an enterprise should also namely, embrace that of facilitating initiatives aimed at job and wealth creation – through entrepreneurship programs which also have a role in determining how directors and executives are remunerated – in addition to corporate governance measures which are currently in place. By way of reference to corporate collapses which have severely and adversely impacted the lives of many "uninsured" stakeholders, this chapter also aims to address how the fulfilment of obligations and commitments to such stakeholders can be secured.

Chapter 6, "Corporate Social Responsibility and Foreign Direct Investment: Legal, Political, and Historical Influences on the Development of Auditing in Malaysia," consolidates on the role of audits and auditing, as well as political influences which have impacted the landscape of Corporate Social Responsibility and Foreign Direct Investment in Malaysia.

As indicated by recent falls and drops in oil and commodity prices, such prices are not simply vulnerable to the economics of supply and demand, but also impacted and dictated by other factors such as political instabilities. Chapter 7 not only investigates the relationship between Foreign Direct Investment and Corporate Social Responsibility, but does so by way of reference to other variables which impact them, namely Central Bank Independence and inflation.

Chapter 9, "Foreign Direct Investment as a Tool for Poverty Alleviation," consolidates on the previous chapter, as well as a very well-known recurring theme of this volume, namely the objective of poverty alleviation. In so doing, it makes reference to how poverty can be addressed through effective implementation of energy reform subsidy programs – particularly with regards to vulnerable stakeholders. It also highlights how stakeholders can be effectively engaged in the Corporate Social Responsibility model as a means of mitigating information asymmetries, information and implementation gaps.

Chapter 10, "Promoting Foreign Direct Investment: Corporate Social Responsibility as a Signaling Device and Tool for Corporate Governance," consolidates on the main themes of the volume by contributing to extant literature on the topic through an illustration and recommendations of how Corporate Social Responsibility could serve as a tool of "extended corporate governance," signaling device, as well as a poverty alleviation tool.

Chapter 11, "Foreign Direct Investment in China: Its Impact on Economic Growth (Revisited)," highlights the role which China has assumed over the years as an emerging economy, its impact of Foreign Direct Investment and global growth and development. In line with recent global developments, it also demonstrates why corporate governance mechanisms such as audits are assuming an ever increasing role in mitigating information gaps resulting from lack of investor confidence and growing mistrust, as well information asymmetries and uncertainties which have the potential to generate shocks, panics and turmoils in financial markets.

Chapter 12, "The Audit Expectations Gap: Mitigating Information Asymmetries and Corporate Social Responsibility as a Signaling Device," explores developments which have taken place within the UK and internationally and contributed to the present state of audit expectations gap, and consolidates on the role of audits as vital mechanisms of corporate governance, as well as recommends and highlights how the audit expectations gap can be mitigated. The chapter seeks to demonstrate why Corporate Social Responsibility endeavors which focus on the mitigation of information asymmetries between the management of an enterprise and local and international investors, also translates to effective corporate social responsibility reporting – in the sense that the engagement of stakeholders - facilitated primarily through legal and ethical responsibilities, ultimately results in the realization of economic and philanthropic responsibilities.

Chapter 13, "Enhancing Regulatory, Financial, Fiscal, and Investment Incentives as a Means of Promoting Foreign Direct Investment," explores how incentives can serve as a means of attracting investment, as well as contributes to the literature on how their incentives could be enhanced.

Whilst survey results, also illustrate that fiscal incentives are the most important type for attracting and benefiting from foreign investment, it is also highlighted that certain scenarios exist whereby investment incentives could be regarded as "compensation for information asymmetries between the investor and the host government, as well as for deficiencies in the investment climate, such as weak infrastructure, underdeveloped human resources and administrative constraints."

In their contribution, "Corporate Social Responsibility: A Manifestation in FDI," which constitutes Chapter 14 of this volume, Patro and Raghunath highlight why they are of the opinion that the concepts of FDI and CSR "have always been double edged tools which either make or break." Further, they add that in such a situation, Indian representatives have a role to play to decide the extent of FDI inflow with economic development at sight. As well as presenting FDI and "Make in India," thus also illustrating how a 48% Growth in FDI Equity Inflows could be registered subsequent to the launch of "Make in India" and how the growth in FDI has been significant following the launch of Make in India initiatives in September 2014, (with 48 percent increase in FDI equity inflows during October 2014 to April 2015), they also accentuate how during the period 2014-15, the country witnessed unprecedented growth of 717 percent, to US $ 40.92 billion of Investment by Foreign Institutional Investors (FIIs).

Chapter 15, "Foreign Direct Investments, Corporate Social Responsibility, and Economic Development: Exploring the Relationship and Mitigating the Expectation Gaps," as highlighted by its author, aims to demonstrate why governments of developing countries must rise up to her responsibilities of infrastructural development, mitigate governance gaps through good governance, combat corrupt and sharp business practices and put in place adequate institutional frameworks and policies to guide and attract foreign activities, and encourage involvement in CSR by corporations – all aimed at not only "making the government to reap the benefits FDI inflows but also promote corporate responsibility and sustainability".

Chapter 16, "Recommendations: Addressing the Imbalances of Corporate Social Responsibility in Developed and Developing Countries," not only aims to recommend means whereby Corporate Social Responsibility can serve as a more effective tool for promoting worthy causes, and ensuring that obligations to the ecosystem and wider stakeholders are facilitated, but also highlight why a redress in the focus of Corporate Social Responsibility, as regards developing countries particularly, needs to be re-evaluated. Further, an alternative model to Carroll's CSR pyramid is recommended.

In following up with the second chapter, which highlights and demonstrates the vital importance and significance of legal objectives, ethical codes and standards, the conclusive section, Chapter 17, "Parliamentary Sovereignty, the Rule of Law, and the Separation of Powers: Involving Other Actors in the Legislative and Judiciary Process," highlights role and significance of legislature in effectively implementing and interpreting those standards and legislation. Furthermore, it highlights why legislature serves as an additional check and accountability mechanism for the judiciary and executive (the Government). Further the chapter contributes to the literature on statutory interpretation by recommending how the forensic expert can be introduced in the judiciary process to facilitate more reliable, relevant and equitable outcomes.

Nothing could be more crucial in future years than a united legislative branch where decisions are reached based on factors which whilst giving consideration to the economic and national interests of the country, also takes into consideration the legacy being left to future generations as a result of environmental matters. In words echoed by outgoing Speaker John Boehner, on the 29th October 2015, "freedom creates possibilities and patience makes it real." Hence amicable and optimal decisions are indeed possible – even if this takes time. Whilst the present decision has the hallmarks and signature of being optimal, a demonstration of its stance may take time before it is amicably and unanimously accepted.

The present steps being taken and the decision can also be lauded on the basis of the need to comply with international agreements, the need to accentuate and demonstrate America's leadership on environmental matters – all well premised and serving as vital foundation for the Paris Climate Summit scheduled for late November/early December 2015. Leadership by example is not only powerful from this respect, but reflects to a greater extent, America's leadership role – as well as its commitment to environmental goals. It is also hoped that many other leading economies will take steps in following this precedent.

Further, the recent keystone XL Pipeline Project decision, by giving thought to wider and broader environmental repercussions, not only sets a very vital example of the legacy that is to be pursued, but also highlights the fact that even where economic benefits are to be derived – particularly in an environment driven by prevailing economic pressures and conditions, such short term beneficial considerations which are aimed at serving as temporary relief measures, may not necessarily warrant devastating environmental or financial consequences which would ensue on the longer term.

Even so, in some cases where pressures attributed to increased borrowings and the justified need to address temporary emergencies - the need for "short term temporary" emergency measures, whilst initially intended to be short term, may drag into longer and more devastating blows for the economy – resulting in broader and far reaching consequences for present and future generations than could ever have been imagined or anticipated.

As highlighted, ultimately, the aim and objective of this publication is to provide an interdisciplinary response which would not only benefit the fields of accounting, economics, law and finance, but which would also encourage and pave way for other inter and multidisciplinary approaches that would contribute immensely in generating innovative and revolutionary solutions to fields of research – particularly those related to Corporate Social Responsibility and Foreign Direct Investment.

Audits and Accounting has continually proven to be a significant field and contributor in the recent Financial Crisis, and corporate collapses. Audit quality has consequences for corporations as well as investors, since audits serve as vital signaling mechanisms which convey sensitive information to the financial markets and investors alike. For these reasons, the role which Corporate Social Responsibility can assume as a model of corporate governance is invaluable.

This volume also contributes to the extant literature by highlighting why a focus on poverty alleviation, as well as entrepreneurship programs which are intended to contribute to wealth and value creation, are necessary as a means of fostering global development and growth, through Corporate Social Responsibility and Foreign Direct Investment – given present economic uncertainties and political instabilities which currently persist around the globe.

As highlighted from the outset, the extent to which environmental considerations are gradually influencing economic objectives is reflected under this section – as evidenced by the recent decision by the United States to reject the XL Pipeline Project.

Elsewhere, consequences of recent global developments, namely, the fall in oil and gas prices are compelling several governments to consider alternative and more economic means of energy production. In the United Kingdom, the British government also announced, in February 2016, its intention to focus on oil and gas reserves in Shetland, Britain's most northerly islands. Over the next ten years, around 150 oil fields face the possibility of being scrapped in the North Sea owing to falling oil prices which make the running of such fields neither economic nor cost-effective. The Shetland, which holds the potential of releasing previously untapped fields, is also expected to provide around 8% of the UK's gas needs in the future.

Plans to facilitate greater exploitation of renewable sources of energy are also on the cards in numerous jurisdictions.

The introductory section will hence commence by highlighting the increased importance of environmental considerations in economic decisions – which ultimately, impact Foreign Direct Investment – as well as corporate social goals and objectives.

Acknowledgment

In acknowledging the Almighty God for His wonderful and continued support, the beauty and wonders of His Creation, the need to respect the sanctity and preservation of the environments with which we have all been blessed, and for which we are all held accountable - some to greater extent than others, this publication and volume is also fondly dedicated to, and commemorates the seventieth birthday of my beloved mum - who for me, and to all who knew her, remains an ultimate role model and embodiment of the ultimate regality.

The publication of this volume would definitely not have been possible without the commitment, teamwork and support of the Project Development and Editorial Team of IGI Global. The editor wishes to express gratitude for the hard work and efforts dedicated towards the quality and product of this publication.

Chapter 5, "Corporate Social Responsibility and Foreign Direct Investment: Engaging Innovation, Auditors, and Stakeholders in Corporate Social Responsibility," is adapted from collaborative work with Professor James (Jim) DiGabriele, "Achieving Amicable Settlements and Possible Reconciliations: The Role of Forensic Accountants in Equitable Distributions." And also many thanks for entrusting me with all his original texts to be incorporated in the original and this chapter.

To my wonderful "General" and incredible gem: "a whole lot of history, we surely do have ... could be the greatest team the world have ever seen...(seriously!)... You and me got a whole lot of history ... So don't let it go – we can surely make some more..."

Many thanks also to the reviewers who have invested much time, as well as expertise in contributing towards the refinement and quality of the volume. Acknowledgements are also to be given to the original publishers and editors of Chapter 11 "Foreign Direct Investment in China: Its Impact on Economic Growth (Revisited)" – The Asian Academic Research Journals (AARJ). This chapter is a radically revised and updated response to the paper that was originally published in 2013 as: "Foreign Direct Investment in China: Its Sectoral and Aggregate Impact on Economic Growth" (AARJSH vol. 1, issue 18, December 2013, ISSN: 2278-859X, first published by Asian Academic Research Associates Journals).

Due acknowledgement is also given to the publishers of the original version of Chapter 12 "Practical Training and the Audit Expectations Gap: The Case of Accounting Undergraduates of Universiti Utara Malaysia", *Journal of Financial Reporting and Accounting*, 2008, vol. 6, issue 1, Emerald Publications.

Finally very many thanks also to all the contributors to this volume for their innovative inputs, original ideas, contributions to the reviews, as well as their investment in generating a high quality volume which it is hoped, will not only contribute to future research practically, as well as theoretically, but will also generate productive results which will make positive contributions to the vital and importance field of Foreign Direct Investment, as well as commitments, increased efforts and more positive attitudes towards improved environmental standards, successful poverty alleviation programs and energy subsidy reforms, all of which are aimed at contributing to global growth and development.

As evidenced by the range and diversity of contributors to this volume, it is hoped that such cooperation and diversity, as illustrated, will also help enlighten about the positive attributes and results that can be generated when global cooperation and collaboration is fostered in the realization of worthwhile objectives which do not only bear regional consequences, but also have far reaching repercussions.

Chapter 1
Investing in the Environment:
A Tale of Three Investments

Marianne Ojo
North-West University, South Africa

INTRODUCTION

Having recently benefited from profits resulting from equity investments – as well as other business ventures, a financial magnate and business enterprise director decided to invest in several jurisdictions. It was the seventies and a huge range of options was presented before the magnate. Furthermore, prevailing environmental and global conditions made investment in certain areas very attractive and profitable at the time.

The first option involved investing in a beautiful island which was located around several other islands which were known for their touristic and natural beauty.

The second option involved another island which also had wonderful landscapes and areas of natural and touristic scenes – however, whose touristic potential had not been fully exploited owing to the availability of, as well as focus on other sources of resource generating income.

The third option involved another jurisdiction whose natural resources were of enviable magnitude – which however, lacked the technology to exploit such resources, and hence, was in need of foreign investment and expertise to maximize the potential of income that could be extracted from such resources. The jurisdiction, although also endowed with areas of natural beauty, had many other priorities and regarded its natural resources as requiring greater focal attention.

The fourth option involved a jurisdiction which was endowed with immense wealth – both in respect of natural resources, as well as touristic attractions. In contrast to the second and third options, no regional or national vulnerabilities to geo-political influences were evident.

The investor decided to commence with negotiations in respect of all options.

DOI: 10.4018/978-1-5225-0305-7.ch001

The response received from the first option was not so favorable – given strict environmental laws which governed the eligibility criteria for foreign investment – as well as other stringent regulations which had to be observed in relation to air and water pollution. Further, the profits which were agreed upon, as compensation to the island for other ventures which were intended to benefit locals, were considered to be uneconomical for the magnate – and as a result, the island authorities decided it was not worth the risk of accepting the offer of investment – when weighed against the resulting losses from damage to the beaches and resulting alterations to the appearance of the island's beautiful landscapes.

The response from the second option was more favorable – however there was a proviso which stated that the investor would have to invest in other sectors as compensation resulting from competitive disadvantage to local competitors. Furthermore, the investor was able to benefit from less stringent environment standards than was the case with the first option.

The third option provided even greater negotiating powers and flexibility for the investor – who not only promised technological and human resource advancement to the jurisdiction, but also regional development in terms of aid for vital local and national infrastructure. As regards, environmental considerations, this was given little attention since technological advancement appeared to constitute greater priority and since social attitudes implied that little appreciation was given to areas of natural beauty or possibilities to develop and exploit such areas of possible natural wonders. Many areas of touristic attractions were located in vicinities which were in need of greater access to tourists – as these areas were not located in the cities. Even though plans were underway to finalize connecting airports, to such areas, the government did not seem particularly keen or interested in the enterprise' offer to collaborate on a "touristic venture". The enterprise was then discouraged from pursuing with negotiations, after having been warned that any funds aimed at developing such projects would be diverted into the wrong channels.

The jurisdiction relating to the fourth option welcomed the investor and the offers provided – on the premises that strict environmental regulations would be observed – whilst contributing to the welfare of the local community. The jurisdiction had greater negotiating power as it already had several options and a longstanding reputation in respect of its touristic and wildlife attraction. Further, it was technologically equipped to maximize the potential of natural resources – and was less susceptible to geopolitical influences and tensions.

The investor weighed all the options and decided to invest in the last three options. Having set the ball rolling, investment commenced and summary reports revealed the following results after one decade:

The second option had generated expected profits for the investor – however, for the jurisdiction which was being invested in, the same could not be said. Even though the jurisdiction, on the whole, benefited from the investment, there were spill-over effects resulting not only from competitive disadvantage to neighboring industries, but also resulting from geo political influences.

As regards the third option, this fared even worse than the second option – particularly in respect of matters relating to environmental considerations, regional and technological disappointments. This was attributed, considerably, to lack of commitment to environmental standards – not only on the part of the investor, but also with regards to the jurisdictional authorities who played little attention to corporate governance practices, rules, regulations or codes of conduct – both in terms of enforcement and compliance. As a result, rather than evidence of visible benefits of foreign direct investment, the jurisdiction appeared to be worse off – aggravated by geo political conflicts and other related influences. Further, it appeared that reported cases new forms of illnesses had plagued communities affected by contaminated water resulting from chemicals and industrial pollution.

In respect of the fourth option, this jurisdiction reaped the greatest rewards both in terms of returns from investment – as well as having retained its environment standards and commitments.

The investor hence, whilst benefiting to a lesser extent from the fourth option, benefited immensely on the whole from all three investing options.

Forty years, after having instigated his negotiations and having commenced investment activities, the investor decided to undertake an inventory on the progress of all the jurisdictions he had initially considered – including the first option – whose jurisdiction had declined his offer.

He visited the island and realized that even given the recent economic slowdown and global pressures, the island had not been affected economically by the global slow down. Further, the island had retained all areas of natural beauty and was still thriving and benefiting from its touristic industry. The island's landscape had been retained to a greater extent – with no apparent construction of industrial areas or unappealing structures in very visible areas.

He also discovered that many of his employees usually went on vacation to this island – and even though he had visited a couple of times, over the years, he had not realized the extent to which the island had developed over the years till he visited exact locations where negotiations had taken place forty years earlier.

In respect of the second option, the investor was not able to visit the enterprise – given the economic pressures and insolvency proceedings which the enterprise currently encountered. Whilst he was updated with reports regarding the sustenance of environmental conditions in the surrounding areas, he was also warned not to visit the area – in view of angry locals who had just received reports that they may face the prospect of losing their jobs. Further he also discovered that owing to competitive disadvantage whose impact had accumulated over the years, and which had resulted to job losses in previous years, that the local community had not developed as had been anticipated. Regional pressures had also contributed to the level of availability of jobs and other sources of income – as well as global economic pressures.

In respect of the third option, the investor – having visited the area, did not recognize the environment which currently existed in comparison to that which welcomed him forty years earlier. In place of vast huge forests which once stood around the industrial site, there were other chemical and industrial areas – with deteriorated living conditions and infrastructures for the local communities.

When he asked the company directors of the firm which had been invested in, for a report on the projects that had been designed to improve locals' living conditions, he discovered that none of these projects had been implemented and that the directors of his firm, as well as those of the firm which had been invested in, had placed greater focus of profits rather than environmental or corporate social matters.

The fourth option proved to be a success story – as it appeared that the jurisdiction had weathered the storms of the global economic crises. In fact, it appeared as though the jurisdiction was located on another planet – immune from all economic turmoil and pressures resulting from the global meltdown. Whilst continuing to serve as a magnet for investors and investing firms, it also benefited from its touristic attractions and areas of natural beauty.

It might be said that all these jurisdictions were presented with investment offers which could have had positive benefits and impacts in these jurisdictions. It can also be said that the choices made by such jurisdictions could not really be criticized since environmental and economic conditions change over time. Hence it is essential to provide for contingencies – since, as evidenced by events which have occurred over the past four decades, global economic conditions have changed considerably over the years. However, current prevailing pressures are indeed no excuse for neglecting greater life changing repercussions resulting from the present neglect of the environment.

Furthermore, whilst some may argue that certain neglects to the environment could be ignored for a while, the detrimental consequences of air and water pollution – over time, will compel many governments to address the problem – particularly where this results in life threatening conditions, greater health, medical costs and burdens for governments, as well as dangerously high levels of smog in many cities.

THE PRINCIPLE OF SELF DETERMINATION

Whilst historically, this has been applied within the context of decolonization, it appears that other contexts relate to the situation in which the Principle can be extended. This particularly being applicable to the context of groups of individuals whose interests and rights – as well as means of livelihood are subjected to external conflicting interests and whose rights cannot be secured or guaranteed by legislation aimed at protecting such interests – as is currently the case with the Kayapo Tribe of the Amazonian Forest.

Whether this can also extend matters involving sovereignty and the EU Referendum, constitutes another topic and volume for discussion.

In the article "The Meaning and Range of the Principle of Self-Determination", a definition attributed to self-determination is as follows (1965:96,97):

"Self-determination to Portugal meant the agreement and consent of the population to a certain political structure, type of State and administrative organization... To Portugal, self-determination meant the consent of the people to a certain structure and political organization. It came about by participation in administration and by participation in political life (also see Report by the Secretary-General: 1963).

Further, the right of self-determination is also considered to "extend to economic, social and cultural matters." (Nawaz, 1965:100).

According to Nawaz (see page 101), the principle of self-determination is considered to "represent an important movement away from the old legal view under which international law rights pertain only to states and governments, and not to groups or individuals." (also see Higgins "The Development of International Law through the Political Organs of the United Nations" 106 (1963).

Given the current plight of the Amazonian Tribes (the Kayapo Tribe), the need for such rights and interests to be represented – as well as secured, such a stance can be justified. Indeed, given the global spotlight and environmental – as well as ethical concerns which are involved, there are plausible justifications for extending the Principle to groups of peoples – even where individual interests are not being represented. This being all the more consequential where global and national interests (even if this is not explicitly admitted) – as well as environmental interests are also involved.

Further, in recognition of other groups whose interests are involved – as is the case with the Kayapo Tribe – particularly in matters of environmental concerns and the need to ensure the protection of such individuals' economic, social and cultural rights – as well as their means of survival, international law and agreements should prioritize the enactment of provisions aimed at securing such interests. Further, the enactment of such legislation is merely a means to the achievement of such goals and objectives. Ensuring effective enforcement and compliance with such legislation and agreements (which should be binding) – by all contracting parties to the agreements, constitutes another task.

And whilst (and if) we neglect the need for environmental considerations - in focusing on economic benefits of job creation, we may come to regret our decisions, and be left to ponder on the consequences of our actions, in the years to come.

REFERENCES

Higgins, R. (1963). The development of international law through the political organs of the United Nations. Oxford Univ. Press.

Nawaz, M. K. (1965). The meaning and range of the principle of self-determination. *Duke Law Journal*, *1965*(1), 82–101. doi:10.2307/1371019

Report by the Secretary-General in Pursuance of the Resolution Adopted by the Security Council at its 1049th Meeting on 31 July 1963 (S15380), U.N. Doc. No. S/5448, at 4 (1963).

Section 1

Pyramid of Corporate Social Responsibility:

The Need for Environmental and Poverty Alleviation Considerations

From economic responsibilities to philanthropic responsibilities, this volume explores the relationship between Corporate Social Responsibility, as exemplified and illustrated through Carroll's pyramid of Corporate Social Responsibility, and how corporate social economic, legal, ethical and philanthropic responsibilities impact Foreign Direct Investment. As well as exploring other economic variables which have an impact on the relationship between Corporate Social Responsibility (CSR) and Foreign Direct Investment (FDI), the volume illustrates why certain elements of responsibilities need to be incorporated, or rather accorded greater priority within the CSR pyramid of responsibility.

Chapter 2
The Importance of National, Regional Laws and Globally Enforceable International Agreements:
The Case of Port Talbot and the XL Pipeline Project

Marianne Ojo
North-West University, South Africa

ABSTRACT

As well as highlighting the importance of effectively engaging different actors and implementing and enforcing rules, principles and standards, at various levels, this chapter contrasts the pyramids of regulatory and punitive strategies, Nestle's pyramid of Shared Value, and Carroll's pyramid of Corporate Social Responsibility in deriving an optimal mix of how regulation should be applied. In deriving such a regulatory mix and recommendation, acknowledgement is accorded to Ayres and Braithwaite's argument that "the greatest challenge facing regulatory design is not to be found at the apex of the pyramid of regulatory strategies – where a variety of well-tested punitive strategies exist – nor at the base of the pyramid, where there is experience of successes and failures of the free market, but that the need for innovation is at the intermediate levels of the pyramid of regulatory strategies. In so doing, the Enforced Self-Regulation Model which involves and incorporates the role of governments in self-regulation, is implemented in recommending desired regulatory designs.

Human beings are part of the environment.
Any harm done to the environment therefore, is harm done to humanity.
Humans are not authorized to abuse (the environment), much less destroy it,
Economic and social exclusion is a complete denial of human fraternity and a grave offense against human rights and the environment.

DOI: 10.4018/978-1-5225-0305-7.ch002

-Address given by Pope Francis before the United Nations General Assembly on the 25th September 2015 following an unprecedented historic speech before the Joint Meeting of the United States Congress on the 24th September 2015, in which environmental issues constituted one of the key issues raised.

FOREIGN DIRECT INVESTMENT AS SHARED VALUE RESOURCE OR THREAT TO THE ENVIRONMENT?

The benefits of international co-operation, which are enhanced through the redress of issues relating to international investment and multi-national enterprises (MNEs), according to the OECD Guidelines, include (OECD, 2011:7):

- Improving the foreign investment climate
- Encouraging positive contribution which MNEs can make to economic, social and environmental progress; and
- Minimizing and resolving difficulties which may arise from the operations of MNEs

Based on general policies stated in the 2011 OECD Guidelines for MNEs (OECD, 2011:19), enterprises are required to take full account of established policies in countries in which they operate – as well as:

- Contribute to economic, environmental and social progress with a view to achieving sustainable development;
- Respect internationally recognized human rights of those affected by their activities;
- Encourage local capacity building through close cooperation with the local community;
- Encourage human capital formation through the creation of employment opportunities;
- Refrain from seeking exemption which is not envisaged in the statutory or regulatory framework related to human rights, environmental, health, safety or other issues;
- Support and uphold corporate governance principles;
- Develop and apply effective self-regulatory practices and management systems which foster an environment and relationship founded on confidence and mutual trust between enterprises and the societies in which they operate;
- Promote awareness of and compliance by workers employed by MNEs as regards company policies;
- Engage with relevant stakeholders in order to promote meaningful opportunities for their views to be taken into account in relation to planning and decision making for projects and other activities that may significantly impact local communities
- Abstain from any improper involvement in local political activities.

In consolidating on the OECD's observations, international cooperation also serves as a means of addressing legal obstacles which emanate from the social, environmental, institutional, political environments and frameworks in which MNEs operate, and which may considerably hinder the maximal realization of corporate social objectives and the above-mentioned contributory benefits of MNEs.

A number of disclosure initiatives have been carried out by companies such as Nestle – as disclosed in its 2013 Summary Report (Nestle, 2013:5) which also provides a highlight of performance indicators, which, in Nestle's view, facilitate the focus for measuring and reporting Creating Shared Value, sustainability, and compliance.

It is frequently the case that many multi national enterprises have their bases of operations in industrial areas which provide the advantages of granting substantial availability of space for such businesses and firms to operate and carry out their activities, as well as limiting air pollution which is typically a feature of many cities. Apart from environmental concerns which may play a role in choosing such points of location, land and space, as well as access and cost to such facilities also play a role for many businesses – local or international. However, such areas are frequently within the vicinity of villages which have restricted access to basics such as water or good water supply – as well as services (which include banking facilities) that can be made readily accessible in larger localities and cities.

In such cases, in addition to firm goals which are aimed at facilitating lower levels of water consumption, lower levels of carbon and other toxic emissions which have potential life threatening consequences, and goals of effectively discharging waste industrial products – such that they present the least threat to the likelihood and means of subsistence of locals,

Goals aimed at facilitating the generation of water resources – and in particular, healthy and safe water supplies, as well as facilities and skills which are aimed at ensuring that such localities are able to sustain and manage those resources effectively, are encouraged. It is well known that the establishment of commendable projects and facilities, on their own, do not suffice as aims of facilitating communal or regional development. A means of ensuring that such projects are sustained on a longer term basis is required. For these reasons, the Nestle initiative and commitment to raising awareness of water access and conservation (see Nestle, 2013:18), as well reports such as those of the United Nations Development Goals Report 2012, which highlights the fact that 783 million people worldwide do not have access to clean water, is to be commended.

As well as highlighting the importance of effectively implementing and enforcing rules, regulations, codes, principles and standards, at regional, national, and international levels, and demonstrating why the engagement of political, social, economic actors is crucial in the aims and objectives of multinational enterprises seeking to realize ultimate and ancillary goals of Corporate Social Responsibility – and primarily that of Shared Value Creation, this chapter is aimed at proposing means whereby regulatory design could be targeted in determining the extent to which mandatory and persuasive rules should apply.

Concepts and Theories Relating to Enforced Self Regulation

Based on the "Creating Shared Value" pyramid in Figure 1 (Nestle, 2014) it is quite easy to comprehend why compliance with laws, business principles and codes of conduct, without doubt, constitutes most fundamental and strategic level of the pyramid since goals and objectives attributed to other levels of the pyramid, namely longer term goals of sustainability, and goasl relating to nutritional, water and rural development, will not be realised to their maximum potential where compliance with regulations and other related laws and principles are not effectively implemented and enforced.

For example, where dangerous emissions and toxic wastes are released into the atmosphere and water drainage channels, the consumption and inhalation of such dangerous chemicals and substances is likely to create greater life threatening conditions than the nutritional initiatives that are sought to be established. In such sense, whilst many multinational enterprises may have commendable goals and objectives, such objectives would be futile where efforts aimed at facilitating compliance with local, national, regional and international standards are not met or effectively implemented and enforced.

Figure 1. Creating shared value pyramid
Source: Nestle in Society "Creating Shared Value (and Meeting Our Commitments) Summary Report 2013, March 2014 at page 4

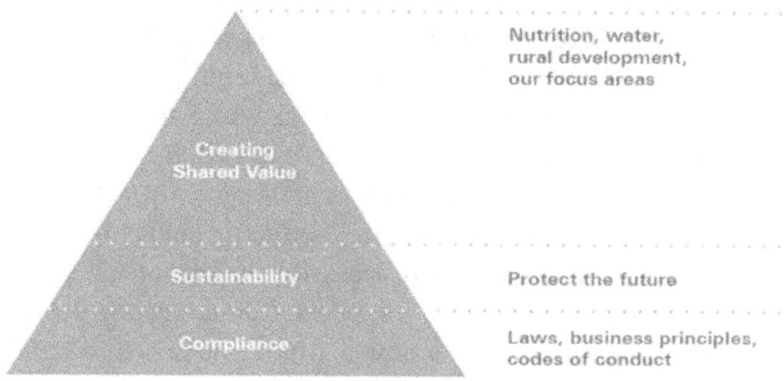

In this regard, it is also important to highlight the importance of effective engagement of stakeholders in the process – particularly the Government, in matters aimed at ensuring that multinational enterprises' principles, codes of ethics and values, are respected. It is also vital to ensure that local, regional and international rules, agreements, codes and standards are effectively complied with.

For this reason, section two, the literature review section, is committed to illustrating how the Government and other economic, social and political actors can be effectively engaged in regulation, compliance, and effective enforcement of rules, principles and standards.

"Optimal governance", it is contended (Esty & Geradin, 2001:31), "requires a flexible mix of:

- Competition and;
- Co-operation between governmental actors, as well as between governmental and non-governmental actors."

According to Ayres and Braithwaite (1995:101), the Enforced Self-Regulation Model is not just:

- A form of responsive regulation whereby negotiation occurs between the state and the individual firms to establish regulations that are particularized to each firm. In the Enforced Self-regulation Model, each firm is required to propose its own regulatory standards in order to avoid harder (and less tailored) standards imposed by the state. This individual firm is "enforced" in two senses:

Under the Enforced Self-Regulation Model put forward by Ayres and Braithwaite, they highlight that the firm is firstly required by the State to do the self-regulation. Second, the privately written rules can be publicly enforced.

Figure 2. Pyramid of regulatory strategies
Source: http://apps.who.int/medicinedocs/en/d/Js2216e/7.9.html

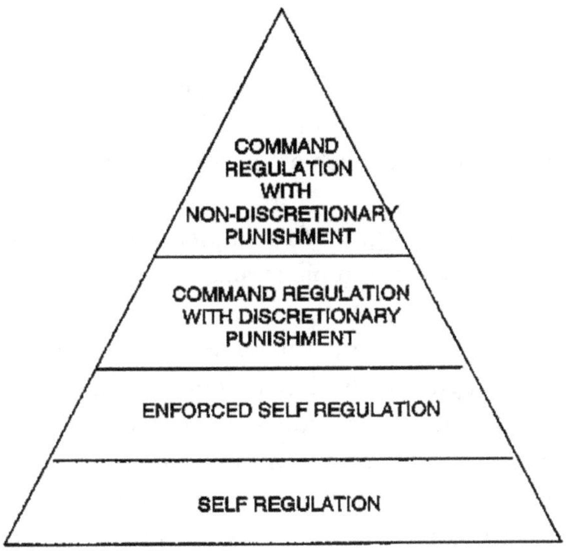

Bridging and Accounting for the Gap Between Carroll's Pyramid of Corporate Social Responsibility (CSR) and the Pyramid of Regulatory and Punitive Strategies

An inverse relationship can be drawn between Carroll's pyramid of Corporate Social Responsibility (CSR) and the pyramid of regulatory and punitive strategies in the sense that:

whereas the base of Carroll's pyramid of CSR denotes greater responsibilities and obligations to comply with economic responsibilities, than is the case with other levels of the pyramid, the base of the pyramid of regulatory and punitive strategies, refers to self-regulation, flexibility of rule application and connotes less severity of punitive measures which are more persuasive (rather than mandatory) in nature. Command and control regulation, applies at the apex of the pyramid, which provides for less flexibility.

In accentuating and consolidating on Ayres and Braithwaite's remarks that the greatest phases of innovation are to be found at the middle and centre of the pyramid (1995:101), this accords with the already discussed argument that the delineation of status and order of importance of director's responsibilities, with particular reference to Carroll's pyramid, is not so clear cut. In certain individual circumstances, economic and legal or ethical responsibilities may carry the same or equal weighting in terms of priority, importance or status - based on the perspectives of the stakeholders. Indeed, the surrounding circumstances or the context in which individual cases are founded, might play an instrumental or influential role in determining the status to be accorded to the various CSR responsibilities as highlighted under Carroll's pyramid.

Whereas economic responsibilities is expected to assume a pivotal position in a majority of cases, serving as a benchmark, some individual and exceptional cases may deviate from this expected standard, Consequently greater innovation may be required where matters involving legal and ethical responsibilities are concerned, in determining sanctions to be applied in such cases.

Designing an Optimal Regulatory Combination

In terms of the types and classes of rules to be applied at various phases of the pyramid, applying all that has been discussed in this section,

A combination of bright line rules and high level principles (Ojo: 2011b) should be applied to the more innovative middle phases of the pyramid - the application of this combination of rules not only reflecting the level of flexibility offered by such a combination, but also the priority accorded to this level or phases of the pyramid.

Principles which offer even a greater degree of flexibility, and are less mandatory and of persuasive nature than hard law, should apply to philanthropic related issues - hence also attracting less severity in terms of punitive measures.

Rules which are more mandatory and binding in nature than the above mentioned classes and categories, and which also offer less degree of flexibility, whilst commanding greater severity in terms of punitive sanctions, should apply to failure to comply with economic responsibilities.

The application of these rules and principles to various phases of the pyramid, not only reflects the need for flexibility where greater innovation is required, but also the inverse relationship in the severity of sanctions to be applied where a relationship is established between Carroll's pyramid of CSR and the pyramid of punitive strategies.

Hence, re-contrasting the CSR pyramid with the pyramid of enforcement and regulatory strategies, as illustrated under this section (Ojo: 2011b):

Within the framework of Self-Regulation and the Enforced Self-Regulation models, mechanisms can be designed whereby compliance, enforcement and monitoring costs faced by medium sized firms could be minimized – such costs, in addition to transaction costs, also constituting reasons why medium sized firms may be discouraged from pursuing joint ventures with their more powerful "Big Four" counter parts. Such regulatory design would not only be aimed at determining the extent to which mandatory and persuasive rules should apply – at different levels of management and based upon the size and structure of audit firms involved, but also to investigate how major barriers to the entry of medium sized firms in the audit market can be addressed – this being of vital importance given the present level of audit concentration in the audit market – as well as its impact on audit quality, objectivity and independence.

This would also facilitate investigation of how Joint Audits, that is joint collaborations between medium sized and the Big Four Audit firms, can be successfully implemented in facilitating timely audit rotation – hence serving as a means of recommending measures and safeguards which are aimed at facilitating more effective corporate governance mechanisms in respect of joint collaborations between medium sized audit firms and the Big Four audit firms.

WHERE ENVIRONMENTAL CONSIDERATIONS OUTWEIGH ECONOMIC BENEFITS: THE XL PIPELINE PROJECT

The month of October 2015 witnessed even more significant and radical changes for the House of Representatives, as well as legislative consequences which heralded the end of a twenty-five year tenure by the outgoing Speaker, John Boehner, and the passing on of leadership to the incoming Speaker, Paul Ryan. It is hoped that this transition will not only further a legacy of achieving the goal of unification to a greater extent within the House, but also facilitate the legislative process to a greater extent than

Table 1. Re constrasting the CSR pyramid with the pyramid of enforcement and regulatory strategies

Level of Pyramid	Type of responsibility based on Carroll's pyramid	Type of Regulation based on pyramid of enforcement and punitive strategies	Applicability of Rules or Principles
Base	Economic Responsibilities: It can be argued that rules which are more mandatory and binding in nature should apply to economic responsibilities - thus reflecting the inverse relationship between Carroll's pyramid of CSR and the pyramid of regulatory and punitive strategies	Self-Regulation	Consisting primarily of principles which offer even a greater degree of flexibility, and are less mandatory and of persuasive nature than hard law
Middle	Legal responsibilities	Enforced Self Regulation	A combination of bright line rules and high level principles
Middle	Ethical responsibilities	Command Regulation without Discretionary Punishment	A combination of bright line rules and high level principles
Apex	Philanthropic Responsibilities: In jurisdictions where CSR approach focuses on philanthropic responsibilities, it could be argued that rules which are mandatory and binding - rather than persuasive in nature, should be applied.	Command Regulation with Non Discretionary Punishment	Rules which are more mandatory and binding in nature than the above mentioned classes and categories

many desire at present. The importance of legislative reforms is undeniably a crucial basis and defining factor for many governments since such decisions can make or break the legacy of such governments.

Even so is the vital need to give priority to environmental considerations in situations where some may deem it less important than economic benefits. Economic benefits – which to a large extent, are induced by prevailing economic pressures and which may not necessarily serve longer term interests of the nation – particularly also in matters of national security.

It was announced on the 6th November 2015 that the keystone XL Pipeline Project and Proposal which was intended to transfer Canadian crude oil from oilfields and ports to refineries in the Gulf of Mexico, such pipelines running through six states, from Canada, was to be rejected. The Project, which involved initiatives from Trans Canada Corp, had been on the cards for seven years, since 2008 – indeed a project which had been inherited from the previous government. However, environmental considerations, as well as economic considerations played a crucial factor in the final decision to reject the project.

Prior to President Obama's statement on the 6th November 2015, in which reasons justifying the rejection of the recommendation were highlighted, the Secretary of State, John Kerry, highlighted that a contributing factor to the decision resulted from the fact that potential environmental costs resulting from the project were more likely to outweigh intended economic benefits.

Even though it was thought that the project would generate jobs, it was also added that the Keystone XL Pipeline "would not serve the interests of the country."

In bolstering why the Project would neither serve as "a silver bullet for the economy nor the express lane to climate disaster", reasons for rejecting the Project, as highlighted by President Obama, are as follows:

1. The Pipeline would not make meaningful long term contribution to the economy in terms of creating jobs;
2. Pipeline would not lower gas prices for American consumers (which according to current estimates, has been down $1.27 over three years);
3. Shipping and transferring dirtier and unrefined crude oil into the United States would not increase America's security.

It was also added that the United States would have relied on oil and gas as transition occurred, however, that such transition was taking place at a much faster pace than anticipated. In addition to accentuating the fact that "cheaper energy from the wind and sun was more beneficial than resorting to more carbon polluted related projects which result in the release of more fossil fuels from the ground" and in taking serious measures to cut carbon emissions, the President also added that the Project would have "undercut America's leadership on environment."

WHERE STRATEGIC ECONOMIC INTERESTS ARE INVOLVED: THE CASE OF PORT TALBOT AND THE DECLINING STATE OF THE UK STEEL INDUSTRY

Over the past months and in particular, since October 2015, the UK steel industry has faced huge challenges in respect of job losses and the impact of a slowdown in global economic conditions. Whilst declining oil prices have impacted volatilities in global financial markets, the UK, to a greater extent, has been affected by the steel industry.

This is not only attributed to recent revelations that have plagued the industry, as well as disclosures in respect of the extent of losses that have compelled the major steel enterprise Tata Group, to cut down costs in the UK – in the form of massive close down operations, but also attributed to the fact that steel constitutes a major component of the UK manufacturing sector – accounting for a tenth of its economic output.

There's a need to distinguish between long-term non disclosures (lack of adequate transparency and deliberate non disclosures) to investors which have little or nothing to do with creative accounting cover ups. Such non disclosures being difficult to sustain or conceal once losses have reached unbearable limits. Whilst certain information are withheld from the public – and in particular financial investors – for purposes aimed at avoiding unnecessary panics, this could be distinguished from creative accounting and fraudulent practices aimed at personal gains. However, a time comes when even certain losses can no longer be sustained by enterprise owners or investors.

Whilst the Case of Port Talbot can be distinguished from that of Enron, on the basis that Enron's collapse occurred at a much swifter pace and involved a major accounting firm – with Port Talbot's fate (as well as that of other affected UK steel companies) being determined primarily by global external factors – in contrast to internal management issues in Enron, both cases can be reconciled on the basis of the magnitude of the impact of their collapses (and possible demise) for the economy – as well as their impact on wider stakeholders.

Wider stakeholders and indirect impact involves cases with suppliers, contractors – as well as town and surrounding localities whose main industry rely on the steel industry. Hence the devastating consequences of Port Talbot's closure should not be under-estimated.

The steel industry in Port Talbot, dating back to a hundred years has grown to become a cultural and indeed, a defining aspect of a community such as Port Talbot – becoming a central and integral aspect of the locals' lives and livelihood. Just like its sister company in Redcar, Teeside, the loss of jobs in that area of the country has impacted lives locally – as well as nationally.

Whilst Scottish steel branches have possible consequences that could have resulted from closures – through temporary nationalization measures and funding from taxpayers, it appears that the rescue of Port Talbot will require more radical measures.

Could better communication between management and stakeholders have mitigated current problems at Port Talbot? To what extent were the information asymmetries which existed between the management and stakeholders and why could it have taken so long for the extent of daily losses to be revealed?

As already highlighted, the Case of Port Talbot is rather complicated as many contributory factors to the current situation have been external (global unpredictable economic conditions which have contributed to the inability to accurately predict future prospects with reasonable certainly – as opposed to merely a management issue or cover up). However many would still argue that signs of an impending problem had been revealed years before and that swifter action could have been taken to mitigate the level of losses that have consolidate over the years.

Estimated losses over the past five years at Tata have been highlighted as £2 billion. Hence it could be said that the problem has been an ongoing long term issue whose roots could actually be attributed to contributory factors which have appeared as far back as 2005. Whilst any company is not expected to sound alarming signals upon the first incidences on economic problems, and whilst hope continues to persist – even in the face of reported daily losses of £1 million, release of such reports to investors or the public, at a much earlier time than is the case at present – where such losses have not accrued to £2 billion, would have facilitated much easily, the process of finding new buyers.

This is not to say that hopes of finding new buyers are no longer realistic – but to accentuate the reasons for Tata's rejection of the rescue plans put forward on the 29th March 2016. It could have been more realistic for quicker rescues in a less volatile financial environment – where global demand for steel had not deteriorated dramatically, where slow-down of growth in countries such as India and China had not reached such levels as is currently the case, and where the costs of running such industries had not been made even more difficult by high energy prices, the strength of the pound, to name a few factors.

Based on BBC reports, in October 2015, Thailand's SSI announced it was closing down its Redcar works with the loss of 2,200 jobs, then parts of Caparo Industries' steel operations went into administration putting 1,700 jobs potentially at risk (BBC, 2016b).

Figure 3 and 4 highlight the extent of the devastating losses – as well as the trends which have followed over the past months – as well as over the past two decades.

Figure 3. Steel job losses in the UK since September 2015
Source: BBC (2016a)

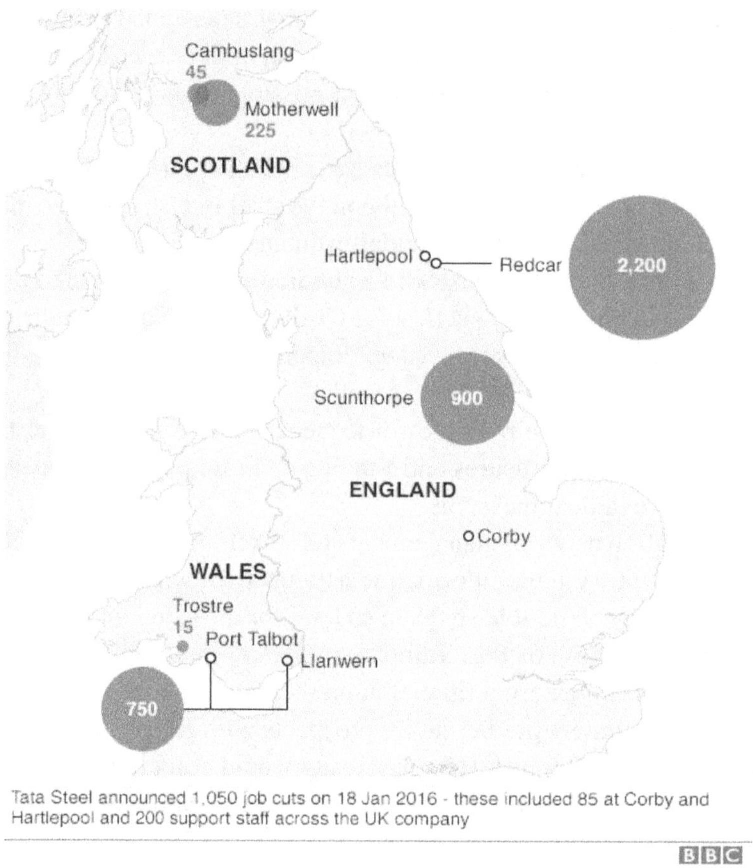

Figure 4. Workers employed in steel manufacturing, 1994-2014
Source: BBC (2016a)

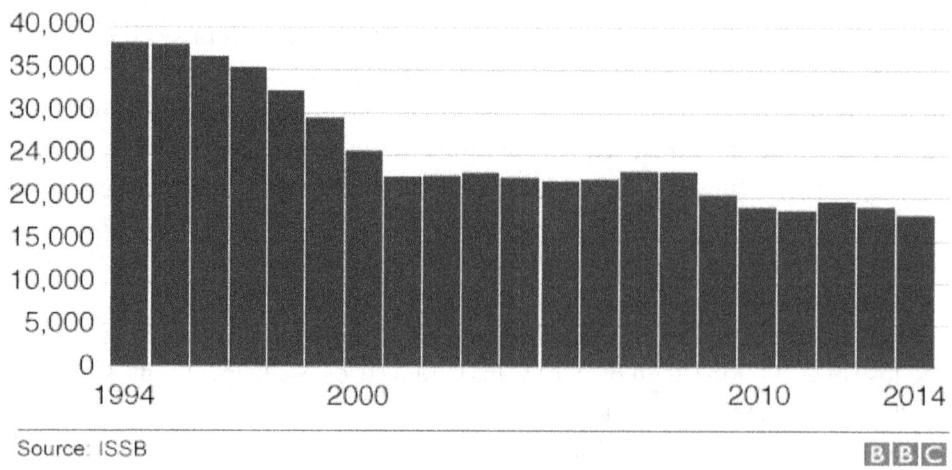

Contributory Factors to the Decline of the UK Steel Industry

The following have been cited as being contributory to the present state of the UK steel industry (see also BBC, 2016a, 2016b):

- Global oversupply of steel, cheap steel imports, high costs and currency volatility.
- Relatively high electricity prices, the extra cost of climate change policies, and competition from China - with allegations that Chinese steel is being sold in the UK at unrealistically low prices.
- It is also reported that demand for steel worldwide has not returned to pre-financial crash levels and that with economies - particularly China's - still seeing weak growth, global demand for steel is set to remain sluggish, falling by 1.7% in 2015 and rising by 0.7% in 2016. Further, global steel prices have fallen sharply and whilst China's own economic slowdown has led Chinese producers to seek export markets, their home demand has stalled. As a result, UK imports of Chinese steel have increased dramatically. In 2014 the UK imported 687,000 tonnes of steel from China compared to 303,000 tonnes the year before.

Further reports have pointed out to the severity of the recent steel crisis as being synonymous to the 2008 Financial Crisis where banks were offered financial assistance in the form of bailouts and nationalization rescue initiatives. It was added that " the key question was whether the Welsh Government could do something other than providing the usual level of support for regeneration and training for workers who have lost their jobs – with the Scottish Government having recently bought two mothballed steel plants in Lanarkshire from Tata before selling them to a private company on the same day." (BBC, 2016c).

Options Currently Being Considered to Rescue Port Talbot

These include the following:

- Government support (either in the form of full or partial nationalization).
- Management buy-outs.
- In the face of data which reveal that UK imports of Chinese steel have increased dramatically – doubling from 303,000 tonnes (in 2013) to 687,000 tonnes of steel in 2014 - even whilst local production suffers, more stringent rules on procurement to compel such firms to buy domestic products. Furthermore, UK steel companies" imports from the EU are much higher – with an estimated 4.7 million tonnes in 2014.
- Possible aid from the European Union – even though current EU rules apply - which restrict how much support governments are able to give particular industries.

In view of recommendations which suggest restriction of steel imports from China, it has also been added by some commentators that the Government, given investments in other areas (which include the nuclear sectors), is cautious of endangering relations with China. To which it should also be added, that strategic economic and national interests, should have a core position in the determination of decisions and steps to be undertaken.

Whilst the XL Line Pipe Project between the United States and Canada, had to be abandoned for reasons principally stemming from the fact that engagement in the project would not serve the economic interests of the country, other factors – including environmental – as well as cost benefit considerations also played a part in the final decision.

The Current State of Anti-Dumping Legislation

Even though the EU imposed anti-dumping duties on Chinese and Taiwanese steel imports in 2015, these were in operation for just six months.

- Dumping occurs if a company sells at a lower price in an export market than in its domestic market. If such dumping injures the domestic producers in the importing country, under certain circumstances the importing country authorities may impose anti-dumping duties to offset the effects of the dumping (UNCTAD, 2003:3).

According to UNCTAD, reasons why companies dump are considered irrelevant as long as the following technical definitions are met (see UNCTAD, 2003: pages 4 and 5):

- Dumping may therefore equally cover predatory dumping (Dumping in order to drive competitors out of business and establish a monopoly);
- Cyclical dumping (Selling at low prices because of over-capacity due to a downturn in demand);
- Market expansion dumping (Selling at a lower price for export than domestically in order to gain market share);
- State-trading dumping (Selling at low prices in order to earn hard currency);
- And strategic dumping (Dumping by benefiting from an overall strategy which includes both low export pricing and maintaining a closed home market in order to reap monopoly or oligopoly profits).

SUGGESTIONS AND RECOMMENDATIONS

In view of the apparently ineffective rules which appear to be in operation, it is therefore evident that more effective anti-dumping rules which are aimed at avoiding unnecessary job losses and which should restrict the levels to which prices can be lowered – such that competitors are not driven out of the market, should be agreed upon by contracting parties.

Where a market or industry is considered strategic to any economy or constitutes a significant proportion of its economic activities and output, and the impact of job losses in such a sector is of colossal magnitude, then as is the case with the banking industry, such manufacturing industries should be considered as "Too Big To Fail" industries which should receive government priority, support in the form of state aids and bail outs - given the likely and devastating consequences which could impact the economy as a result of the collapse of such a pivotal and strategic industry.

This chapter has demonstrated the importance and impact of lack of regulations and/or compliance with regulations – at local or international levels. Whereas stringent rules on carbon emissions or regulations imposing costs – resulting in higher productivity costs, may need to be relaxed, efforts should be made such that international trade agreements contain provisions which are effectively implemented and complied with, such that enterprises, and particularly strategic enterprises, are not priced out of the industry. More importantly, other governmental measures which serve as safeguards should be in operation to ensure that job losses on huge scales and magnitude are mitigated or avoided.

In respect of long term viable plans, subsidy proposals appear to have been ruled out – with debates on the viability of measures such as nationalization. Full – as well as partial nationalization could constitute initial rescue efforts – with gradual sale to private companies. This would ensure a longer term solution which would not involve continual drain of taxpayer funds. Enterprises should also continually ensure that current disclosure requirements meet and satisfy the demands of external and broader stakeholders. Meanwhile it remains to be seen, just how strategically and of economic importance Port Talbot's rescue will be – as will be demonstrated in the months to come.

With the XL Pipeline Project and Proposal which was intended to transfer Canadian crude oil from oilfields and ports to refineries in the Gulf of Mexico, such pipelines running through six states, even though it was thought that the project would generate jobs, it was also added that the Keystone XL Pipeline "would not serve the interests of the country."

CONCLUSION

Operation "Saving Port Talbot" – as well as the redemption other interests which are pivotal to the economy of the UK – appear to be of strategic and national importance. For this purpose, a distinction, as drawn between Enron and Port Talbot – can also be drawn between the XL Pipeline Project and Port Talbot.

Meaningfully and effectively implementing codes of conducts, standards and regulations which drive a business, and particularly multinational enterprises can have important consequences for basic goals such as profit maximization for such enterprises – however they also play determine the extent to which corporate social responsibility objectives are realized. Without effective compliance and enforcement strategies, which embrace a range of disclosure requirements that are aimed at maximally engaging stakeholders in the corporate social responsibility process, CSR objectives which are also facilitated by such corporate governance mechanisms of disclosure and accountability, will be hindered in achieving their maximum potential.

There is substantial evidence to bolster the claim that "governments are cooperating with each other and with other actors to strengthen the international legal and policy framework in which business is conducted (OECD, 2008:10)." Having considered the importance of addressing legal impediments to the realization of Corporate Social Responsibility objectives, environmental concerns, also constitute one of those vital issues which still need to be addressed.

Such issues and areas of focal points include (OECD, 2011:42):

- Collection and evaluation of adequate and timely information regarding the environment, health and safety impacts of MNE activities;
- Taking into account concerns related to cost, business confidentiality and the protection of intellectual property rights;
- Continually seeking to improve corporate environmental performance at the level of the enterprise.

An international cooperative environment represents a huge step forward, not only in overcoming legal obstacles faced by MNEs in achieving their corporate social goals, but also a means of facilitating the development of new, innovative techniques whereby such goals can be achieved in a more effective and timely fashion.

Economic Considerations

Economic considerations which were taken into account, and which also partly constitute a basis for the decision to reject the keystone XL Pipeline Project include the following:

- Present economic data released on the 6th November 2015, which revealed a drop in employment to pre-Crisis level figures of 5%. As well as the addition of a net value of 271,000 jobs in October 2015 to the US economy, such figures indicate a high probability that the Fed would raise interest rates in December 2015 – for the first time in a decade.
- The prevailing low gas prices – which justified the case that gas prices would not be lowered.

The rejection of the Proposal, it is added, also "ends a seven year political fight" as considered by some, over the collaborative Canadian-Texas project however;

In view of responses from some prominent figures from the Senate – including a Presidential candidate, as well as some members from the House of Representatives, there are still possibilities that the project could be resurrected by the next government and that the present decision to reject the proposal could have been "deemed" to have been significantly impacted by present economic data – as well as current global events. It is acknowledged that Canada needed markets and the partnership for oil production – however, do some economic benefits merit certain potentially devastating environmental repercussions? Long term interests and longer term repercussions cannot be valued solely on a monetary basis and some damages are indeed irreversible and irreparable.

As accentuated under the Preface section, nothing could be more crucial in future years than a united legislative branch where decisions are reached based on factors which whilst giving consideration to the economic and national interests of the country, also takes into consideration the legacy being left to future generations as a result of environmental matters. Further, the present steps being taken and the XL Pipeline Project Decision should also be applauded and welcomed on the basis of the need to comply with international agreements, the need to accentuate and demonstrate America's leadership on environmental matters – all well premised and serving as vital foundation for the 2015 Paris Climate Summit.

REFERENCES

Annual Report on the OECD Guidelines for Multinational Enterprises 2010 Corporate Responsibility: Reinforcing a Unique Instrument. (2010). OECD Publishing.

Annual Report on the OECD Guidelines for Multinational Enterprises 2014 Responsible Business Conduct by Sector. (2015). OECD Publishing.

Ayres, I., & Braithwaite, J. (1995). *Responsive Regulation: Transcending the Deregulation Debate*. Oxford, UK: Social Legal Studies.

BBC. (2016a). Tata: Government considers 'all options' for Port Talbot. *BBC news*. Retrieved from: http://www.bbc.co.uk/news/business-35923626

BBC. (2016b). Britain's steel industry: What's going wrong? by Tim Bowler Business reporter. *BBC News*. Retrieved from: http://www.bbc.co.uk/news/business-34581945

BBC. (2016c). *Port Talbot Tata Steel: Assembly set for crisis recall*. Retrieved from: http://www.bbc.co.uk/news/uk-wales-politics-35923463

BBC. (2016d). *Tata Steel plans to sell loss-making UK plants*. Retrieved from: http://www.bbc.co.uk/news/business-35922046

Carroll, A. B. (1991, July-August). The Pyramid of Corporate Social Responsibility: Toward the Moral Management of Organizational Stakeholders. *Business Horizons*.

Daily Telegraph. (2016). *Steel industry dealt hammer blow as Tata withdraws from UK*. Retrieved from: http://www.telegraph.co.uk/business/2016/03/29/port-talbot-steels-itself-for-tata-decision/

Esty, D. C., & Geradin, D. (2001). *Regulatory Competition and Economic Integration: Comparative Perspectives*. Oxford University Press.

Nestle. (2014). *Nestle in Society: Creating Shared Value (and Meeting Our Commitments) Summary Report 2013*. Nestle.

OECD. (2008). *OECD Guidelines for Multinational Enterprises*. OECD Publishing.

OECD. (2011). *OECD Guidelines for Multinational Enterprises*. OECD Publishing. 10.1787/9789264115415-en

Ojo, M. (2011a). Cooperative and Competitive Enforced Self-Regulation: The Role of Governments, Private Actors and Banks in Corporate Responsibility. *Journal of Financial Regulation and Compliance, 19*(2).

Ojo, M. (2011b). Building on the trust of management: overcoming the paradoxes of principles based regulation. Law and Prosociality, 30(7).

Ojo, M. (2015). *Regulating Self-Regulation: Audits and Accounting Mechanisms*. Science Publishing Group. Retrieved from: http://www.sciencepublishinggroup.com/book/B-978-1-940366-52-4.aspx

UNCTAD. (2003). *Dispute Settlement: World Trade Organization, Anti-Dumping Measures*. New York: United Nations Publications.

Chapter 3
Corporate Social Responsibility as a Tool for Poverty Reduction:
Globalization, Corporate Social Responsibility and Poverty Revisited

Maria DiGabriele
New York University, USA

ABSTRACT

This chapter is aimed at addressing gaps highlighted as being inherent in the current model of Corporate Social Responsibility. In so doing, it proposes means whereby the current CSR model can be harnessed more efficiently to achieve and realize the goal of poverty reduction - particularly in developing countries.

INTRODUCTION

In his article, Jenkins (2005) states that the principal way whereby Corporate Social Responsibility might contribute to government revenue, is through the discouragement of bribery of public officials by companies (Jenkins, 2005, pg. 539). However, he also adds that this does not prevent nor deter companies' ability to divert profits and avoid taxation through "legitimate means such as transfer pricing and the use of tax havens." In highlighting the gaps which persist in the current CSR model, the following arguments are propounded (Jenkins, 2005, pg. 539-540):

- The silence of current CSR model on the above issues, as well as the assertion that "the dominant view is that companies are perfectly entitled to minimize their tax burden through legal means,"
- The lack of an express focus on poverty reduction.

Further he recommends the consideration, as regards whether the CSR model could be "extended to incorporate poverty reduction as a key element" - in addition to other elements such as labor rights and environmental protection.

DOI: 10.4018/978-1-5225-0305-7.ch003

In adding that characteristics of CSR which restrict its ability to address poverty include "the way in which CSR prioritizes the business case" (Jenkins, 2005, pg. 540), this mirrors the argument highlighted in chapter two, namely, that legal and ethical considerations, within the sphere and context of Carroll's pyramid of Corporate Social Responsibility, should assume greater prominence and priority than is currently the case - with such considerations being accorded the same, or even greater priority, based on individual circumstances, than economic and profit maximization objectives.

Even though his third proposition that "the centrality of stakeholders within CSR also limits its usefulness in approaching poverty,"[1] such a "limitation" as well as the second limitation, could be transformed positively in such a way that would generate more beneficial responses in addressing poverty.

The stakeholder theory, by definition, provides a broader scope in extending the ambit of those who can be designated as falling under the definition of a stakeholder - in contrast to the traditional principal agent theory and model. Such stakeholders should not just extend to members of the general public who may be creditors, suppliers, or are likely to be affected by economic decisions of the corporation, but should also embrace individuals who are affected by environmental, social impacts and repercussions of the corporation's activities.

Furthermore, devastating consequences resulting from the failure of a corporation to adequately implement and comply with prescribed rules, codes of conduct related to corporate governance, ethical codes, as well as other legal rules, which also adversely impact the wider community at large, should be categorized within the scope of the stakeholder theory.

The ensuing section traces the developments which have resulted in a broader definition of a stakeholder, in prescribing how Corporate Social Responsibility could be harnessed more effectively, as a tool for poverty reduction.

BACKGROUND AND LITERATURE REVIEW

Conceptual and Theoretical Frameworks

One definition of Corporate Social Responsibility is provided by Hopkins is as follows (Hopkins, 2004):

- CSR is concerned with treating the stakeholders of the firm ethically or in a responsible manner. 'Ethically or responsible' means treating stakeholders in a manner deemed acceptable in civilized societies. Social includes economic responsibility. Stakeholders exist both within a firm and outside. The natural environment is a stakeholder. The wider aim of social responsibility is to create higher and higher standards of living, while preserving the profitability of the corporation, for peoples both within and outside the corporation.

Whilst the negative aspects of legislation are highlighted by Hopkins, the following are identified benefits and attributes of legislating Corporate Social Responsibility (Hopkins, 2004):

- It would help to avoid the excessive exploitation of labor, bribery and corruption.
- Companies would know what is expected of them, thereby promoting a level playing field.

- Many aspects of CSR behavior are good for business (such as reputation, human resources, branding and making it easier to locate in new communities) and legislation could help to improve profitability, growth and sustainability.
- Some areas, such as downsizing, could help to redress the balance between companies and their employees.
- Rogue companies would find it more difficult to compete through lower standards. The wider community would benefit as companies reach out to the key issue of underdevelopment around the world.

As highlighted by Ojo (2016),

Legal and ethical responsibilities, as corporate governance facilitating tools and mechanisms, through stakeholder engagement, are crucial to achieving:

Economic responsibilities – which are vital and pivotal to achieving philanthropic goals of:

- Addressing environmental concerns and
- Furthering poverty alleviation initiatives.

Corporate Social Responsibility, hence, should not merely apply to corporations, but also other actors - namely food chains and stores - which have the potential to serve in a formidable role in the fight against food and packaging waste. The process of facilitating green growth and efforts aimed at reducing food and packaging waste, not only serves to further environmental initiatives and goals, but also promotes the process of value and job creation.

ISSUES, CONTROVERSIES, PROBLEMS

The Stakeholder Theory: Who Does it Extend to?

According to Kaplan (2010), the Balanced Scorecard has been extended and broadened as a concept, as well as "a management tool for describing, communicating and implementing strategy."

Seven non-financial metrics and one financial metric, it is added, were recommended by a project team, as performance measures of divisional performance and these are as follows (Kaplan, 2010, pg. 5):

- Profitability
- Market Share
- Productivity
- Product leadership
- Public responsibility (which includes legal and ethical behavior, as well as responsibility to stakeholders, including shareholders, vendors, dealers, distributors, and communities)
- Personnel development
- Employee attitudes

- Balance between short range and long range objectives

The roots of the Balanced Scorecard, it is further contended, can be traced to these eight objectives.

Criticisms, however, have been directed at the Balanced Scorecard, as regards the Balanced Scorecard Theory, as regards its ability to provide managers with purposeful goal facilitating tools (Jensen, 2001).

In proposing the stakeholder theory as "another multi-dimensional approach" for enterprise performance measurement, Kaplan states that stakeholders are defined as groups or individuals inside or outside the enterprise, who have a stake or can influence the organization's performance (Kaplan, 2010, pg. 14).

Furthermore, five stakeholder groups are generally identified, namely (Kaplan, 2010):

- Shareholders
- Customers
- Communities
- Suppliers
- Employees

As illustrated under the chapter "Corporate Social Responsibility and Foreign Direct Investment: The Importance of Compliance with National, Regional Laws and Globally Recognized Standards", "the importance of effective engagement of stakeholders in the process – particularly the Government, in matters aimed at ensuring that multinational enterprises' principles, codes of ethics and values," are respected, should be taken into consideration. Further, as highlighted under the chapter, it is also vital to ensure that local, regional and international rules, agreements, codes and standards are effectively complied with.

In line with the theme of this volume, the engagement of stakeholders, and particularly, wider and more vulnerable stakeholders, could serve as a possible corporate governance tool and avenue, not only in the mitigation of asymmetric information between the principal and agent, but in also in poverty reduction for those who are likely to be vulnerable to consequences which ensue where corporations place economic and profit maximization aims well above legal and ethical responsibilities of the firm.

As highlighted by Rodriguez et al (2006), "scholarship on corruption would benefit from more attention to definitions." Corruption, it is further argued by them, "is still most commonly defined to preclude private corruption though it is clear that both government corruption and private corruption often go hand in hand and stem from the same underlying institutions. Moreover, an understanding of private corruption is vital to any assessment of the role of business in society and of the effects of firms on the environment of corruption." The difficulties of asymmetric information, as a contributory obstacle to the study of antecedents and consequences of CSR is further identified (Rodriguez, Siegel, Hillman & Eden, 2006). In their opinion, such asymmetric difficulties, as well as "lack of candid information" has contributed to the difficulties in delineating and accounting for the varying rationales for CSR, which could be private or social.

Empirical issues which they also raise as being in need of redress, comprise (Rodriguez, Siegel, Hillman & Eden, 2006):

- Problems with measurement of the costs and benefits of CSR activities continue to cloud our understanding of the strategic implications of CSR.

- The continuing confusion over definitions and the impossibility of measuring what cannot be define since varying and inconsistent definitions, in their opinion, contribute to empirical results that cannot reliably be compared.

SOLUTIONS AND RECOMMENDATIONS

As rightly observed and highlighted in the foreword contribution, the Prisoner's Dilemma, a situation whereby "whereby purely self-interested action leads to an inefficient outcome" (Goyal, 2006), constitutes another persisting issue that needs to be addressed. An example of means whereby vulnerable and poverty prone stakeholders are effectively engaged is also provided whereby villagers are engaged in projects, sponsoring of education and training is provided by corporations as means of addressing possible asymmetries resulting from information gaps and implementation gaps.

However, Goyal (2006) also adds that:

- Even though such activities contribute to social capital, a higher stock of which raises a firm's productivity, and although a firm has the option of free riding on others' contribution to social capital, if all do so social capital will be under-supplied, and all will be worse off – an example of what is said to constitute the Prisoner's Dilemma.

In addressing this issue, "a longer-term perspective, with more weight for the future, and punishment for those who deviate from cooperation is proposed" (Goyal, 2006). As emphasized by the theme of this volume,

And according to Sacconi (2004), corporate social responsibility can be defined as:

- A model of extended corporate governance whereby those in control of the firm have responsibilities that range from the fulfillment of their fiduciary duties owed towards the owners (principal) to the fulfillment of analogous fiduciary duties owed towards all the firm's stakeholders.

Jensen (2001), argues that:

- To the extent that the stakeholder theory says that firms should pay attention to all their constituencies, that the theory is unassailable, and that to this extent, the theory is completely consistent with value maximization or value-seeking behavior.

In seeking to reconcile both views, it is illustrated that "firms can effectively involve the engagement of stakeholders as a means of attaining value maximization objectives - even under the stakeholder theory, where corporate social responsibility is involved and where certain other considerations which involve the effective implementation of self-regulation, bright line rules and principles are appropriately incorporated in facilitating better communication between the principal and stakeholders of the firm" (Ojo, 2016).

In illustrating the role of corporate social responsibility as "a model of extended corporate governance" reference is made by Sacconi to the self-regulation approach to corporate social responsibility which he distinguishes into (Sacconi, 2004):

- Self regulation based on a discretionary approach.
- Self regulation based on voluntary compliance with explicit norms.

As highlighted (Ojo, 2016),

- If adopted with the engagement of stakeholders at appropriate stages, as well as the incorporation of applicable and most suitable forms of rules during such phases of the mediation process between agents and stakeholders, such that flexibility is facilitated in the process to allow for contingencies whilst also compelling effective enforcement and compliance mechanisms, corporate social responsibility should be fostered through the outcomes emanating from better, focused planning, control, decision making, as well as more effective accountability, compliance and enforcement mechanisms.

FUTURE RESEARCH DIRECTIONS

As highlighted and identified under the literature review section, conceptual and theoretical issues which have not been fully addressed under this chapter, as well as the following empirical issues and areas should constitute areas for continued research and focus, notably:

- Those problems with measurement of the costs and benefits of CSR activities which continue to distort an understanding of the strategic implications of CSR.
- Clarification of the confusion over definitions and the impossibility of measuring what cannot be defined since such varying and inconsistent definitions contribute to empirical results that cannot reliably be compared.

CONCLUSION

Sacconi proposes that stakeholders should be engaged in all phases of the CSR management function and that effective dialogue should occur within these stages (Sacconi, 2004):

1. Creating and establishment of the social contract (which clearly stipulates the firm's fiduciary duties towards its stakeholders)
2. Internal management and implementation - with the presence of external members on internal board or committees - both corporate board of directors or those set up "ad-hoc" to address corporate social responsibility
3. Social accountability - this stage aiming to identify areas of effective interest of stakeholders
4. Verification by an independent third party - as distinguished from auditors - with an independent third party controlling the verification of this phase

As argued, stakeholder engagement should be regarded as a tool, "not only in mitigating information asymmetries, but also in compelling greater accountability on the part of the agents, facilitating avenues and platforms whereby incentives are created, as well as establishing negotiations and agreements which constitute the bases on which longer term based planning, goals, decision making and control are realized" (Ojo, 2016). Through such a tool and platform, the agent's incentives and objectives should be better aligned with those of the principal - hence discouraging the pursuit of short term interests on the part of the agents."

Furthermore, as highlighted:

- The stages during which hard law and principles should be incorporated in the mediation process between stakeholders and their agents, should involve a careful consideration of the role of certainty and predictability at those stages. Since incomplete contracts are inevitable and are necessary to facilitate flexibility - given unforeseen contingencies that need to be provided for, principles should constitute the basis for regulation where events which have a greater degree of unpredictability and uncertainty are concerned (Ojo, 2016).

The roles of Corporate Social Responsibility, as an extension of corporate governance, and a tool for the engagement of wider stakeholders – particularly those more susceptible to poverty and the failure of corporations to adopt and implement required standards and codes which serve to mitigate practices associated with bribery and corruption; as well as a signaling mechanism, have been highlighted in this chapter. Effective engagement and involvement of such vulnerable stakeholders in the corporate process - those who are most susceptible to corporate failures and collapses as well as a focus on poverty reduction as a key element and objective of Corporate Social Responsibility, would not only represent a step towards greater realization of goals of poverty reduction, but would also serve to ensure that more positive characteristics of Corporate Social Responsibility, those related to goals of facilitating environmental protection are enhanced through greater cooperation between governments and authorities, as well as greater compliance with legal standards, regulations, codes and principles.

REFERENCES

Atkinson, A., Waterhouse, & Wells. (1997). A Stakeholder Approach to Strategic Performance Measurement. *Sloan Management Review*.

Diawara, K., & Lavallée, S. (2014). Corporate Social Responsibility (CSR) in the Ohada Law. *Journal of Business Law and Ethics, 2*(2), 39-62.

Goyal, A. (2006). Corporate Social Responsibility as a Signalling Device for Foreign Direct Investment. *International Journal of the Economics of Business, 13*(1), 145–163. doi:10.1080/13571510500520077

Hopkins, M. (2004). *Corporate Social Responsibility: An Issues Paper*. Working Paper No. 27. Policy Integration Department World Commission on the Social Dimension of Globalization International Labor Office Geneva.

Jenkins, R. (2005). Globalization, Corporate Social Responsibility and Poverty. *International Affairs, 81*(3), 525–540. doi:10.1111/j.1468-2346.2005.00467.x

Jensen, M. (2001). Value Maximization, Stakeholder Theory, and the Corporate Objective Function. *Journal of Applied Corporate Finance*, (Fall), 821.

Kaplan, R. S., & Norton, D. P. (2008a). Mastering the Management System. *Harvard Business Review*, (January), 6257. PMID:18271319

Kaplan, R. S., & Norton, D. P. (2008b). *The Execution Premium: Linking Strategy to Operations for Competitive Advantage*. Boston: HBS Press.

Neely, A., & Adams, C. (2002). *Performance Prism: The Scorecard for Measuring and Managing Stakeholder Relationships*. Financial Times/Prentice Hall

Ojo, M. (2016). *E Commerce As a Tool For Resource Expansion: Postal Partnerships, Data Protection Legislation and the Mitigation of Implementation Gaps*. IGI Global Publications.

Rodriguez, P., Siegel, Hillman, & Eden. (2006). *Three Lenses on the Multinational Enterprise: Politics, Corruption, and Corporate Social Responsibility*. Number 0608.

Sacconi. (2004). *Corporate Social Responsibility (CSR) as a Model of 'Extended' Corporate Governance: An Explanation Based on the Economic Theories of Social Contract, Reputation and Reciprocal Conformism*. Author.

ENDNOTE

1 The second limitation put forward being accredited as resulting from "the origins of the current CSR movement as a response to criticism of the environmental and social impacts of transnational companies (TNCs)."

Section 2

Ethical Codes and Legal Considerations:

Rules and Regulations

Chapter 4
IFRS Harmonization and Foreign Direct Investment

Javier Vidal-García
University of Valladolid, Spain

Marta Vidal
Complutense University of Madrid, Spain

ABSTRACT

IFRS refers to International Financial Reporting Standards, which are the guidelines that provide the framework for accounting works. The principles are also known as the International Accounting Standards (IAS). This global financial concept was first introduced in 2001 to equip investors with analyzed accounting statements. In this Chapter we review the relation between IFRS and Foreign Direct Investments (FDIs). We review the relevant literature that analyses the effects on IFRS on FDIs and cross-border acquisitions. The economic literature states that the introduction of IFRS has presented an important increase in FDIs. The evidence shows that IFRS adopting countries attract investments from countries that implemented IFRS and non-IFRS implementing countries.

INTRODUCTION

IFRS refers to International Financial Reporting Standards, which are the guidelines that provide the framework for accounting works. The principles are also known as the International Accounting Standards (IAS). This global financial concept was first introduced in 2001 to equip investors with analyzed accounting statements. In this Chapter we review the relation between IFRS and Foreign Direct Investments (FDIs). We review the relevant literature that analyses the effects on IFRS on FDIs and cross-border acquisitions. The economic literature states that the introduction of IFRS has presented an important increase in FDIs. The evidence shows that IFRS adopting countries attract investments from countries that implemented IFRS and non-IFRS implementing countries.

DOI: 10.4018/978-1-5225-0305-7.ch004

BACKGROUND AND LITERATURE REVIEW

The notion of unifying accounting principles dates back to the early 19th century. It is at this time that the concept of international financial standards originated, specifically during the first Global Congress of Accountants held at St. Louis in 1904 (Fritz & Lammle, 2003, p. 3). At the conference, the need for harmonization and cooperation in the accounting field was emphasized. Despite the initiative, differences in the accounting principles still abound, mainly because the dissimilarities in legal systems, the manner in which providers of capital operate, taxation systems, national cultures, and general accounting practices. The differences hindered investors from obtaining clear financial information, which is vital for strategic planning. Thus, international trade was constrained; countries experienced unequal opportunities as a result of the dissimilarities. In this regard, the inequalities and unclear financial statements were the main reasons behind the call for financial standardization.

1. The Accounting Harmonization Process

In harmonizing the accounting standards, different approaches were and still are being employed (Fritz & Lammle, 2003, p. 3). To enable accurate depiction of the process, harmonization can be viewed from different angles. First the process can be shown as a timeline and then depicted as a series of trait junctions. The timeline follows the steps and achievements made by the International Accounting Standards Committee (IASC) since the early 1960s.

1.1 Pre-Stage of the Harmonization Process

Jacob Kraanyehorf was the pioneer of financial unification. He released his first concept paper on the subject in 1959; through the document, Kraanyehorf campaigned for the international acceptance of economic unification (Fritz and Lammle, 2003, p. 21). To strengthen his proposal, he noted the advantages of a unified financial front such as elevated global loaning and easy trading that come with identification and appreciation of differences among countries. As a result of Kraanyehorf efforts, the International Accounts Study Group (IASG) was formulated in 1966 to help analyze and eliminate the differences in financial documentation between Canada and the United Kingdom. The Americans were not as enthusiastic about harmonization in the early 1960s, but changed their viewpoint in 1972 after one of their professional accounting bodies held discussions with six other nations, including Germany, Japan, China, the United Kingdom, and Canada (Fritz and Lammle, 2003, p. 21).

1.2 Harmonization between 1973 and1987

The International Accounting Standards Committee (IASC) was slowly developed between 1973 and 1987. This body was responsible for a considerable number of the standards set during the 14-year period. Particularly, the institution dealt with the problem of inventory recording. In this case, the main objective of the IASC was to ascertain compatibility between the new set guidelines and those established by the IASG (Fritz & Lammle, 2003, p. 23). Besides that, during the period, the unpopular global measurement methods, such as the austerity metrics, were eliminated. All standards were incorporated through a democratic process; if the set quorum was not achieved, the member states had the right to use any other desired algorithm to enact changes to the accounting principles. Unfortunately, the IASC actually ended up endorsing only mainstream financial procedures, instead of performing actual harmonization.

1.3 Harmonization between 1987 and 1993

This period marked the second generation of the IASC's developments. In 1987, the harmonizing group initiated membership with the International Organization of Security Commissions (IOSCO). A year later, the Financial Accounting Standards Board (FASB) joined the membership committee. The more other regulatory organizations acceded to the principles promoted, the further procedural standardization advanced. The member bodies dealt with financial matters in the same manner and thus the second harmonization process was characterized by further reduction of the set IASC options. That said, the IASC financial recording principles of 1989 were employed on a trial basis, hence the union of guidelines was rarely implemented. In this respect, the existence of comparability and a right to choose constrained the unification process; member organizations basically operated independently (Fritz & Lammle 24).

1.4 Harmonization between 1993 and 1998

The third IASC harmonization process began in 1993 after the agency and IOSCO agreed on a specific catalog of core guidelines for integration of financial statements (Fritz & Lammle, 2003, p. 25). By the end of 1994, the IOSCO had initiated and completed an analysis on all standards set by the IASC. By doing that, the body identified several niches and standards that required modifications to increase the openness, truthfulness, and accuracy of reporting. In 1995, both agencies jointly went through the reviews to create a joint list of unified principles. It is also at this time that the European Union (EU) decided to support the unification process. In addition, the EU decided not to segregate itself and thus eliminated its independent accounting standards. Finally, the harmonization process came to an end in 1998.

1.5 Harmonization 1998 Onwards

The current harmonization process began mainly in the new millennium. In May 2000, the IOSCO instructed its member states to permit the IASC to prepare for them international listings and offerings. The body also created a 26-question questionnaire that examined the acceptability of the financial documentation process under harmonization. The creation of the Euro – the EU's currency – in 1999 also increased the push for global accounting standards and thus more reviews and changes were made. Examples of the changes include the formulation of an inclusive body of accounting, emphasis on high levels of transparency and comparability as well as rigorous interpretations of financial statements (Fritz and Lammle, 2003, p. 27). The changes facilitated complete statement analysis in different languages and through multiple algorithms. The standard enforcement is now structured as shown below (see Figure 1).

1.6 Harmonization through Socio-Economic Aspects

In relation to trait junctions, the harmonization process has to be analyzed through socio-economic aspects. In this respect, the harmonization process can be broken down into material and formal harmonization, mutual recognition, reconciliation, and standardization. Material harmonization refers to the

Figure 1. Standard enforcement of accounting principles

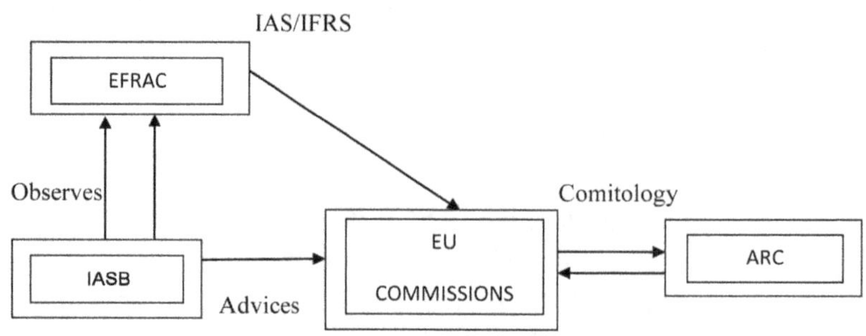

use of standard materials, such as tick marks and opinion letters, to ensure financial research follows a common theoretical and practical angle (Fritz & Lammle, 2003, p. 31). Formal harmonization refers to the broad acceptance and analysis of domestic or independent rules and regulations used by different states (Fritz & Lammle, 2003, p. 31). In the process of conducting formal harmonization, divergence and similarities were considered in the interpretation process, hence allowing statistical data to have similar conclusions irrespective of the rules and regulations applied.

Mutual recognition is the acceptability of statements across borders despite the fact that preparation of the documents may not have been done in accordance with accounting guidelines of the destination state. For instance, Canada and the United States employ different accounting principles domestically, but a document prepared by either country would be accepted by the stockbrokers of both nations. In this respect, mutual recognition curtails the harmonization process to some extent because it negates the need for similar core principles.

The reconciliation guidelines state that an expanding or foreign enterprise has the right to prepare documents in accordance with its local accounting standards so long as it additionally prepares records for use in the accounting of critical principles in the destination state (Fritz & Lammle, 2003, p. 33). As states reconcile critical principles, the harmonization process is able to identify the major dissimilarities in the accounting procedures. To elaborate further, an enterprise using IFRS guidelines can only venture into the United States if it prepares secondary Generally Accepted Accounting Principles (GAAP) documents.

Through standardization, all members participating in an accounting interaction set a number of principles that each party must comply with (Fritz & Lammle, 2003, p. 33). Thus, every act is binding, homogenous, and regular. In other words, standardization does not leave room for variation, misinterpretations, or unevenness. Given that the transactions in consideration affect international players, then one accounting principle of the participant states is applied universally. The summary of the concepts and processes involved in the harmonization through socio-economic aspects is shown below (see Figure 2).

Figure 2.

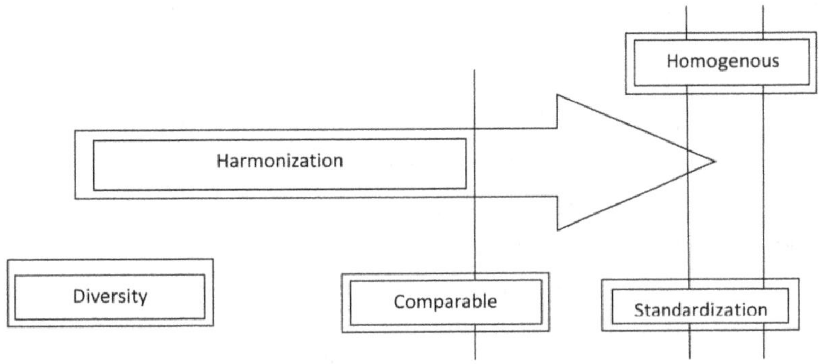

MAIN FOCUS OF THE CHAPTER: ISSUES, CONTROVERSIES, PROBLEMS

2. Economic Value of the IFRS

The push for common international financial reporting standards is based on the fact that successful implementation of the policy will result in economic benefits including creation of value relevance for fair value and minimization of reporting costs. The integration of the IFRS guidelines in financial reporting has elevated the quality of fair worth with respect to financial assets and liabilities. Value relevance is an important analytical aspect used in the testing of book data, mainly within the balance sheet. The financial concept is vital because it has a direct implication on equity and market values. Assets and liabilities are the basic variables of interest, thus harmonization of the elements allows open share pricing (Okpala, 2012). In this respect, value relevance is examined using the valuation model through which market and equity worth in balance sheets are regressed (Okpala, 2012). The US banking industry is an example of a market in which value relevance is constantly applied to examine the robustness of the IFRS in contrast to the US GAAP. Through the IFRS' fair value principle macro hedging in the United States was raised, thus facilitating more funding on asset demand that in turn enhances revenue generation.

Adoption of the IFRS minimizes the reporting costs of financial documentation given that enterprises within a trade pact do not operate as the sole entities (Okpala, 2012). Compliance with the standardized regulations enables the streamlining and cohesion between foreign companies, hence enabling comparisons, benchmarking, and company status-derivation on a simplistic level that does not necessitate the hiring of external consultants or auditors, which comes with extra costs. The harmonization process also puts a company in an advantageous position over its competitors through open financial reporting. The standards also help to identify new innovative production and marketing procedures that give better results.

The adoption of the IFRS has other economic benefits. It facilitates the transcending of international boundaries, hence making mergers and acquisitions of enterprises easier. The standardized guidelines aid in identification of organized and suitable partners, thus increasing opportunities of accessing foreign capital. In other words, companies can trade, move, and secure their capital and shares in different stock exchanges (Okpala, 2012). In relation to that, a majority of stock exchanges requires statements to be prepared under the IFRS process. By late 2010, more than 127 non-European states had accepted to use the IFRS guidelines as the standard reporting principles.

The IFRS is applied to take advantage of the progressive nature of companies and in the process it has been shown that only big audit firms can provide the expertise required for international cohesion. The standards have curtailed the developments of small establishments because such entities are often inexperienced or lack familiarity with cross border rules and regulations (Okpala, 2012). Consequently, the harmonization encourages the establishment of second tier firms, particularly because of the complexities involved in reconciliation. Fortunately, the application of macro-hedging and fair value estimates on financial assets and liabilities give more structured and defined information on the status and capacities of institutions, thus removing the need for external audits. This reduces the burden for smaller enterprises.

To some extent, the IFRS facilitates fraud deterrence. Fraudulent accounting is a menace that has eaten into the profits of international organizations. Several companies, for instance, AIG, have suffered considerable losses from fraudulent practices such as offshore trading. The harmonization of financial reporting, done through the IFRS' principles, has facilitated the reduction of fraud cases. Particularly, the push for high levels of document transparency and openness has made it easy to identify malpractices (Okpala, 2012). Therefore, companies cannot falsify their financial capacities to lure investors. Similarly, an organization cannot defraud its employees and vice versa, because of the specified relationship guidelines that state that functionality is mutually exclusive and firms have direct liability over protection of labor rights.

3. Political Value of the IFRS

In addition, the IFRS guidelines play a major role in politics. Politics or policy-making is a socio-economic function undertaken by state leaders to ensure that the best interests of citizens are protected. The incorporation of the IFRS accounting standards is a political strategy. The Gunadarma University conducted research on the subject in 70 countries and discovered that the IFRS guidelines ensure political stability through economic progression (Alexander, Fajri & Kurniawan, 2009, p. 168). This is because the standards determine the political approach that a country's administrators will employ. Though political stability was identified as a null factor in the integration of IFRS, the standards were noted as determinants of the level political constancy (Alexander, Fajri & Kurniawan, 2009, p. 168). This suggests that the better the economic capacity of a country, the more stable its governance is. Hence, the harmonization of reporting principles enhances the economic capacity of a state.

In relation to that, since the onset of the new millennium, countries have had different perspectives on the global standards and, therefore, comply to varying extents to the guidelines, particularly because of the dissimilarities in culture, technology, governance, and endowment with natural resources (Alexander, Fajri and Kurniawan, 2009, p. 168). Jurisdictional differences in the IFRS implementation result in immediate political response. For instance, if a certain domestic market performs better in terms of revenue generation than the international market, the political rhetoric would be against using the IFRS. Such a measure would be taken to discourage foreign penetration and at the same time safeguard local resources. Conversely, if the domestic economy performs poorly in comparison to the international market, the politicians would support the integration of the IFRS standards to lure investors.

4. The Global Acceptance of the IAS/IFRS Accounting Standards

Given the political and economic benefits of accounting harmonization, there is widespread or universal acceptance of the IAS reporting standards. The guidelines equip investors with the required flexibilities that enable expansion into foreign markets. For instance, through the IFRS, companies have enhanced their levels of capital security and have access to proficient audit consultancies. To highlight the degree of the global acceptance, the IAS guidelines have to be analyzed chronologically and in terms of the functions of the accounting standards.

The global acceptance of the IFRS guidelines can best be depicted in a chronological manner, from the introduction of the principles to present day enforcement. As earlier shown, the adoption of unified reporting standards was a gradual process that began in the late 50's and still continues to date. In 2002 all the member states of the EU voted unanimously to adopt the IFRS standards (Carmona & Trombetta, 2008). Hence, all the companies trading in the European Security Market were required to abide by IAS guidelines, while foreign or non-European investors had to adhere to the US GAAP. In 2005, the Australian Accounting Standards Board (AASB) followed suit; the agency recommended that all standards and reporting interpretation methods in the country be tailored to comply with IFRS guidelines (Carmona & Trombetta, 2008).

Some regions continue to lag behind in terms of implementation of the IFRS guidelines. Particularly, countries in South West Asia and Middle East and North Africa (MENA) regions have been slow in adopting the standards. For instance, Tunisia, Korea, Mongolia, and Morocco are still in the process of integrating the IFRS principles. The main impediment in the MENA region is Sharia Law, which compels Muslims to apply different accounting principles. Other nations are just beginning the transformation process. At the present, all banking institutions and enterprises within Russia are required to prepare financial statements using the IFRS regulations. Since 2005, New Zealand has adopted 36 novel accounting rules as well as 12 interpretation algorithms, all of which were derived from the IFRS guidelines (Carmona & Trombetta, 2008). The other accounting standards in use in the country are all past guidelines that were equivalent to the IAS principles.

Other significant markets also adopted the policies recently. The eighth largest market in terms of capitalization, Hong Kong, has been aligning its standards with the IFRS guidelines since 1990. In 2008, the Canadian Accounting Standard Board adopted the IFRS principles on a trial basis for a five-year period (Carmona & Trombetta, 2008). As a result, the United States is the only G4 country that does not comply with the harmonized practices. By the time Canada acceded to the standards, Japan and China had already begun gradually adopting the principles a decade earlier.

The distinctive element of the IFRS/IAS guidelines is its principle-based approach; domestic standards employ a rule-based approach. A principle-based approach overrides secondary rules that increase data complexities (Carmona & Trombetta, 2008). In addition, its associated restrictions, precedents, and exceptions are clear and precise unlike the criteria thresholds of rule-based systems. Hence, the principle-based approach offers generic practices that address controversial issues, while simultaneously ascertaining ambiguity (Carmona & Trombetta, 2008). The approach also allows the diverse and broad nature of harmonization to be viewed from a narrow and simplistic perspective, thus enhancing report comprehension. For example, according to principle 19 of the IAS that addresses employee benefits, integration of the corridor approach eases documentation of losses and gains that in turn reflects on the net income for any portion that surpasses the corridor.

5. Effects of Mandatory IFRS Adoption in the EU Commerce

The European Union officially adopted the IFRS standards in 2005 and, as a result, all European companies listed on the unified stock exchange were forced to abandon their domestic national accounting standards in favor of the new reporting principles. The adoption of the new accounting practices had implications on loans and advances, particularly due to changes on fair value estimation. The fair worth of loans and advances became vital and relevant derivatives for the determination of a bank's performance (Dimos, 2011, p. 100). In addition, the fair values gave a clear picture of a firm's economic position by highlighting its financial capacities. In other words, the values on loans, advances, and debts showed that fair value was a functional indicator of an institution's financial health as well as its revenue generation variability. Hence, the nations with strong financial institutions found it easy to adopt the IFRS, while the reverse is true.

Besides that, (Dimos, 2011, p. 102) conducted an analysis of several European banks over a five-year period and discovered that the adoption of the IFRS resulted in lower equity-capital costs. Even the European states that fared poorly in IFRS enforcement recorded the reduction in equity-capital costs; possibly the benefits resulted from the complete implementation of the IFRS principles by neighboring nations. The capital costs may have also reduced because of the changes in measurement and presentation methods along with the asset holding to maturity function prior to the commencement of a financial transaction (Dimos, 2011, p. 102). The measurement and presentation of all assets and liabilities incorporated a mixture of fair value and remunerated expenses that in turn increased the accuracy of status depiction. Hence, the investors and entrepreneurs could effectively and efficiently carry out share pricing. This in turn elevated trading within the region. The act of holding stock to maturity ensures that trading is done in instances when the shares fetch the optimal market values, thus maximizing revenue generation (Dimos, 2011, p. 102). In addition, the practice encourages provision of bank advances and loans, hence also increasing revenue generation in the long term.

Adoption of the IFRS by the EU also improved the hedge accounting process. The purpose of hedge accounting is to pair up gains and losses to reduce risk. According to the IAS, hedging accounting can be classified into cash flow, fair value, and net venture on alien operation hedging (Dimos, 2011, p. 104). Fair value hedges mitigate an institution's exposure to fair value risks, cash flow hedges protect a firm from poor cash flows, and the net investment hedges on foreign soil ensures that a company's interest or total assets are free from exposure in the novel territory. The effectiveness of the risk management functions of the IFRS facilitated by the modified hedge accounting process improved the financial performance of European institutions. The banking sector benefited by receiving expansion guarantees, thus encouraging ventures into South West Asia and the MENA regions that lagged behind financially because of adopting religion-based accounting principles. In this respect, macro hedging has extensively been promoted by the EU's banks.

A report from ICAEW (2015) examines the findings of about 200 research papers on the effects of mandatory IFRS adoption in the EU. The report aims to add to the debate on the future of IFRS in the EU. The report shows that there is evidence of benefits following IFRS adoption in relation to financial reporting transparency and comparability, the cost of capital, market liquidity, corporate investment efficiency and cross-border capital flows. The report points out that the benefits found are uneven, varying with the institutions and incentives that apply for different companies in different countries.

6. Multinational Companies and Accounting Convergence

The movement towards a global economy has increased the need for global accounting standards. The growth of multinational companies has enhanced the need of such standards. The Securities and Exchange Commission (SEC) has influenced the topic of converging US GAAP and international accounting standards. The commission has allowed foreign companies to use IFRS in financial reporting without having to reconcile US GAAP and international standards. In addition, it has sought to unite world regulators on the convergence of global accounting standards. The convergence and harmonization of IFRS and American GAAP into a single set of accounting standards would benefit multinationals significantly.

According to the United Nations Conference on Trade and Development (2008), the decision to adopt IFRS is determined by a cost-benefit trade-off between some factors. Firstly, it recognizes the benefits of the investors. Secondly, it recognizes the recurring cost savings on the multinationals. The third trade-off involves the one time transition cost that multinationals and the national economy have to incur. The cost involves the adjustments to the institutions of a specified country. Multinational companies have enhanced the spread of IFRS. They provide a significant channel for foreign direct investment into most economies. They were involved in the formulation of the standards. In addition, their support has been essential to the success of the standards. Due to the important role that they play in the national economy, it is impossible to imagine if the standards would have been so successful had they opposed them.

Furthermore, governments should let multinational companies to decide whether and when to adapt the IFRS. The companies incur the heaviest burden of the process. In addition, they hold the key to determining the success of implementing the standards.

Countries should embrace the model that Russia has adopted. Their financial reporting standards should be implemented in a dual manner. Firstly, the national GAAP should be upheld as alternatives to the IFRS. Secondly, countries should adopt the IFRS. Having the two options will enable the country to comply with the needs of the international financial community without undermining its local practices. In addition, it would save domestic organizations from incurring the expense of adopting international standards that would have no real impact on their operations.

The accounting scandals that have occurred in major multinationals such as Enron and World Com have highlighted the need for high quality international accounting standards. The need for the standards has been increased by the expansion of the internalization of the securities market.

The Securities and Exchange Commission (SEC) has joined forces with the European Commission and the Japan Commission to increase the globalization of international accounting standards. However, the threat of increased global power for the SEC is a contentious issue. The formation of the International Accounting Standards Committee Foundation (IASCF) is expected to solve the problem of a super powerful SEC.

The process of globalization has combined with the increased awareness of capital markets to increase the need for the convergence of accounting standards (Fortin, Barros, & Cutler, 2010). In addition, the size of investors has increased significantly. For example, foreign institutional investors are investing in significant global volumes. Furthermore, the television and online media have enabled the public to track the movements of share prices in the global market. The convergence of accounting standards would enable investors to make quick investment decisions.

Multinational organizations have adopted institutional entrepreneurship. The institutional entrepreneurs are organizations that use their resources to advocate for change. They have been change agents on the subject because they perceive the value in the implementation of international accounting standards.

7. IFRS Adoption, FDI and Institutions

An evaluation of the data on international trade and financial reporting standards demonstrates that the development of institutions in a country has a greater impact than the mere adoption of the standards.

Although adopting the standards has a positive immediate impact, it does not have a long-term influence. According to the United Nations Conference on Trade and Development (2008), investors consider multiple factors when making an investment decision. As a result, the presence of one positive factor is not enough. The observation can be used to explain why the implementation of the standards in developing countries has a limited impact. Governments should instead match the adoption of the standards with a number of key factors. Firstly, they should work on strengthening the institutions in the country. Most developing countries have weak institutions controlled by the government. They should ensure that there is a strict separation of powers between the arms of government. They should also promote the rule of law. Countries with low corruption rates will benefit from increased FDI. There should be a strong focus on the implementation of property law and the enforcement of contracts.

The World Bank has made more countries to adopt the standards. Most countries are forced to adopt the standards in order to receive funding from the institution. As a result, the standards have been driven by international forces as opposed to a deliberate desire among the countries to increase the integrity of their standards.

Another key thing to note is that the developing countries as opposed to their developed counterparts drive the overall increase in FDI. The observation is because foreign direct investment is skewed in favor of emerging markets. In addition, most developed countries already have similar financial reporting standards.

The success of the international financial reporting standards is dependent on government institutions. Governments adopt the standards and commit themselves to enforce them in their jurisdictions. However, the implementation of the standards requires the participation of all the stakeholders. In most instances, the government would have to give the organizations within its jurisdiction sufficient time to implement the new standards. The relevant government institutions will have to police the organizations.

Financial standards setters, regulators and policy-makers have a significant interest on the impact of financial reporting standards on the economy (Tsamenyi & Uddin, 2008). The interest can be attributed to the economic consequences associated with the financial information. The financial information influences the behavior of investors by determining their portfolio selection. Firms have a significant interest in the information because it determines the pricing of securities that in turn affect their ability to get additional funding. The regulation of financial reporting mechanisms is a significant mechanism that determines the operation of securities markets. The markets are a significant channel of foreign direct investment.

Adoption of IFRS has been influenced by the desire to among transitional economies to adopt corporate governance practices that would give them global intimacy (Tsamenyi & Uddin, 2008). The move acknowledges the modernization of developing economies. The practice is bound to result in greater financial transparency. Achieving a high level of transparency will encourage international trade and FDI. The adoption of the practices has been both mandatory and voluntary. However, a country's adoption of the standards was not affected.

The increased push for more countries to adopt International Financial Reporting Standards requires a determination of their impact on international trade. The practice results in increased foreign direct investment and international trade because it fosters transparency and comparability. International investors are keen on investing in countries whose financial practices are understandable. Furthermore, they desire to work in countries that have high levels of transparency. The countries with transparent institutions have the ability to attract investors from diverse countries (Fortin, Barros, and Cutler, 2010). For example, the United States has a code of standards that investors and companies working abroad should follow. If they engage in questionable financial practices, then there is the possibility that they could be sued for their actions. As a result, they are keen on entering into countries with clear financial practices.

In addition, the practice enhances the ease of doing business. The standards will enhance the process of doing business because agents will understand each other more. Furthermore, the adoption of such standards will reduce information cost. International trade and foreign direct investments are often hampered by the high cost of acquiring the right information. In cases where there are different accounting standards involved, the investors are forced to invest in consultants. The price of hiring consultants increases the investment cost significantly.

In 2010, 120 countries decided to adopt the International Financial Reporting Standards and made a commitment to enforce them in their jurisdictions (Lasmin, 2011). In the same year, foreign direct investment in foreign countries increased significantly. As a result, an increase in people who support the adoption of uniform accounting standards has been noted. However, there is no sufficient data to prove that developing countries benefit from adopting the standards. According to the United Nations Conference on Trade and Development (2008), developing countries are not likely to receive more FDI inflows and increased international trade by adopting the standards. This is because international trade is determined by many different factors. In contrast, the European countries benefited the most from the adoption of those standards.

The process is characterized by several challenges. For example, the United Nations Conference on Trade and Development (2008) notes the high cost involved in adopting the standards for the organizations involved due to the overhauling of systems and training costs involved. Furthermore, the organizations would be forced to implement many changes in their financial practices. However, the benefits of benchmarking with their peers from any part of the world are enough to offset the high cost. In addition, adopting the standards would allow a multinational company to have consistent reporting standards with its subsidiaries. The move would improve international communications. Moreover, it would result in a better quality of reporting. The decision-making process within the organization will also be improved in a significant manner.

However, it is clear that there should be further research on accounting standards harmonization process in Europe and other countries. Furthermore, a deliberate effort to address the unwanted effects of adopting IFRS standards is crucial. The process will lead to a better understanding of IFRS standards on national and international economies.

8. When do the Adoption and Use of IFRS increase Foreign Investment?

A significant challenge that firms face when attracting foreign investment is the asymmetry of information between foreign and direct investors. IFRS gives firms the opportunity to reduce the asymmetry. The move will increase their attractiveness among foreign firms. However, significant differences are noted in the manner that firms implement the IFRS standards. The observation is because firms have different reporting practices. Firms with strong reporting standards tend to attract many foreign investors. In contrast, those with weak reporting standards only attract little foreign investment (Bowe, Miletkov & Wintoki, 2013, p. 3). The countries that have weak investor protection systems would not benefit significantly from the adoption of the standards if the practice were not matched with a deliberate process to reform the institutions of the organization.

Foreign investors consider many factors before investing in a country. For example, the country must demonstrate its respect for the rule of law. Strong property laws and a commitment to enforce contract characterize countries that respect the rule of law. Since corruption increases the cost of doing business significantly, most investors are keen on investing in countries with low levels of corruption. Consequently, an enabling environment is necessary for the IFRS to increase foreign investment. As a result, countries looking to benefit from the adoption of the standards should ensure that a deliberate process to create an enabling environment that protects investors accompanies them.

In addition, IFRS are effective in countries with high quality auditing standards. Auditors play noteworthy role in ensuring that organizations comply with the financial practices of their countries. Foreign investors rely on auditor reports to enable them make appropriate investment decisions. In the event that a country with high quality auditors adopts IFRS, then it can attract many foreign investors.

A critical evaluation of IFRS standards shows that they were designed for developing and mature capital markets. Although it is clear that financial statements assist investors to make critical investment decisions, countries with no stock markets should not adopt IFRS. Financial statements help users to estimate the value of securities when they are buying or selling. Financial reporting should not exist in developing markets. The accounting systems in a particular country are determined by its socio-economic and political history. The fact that some economies differ significantly from others shows that the adoption of the standards is only effective in some countries.

In order for IFRS to be effective, it is important to modify some aspects in order to make it suitable to the accounting needs of the country. The European Union and other countries have adopted modifications that ensure that the standards address their needs. If the standards are suited to a given country, then they are likely to succeed in attracting foreign investment.

Many countries have adopted the European Union-based IFRS standards. Understanding the reasons that motivate their actions provides a strong indication of the future of the standards. An evaluation of the countries that have adopted the standards shows that more powerful countries are less likely to adopt them. The countries have a strong economy that has good corporate governance systems. As a result, they fail to perceive any value in adopting additional standards. The approach explains why the developing countries represent a significant portion of the states that have adopted the standards.

The indifference that powerful countries have towards the standards is due to their unwillingness to surrender standard setting authority to an outside entity. In most instances, countries try to avoid surrendering any authority to independent entities. For instance, the United States has been reluctant with the adoption of the IFRS (MAFK International, 2013). However, with hundreds of countries adopting the standard, the United States is likely to replace its US GAAP standards with the new accounting practices (MAFK International, 2013).

The network effect that is associated with the adoption of the standards provides a powerful motivation for other countries to join them. A country is more likely to adopt the IFRS standards if other countries within their geographic region did the same. In addition, if trade partners adopt the standards, then a country would be under intense pressure to act similarly. Consequently, the practice has been driven by strategic considerations as opposed to a willful desire to demonstrate financial prudence.

Furthermore, the increasing number of countries adopting the standards has led to higher network effects. The argument postulates that some countries are forced to adopt the studies so that they can benefit from the effects of a global economy that focuses on the creation of a unified financial code.

However, there is no evidence to show that changes in the trade and foreign direct investment have any direct impact on the decision of a country on the subject. In contrast, the adoption is due to the economic theory of networks. The theory postulates that the value of something such as a product or service increases when it is adopted by a wide group of people. The adoption of the standards has occurred in a gradual manner. Countries did not adopt the standards at once. Instead, the adoption process has been gradual. As more countries embrace the standards, their counterparts have to adopt them in order to avoid missing a new global reality.

The strength of the governance and corporate structures in a country determine whether they are likely to adopt the IFRS standards. Countries, whose governments have the ability to make timely-decision making, are more likely to adopt the standards. In addition, they are more likely to embrace the standards if the cost of switching to the new standards is expensive.

The implementation of the standards does not result in a significant reduction in information costs for advanced economies. The observation demonstrates that the developing economies would benefit the most from adopting the standards. As a result, it is evident that adopting the standards is driven by strategic considerations.

Countries understand that widespread adoption of the standards is integral towards creating a global accounting standard that benefits everyone. The standards will result in a significant reduction in the investment decision. In addition, it would lead to a reduction in the cost of accessing the information (MAFK International, 2013). Many countries realize the importance of being part of the global economy. They hope that by adopting the standards they are likely to create an environment that matches the emerging trends in the international arena.

9. IFRS, Foreign Direct Investment, and Corporate Social Responsibility

Although there is not a standard definition of corporate social responsibility, the term is widely known as contributing to a better society through company actions in the benefit of the workforce and local community. This means the adoption of voluntary codes of conduct and rules of behavior by companies which go beyond public legislations. There is a strong relationship between corporate social responsibility and foreign direct investment as the increase of foreign direct investment has fostered the growth of corporate social responsibility. Corporate social responsibility is an important determinant for multinational companies to start operations. FDI increases the working conditions due to established CSR initiatives (see Frost & Ho, 2005; Goyal, 2006; Kolk & van Tulder, 2010).

Some authors claim that FDI and CSR have played an important role for poverty reduction, as well as having an impact on salaries and working conditions in developing countries (see Brown *et al*, 2004). On the other hand, other authors explain that corporate social responsibility is the reaction to the social dissatisfaction from globalization (see Jenkins, 2005; Gonzalez-Perez & McDonough, 2007). CSR policies have increased as a result of globalization creating a sense of responsibility creating a sense of responsibility engaging companies in an improvement of the societies where they operate. There is also a relationship between CSR and economic performance of companies (see McWilliams & Siegel, 2000, 2001; Carter, 2005). Although it is not clear if companies are successful as a result of the CSR implementation or if companies implemented CSR policies due to their economic success.

It is often suggested that there is a mutual relationship between society and economic actors. In this sense, Edwards (2004) explains society needs to access the surplus of market economies in order to have sustainable social objectives, he points out that society needs markets and these markets need a strong civil society to develop. Goyal (2006) points out that corporate social responsibility can create a sense of responsibility for companies entering new countries to cooperate in poverty reduction and social welfare. Thus, an increase in FDI will promote growth of CSR practices, and a higher degree of responsible business initiatives will attract new FDI.

Emerging economies are still perceived as risky places to invest, although multinationals countries are actively investing in many developing countries. Countries which are rich in resources are a strong motivation for investment. Most developing countries depend on FDI inflow to transform their fast growing economy. These countries hope that a higher inflow of FDI will improve their economy and increase the standard of living of their population with more employment opportunities. The implementation of the appropriate macroeconomic policies together with the liberalization of the economy, and privatization are the key factor to attract FDI to emerging economies (See Ajayi (2008)). Unemployment and poverty are the major challenges faced by developing economies, being the high unemployment the main determinant of low standard of living in these countries. Thus, developing countries have a strong incentive to attract foreign companies to invest and to use trade in favor of their country´s interest.

Most developing countries have implemented policy reforms with the intention to create great business atmosphere for foreign investors. The leaders of developing countries work to attract more FDI to alleviate poverty. Creating job opportunities in a country would contribute to alleviate poverty. The higher economic growth would increase employment, improving the standard of living and reducing poverty. Furthermore, FDI can contribute to the improvement of infrastructure by host countries. Another factor which contributes to poverty alleviation is the taxation of foreign subsidiaries. Taxes from foreign companies would increase the revenues of the host country. This tax revenue can be used to finance poverty reduction initiatives or creating a safety net for the poor. In this sense, Prahalad (2002, p. 42) stated that "By stimulating commerce and development at the bottom of the economic pyramid, MNCs could radically improve the lives of billions of people and help bring into being a more stable, less dangerous world".

INVESTMENTS THROUGH EMPLOYMENT OPPORTUNITIES: SOLUTIONS AND RECOMMENDATIONS

10. The Effect of IFRS on Cross-Border Acquisitions

One of the biggest arguments advanced by proponents of the IFRS is its ability to create an efficient capital allocation process through greater cross-border investment. An evaluation of investment data shows a significant increase in the level of investment due to the adoption of the IFRS standards. The observation is consistent with the fact that investors benefit from a significant reduction in information symmetry due to the increase in the comparability of financial reports.

In addition, a strong implementation of the IFRS standards may result in a significant increase in mutual funds investment. The countries that have strong implementation credentials tend to attract many investments from both individual and institutional investors. In contrast, countries with weak implementation capacities realize no significant impact from the adoption of the standards. Achieving financial comparability is bound to have a net positive result of cross-border trade. Comparability refers to achieving uniformity in accounting practices between two different countries (DeFond, Hu, Hung & Li, 2010, p. 1). High comparability levels will reduce the cost of accessing information. As a result, increased investment in firms will be noted.

However, two factors should qualify any claim about the impact of achieving financial comparability. In jurisdictions where the enforcement of the standards is mandatory, the success of the new accounting standards is dependent on the management credibility of the new organizations (DeFond, Hu, Hung &

Li, 2010, p. 1). Management credibility involves the ability of the management to implement the new accounting standards. Financial reporting practices vary significantly amidst countries. In addition, managers have a lot of flexibility in determining the implementation of accounting standards.

The second qualifying factor involves the magnitude of the increase in uniformity. A large increase in uniformity will result in increased financial comparability. The magnitude varies from one country to another (DeFond, Hu, Hung & Li, 2010, p. 2). As a result, the adoption of IFRS standards is bound to result in varying implications in different countries.

(Henock & Oktay, 2015) examine the effect of IFRS on foreign direct investments (FDIs) by analyzing whether the 2005 mandatory adoption of IFRS leads to an increase in cross-border acquisitions in the adopting countries. They find that the adoption of IFRS led to a significant increase in FDIs, which is consistent with the primary objective of IFRS.

FUTURE RESEARCH DIRECTIONS

The European Union provides an effective case study for analyzing the impact of the implementation of the IFRS standards on a large scale. In the European Union, the implementation of the IFRS standards was mandatory. As a result, they were implemented in many firms at the same time. An analysis of the information is based on mutual fund investments. In most instances, mutual fund investors are sophisticated investors who make their investment decisions based on a comprehensive analysis of financial information.

CONCLUSION

The impact of adopting the IFRS standards is limited to domestic investors. The investors have access to alternative channels of communication. For example, they can obtain information from industry analysts or mangers. Similarly, the increase in cross-border transactions is due to the activities of foreign- owned organizations. The organizations tend to have a presence in multiple foreign markets. Consequently, they have a significant interest in benchmarking with a large number of firms.

The effects of adopting IFRS on cross-border trade are dependent on the economic institutions in the countries involved. Furthermore, the management incentives in the country determine the process. The enforcement of the IFRS standards is bound to play a significant role in determining if the implementation of the organization is bound to have a significant effect. Some countries have strong financial regulatory bodies that ensure all the organizations in the country implement the standards. Others have weak institutions that lack the resources or ability to ensure that all firms in a country implement the new standards. In the former countries, a significant increase in cross-border trade is noted while in the latter countries, the impact will be limited.

Multinational companies contribute to economic development through investments, taxation, jobs, and the transfer of technology and skills. As the level of corporate social responsibility is strongly related to FDI inflow for developing countries, there should be a higher degree of cooperation between local governments and multinational companies to improve FDI inflow and reduce poverty. Local governments should implement programs to engage foreign companies to hire and train their local employees with the view of increasing long-term employability. Initiatives followed by developing countries should include liberalization of trade, increase export-led growth, and privatization of public companies.

REFERENCES

Bowe, H., Miletkov, M., & Wintoki, B. M. (2013). *When does the adoption and use of IFRS increase foreign investment?* University of Virginia Working Paper.

Brown, D. K., Deardorff, A. V., & Stern, R. M. (1998). Trade and labour standards. *Open Economies Review*, *9*(2), 179–194. doi:10.1023/A:1008268419257

Carmona, S., & Trombetta, M. (2008). On the global acceptance of the IAS/IFRS accounting standards: The logic and implications of the principle-based system. *Journal of Accounting and Public Policy*, *27*(6), 455–461. doi:10.1016/j.jaccpubpol.2008.09.003

Carter, C. R. (2005). Purchasing corporate responsibility and firm performance: The key mediating roles of organisational learning and supplier performance. *International Journal of Physical Distribution & Logistics Management*, *35*, 177–194. doi:10.1108/09600030510594567

DeFond, M., Hu, X., Hung, M., & Li, S. (2010). *The impact of mandatory IFRS adoption on foreign mutual fund ownership: The role of compatibility.* IAS Working Paper.

Dimos, A. (2011). *IFRS and European commercial banks: Value relevance and economic consequences.* (Doctoral thesis), University of Birmingham, Birmingham, UK.

Edwards, M. (2004). *Future positive: International co-operation in the 21st century.* London: Earthscan.

Fritz, S., & Lammle, C. (2003). *The international harmonization process of accounting standards.* (Master's thesis), Linkoping University, Linkoping, Sweden.

Frost, S., & Ho, M. (2005). Going out: The growth of Chinese foreign direct investment in Southeast Asia and its implications for corporate social responsibility. *Corporate Social Responsibility and Environmental Management*, *12*(3), 157–167. doi:10.1002/csr.98

Goyal, A. (2006). Corporate social responsibility as a signalling device for foreign direct investment. *International Journal of the Economics of Business*, *13*(1), 145–163. doi:10.1080/13571510500520077

Henock, L., & Oktay, U. (2015). *The effect of IFRS on foreign direct investments: Evidence from cross-border acquisitions.* SSRN Working Paper.

ICAEW (2015). *The effects of mandatory IFRS adoption in the EU: A review of empirical research.* ICAEW's Financial Reporting Faculty.

Jenkins, R. (2005). Globalization, corporate social responsibility and poverty. *International Affairs*, *81*(3), 525–540. doi:10.1111/j.1468-2346.2005.00467.x

Kolk, A., & Van Tulder, R. (2010). International business, corporate social responsibility and sustainable development. *International Business Review*, *19*(2), 119–125. doi:10.1016/j.ibusrev.2009.12.003

Lasmin. (2012). The unwanted effects of international financial reporting standards (IFRS) adoption on international trade and investments in developing countries. *Journal of Economics and Economic Education Research, 13*(1).

McWilliams, A., & Siegel, D. (2000). Research notes and communications: Corporate social responsibility and financial performance: Correlation or Misspecification? *Strategic Management Journal, 21*(5), 603–609. doi:10.1002/(SICI)1097-0266(200005)21:5<603::AID-SMJ101>3.0.CO;2-3

Okpala, K. E. (2012). Adoption of the IFRS and financial statements effects: The perceived implications on FDI and global economy. *Australian Journal of Business and Management Research, 2*(5), 76–83.

Prahalad, C. K. (2002). Serving the world's poor profitably. *Harvard Business Review, 9*(48). PMID:12227146

Tsamenyi, M., & Uddin, S. (2008). *Corporate governance in less developed and emerging economies.* Bingley: JAI Press. doi:10.1016/S1479-3563(08)08018-3

ADDITIONAL READING

Ajayi, S. L. (2008). *Foreign direct investment in Sub-Saharan Africa: Origins, targets, impacts and potential.* African Economic Research Consortium.

Alexander, M., Fajri, S. N., & Kurniawan, C. R. (2009). Political influence towards IFRS implementation in Asia. *The 3rd Uzbekistan-Indonesia International Joint Conference on Economic Development and Nation Character Building to Meet the Global Economic Challenges* 1.1, 167-170. Print.

Fortin, H., Barros, A. C., & Cutler, K. (2010). *Accounting for growth in Latin America and the Caribbean: Improving corporate financial reporting to support regional economic development.* Washington, D.C: World Bank.

Gonzalez-Perez, M. A., & McDonough, T. (2007). More than bananas: Social responsibility networks and labour relations in the banana industry in the Uraba region of Colombia. Organización Internacional del Trabajo, editor, Trade Union strategies towards globalisation.

United Nations Conference on Trade and Development. (2008). Practical implementation of international financial reporting standards: Lessons learned. Country case studies on IFRS. *New York: United Nations.*

KEY TERMS AND DEFINITIONS

Accounting Harmonization: A process of increasing the comparability of accounting practices worldwide. Harmonized standards should improve the compatibility of financial information from different countries.

Corporate Social Responsibility: A company initiative to take actions to improve the environment and social wellbeing.

Developing Country: A country with an underdeveloped industrial environment, together with a low Human Development Index (HDI). It is also called less developed country or underdeveloped country.

Foreign Direct Investment: An investment made by a company located in one country, into a company based in another country.

International Trade: The exchange of goods and services between countries.

Multinational Company: A company that has operations and assets in at least one country outside its home country. It is also referred as "transnational corporation".

Poverty Reduction: Promotion of several measures, economic and humanitarian, that will eliminate poverty.

Chapter 5
Corporate Social Responsibility and Foreign Direct Investment:
Engaging Innovation, Auditors, and Stakeholders in Corporate Social Responsibility

Marianne Ojo
North-West University, South Africa

ABSTRACT

As well as highlighting how corporations and multinational enterprises can be effectively engaged in entrepreneurship and innovation, as a means of fulfilling corporate social responsibility goals and objectives, this chapter aims to propose means whereby auditors could fulfil corporate governance roles more effectively. Having drawn vital lessons from past corporate collapses and the devastating of these in terms of unemployment - particularly for uninsured wider stakeholders, a vital goal of an enterprise should also namely, embrace that of facilitating initiatives aimed at job creation – through entrepreneurship programs which should also have a role in determining how directors and executives are remunerated – in addition to corporate governance measures which are currently in place. By way of reference to corporate collapses which have severely and adversely impacted the lives of many "uninsured" stakeholders, particularly in developed countries, the chapter also aims to address how the fulfilment of obligations and commitments to such stakeholders, can be secured.

INTRODUCTION

Whilst Corporate Social Responsibility is considered to be generally used as "an umbrella term to describe the complex and multifaceted relationships between business and society and to account for the economic, social and environmental impacts of business activity", another definition which incorporates the role of corporate governance, regards corporate social responsibility as:

DOI: 10.4018/978-1-5225-0305-7.ch005

- A model of extended corporate governance whereby those in control of the firm have responsibilities that range from the fulfilment of their fiduciary duties owed towards the owners (principal), to the fulfilment of analogous fiduciary duties owed towards all the firm's stakeholders (Sacconi, 2004:6).

Whilst the focus accorded to CSR in developed countries, appears to revolve round its role in facilitating greater accountability to stakeholders, particularly given the devastating consequences of corporate collapses on wider stakeholders, as well as the need for more effective corporate governance mechanisms, the focus of CSR as a means of philanthropy and charitable donations, appears to be a more predominant feature in developing countries (Jamali & Mirshak, 2007: 243-262). The role which political environments may play in obstructing the desired objectives of contributing positively to the economies of the host countries, where matters relating to Foreign Direct Investment are involved, and where regulations, standards, principles and codes of conduct are not complied with, will also be considered in this chapter – by way of reference to the vital role assumed by legal and ethical responsibilities within the framework of Carroll's pyramid of Corporate Social Responsibility.

It will be argued that even though economic responsibilities assume a primary role in certain cases, that basic goals of profit maximization will not attain their potential where rules, regulations, codes and principles are not effectively complied with or enforced. Herein lies the need for vital corporate governance mechanisms whose effectiveness is further bolstered by the role of external auditors in the corporate governance process.

AIMS AND OBJECTIVES OF THE CHAPTER

In line with the main objective of this chapter, namely highlighting how corporations and enterprises, national or multinational, can be effectively engaged in entrepreneurship and innovation, as a means of fulfilling corporate social responsibility goals and objectives, the chapter also seeks to:

1. Recommend means whereby audits, auditors, and forensic accountants could be engaged more effectively, in enhancing and complementing corporate governance mechanisms in more advanced economies.
2. To illustrate how CSR can benefit locals in developing countries, more effectively, by specific reference to Foreign Direct Investment, as well as the goals of charitable donations and projects.
3. To illustrate and recommend how CSR can be effectively enhanced to particularly, better serve the needs of developed countries by enhancing their corporate governance structures.

Given these considerations, as well as profound evidence of lack of operation of effective corporate governance mechanisms and structures in developing countries, should there not be a re-think in the role and focus of CSR in developing countries?

Whilst charitable projects could still feature prominently as goals, such goals require a vehicle whereby their realization could be facilitated and achieved. Such a vehicle assuming the form of effective corporate governance mechanisms and structures.

Hence whilst charitable projects may still constitute the ultimate goal, greater focus, than is presently the case, should be accorded to the role which CSR can assume in facilitating the operation of more effective corporate governance mechanisms, which in turn, will facilitate the goal of charitable donations and ensuring that intended targets receive such donations.

Background and Literature Review

Meaningfully and effectively implementing codes of conducts, standards and regulations which drive a business, and particularly multinational enterprises can have important consequences for basic goals such as profit maximization for such enterprises – however they also play determine the extent to which corporate social responsibility objectives are realized.

Without effective compliance and enforcement strategies, which embrace a range of disclosure requirements that are aimed at maximally engaging stakeholders in the corporate social responsibility process, CSR objectives which are also facilitated by such corporate governance mechanisms of disclosure and accountability, will be hindered in achieving their maximum potential.

Therein lies the principal objective of this section: not only to highlight why corporate goals of profit maximization may not achieve their maximum potential, but also to illustrate why in certain cases, rules and regulations – which can be found closer to the apex of Carroll's pyramid of Corporate Social Responsibility, may assume a more primary function that economic responsibilities which are found at the base of the pyramid. In highlighting the importance of rules, codes, principles and standards and effectively implementing and enforcing these, this chapter also incorporates the role of audits as corporate governance mechanisms for facilitating disclosure requirements and complying with International Financial Reporting Standards – such that directors and management of enterprises are held accountable – as well as enhancing greater transparency into the process.

Nestle Creating Shared Value and Carroll's CSR Pyramids

A number of disclosure initiatives have been carried out by companies such as Nestle – as disclosed in its 2013 Summary Report which also provides a highlight of performance indicators, which, in Nestle's view, facilitate the focus for measuring and reporting Creating Shared Value, sustainability, and compliance.

Based on the "Creating Shared Value" Figure 1, analyses and deductions can be made about the different levels of the pyramid:

That compliance with laws, business principles and codes of conduct, without doubt, constitutes the most fundamental and strategic level of the pyramid since goals and objectives attributed to other levels of the pyramid, namely longer term goals of sustainability, and goals relating to nutritional, water and rural development, will not be realised to their maximum potential where compliance with regulations and other related laws and principles are not effectively implemented and enforced.

That a contrast can be drawn between the Figure 1 and Carroll's pyramid of regulatory strategies.

In this regard, a contrast with Carroll's pyramid of regulatory strategies is illustrated in Figure 2.

Where economic responsibilities exclude the consideration of vital obligations such as codes of ethics - that are intended to serve as safeguards in ensuring that directors and management do not abuse their positions of authority - to the detriment of stakeholders, then, profit maximization goals and objectives will fail to achieve their full potentials.

Figure 1. Creating shared value pyramid

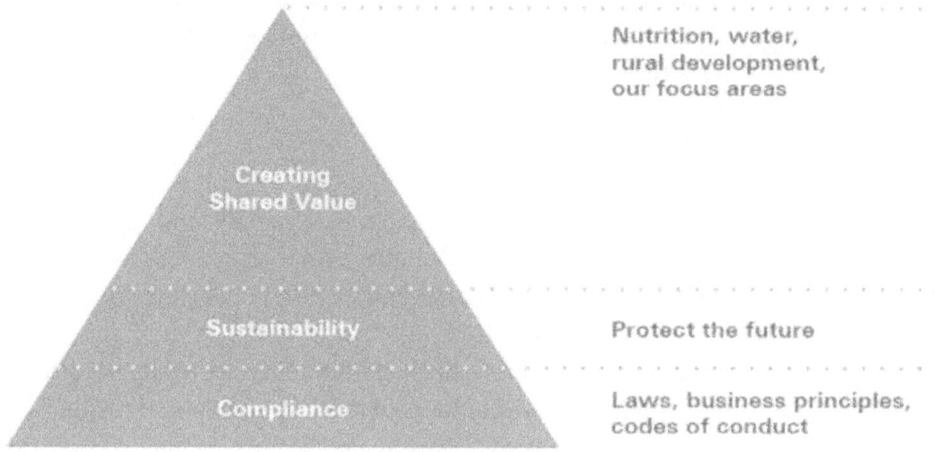

Figure 2. Carroll's Pyramid of Corporate Social Responsibility
Source: Danjsmee, 2012

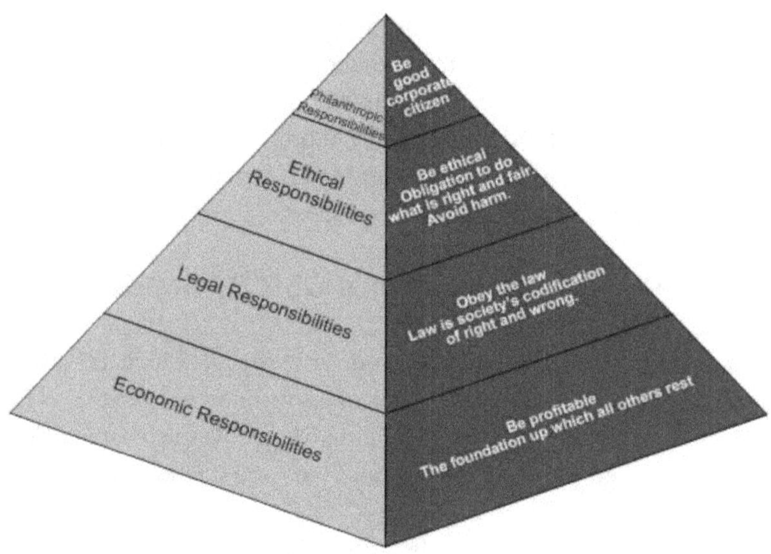

Hence ideally, economic responsibilities should also embrace legal and ethical responsibilities. Where such economic responsibilities are executed, such that they take into account goal maximization objectives, which do not serve self-interest or self-dealing purposes, such that other ultimate objectives - such as philanthropic goals are realized, then the supremacy of economic responsibilities becomes justified.

Hence, a more representative picture of Carroll's Pyramid of Corporate Social Responsibility, which highlights the dependency of the various layers and responsibilities is represented through Figure 3 which presents overlapping layers of responsibilities:

Figure 3. Overlapping layers and strata denote interdependence of responsibilities in their ability to function effectively

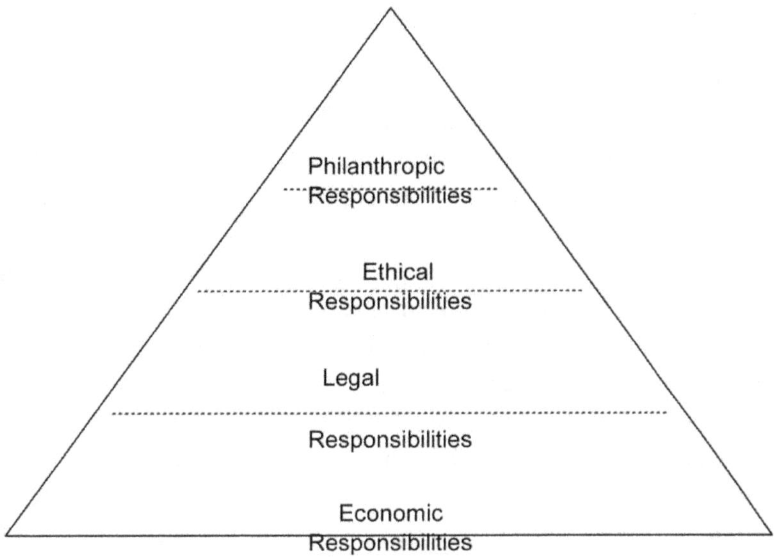

- Philanthropic Responsibilities
- Ethical Responsibilities
- Legal Responsibilities
- Economic Responsibilities

As already highlighted under the introductory section of the literature review,

Without effective compliance and enforcement strategies, which embrace a range of disclosure requirements that are aimed at maximally engaging stakeholders in the corporate social responsibility process, CSR objectives which are also facilitated by such corporate governance mechanisms of disclosure and accountability, will be hindered in achieving their maximum potential.

The 2011 OECD Guidelines place emphasis on the following (OECD, 2011):

- The importance of information being prepared and disclosed in accordance with high quality standards of accounting and financial and non-financial disclosure;
- The importance of such disclosure improving the ability of investors to monitor the enterprise through the provision of increased reliability and comparability of reporting, as well as improved insight into enterprise performance;
- That annual independent audits recommended by Guidelines, should result in improved control and compliance with standards and regulations (by the enterprise).

The above requirements and provisions would not only result in the generation of improved and effective implementation and enforcement of rules, regulations, standards or codes, but also facilitate the realization of Corporate Social Responsibility goals and objectives.

Mitigating Expectation Gaps: Audits as Mechanisms of Corporate Governance in Facilitating Disclosure, Accountability, Financial Reporting and Enhanced Disclosures

Audit committees should ideally be comprised of shareholder representatives, as well as Board representatives - a move which may well serve to benefit shareholders and enhance their say in matters relating to decision making and planning. This would also not only confirm the increased focus on shareholder interests as is the case with the "Say-On -Pay-Voting", but also effectively engage shareholders in the corporate governance process.

According to a report by the FEE's discussion paper on the functioning of audit committees (FEE:2012), the external auditor's presence at audit committee meetings varies in different countries of the EU - whilst some countries encourage audit participation at audit committee meetings to foster the communication between them, in other countries the external auditor attends the meetings when the audit committee finds it relevant to have the auditor present.

External auditors do not only serve as vital facilitators of transparency, accountability, disclosure of financial statements prepared by the management and directors of an enterprise, but also incorporate some degree of credibility into the financial reporting process through audits prepared by them since such audits should serve as indicators to investors, and other stakeholders of the enterprise, of the financial performance of the enterprise and that information provided by such audits can be accurately relied upon.

Disclosure is classified under two recommendations, pursuant to paragraphs 32 and 33 of the 2011 OECD Guidelines (OECD, 2011:29):

The first set of disclosures:

- Calls for timely and accurate disclosure on all material matters relating to the corporation, including the financial situation, performance, ownership and governance of the company as well as;
- Disclosure of adequate information in relation to remuneration of board members and key executives, related party transactions and material foreseeable risk factors

Whilst the second set of disclosure practices are required in those areas where reporting standards are still developing, namely:

- Areas related to social, environmental, and risk reporting, as well as bio-diversity as exemplified with greenhouse gas (GHG) emissions, indirect, current, future, corporate and product emissions.

The first set of disclosures is particularly relevant to those stakeholders and investors whose classification and designation can be considered to have such vicinity and features that they fall within the domain of the traditional principal agent theory, whilst the second set of disclosures, given their applicability to environmental matters – as well as future and most likely unforeseeable events, could be considered to affect a broader range of stakeholders whose ambit extends beyond the scope of the traditional principal agent relationship.

In this sense the importance of timely, accurate disclosure of material information, as well as remuneration related information, is distinguished in providing crucial information for more immediate stakeholders for long term planning, as well as shorter term perspectives and strategic decision making which could embrace the assessment of the appropriateness of incentive schemes for Board members – based on the performance of the enterprise.

The Sarbanes Oxley Act of 2002 (SOX) is a landmark legislation which was introduced following the collapse of Enron – which is not only notable for the fraudulent practices and cover- ups involving directors and management, but also the involvement of auditors in creative accounting practices.

Under Title IV of SOX [section 401 (j)], Enhanced Disclosures, material off balance sheet transactions are required to be disclosed - along with arrangements, obligations and other relationships of the issuer, in the annual and quarterly financial reports.

Further, in the efforts to facilitate enhanced transparency and disclosure, a crucial mechanism of corporate governance, namely internal controls, constitute the focus of section 404 whereby it is required that an internal report is to be generated which:

- Stipulates the responsibility of management for establishing and maintaining an adequate control structure, as well as financial reporting and;
- Provides an assessment of the effectiveness of the internal control structure and procedures of the issuer for financial reporting to be generated.

Three key mechanisms, as indicated in the 2014 Nestle Report, are highlighted as confirming compliance with Nestle policies, national regulations, namely:

- Internal corporate audits.
- External audits carried out by Bureau Veritas.
- FTSE 4 Good's Independent verification process.

By engaging stakeholders in the corporate governance process, suppliers are also required to conduct an "ethical audit" which represents and conveys "adherence with national and international laws and standards" as well as the minimum standards which have been set out in the Nestle Supplier Code (see Nestle, Full Report, 2014: 72).

Such audits are carried out by approved independent verification firms which incorporate the use of either (Nestle, Full Report, 2014: 72):

- The Sedex Members Ethical Trade Audit (SMETA) Four Pillars guidelines; or
- The Ecovadis methodology.

The audit process involves:

- Site visits which take place on a rolling basis using consistent audit criteria that embrace labour standards, safety and health, environment and business integrity;
- Reporting process, whereby, after the above mentioned site visit, the auditor provides a report for the supplier – and for Nestle- identifying issues of non- compliance;
- The resolution stage, in which Nestle provides support to the supplier to address and mitigate identified gaps – in relation to Nestle's standards. Such support assuming the collaboration on an agreed course of action.

Further, where the supplier does not improve conduct within the scope of agreed time frame, Nestle has the discretion to remove such suppliers from its food and supply chain and new partnerships with other suppliers are sought and forged.

According to Ayres and Braithwaite, the middle levels of the pyramid of regulatory strategies are those areas which require the greatest innovative mix.

They add that (Ayres & Braithwaite, 1992:101):

- Perhaps the greatest challenge facing regulatory design is not at the apex of the pyramid of regulatory startegies, where a variety of well- tested punitive strategies exist – nor at the base of the pyramid, where there is experience of successes and failures of the free market and of self regulation in protecting consumers. The need for innovation is at the intermediate levels of the pyramid of regulatory strategies.

In addressing such a "gap", the Enforced Self Regulation Model is proposed (Ojo, 2011).

The engagement of auditors at the innovative stages of the pyramid of regulatory strategies – as well as those phases or strata within Carroll's Pyramid of Corporate Social Responsibility that are more subject to innovation, namely the legal responsibilities and ethical reponsibilities phases, is also proposed as a means of facilitating consistency and comparability in the adoption, implementation and application of regulations, codes and standards.

This is not to undermine other levels of Carroll's Pyramid of CSR, but to accentuate the need to safeguard the more manipulative-prone and innovative phases from potential practices of creative accounting – as well as bribery and corruption.

Stakeholder engagement is also vital at the intermediate levels of the pyramids of Corporate Social Responsibility - where matters relating to legal and ethical considerations, and failure to comply with such responsibilities, are involved. Furthermore, the audit expectations gap, arising from information asymmetries, can be mitigated through the engagement of stakeholders in the corporate governance process.

Nestle also acknowledges the "effective dialogue with stakeholders" as being central to Creating Shared Value – with its stakeholder engagement program also being considered as a facilitator in formulating responses to common challenges, propelling and propagating performance improvements, as well as ultimately "fortifying collective action" (Nestle, 2014).

ISSUES, CONTROVERSIES, PROBLEMS

Mitigating Expectation Gaps and Information Asymmetries: Valuation Standards and Accounting Methods As Reliable Indicators of Value for Business Ownership Interests

Revenue recognition, particularly in terms of the timing of revenue, as well as valuation, are prominent areas in accounting which are highly susceptible to manipulation in view of the level of judgment, resulting in impaired objectivity, required in implementing corporate related activities. As a result, management override, inadequate and unaccounted for practices are exercised in relation to such accounting related policies and procedures. Clear, consistent policies are therefore required in order to recognise revenue appropriately, detect possible cases of fraud, ommissions and error. As well as facilitating the detection of such omissions, Forensic Accounting and valuation standards constitute formidable tools in efforts aimed at promoting clear, consistent and reliable policies - through the implementation and the enforcement of reliable, consistent and comparable standards – particularly valuation standards.

Attempting to Enhance Comparability and Consistency: IFRS Business Combinations

Creative accounting practices and the use of Special Purpose Vehicles were prominent amongst the attributable causes of corporate collapses such as those relating to Enron and Lehman Brothers. Hence the importance of consistency, transparency and reliability in accounting valuation is crucial to ensuring that manipulative related practices are not carried out to cover-up fraudulent acts. IFRS 3, Business Combinations, addresses matters relating to business combinations and the initial recognition of goodwill, and relates to Special Purpose Entities.

It seeks to:

- Enhance the relevance, reliability and comparability of information provided about business combinations and their effects;
- Establish the principles on the recognition and measurement of acquired assets and liabilities, the determination of goodwill, as well as necessary disclosures.

The following principles are established by IFRS 3 in relation to the recognition and measurement of items arising in a business combination:

- Recognition principle
- Measurement principle

Furthermore, whilst IFRS is to be applied when accounting for business combinations, the following constitute some conditions to which it does not apply:

- The formation of a joint venture (IFRS 3.2a).
- The acquisition of an asset or group of assets that is not a business, although general guidance is provided on how such transactions should be accounted for.
- Combinations or businesses under common control (IFRS 3.2 b).

Qualitative Characteristics of Accounting Information

According to KPMG's Briefing (2010:3):

- The fundamental qualitative characteristics have changed from the IASB's existing framework published in 1989 (the 1989 framework). While *relevance* is in both, *faithful representation* has replaced reliability in the new conceptual framework. This change is the result of the IASB's desire to clarify the meaning of reliability. The Boards decided it was better to use a new term rather than to try to clarify the use of "reliability".
- However, faithful representation excludes substance over form and prudence, which are part of the 1989 framework's definition of reliability. The Boards concluded that *substance over form* is redundant as a separate characteristic; faithful representation means that the information presents the substance. Representing the form that differs from the substance could not result in a faithful representation. *Prudence* was removed as it is considered to be in conflict with neutrality.

- *Comparability, verifiability, timeliness* and *understandability* are considered to be complementary to the fundamental qualitative characteristics and should be used to enhance the decision-usefulness of the information reported. These characteristics are differentiated from the fundamental characteristics because if information is not relevant or not faithfully represented, then the enhancing qualitative characteristics cannot make information useful.

PwC (2013:1) highlights the importance of ensuring consistency and comparability with subjective and more judgmental based concepts and elements within the conceptual framework of accounting:

- A conceptual framework is an important basis for the development of accounting standards that are both principles based and internally consistent. Some argue that such consistent conceptual basis has been missing in recent board deliberations. Debate about the definition of assets and liabilities, other comprehensive income and the relevance of disclosures might be traced back to an insufficient basis in the existing framework. Also the recent financial crisis has put pressure on the definition of performance and 'fair value' as a measurement model.
- The old qualitative characteristics (understandability, relevance, reliability and comparability) were replaced by two fundamental qualitative characteristics, relevance and faithful representation, and four enhancing qualitative characteristics.

However, some IFRS, despite their efforts to enhance relevance and comparability, still have certain judgmental elements in their application. For example, as already highlighted, with IFRS 3 (Business Combinations):

- The objective of the IFRS is to enhance the relevance, reliability and comparability of the information that a reporting entity provides in its financial statements about a business combination and its effects.
- It does that by establishing principles and requirements for how an acquirer: (a) recognizes and measures in its financial statements the identifiable assets acquired, the liabilities assumed and any non-controlling interest in the acquiree; (b) recognizes and measures the goodwill acquired in the business combination or a gain from a bargain purchase; and (c) determines what information to disclose to enable users of the financial statements to evaluate the nature and financial effects of the business combination.

The establishment of principles does not only contribute to further judgmental based elements, but also the aforementioned exemptions/exceptions granted in respect of recognition and measurement principles – notably of which include certain assets and liabilities which are required to be recognized or measured in accordance with other IFRSs, rather than at fair value.

Having considered the aim of IFRS 3 in attempting to enhance relevance, reliability and comparability of information provided about business combinations and their effects, the reliability of accounting valuation methods will be addressed in the following section - by way of reference to the Daubert standard of evidentiary reliability.

SOLUTIONS AND RECOMMENDATIONS

The Daubert standard of evidentiary reliability codified in Federal Rule of Evidence 702 defines the admissibility of expert testimony based on the following:

If scientific, technical, or other specialized knowledge will assist the trier of fact to understand the evidence or to determine a fact inissue, a witness qualified as anexpert by knowledge, skill, experience, training, or education, may testify thereto in the form of an opinion or otherwise, if (1)the testimony is based uponsufficient facts or data, (2) the testimony is the product of reliable principles and methods, and (3) the witness has applied the principles and methods reliably to the facts of the case.

While Daubert is the law in federal courts and more than fifty percent of the states, the Frye standard still remains the general acceptance test for the determination of the admissibility of scientific evidence in the remaining venues. Frye does require expert testimony to be founded in generally accepted scientific principles that are recognized in the particular field; and there must be evidence that the technique has been used. According to a recent study, those states not adopting Daubert are California, Colorado, District of Columbia, Florida, Kansas, Maryland, Nevada, NewYork, North Dakota, Pennsylvania, South Carolina, Washington, and Wisconsin.

Arizona was originally included in the above list; however in May 2010 it adopted the Daubert standard for admitting expert testimony and expert evidence.

Daubert and Frye are cornerstones in establishing the reliability, and ultimately, admissibility of expert testimony. This section of the chapter illustrates how valuation standards, which serve in the role of providing evidentiary reliability, dictate the use of Rules of Thumb. This concept is further explored in the case of Devries v. Devries which specifically highlights opposing arguments regarding the use of Rules of Thumb, their prescribed application according to valuation standards, and the challenges made against their reliability inthe value calculation of goodwill. The limitations of the outcome of the Devries' case in light of Daubert and Frye are then addressed and the potential role of rules of thumb in future cases are highlighted.

VALUATION STANDARDS, RULES OF THUMB, AND RELIABILITY

The methods of valuing closely held companies are segregated amongthree broad approaches: the asset approach, the income approach, and the market approach. Specific valuation methods reside in each of the broad categories. The capitalization of earnings method is an example of a valuation technique that is a component of the income approach.

The capitalization of earnings method calculates firmvalue byestimatingthe subject businesses' current annual earnings and dividing that benefit stream by the capitalization rate. The capitalization rate is derived by reducing the required percentage rate of return on the investment in the business by a long term sustainable growth rate. As with all valuation methods, the reliability of a calculation or conclusion of value is sensitive to the assumptions driving the model. In the case ofthe capitalization of earnings method, items that are likely to be scrutinized are the components of the capitalization rate that will moderate a higher or lower value. In a trialsetting, the reliability of these assumptions will usually be the focal point of determining the credibility of the expert's findings.

Valuation standards issued by the American Society of Appraisers (ASA), National Association of Valuation Analysts (NACVA), and the American Institute of Certified Public Accountants (AICPA) are consistent, recognizing the asset approach, the income approach, and the market approach as reliable indicators of value for business ownership interests. However, all three have a common thread in that they encourage rules of thumb to be considered only with other valuation methods.

The NACVA addresses the rules of thumb in development standard 3.8 by stating that "typically, a rule of thumb or benchmark indicator is used as a reasonableness check against the values determined by the use of other valuation approaches. For Valuation Engagements, it should not be used as the only method to determine value of the subject interest."

The ASA Business Valuation Standards focus on the use of rules of the thumb in section five of the market approach to business;

"Rules of thumb may provide insight into the value of a business, business ownership interest, security or intangible asset. However, value indications derived from the use of rules of thumb should not be given substantial weight unless they are supported by other valuation methods and it can be established that knowledgeable buyers and seller place substantial reliance on them."

The AICPA Statement on Standards for Valuation Services No.1 (SSVS1) became effective January 1, 2008. Guidance on rules of thumb resides in paragraph 39 of SSVS 1.

It states that, "Although technically not a valuation method, some valuation analysts use rules of thumb or industry benchmark indicators in a valuation engagement. A rule of thumb is typically a reasonableness check against other methods used and should generally not be used as the only method to estimate the value of the subject interest."

A practical interpretation of the above groups' recommendations on the use of the rules of thumb as a sole valuation indicator can be understood as follows: a rule of thumb should be used as a "sanity" check against valuation methods dwelling in the asset approach, income approach and market approach.

Valuation standards are designed as guidance for members, however they also serve as a form of evidentiary reliability. From both a Frye and Daubert perspective valuation standards are both generally accepted and peer reviewed. Inlight of these valuation directives a California court, in the case of Devries v. Devries, chose to use a rule of thumb type formula to calculate the value of goodwill for a construction business.

As a form of evidentiary reliability, valuation standards, hence not only contribute to enhancing comparability, consistency, disclosure and transparency of accounting information, but also serve as formidable mechanisms in mitigating the audit expectations gap.

FUTURE RESEARCH DIRECTIONS

In a computer age where files, documentation and evidence can easily be deleted or destroyed, forensic accounting is a rapidly growing field which has the potential to play crucial roles in detecting fraudulent practices, as well as facilitating accountability in audit trails, investigations aimed at detecting fraudulent practices. It will be quite interesting to see the role it can be maximally and effectively harnessed to play in future cases – particularly corporate collapses which involve the sophisticated destruction and cover-ups of evidence, documentation, management override, as well as the generation of fictitious invoices and other transaction related material.

CONCLUSION

Even though auditors played a huge role in Enron's collapse, recent corporate collapses and the Financial Crisis have also continued to highlight management responsibility and the need for improved corporate governance mechanisms - particularly where material misstatements, fraud and error are involved in the generation of financial statements (directors' and management responsibility) and the verification of those statements (auditors' responsibility).

The restriction of volumes of damaging activities on ecosystems - particularly in very vulnerable areas, could be facilitated through contracts or agreements which stipulate compensation clauses that could be awarded on the basis of the extent of costs suffered by locals or repercussions for the environment (costs which may or may not yet be quantifiable). In this respect, the engagement of wider stakeholders - even those unlikely stakeholders, in the design and negotiation of such contracts is necessary. Of greater importance is the need to ensure that safeguards, which address political, corporate and other institutional obstacles which could hinder the realization of fulfilment of contractual obligations, are in place. Such safeguards can be best facilitated where effective corporate governance mechanisms exists – such that regulations, codes of conduct, principles and laws are not only implemented and enforced effectively, but also ensuring that effective corporate governance mechanisms are in place to facilitate greater transparency, disclosure practices and accountability in the corporate governance process. However, as demonstrated time and time again in corporate collapses which played prominent roles in the recent Financial Crises, there is a limit and boundary to which management can be controlled – even with corporate governance mechanisms. For this reason, the engagement of forensic accounting in detecting corporate fraud is a much needed tool in combatting corporate malpractices – particularly high-level collaborations and technologically skilled and designed cover-ups.

ACKNOWLEDGMENT

This chapter is an updated, revised collection of material previously co-authored with James A. DiGabriele in:

DiGabriele, James A. and Ojo, Marianne, Achieving Amicable Settlements and Possible Reconciliations: The Role of Forensic Accountants in Equitable Distributions (June 29, 2013). Achieving Amicable Settlements and Possible Reconciliations: The Role of Forensic Accountants in Equitable Distributions, J. DiGabriele, M. Ojo, Amazon Books, Kindle Publishing April 2014. Available at SSRN: http://ssrn.com/abstract=2287197

REFERENCES

Annual Report on the OECD Guidelines for Multinational Enterprises. (2010). *Corporate Responsibility: Reinforcing a Unique Instrument.* OECD Publishing.

Annual Report on the OECD Guidelines for Multinational Enterprises. (2014). Responsible Business Conduct by Sector. OECD Publishing.

Ayres, I., & Braithwaite, J. (1992). *Responsive Regulation: Transcending the Deregulation Debate.* Oxford University Press.

Carroll, A. B. (1991, July-August). The Pyramid of Corporate Social Responsibility: Toward the Moral Management of Organizational Stakeholders. *Business Horizons.*

Daily Telegraph. (n.d.). *Arthur Andersen Returns Twelve Years After Enron Scandal.* Retrieved from http://www.telegraph.co.uk/finance/newsbysector/banksandfinance/11069713/Arthur-Andersen-returns-12-years-after-Enron-scandal.html

Danjsmee. (2012). Retrieved from: https://danjsmee.wordpress.com/2012/12/10/the-approach-to-csr-more-important-than-csr-itself/

Daubert v. Merrell Dow Pharmaceuticals, Inc., 509 U.S. 579 (1993)

DiGabriele, J. A. (2011). Evidentiary Reliability, Valuation Standards, and Rules of Thumb. *American Journal of Family Law, 25*(1), 16–22.

DiGabriele, J. A., & Ojo, M. (2013). Objectivity and Independence: The Dual Roles of External Auditors and Forensic Accountants. *Journal of Forensic and Investigative Accounting, 6*(2). Retrieved from http://papers.ssrn.com/sol3/papers.cfm?abstract_id=2231524

FEE. (2012). *The Functioning of Audit Committees.* Discussion Paper June 2012. Retrieved from http://www.fee.be/index.php?option=com_content&view=article&id=519&Itemid=106&lang=n

Frye v. United States, 293 F. 1013 (D.C. Cir.1923)

IFRS. (2013). IFRS News: IASB issues Discussion Paper on Conceptual Framework July/Aug 2013 IFRS 3. *Business Combinations.* Retrieved from http://www.iasplus.com/en/standards/ifrs/ifrs3

Jamali, D. (2010). The CSR of MNC Subsidiaries in Developing countries: Global, Local, Substantive or Diluted? *Journal of Business Ethics, 93*(S2), 181–200. doi:10.1007/s10551-010-0560-8

Jamali, D., & Mirshak, R. (2007). Corporate social responsibility: Theory and practice in a developing country context. *Journal of Business Ethics, 72*(1), 243–262. doi:10.1007/s10551-006-9168-4

Jamali, D., & Neville, B. (2011). Convergence versus Divergence of CSR in Developing Countries: An Embedded Multi-layered Institutional Lens. *Journal of Business Ethics, 102*(4), 599–621. doi:10.1007/s10551-011-0830-0

Kaufman, M. S. (2006). *The Status of Daubert in State Court.* Atlantic Legal Foundation. Retrieved from http://www.atlanticlegal.org/daubertreport.pdf

KPMG. (2010). *Briefing Sheet Conceptual Framework for Financial Reporting Chapters 1 and 3, October 2010 Issue 213 NACVA, Standard 3.8.* Retrieved from http://www.nacva.com/PDF/NACVA_Standards.pdf

Nestle. (2014). *Nestle in Society: Creating Shared Value (and Meeting Our Commitments) Summary Report 2013.* Author.

OECD. (2005). Guidelines on Corporate Governance of State Owned Enterprises 2005. OECD.

OECD. (2011). *OECD Guidelines for Multinational Enterprises*. OECD Publishing. doi:10.1787/9789264115415-en

Ojo, M. (2006). Avoiding Another Enron: The Role of the External Auditor in Financial Regulation and Supervision. In Global Auditing: Concepts and Concerns. ICFAI University Press.

Ojo, M. (2011). Cooperative and Competitive Enforced Self Regulation: The Role of Governments, Private Actors and Banks in Corporate Responsibility. *Journal of Financial Regulation and Compliance*, *19*(2).

Ojo, M. (2015). *Regulating Self-Regulation: Audits and Accounting Mechanisms*. Amazon Publishing.

Reputation and Reciprocal Conformism Securities and Exchange Commission. (2002). *Study Pursuant to Section 108(d) of the Sarbanes-Oxley Act of 2002 on the Adoption by the United States Financial Reporting System of a Principles-Based Accounting System*. SEC.

Sacconi, L. (2004). *Corporate Social Responsibility (CSR) as a Model of 'Extended' Corporate Governance: An Explanation Based on the Economic Theories of Social Contract*. Academic Press.

Sarbanes-Oxley Act of 2002

Spulber, D. (2014). *The Innovative Entrepreneur*. New York: Cambridge University Press. doi:10.1017/CBO9781107239012

Visser, W. (2008). Corporate Social responsibility in Developing Countries. In A. Crane, A. McWilliams, D. Matten, J. Moon, & D. Siegel (Eds.), *The Oxford Handbook of Corporate Social Responsibility* (pp. 473–479). Oxford, UK: Oxford University Press.

Section 3

Monetary Policy Factors, Environmental Factors, and Other Variables which Govern the Interplay between Corporate Social Responsibility and Foreign Direct Investment

Chapter 6

Corporate Social Responsibility and Foreign Direct Investment:
Legal, Political, and Historical Influences on the Development of Auditing in Malaysia

Ali Azham
Universiti Utara Malaysia, Malaysia

Marianne Ojo
North-West University, South Africa

Lee Teck Heang
Tunku Abdul Rahman University (UTAR), Malaysia

Nor Zalina Mohamad Yusof
Universiti Utara Malaysia, Malaysia

ABSTRACT

As well as highlighting the importance of corporate governance mechanisms such as audits in facilitating Corporate Social Responsibility objectives and Foreign Direct Investment – where corporate social objectives are not unduly compromised, this chapter applies the political economic theory introduced by Tinker (1980) and refined by Cooper and Sherer (1984), which emphasizes social relations aspects of professional activity rather than economic forces alone. In a case study format where qualitative data was gathered mainly from primary and secondary source materials, the study found that the function of auditing in the Malaysian society in most cases is devoid of any essence of mission; instead it is created, shaped and changed by the pressures which give rise to its development over time. The largely insignificant role that it serves is intertwined within the contexts in which it operates. Furthermore, chapter is aimed at highlighting the importance and role of external audits – particularly in the aftermath of the 2008/09 global Financial Crisis.

DOI: 10.4018/978-1-5225-0305-7.ch006

INTRODUCTION

The activity of external auditing as conducted by audit firms intervenes between the preparation of financial and non-financial information relating to a particular entity by management and the (supposed) use by many different groups of users of this audited information. In Malaysia, this audit is characterized by little publicity and little public clamor for needed changes. There may be a few lone voices from both the public and private sectors asking auditors and their representative bodies, the Malaysian Institute of Accountants (MIA) and the Malaysian Association of Certified Public Accountants (MACPA) to do a better job, but that seems to be where the "story" ends.[1] From time to time there would also be certain exposures/revelations' which provide proof that external audit in the country is in need of a certain level of revamp.

Examples include the revelation made by the Central Bank of Malaysia that the main issues of contention between the Central Bank and the external auditor were a consequence of the auditor having compromised his or her independence in two proven areas of financial reporting: disclosure and the provisional figure for bad and doubtful accounts (Central Bank, 1987, p. 6). On the former issue in particular, there had been cases where the auditor either worked together with management or agreed with management efforts at "window-dressing" the accounts leading to inadequate disclosure of significant changes in accounting policy and/or unneeded adjustments to certain disclosed items. A few years later in 1991, it was an auditor himself, Mr. Khoo Eng Choo, a senior partner of Price Waterhouse, who mentioned that there were local auditors who "... have been found not to have exercised sound professional judgement" (Choo, 1991, p. 23). He also made the following revelation (p. 23): "It is also unfortunate that sometimes some members of the profession have sunk to the level of enabling some unscrupulous members of the business community to dictate to them the approach 'Just your signature' is enough. They become poodles or lapdogs of these businessmen. These members are tarnishing the image of the profession and have failed in their duties."

However, even with these revelations, the one single case/only incident where a Malaysian auditor has been brought to court took place in the mid-1960s when a group of company shareholders unhappy with the losses they had incurred, sued the auditor.[2] Thus, during economic recessions in the 1980s, when many businesses were forced to close down and cases of financial improprieties by directors and top management were disclosed, Malaysian auditors avoided being taken to court. In this regard, the then finance minister Datuk Paduka (now Tun) Daim Zainuddin was quoted by the New Straits Times[3] (12 Sept. 1987) as saying that "... it is a miracle that no member of the public or any interested party has sued auditors for being professionally negligent taking into account the various "swindle" cases recently...." The blissful existence of Malaysian auditors certainly contrasts that experienced by teachers/ lecturers, government servants, politicians, Malay rulers, nurses who have all by the early 1990s entered the limelight of adverse publicity. Other professionals, such as physicians and lawyers have also in recent years, been confronted with adverse public scrutiny.[4]

Indeed, if there is any profession or group of people in the country which seems to have been able to operate with little challenge to its practices, it is the so-called company auditors. This in fact had led Oh Chong Peng, the then vice-president of the MACPA and also a senior partner of Malaysia's Coopers and Lybrand, to argue that there was still not enough pressure coming from the Malaysian society in order for the auditor to extend his or her responsibilities - despite the recent numerous cases of failures of companies, both listed and unlisted, where auditors had failed to give warning by qualifying in their audit reports that such companies were not going-concerns (Peng, 1989). Thus, he pointed out, there was little need for the accounting profession to put forward reactive measures. Similar sentiments may also be found in the remarks made by his colleague, the then MACPA president, Subimal Sen Gupta (The Malaysian Accountant, July 1987, p. 4). The latter figure had also pointed out that even the regulatory authorities were oblivious to the on-goings (more appropriate)/goings-on in audit.[5]

What is happening in Malaysia is considerably different from that experienced by auditors in countries such as the United States, Britain, Canada and Australia. In these countries, they are often criticized for business and corporate failures and a number have had to pay large damages or settle out of court with plaintiffs accusing them of committing audit failures. Besides the court, regulatory agencies and other groups have also played their part in demanding that the profession move in an expeditious fashion to meet its responsibilities as perceived by the public (see Flint, 1983; Bruce, 1988; Humphrey et al., 1992; Jacob, 1992). In these countries, even where external economic factors force businesses into liquidation and there is little proof of auditors' failure to conduct audits properly, the auditors have nonetheless become implicated in the failure.

Malaysia's auditing experience when compared to other Asian countries such as South Korea, Hong Kong, India and Singapore, is a source of surprise. This is because unlike what has happened in Malaysia, auditors in these countries have experienced tough times with their authorities.[6] In the case of South Korea and Singapore, the auditors concerned have also been brought to court by disgruntled investors.[7]

This chapter thus aims to explain this Malaysian audit phenomenon by applying the alternative contextual view of accounting i.e. the theory of political economy, with the theory of political economy introduced by Tinker (1980) and refined for accounting by Coopers and Sherer (1984). Attempts are made to understand how the distribution of power in the society and the social, political and institutional structures that mirror that distribution of power have impacted the functioning of audit in Malaysia across a period of forty years, from the gaining of independence from the British in August 1957 to the time just before the emergence of the Asian Financial Crisis in the third quarter of 1997. In other words, auditing is understood here to be interrelated with the dynamics of the wider sociopolitical and economic context of which it is an integral part. It is considered to be a mutable phenomenon, interacting with a dynamic, mutable context (Hopwood, 1987). By examining the social, economic and political environments surrounding auditing together with developments within auditing itself, it is hoped that the original, present and potential functions of auditing in Malaysia will be disclosed fairly - perhaps in the spirit of the following remark by Burchell et al. (1980, p.13): "... accounting, it would appear, is made to be purposive rather than being inherently purposeful."

While this is a country-specific study, it also provides a contribution within the framework of international comparative auditing research (professionalization or professional developments) by adding to studies of the causes and effects of auditing variation between countries classified under the typology of fast developing economies. Another form of contribution of this work is concerned with the issue raised by Willmott (1991, p. 109): that the study of auditing "has been seriously neglected and marginalized, even as evidence of 'failures' mounts and doubts about the independence of auditors grow". It is thus hoped that this chapter will be able to contribute in some way towards enriching this very important area. Finally, by carrying out this research, it is specifically hoped that the profile of auditing will be raised in Malaysia to direct the attention of more influential parties (e.g. politicians, civil servants, journalists, consumer groups) to probing questions about the operation and adequacy of existing audit regulatory arrangements (Sikka et al., 1989; Willmott, 1985) with focus also directed to other areas related to the audit practice.

The chapter begins with a discussion of the theory of the political economy of accounting. It is then followed by a section on data collection. A section describing the ongoings/goings-on in the audit arena and related areas follows right after. This section includes the following headings: the early beginnings, the NEP era and the post-NEP era of 1987-1997. In attempting to make sense of what has taken place, the subsequent section applies the theory of the political economy of accounting to that section where the discussion is imparted into two parts: the pre-NEP era and the NEP plus era. The chapter then ends with a section on conclusions.

BACKGROUND AND LITERATURE REVIEW

The Political Economy of Accounting

The political economic theory was introduced by Tinker (1980) and refined by Cooper and Sherer (1984) to explain accounting experiences. Tinker (1980) in introducing a classical political economic approach to financial reporting, proposes that the social relations of production work together with the economic forces of production as two related dimensions of capital shaping the social and economic life of a nation. He points out that in any society, the coming together of the two modes of production is discernible in the particular socio-political and economic institutional forms and arrangements. The use of political economic theory that recognizes the presence of social relations makes it less cumbersome to understand the economic forces of production that are operating at any particular time period and in any society. Tinker explains that such relations are reflected through a set of institutional forms and arrangements that are constructed to interact with economic relations (i.e. the type of economy). Therefore, in order to understand what is going on in the economic sphere, which may include the external audit function, researchers need to identify the related socioeconomic and institutional environments. Interpretation of a nation's specific economic features will be less clearer if insufficient attention is given to the surrounding social and political processes.

With regard to accounting activity in particular, Cooper and Sherer (1984) point out that a political economy of accounting is useful in order to understand how the accounting process interacts with its social, economic and political environment. They write as follows (p.208):

... the objectives of and for accounting are fundamentally contested, arise out of recognition that any form of accounting contains representation of a specific social and political context. Not only is accounting policy essentially political in that it derives from the political struggle in society as a whole but also the outcomes of accounting policy are essentially political in that they operate for the benefit of some groups in society and to the detriment of others.

Thus, it is assumed that no basic harmony of interests exist in the current society. Auditing practice is viewed as favoring specific dominant interests in the society and disadvantaging others. That is, what transpires in the audit process would be in accord with the expectations or goals of these dominant parties. Cooper and Sherer (1984) have also identified the presence of several key variables which they claim affect the value of financial accounting reports including power-play in society and historical specificity. On the former, they argue that social-relations of power and conflict[8] determine the significance of accounting, which in turn affects such relationships. Instead of assuming a basic harmony of interests in a society where power is widely diffused and which results to the unproblematic view of the social value of accounting reports, the political economy approach supports the following contrasting views: either that society is seen as clearly controlled by a well-defined elite or that there is a continuing conflict in society between antagonistic classes.[9] Both views of elitist domination and pluralist anarchy indicate/testify to the contested value of accounting reports and practices. Thus, accounting reports are hardly impartial and objective, nor is the accountant in the position of a disinterested and innocuous historian.

The latter variable of historical specificity stresses the importance of the specific historical and institutional environments comprising the social and political structures and cultural values of the society that provide the context for the delivery of accounting reports. There is recognition that "disequilibrium is a standard feature of the economy" as proven by the presence of a few large corporations dominating the economy and that the state plays paramount roles in various fields including that of intervening in the determination of accounting policies. The historical focus in particular should assist efforts in understanding the changing roles of accounting practice and emphasizes the importance of historical specificity for a fair assessment of the social value of these roles.

In summary, a political economy of accounting focuses on the institutional environment which supports the existing system of corporate reporting. It looks at the accounting function within the broader structural and institutional environment in which it operates. It stresses that political issues cannot be divorced from economic analysis in relation to social choices. It revolves around power and whose interests predominate in society which inevitably impact upon auditing. Thus, under the political economy approach, the focus on social relations leads to the proposition that certain parties possess special interests that often influence the audit process.

Also, with political economy as the theoretical framework, the rationale for Malaysia's audit function may be discovered by linking the history of the nation's audit practice with the nation's history within the social, economic and political spheres. Thus, the understanding is viewed as coming about not through the study of separate and overt elements of the audit infrastructure and its technical outputs, but through a more comprehensive and in depth study of these and other items considered crucial to such an understanding. The assumption held throughout is that audit activities taking place within a certain length of time are associated with a unique configuration of social, economic and political conditions. That is, these activities are products of social, economic and political realities and that differences in audit activities across several time periods may be traced to changes in these realities. It is very much recognized however, that the "story" told is most probably only one of many. As succinctly noted by Carnegie and Napier (1996, p. 30): "Researchers starting from quite distinct theoretical perspectives and with disparate moral and political attitudes could well narrate virtually the same chronology of "facts": how those facts are interpreted is likely to differ widely."

Data Collection and Methodology

The study relies on qualitative data gathered by utilizing the technique of documentary analysis. All the documents referred to, lend insight into the perspectives, assumptions, concerns and activities of those who produced them. The primary written materials assessed and analyzed comprise mainly of the annual reports of accounting bodies such as the MIA and the MACPA and government documents such as the numerous Malaysian Plans. The secondary written sources relied on to provide data on Malaysia's auditing are few and far between. There are conference materials at the ASEAN level where materials on Malaysia's auditing are discussed and a few others at national level and books by Gul (1983) and Enthoven (1973, 1977).

Where it concerns the nation's social, economic and political environments, numerous secondary written sources were accessed including various authoritative sources published over the years in and out of the country. The same was done in investigating developments in the nation's history and in systems of relevance to audit: corporations, government and capital funds.

Much of these materials were collected during the field work which took place in the first six months of 1997. However, the rest, especially in the area of accounting/auditing in Malaysia, were collected long before the field work began and culminated with the publication of a book published locally (see Azham, 1994).

Finally, it needs to be mentioned that this study forms part of a wider study on accounting development in Malaysia in which in-depth interviews with selected personalities were conducted. A number of these personalities were leaders of Malaysia's accounting profession. Where appropriate, materials from these interviews are also introduced in this chapter to consolidate the points raised. These cases are however very few and far between. Details regarding the interviews may be found in Azham (2002).

Audit in Malaysia over the Years

In the following section, the early beginnings of audit development and the trials and tribulations faced by a number of players in the audit arena in later years are described. It begins with audit developments taking place right after the independence of the Malay Federation. It is followed by the on-goings/goings-on in the audit arena during the years when the New Economic Policy (NEP) took place. The section concludes with a description of what happened during a period of just over ten years prior to the onset of the Asian Financial Crisis in the third quarter of 1997. With an application of the theory of political economy of accounting, this section also describes developments taking place in areas surrounding the audit arena, such as the government and corporate sectors, and their impacts. In order to distinguish this discussion from the one following, more emphasis is however, placed on developments taking place within the audit arena.

The Audit Beginning of a Newly Independent Nation

The passing of the Companies Act 1965 and the Accountants Act 1967 facilitated the emergence of the initial pattern of audit system, replacing a pre-existing pattern where there was no law to govern the operations of companies throughout the newly formed federation[10] and a national accounting body to represent all qualified accountants in the country. These Malaysian Acts are similar to those found overseas. The Companies Act 1965 drew mainly on two sources: the Victoria Companies Act of 1961 and the British Companies Act 1948 (Walton, 1986).[11] The former in turn was based upon the UK Companies Act 1908, 1929 and 1948 while the latter on the UK Companies Act 1929. The Act placed the requirement on companies to disclose more than ever before. It also requires companies to keep accounting records so as to have true and fair statements prepared and that record keeping should be executed in such a way so as to enable the records to be conveniently and properly audited. In matters of auditing, the Act stressed the need for the auditor to be independent. This is illustrated in cases where he or she is not allowed to be an officer or director or had shareholding (either direct or indirect) with the companies audited. In addition, the auditor was given very broad powers in relation to matters of inspecting records and obtaining information for the audit and had the right to attend and address general meetings of the company. As in the earlier Companies Ordinance 1946, the academic and professional qualifications of the auditor were not specified. However, under section 8 of the Companies Act, a person had to apply to the Finance Minister in order to gain license to become a company auditor.[12] In order to get the license, he or she besides being a Malaysian resident, had to be able to satisfy the Finance Minister of his or her good character and competence to perform the duties of an auditor. The passing of the Accountants Act 1967 roughly a year after the Companies Act came into existence had ensured however that being a member of the MIA was a requirement before one could be given the permission to audit although the Companies Act 1965 has not made that clear (Shing, 1981, p. 32; Abu-Hassan, 1986, p. 4). The Accountants Act 1967 resembles the Singapore Society of Accountants Ordinance 1963 which in turn was based upon the New Zealand Society of Accountants Act - the main difference being that the Malaysian Act was "much briefer" and thus "less explicit" than the Singaporean Ordinance (Hai, 1970/71, pp. 27-28). With the Accountants Act 1967 coming into existence in September that year, the MIA emerged as the nation's accounting statutory body.

Section 6 of the Act notes five functions of the MIA including the responsibility to regulate the practice and promote the interests of the profession and to determine the qualifications of persons for purposes of admission as members. With regards to the latter in particular, the MIA is required to maintain a register of accountants. These accountants fall under one of three categories of membership: public, registered and licensed accountants.[13] To ensure that only qualified people whose principal place of residence is Malaysia can act as public and registered accountants, the MIA through the Accountants Act has made it illegal under Sections 22 and 23 for anybody to hold him/herself out as a public, registered or licensed accountant or adopt, use or exhibit these titles or others such as auditors, tax consultants and tax adviser.[14] Any transgression would mean the person being held liable for a maximum fine of RM 1000 or imprisonment for up to one year for the first offence and with subsequent transgressions being liable for a maximum fine of RM 2000 or imprisonment of two years. In short, as stated in the House of Representatives' Parliamentary Debates (Vol. IV, No. 12, Col. 2409 dated 25 Aug. 1967), the Act is intended to make provision for the adequate control of the accounting profession as a whole, and this control is to be entrusted to the MIA, under the establishment of the Act. Finally, the accounting body MACPA, as opposed to that of the MIA, was established through the initiative of the private sector. To be more precise, in less than one year after independence, on 26 July 1958, twenty local accountants who were formerly members of the Malayan branch of the Association of Chartered and Incorporated Accountants (ACIA) and the Malayan branch of the Association of Certified and Corporate Accountants (ACCA), both established in 1936, came together and incorporated the Malayan (later Malaysian) Association of Certified Public Accountants (MACPA) in Singapore under the Straits Settlement Companies Ordinance 1940 (CERPASS, Dec. 1967, p. 51). The MACPA was modelled upon the Institute of Chartered Accountants of England and Wales (ICAEW) and is a good example of those accounting professional bodies described by Parker (1989) as following the British institutions of professional accountancy.

Fulfilling the Need of Foreign Investment: Auditing in the NEP Era

The newly independent nation appeared set on ensuring that activities in the nation's audit arena would fulfill the need for foreign investors. The same appeared to be the case in the related area of taxation where the government in its attempts to attract industrial investment from overseas had brought upon itself the criticism of providing foreigners with excessive tax exemptions (Lim, 1973, p. 261; Edwards,

1975, Section 5.2). Specifically, among limited companies in the manufacturing sector in 1971, the effective rates of direct taxation on profits were 67.6 percent and 39.9 percent for local and foreign companies, respectively. As for all limited companies in 1971, the rates were 59.8 percent and 39.5 percent, respectively (Jomo, 1986, p. 222). All this apparently took place when the rates of reinvestment[15] by foreign-owned companies were much less compared to local-owned companies (see Hirschman, 1971, pp. 26, 30, Table 6; Peng, 1979, p. 192, Table 4.4; and Lindenberg, 1973). With the occurrence of conflicts between Malays and Chinese in 1969, it was realized that for the long term good of the country, changes needed to take place in the nation's economy and other sectors of Malaysian life. Thus, the subsequent implementation of the New Economic Policy (NEP) in 1971 heralded a new era where foreign interests now had to play a secondary role to those inside the country – in particular that of the government which entered the corporate sector in full steam. This had a profound impact on the audit arena as is discussed under the next section.

For years, there had been underlying tensions between the Malays and Chinese. In May 1969, the tensions boiled over/escalated to a point with the Malays and the Chinese being involved in riots on the streets of Kuala Lumpur and resulting in nearly two hundred deaths and hundreds more injured.[16] The racial riots had jolted many parties to the realisation that more riots could take place in the future as long as the country remained the same socially, politically and economically. Thus, drastic measures had to be taken in many fields. In the socio-economic field, the NEP was initiated in 1971 with the goals of eradicating poverty - regardless of race and irrespective of geographical location - and reducing imbalances in income, employment and ownership of assets among the various races in the country. In attempting to meet these objectives by 1990, the government implemented a number of strategies.

Among the notable ones are the pursuance of an ownership and employment restructuring program imposed on both non-indigenous domestic and foreign owned firms (Zainal-Aznam, 1991a; Jesudason, 1989; Woon & Kam, 1989; Onn, 1989; Means, 1986; Chan & Horii, 1986; Redha, 1985; Woon, 1982). As a result, laws such as the Petroleum Development (Amendment) Act and the Industrial Coordination Act were passed in 1975 which had the goal of greater government control over industries. Large and powerful merchant agency houses such as Guthrie and Sime Darby now had to employ more Malays to fill the quota, restructure their capital to meet the Malay equity requirements and enter into joint ventures with entities established by the government.

With foreign interests no longer being of paramount importance in the nation's economy, the earlier "carrots" such as the Companies Act 1965 (which requires companies to undergo audit annually) and the Accountants' Act 1967 (which resulted in the establishment of the MIA as the national accounting body in 1967) were (left unapplied)/inactive until the second half of 1980s – when changes to a large extent, were made to the NEP. Thus, the promising beginnings in the audit arena of the 1960s had gone nowhere by the end of the decade. Perhaps this was inevitable in a context where the strong presence of the government and the increasing involvement of local Chinese in the corporate sector signified that these corporations were owned, managed and funded by people from their own respective Malay and Chinese communities who shared goals that were not only economic but also social and political. The enterprises were registered as companies but in reality they were unlike those known as companies in the Western sense of the word "company" with conflicting interests from different parties. There was thus little need for the "independent" auditor and accordingly a strong, capable representative professional cum regulatory body to be around.

The MIA in Doldrums

Following the appointment of the then Accountant-General[17] as the MIA's president on 31 May 1968, no single AGM was conducted in the following two decades. The MIA under the leadership of the Accountant General, which finally came to an end in April 1987, presumably took over the role of "registering body".[18] However, this role was delegated to the audit firm Price Waterhouse. In 1982, the MACPA took over this responsibility.[19]

The role of the MIA as "registering body" in those two decades was well articulated by the MIA president, Haji Hanifah Noordin, just before the first MIA annual general meeting in 1987. He said that ".... the earlier members of the [MIA] council could not be entirely blamed for the inactive state of the MIA because in the earlier years it was felt that it should only be involved in its limited role of registering accountants in the country" (Business Times, 10 Sept. 1987). Unfortunately, the MIA did not execute that function successfully. In other words, there were those fully qualified to register with the MIA who had failed to do so. Thus, just a few months after the MIA was activated in 1987, it was discovered that as of 29 February, 1988, of the country's 6000 or so qualified accountants, only 4453 had registered themselves with the MIA (NST, 20 March 1988). The remainder who did not register were comprised of 600 members of the MACPA, 800 of the Chartered Association of Certified Accountants (CACA) and 200 accounting graduates from local universities. It may be said with certainty that nothing substantial had actually taken place in the 1970s except for the passing of Accountants' Rules in 1972 which, however, were not enforced due to the nonexistence of the statutory investigative and disciplinary committees which could only be formed by the MIA after an AGM. Thus, as reported by The Malay Mail (13 Jan. 1988), just a few months after the MIA was activated in 1987: "The recently activated Institute has formed investigation and disciplinary committees in September to regulate the profession - after 20 years of existence." And the MIA president himself mentioned in a seminar paper (Hanafiah, 1990, p. 17): "There was no enforcement of the Accountants Act 1967 in its twenty years of dormancy." In the meantime, with a very discouraging picture for auditing helmed by a body behaving as if it was representing the majority if not all of the company auditors then, various debilitating outcomes took place in the nation's audit arena not only within the next ten years, but also in the 1970s, and continued well into the following decade. Two of such notable outcomes are the disciplinary chaos and the proliferation of unqualified accountants/auditors.

Disciplinary Chaos

The investigation and disciplinary committees of the MIA were not established until September 1987 after its first AGM. As a result, in the area of professional ethics and their enforcement, the Malaysian accounting profession, up to the late 1980s when the MIA was activated, appeared to be in a state of chaos. This is perhaps illustrated by the remarks made by the then MACPA president, Subimal Sen Gupta in 1986 where he mentioned that the MACPA as a "private body" could only be strict with members who did not comply with the body's ethical code and that the body had no control over those who were not members but who deserved to be disciplined. He also said (The Malaysian Accountant, Oct. 1986, p. 4):[20]

The MACPA has no control over the issue of the audit license to individuals which qualifies them to act as Approved Company Auditors. This license is issued by the Ministry of Finance by reference to the Malaysian Institute of Accountants (MIA). I therefore appeal to both these bodies to take cognisance of the disciplinary actions taken by MACPA against its members by taking appropriate action against them if they are also members of the MIA and holders of the audit license. More importantly perhaps there should be a mechanism for taking action against those who are not members of MACPA. The MACPA will be pleased to assist in this respect.

It is also worth noting what was revealed in the letter published in 1988 in the NST. In the letter written by a person who signed him/herself as "Disgusted", he described the mess in the then audit practice (NST, 6 Aug. 1988): "In the past, any attempt [by the MACPA] at disciplinary control over errant members resulted in those members discontinuing their membership with the MACPA and continuing to practice as public accountants as they are allowed to do under the Accountants Act 1967."

Proliferation of Unqualified Accountants/Auditors

The 1967 Accountants Act states that only those with recognized qualifications may practice or call themselves accountants/auditors. However, with the MIA not fulfilling its policing role, unqualified accountants holding either unrecognized qualifications, part qualifications or no qualification had the opportunity to appear and grow with the then expanding economy in the 1970s and early 1980s. As stated in the MIA 1988 Annual Report (p. 13): "The problem of unqualified accountants, both in practice and in commerce and industry, had proliferated to serious proportions during the period of inactivity of the Institute." In early 1988, the MIA president disclosed that a study completed in 1981 (by what appeared to be the MACPA) found that there were 200 to 300 people who were not qualified accountants who were active as public accountants, auditors and tax advisers in the country (Berita Harian, 13 Jan. 1988). The number of unqualified accountants was amended later on in late 1988 to 3,000 with those employed totaling 15,000 (NST, 5 Nov. 1988). Most of the unqualified public accountants were also now identified to have come from corporate secretarial and administrative firms (The Star, 5 Nov. 1988).

Also in 1988, the MIA had pointed out that unqualified accountants acting as auditors would collaborate with the qualified auditors in the sense that the latter would be paid a token fee (normally a 30 percent cut) for certifying and endorsing financial statements that had presumably been audited earlier by the unqualified auditors (NST, 20 March 1988). In the MIA 1988 Annual Report, the following was stated (p. 14): "The unqualified accountants would not have been able to function if not for some of our errant members who are prepared to sign the accounts prepared by them without any question at all." In 1993, the MIA estimated that there were between 50 and 100 licensed accounting firms collaborating with unqualified accountants (NST, 28 Jan. 1993).[21]

Overall, audit practice in Malaysia during the NEP era was in an uncertain and unsatisfactory state. While the MIA remained largely uninfluential, the privately organized MACPA with its power limited to only a fraction of the accountants population in the country and controlled by the internationally affiliated audit firms whose clients would include foreign investors, was left free by the government to do what it felt was right with hardly any interference or much expectation from the government. This led to the picture that financial reporting and the related matter of external auditing was largely superfluous in a society where the government as the main engine of the economy was not just the regulator but also the so-called user and preparer of audited statements - except in cases where there was a need for funds from foreigners to invest in the manufacturing sector who thus for one reason or another demanded the presence of company audit and thus the external auditor.[22] The events of the 1970s, the May 13th 1969 Tragedy and the subsequent implementation of the NEP pushed the government to get heavily involved in the nation's economy.

In the 1980s, the two economic recessions in the first six years of the decade and the financial debacles of numerous companies including those owned by the government forced the government to turn to the private sector to take over its role as the engine of the nation's economy. Therefore, whereas growth was previously based on expansionary public expenditure, from the late 1980s onward most of the economic growth was to be attributed to private sector activities – with perhaps the expected inevitable impacts on the nation's audit practice.

Accounting's Rejuvenation with the End of the NEP?

There were two economic recessions experienced by the country during the 1980s. The first one was mild and took place in 1981-82 when the rest of the world also experienced recession. In response, the government embarked on a number of strategies to stimulate the economy (Yan, 1994, p. 314; Abdullah, 1986). These efforts did not bear much fruit when the subsequent economic slowdown in industrialized countries impacted on the then fragile Malaysian economy. Thus, another recession took place in 1985-86. This recession was marked by reduction in national income, government revenues, consumer spending and investment and the worst scenario that the nation had to face since independence (Mohd. Salleh, 1994, pp. 622-623). At its wake, the government intensified efforts to attract foreign investors to the country's manufacturing sector. Thus, almost all NEP requirements were waived for export-oriented manufacturing industries. There was the "de-emphasizing" of the restructuring prong of the NEP,[23] which led to a more liberal treatment of private enterprises, especially direct foreign investment, and a softening stance towards restructuring the ownership of share capital of companies and raising the threshold for manufacturing companies so that they escaped the requirements imposed by the Industrial Coordination Act (ICA) (Zainal-Aznam, 1994, p. 597). Thus, the NEP had to some extent, come to an end around this time and not in 1990 as planned in the early 1970s.

With a few facets of the NEP pretty much set aside and the private sector now to assume the role of the engine of the economy, the government began a series of programs to facilitate the expansion of private sector businesses. These included the implementation of various strategies to upgrade the operation of the KLSE (see Azham, 1994) and a major amendment to the Companies Act 1985 in the second half of 1980s. The former had apparently helped in ensuring the KLSE to grow by leaps and bound in the late 1980s (see Kuala Lumpur Stock Exchange and Malaysian Strategic Consultancy Sdn. Bhd., 1992, pp. 2829) and also later in the first half of 1990s.[24] However, the major amendment to the Companies Act seems not to have resulted to any significant changes in the manner intended for audit practice in the country. The same may be said on the revival of the MIA in 1987. This and more are discussed under the next heading.

Companies Act's Amendment

In 1985, the Companies Act was substantially revised (Sum & Wishart, 1989). Apparently the aim among others is to attract foreigners to invest in the country, through placing greater emphasis on the need for those associated with companies to be more accountable, and to provide greater protection for minority shareholders, who would include these foreigners. The revised Act which became effective from 1 February, 1986 made extensive changes to the existing Ninth Schedule to incorporate those elements that are regarded as best accounting standards and practices leading towards a much higher disclosure level than previously. Where it concerns auditing in particular, the 1985 amendment requires for the first time all public accounting firms and individual partners of such firms to register with the Registrar of Companies (ROC). Each partner is allocated a number that must be cited in all audit reports. In addition, the amendment increases the range of persons excluded from acting as auditor. It appears that the purpose of this provision is to identify and sanction those company secretaries operating as auditors (Phenix, 1986, p. 12).

Furthermore, the term of an audit license is reduced from three to two years and the procedure for granting licenses overhauled to make it a more effective method of monitoring and policing standards of auditing. Finally, an auditor is required to report to the ROC if he or she were to find that there has been a breach or non-observance of any provisions of the Act. The onus is on the auditor to justify why he has not reported a breach of the Act to the Registrar. This seems to be a major break with the tradition in Malaysian Company Law as it is based on the British system, although it can be found in the corresponding sections of the Australian and Singaporean Acts. Failure to report could result in a requirement for the auditor to justify in a court of law his or her opinion that the breaches have been otherwise adequately dealt with by either one of these two approaches: by a comment about such matter in his or her audit report or by bringing the matter to the attention of the company directors. The fulfilment of either of these two approaches ensures that the reporting duty of an auditor to the Registrar is a limited one. Nevertheless, the significance of this requirement is that Malaysian auditors are now provided with a channel to report non-observance of the Act. Previously, the auditor could only use the audit report and by the time the report was presented to the members of the company, the damage caused by the transgressions might well have been irreparable. Section 174(8) of the Act also makes it clear that the auditor preparing the report would be protected by the law. This particular 1985 amendment to the Companies Act 1965 has increased the auditor's statutory responsibilities in certain respects but at the same time provided the auditors with some additional protection. With or without the protection however, it appears that auditors as represented by the MIA, are not that happy with the additional reporting responsibility. This was openly remarked by the MIA president at a seminar. He mentioned (Hanafiah, 1990, p. 10): "In recent years this legislative intervention in the area of disclosure of certain matters to the regulatory authorities seems to be the trend. It is hoped that the public perception of the accountants' independence is not impaired as a result of such legal interference in the accountant-client relationship."

Perhaps more important than whether or not the auditors are happy with the additional reporting responsibility concerns the question of whether auditors who show their failure to abide with the reporting duty to an external party have in fact been taken to task by the authorities through criminal charges of fraud/conspiracy. At the present time there has been no news of such action by the government. In the early 1990s however, the then minister of domestic trade and consumer affairs noted the following at a conference after saying that auditors had moral and legal responsibilities towards shareholders to report any irregularities to the authorities (NST, 29 Jan. 1991): "My ministry cannot implement and enforce the relevant laws effectively without the feedback and co-operation from your members. For your information, in the past five years the Registrar of Companies only received two reports under this section." The following year, he said (NST, 17 Dec. 1992): "Auditors are still avoiding their responsibilities under the law to report any breach or non-compliance of the Companies Act 1965 to the Registrar of Companies." He also said that although only a handful of such reports had been received from the auditors, the ROC's inspection and enforcement work had revealed that a lot more companies had failed to comply with the law. He warned auditors that "appropriate action" would be taken against those who did not carry out their duties conscientiously. He said that the law - Section 174(8) - had made it clear that an auditor who failed to make such report was liable to spend two years in jail and/or pay RM 30,000.

MIA's Revival

Though interviews provided a very confusing picture of the reasons and parties involved in the activation of the MIA (see Azham, 2002), the available documents were very clear in stating that it was the government which wanted the MIA to be active so that it could play the role of national accounting body as envisaged by the Accountants Act 1967 (Akauntan Nasional, July 1992, p. 5; Berita Harian, 13 Jan. 1988). The exact reasons for the MIA being activated and the important role played by the government in ensuring the activation were revealed in the "MIA 1988 Bounded Document". It was stated (pp. 5-6) that when the then federal cabinet rejected the MACPA proposal for the merger of the MACPA with the MIA,[25] the MIA was "directed" by the government to be active. The document went on to state that the government did so because of the state of the then accounting profession reflected in various financial scandals which resulted with a loss of confidence in the profession among the general public and foreign businessmen. This document also pointed out that the government would like the MIA to be activated due to the proliferation of unqualified accountants who had caused the government to incur millions of ringgit of losses as a result of falsification of their clients' accounts.

It is also noteworthy that the then Finance Minister on the night before the inaugural AGM of the MIA in 1987, had mentioned what appeared to be the goals set by the government for the MIA to achieve once it was revived (The Malaysian Accountant, Oct-Dec. 1987, p. 8): "As the Minister responsible for implementing the Accountants Act it is my hope that members of the Institute will make the MIA an effective professional body responsible for looking after professional standards, education and training and supervision over the professional conduct of members."[26] He continued saying that cases of fraud in the corporate and financial sectors in the country had raised questions on the role played by the auditors. He pointed out that auditors owed a professional duty to the investing public to point out any illegal activity in the company and come out with appropriate audit reports. He stressed the following picture of what the government envisaged for the accounting profession: "As for the government, it would like to see an accountancy profession that is capable of providing professional work of the highest standard in serving the various needs of the sophisticated business community and earning the trust and respect of society."

Though these remarks point clearly the role and responsibilities of the MIA after its activation, it is quite difficult to say that overall the MIA in its first decade of being active has been successful in fulfilling them. In fact, it can be argued that the MIA has failed to achieve much as a regulator of the profession. Instead it has been preoccupied with various efforts to promote the profession. These and more are discussed next.

MAIN FOCUS OF THE CHAPTER: ISSUES, CONTROVERSIES, PROBLEMS

Regulatory Failure

The fact that since the early 1980s white-collar crime in its various forms has proliferated in the country is well known (see Koon, 1994). Right after the MIA was activated, it appears that various parties in the country have made their feelings known that they would like members of the accounting profession to conduct themselves with professional integrity. Among these speakers, Datuk Paduka (later Tun) Daim Zainuddin and Tun Ismail Ali had in fact mentioned the MIA by name as the party to play the required role in this field (see endnote number 2). Indeed, it was none other than the MIA president himself who concurred with the idea of the important role to be played by the MIA in this matter. On the night before the MIA's first AGM in 1987, the MIA president mentioned what he has continued to repeat over the next three years: the MIA aims to be a strong regulatory body (see MIA 1988 Annual Report, p. 6; MIA 1989 Annual Report, p. 7; Hanafiah, 1990, p. 15). Specifically on that night of 1987, he said (The Malaysian Accountant, Oct-Dec 1987, p. 10):

Speaking of image, the Institute must endeavour to restore the credibility the profession has lost in the eyes of the public. Several corporate failures such as the recent co-operative scandal can be attributed to apparent audit failures. These must be pursued and investigated by the Institute in order to discipline those members who have been negligent and to clear the names of those who have not been negligent. Only the MIA can do this as it has been endowed with such disciplinary powers encompassing the whole profession under the Act.

He stressed that after the inaugural AGM when the MIA was then able to establish/create its investigation and disciplinary committees, that the council would have to make "a determined effort" to clean up the image of the profession. The MIA president even mentioned that to ensure a more effective policing by the MIA in the future, there would be a joint investigation and disciplinary body comprising representatives from the Treasury, Registrar of Companies and Registrar of Cooperatives. He also volunteered to have the MIA take over the "policing" task over the auditors handled by "a monitoring committee" in the Finance Ministry.

With this apparent early desire to be a strong regulator, a few months after the MIA first AGM, The Malay Mail (13 Jan. 1988) reported that following complaints against 15 accountants lodged by companies, fellow accountants and government departments. The MIA was going all out to clean up the act of errant accountants. The MIA president was reported to have said that 15 accountants were under investigation for alleged malpractice and criminal breach of trust. He also said that the accountants faced being de-registered while court prosecution awaited those who had violated the Accountants Act 1967. And in 1988 and early 1989, there were a number of reports in the NST on what the MIA leaders would do to errant members. The headlines of the news reports said all: "MIA May Expel Members Who Break the Rules" (21 June 1988); "MIA Warns Members of Stern Action" (15 July 1988); "MIA May Expel Those Abetting Fraud" (17 Oct. 1988); "MIA to Haul Up Accountants Not Following Rules" (28 Feb. 1989). Also on 14 July 1988, reports with the following headlines appeared: "Warning from the MIA" (Business Times) and "MIA to Get Rid of Black Sheep" (The Star). In the former, the MIA president was reported as saying that the MIA would not condone members who "... persistently refuse to comply with the statutory requirements, accounting and auditing standards adopted by the Institute."

However later after the MIA's code of ethics was made effective in April 1990, hardly anything like those stated above had come out from the MIA.[27] And if a check were to be made of the MIA Annual Reports over the years, one would discover that since the first AGM in September 1987 until the AGM in 1996, the MIA's disciplinary committees had only taken disciplinary actions against members for the years 1987/88, 1991 and 1992. In other words, in the later years after its activation, it appears that the MIA had not found it "fit" to discipline any members where complaints were filed against. Specifically, for the years 1987/88, 1991 and 1992, four members were disciplined by the MIA each year for a total of 12 members in its first ten years of active life.[28] Between 1993 and up till the AGM in 1996, it had failed to impose disciplinary actions against its members although the MIA Annual Reports showed that "every year" since 1987 (except for the years 1989 and 1990 when not much details were disclosed in the MIA Annual Reports on the works done by its investigative and disciplinary committees)[29] the total number of cases investigated, under review or pending had in fact reached 25 (1996), 30 (1995), 25 (1994), "more than ten" (1993), 29 (1992), 28 (1991), 39 (1990) and 23 (1987/88).

Related to the topic of failing to ensure that its members are in fact doing a better job as accountants or auditors and that necessary actions are taken against the errant ones, the MIA has also failed to implement the very ideas that its leaders themselves claimed needed to be put into action in order to strengthen the nation's audit practice. One of these ideas concerned the practice of quality review of audit firms. The MIA 1992 Annual Report (p. 7), Mingguan Malaysia (12 Apr. 1992), Akauntan Nasional (May 1992, p. 26; Nov/Dec. 1992. p. 31; June 1993, p. 22), NST (28 July 1992) and finally the MIA 1993 Annual Report (p. 15) provided evidence of the MIA leaders giving glowing details of the need for a quality review programme. Interviews with a number of the MIA council members produced conflicting stories on why the MIA had failed to implement it. Another area that the MIA had failed to put into action is concerned with its various proposals in 1992 related to the subject of the auditor's independence which the MIA president claimed "ought" to have been implemented with a few other measures to strengthen the profession (Akauntan Nasional - Conference Times, 15 July 1992, p. 1; Business Times, 15 July 1992). It is worth noting the following remark that he made when talking about the various proposals (Akauntan Nasional, 15 July 1992): "There is no strong financial centre in the world that is not supported by a strong and well developed accountancy profession. Therefore now is the time for action. Now is the time for us to develop ourselves and to give our profession a lift."

Also, in at least one case the MIA had appeared to under perform as compared to its earlier/previous fine efforts. This is concerned with the Continuing Professional Development (CPD) that was made effective from 1 March 1992 (Akauntan Nasional, March 1992, p. 22). See the Akauntan Nasional (Nov. 1990, p. 20), NST (6 Nov. 1990) and Akauntan Nasional (Nov/Dec 1992, pp. 30-31) where the MIA president stressed why the MIA needed to have the CPD made compulsory. However the MIA 1995 Annual Report (p. 26) disclosed that "changes" that had been introduced in November 1994 and made effective from 1 January, 1995 ensured that what took place in the past, where the MIA secretariat was the entity responsible for CPD record-keeping, had been replaced with members themselves being made responsible to do the record-keeping individually. There was no longer any need for each member to submit an annual CPD report in a prescribed form. Instead, members would be selected at random and asked to produce evidence of compliance.

Successful Promoter

After its activation, the MIA had shown the tendency to promote the interest of its members in a number of ways. In October 1988, the MIA submitted a memorandum to the Finance Minister requesting that the government look into the desirability and possible methods of limiting the accountant's personal liability for negligence claims. The government did not bother to respond to this MIA's proposal. As if the government's indifference was not embarrassing enough, and notwithstanding the apparent positive state experienced by local auditors, the MIA had also on 30 January, 1991 launched a professional indemnity insurance scheme for its practising members (Akauntan Nasional, July 1992, p. 6). But the MIA had failed to get good response from its practising members. After nine months, only 10 percent of the some 800-member firms had signed up (NST, 30 Sept. 1991). Thus, the MIA president said that the MIA council would have to consider making it mandatory for all member firms to be covered by the scheme (NST, 19 Oct. 1991).

The MIA in what appeared to be an all out effort to protect its members' public accounting activities had also started early in 1988 a fight against the unqualified/unregistered accountants. From February to November 1988, the MIA resorted to lodging police reports and at times the MIA senior staff members would join the police to raid the premises of these unqualified accountants. The MIA also hired lawyers to bring the matter to court. By the end of 1988, MIA had lodged 92 police reports and the police had raided 19 firms (NST, 5 Nov. 1988). This approach taken by the MIA received a certain level of condemnation from various parties. For example, the Editorial to the Business Times (5 March 1988) had noted the following: "Until MIA comes out with its own examinations to allow these unregistered accountants to gain local recognition too, it is argued that such a tough stance may not be entirely fair." The crackdown ended when the Malaysian Institute of Corporate Secretaries and Administrators (MICSA) representing unregistered accountants sent a letter of appeal to the then Finance Minister for a review of the actions taken by the MIA (NST, 5 Nov. 1988). Later in 1992, the MIA launched the Malaysian Association of Accounting Technicians (MAAT) to house most of these accountants - a move that with hindsight did not need the MIA to initiate such a crackdown in the first place. That was precisely what the MIA president claimed in 1989. He said (Akauntan Nasional, Sept. 1989, p. 24): "... with the benefit of hindsight and the number of bogus accountants involved – which is estimated at some 3,000 - the Institute should have formed the proposed Malaysian Institute of Accounting Technicians (MAAT) first." Finally, the MIA in promoting the accounting profession had also proposed institutionalising its minimum audit fees schedule (see MIA Council, 1994).

The new ruling that governed all MIA practising members was supposed to be effective from 1 January 1992 (Akauntan Nasional, Feb. 1992, p. 19), but it was later moved to 1 April 1993 (Akauntan Nasional, May 1993, p. 16). At the end it was turned into a mere "guideline" as of 1 September, 1994. This was because as soon as the minimum fees schedule was implemented, the uproar began. The Perak Chinese Chamber of Commerce president suggested that the MIA defer its proposal to implement its minimum audit fees schedule on 1 April, 1993 (NST, 17 Feb. 1993). He claimed that the MIA minimum audit fees were too high and unfair and would be a burden for small and medium businesses. He stressed that the government should amend the Accountants Act of 1967 to prevent such exploitation of small businesses by the MIA. The following year, the Federation of Malaysian Manufacturers (FMM) issued a statement urging the MIA to review the audit fees schedule (NST, 18 Feb. 1994). The final showdown took place on 19 January, 1994 when the Associated Chinese Chamber of Commerce and Industry Malaysia (ACCCIM), the FMM and the MIA plus a few other interested parties met the domestic trade and consumer affairs ministry officials including the ministry's secretary-general to discuss the new fees structure (NST, 11 Feb. 1994). A few months after this meeting, the MIA president announced that the MIA would drop its minimum scale of audit fees effective as from 1 September, 1994 and instead maintain it as a guide for its practising members (NST, 2 Aug. 1994).

It would not be considered an exaggeration to say that the MIA after its activation, did not seem to provide much confidence that it was able to regulate itself well. This seems to illustrate what Friedland (1989, p. 74) says to be "the tremendous reluctance" across accounting professional bodies in the Far East to prosecute their members. The MIA had also failed to implement certain projects that its own leaders argued were necessary for strengthening the nation's audit practice. As if these were not disturbing enough, the MIA in the related field of increasing the number of qualified accountants/auditors, had shown that its conducts had left much room for improvement.[30]

All in all, the MIA during the ten year period following its activation in 1987 had largely failed to provide much confidence in its role as audit regulator. Unfortunately, the authorities did not seem to do much to help improve matters. From several documented sources, it seems that the government was not happy with the MIA during the first few years after its activation and had in fact initiated some actions but never really implemented those actions. The government's half-hearted reaction to the MIA's self-regulatory failure in particular and the quagmire in the profession in general may be reflected in speeches delivered by the then Deputy Finance Minister Loke Yuen Yow in July 1988 (as can be found in Appendix 12 in the "MIA 1988 Bounded Document") and later in 1990 (Akauntan Nasional, Oct. 1990, p. 21) and also in the speech by the then Finance Minister, Tun Daim Zainuddin, in September 1989 (Akauntan Nasional, Sept. 1989, pp. 21-23). After the Finance Minister stepped down in 1991, it seemed that not much could perhaps be expected from his successor. As a whole, the person who replaced him and who had also held the post of deputy prime minister had not been critical of the performance of the MIA as a regulator. In fact, he seemed to have a high regard for Malaysia's audit firms and the related standard of financial reporting of Malaysian companies (see Akauntan Nasional, Sept/Oct 1991, p. 23; The Malaysian Accountant, June 1994, p. 14). From the time he took over from Tun Daim Zainuddin, only once - in the very year when he assumed the post - was he critical of the audit executed by local auditors. At the 7th National Accountants Conference, he mentioned that the government viewed the lack of credibility of the auditors as a serious matter since many auditors had followed the instruction of company directors or top management of the companies in ensuring that the financial statements reflected a misleading picture of the company affairs (Utusan Malaysia, 19 Sept. 1991).

It may be safe to say that the economic recessions of the 1980s had to some extent disrupted the pre-existing political, corporate and financial systems in Malaysia. It had also created a perceived need for "structural" (as oppose to in-depth) changes to the audit system. The fact that changes in the audit process focus more on form or appearance but not so much on substance, had ensured that not much could perhaps be expected from auditors and their representative accounting body, the MIA. The next section attempts to address the issue of why Malaysia has been so unfortunate in the audit arena.

Towards Understanding Audit in Malaysia: Environmental Influences on the Development of Auditing

The objective of this section of the chapter is to explain the distinctive audit phenomenon in Malaysia by tracing the historical development of the audit function from 1957 to 1997 and analyzing environmental influences on this development. In the previous section, the delineation of what took place in the audit arena over the forty year period was divided into three parts. These three parts may now be condensed into two eras namely: pre-NEP and NEP Plus. Both periods have provided evidence of the relevance of the theory of political economy of accounting.

Audit during the Pre-NEP Era

During the pre-NEP era, the passing of the Companies Act of 1965 and the Accountants Act of 1967 appeared to signify that the economy was being set up to operate under a laissez-faire kind of environment by the government - with the assistance of the private sector as shown by the formation of the MACPA in 1958. The authorities and other parties made the necessary moves of ensuring that existing foreign investments stayed put and providing for much more investment to flow in through the manufacturing sector. The Parliamentary Debates (Vol. II, no. 8, Col. 1558 dated 9 Aug. 1965) stated specifically that the Companies Act 1965 had two objectives: to protect investors and to attract "foreign investors" into the country. Specifically, it was in the interest of foreigners who were shareholders and bankers to the merchant agency houses that the right audit infrastructure needed to be in place.

With the eruption of violence between Malays and Chinese in 1969, the Malaysian economy witnessed a change in direction away from a full free enterprise economy to that spearheaded by the government. Even after the NEP era was supposed to have come to an end in 1990, the nation's economy remained much in the hands of the government or those who were closely associated with it. As a consequence, the picture that emerged showed that to a very large extent, audits had little rationale for existence. In other words, the sorry picture of the audit from the 1970s onward provides evidence of the minimal value placed on auditing in the Malaysian society. To paraphrase Hopper et al. (1987), auditing development has been implicated in the broader ideological and political struggles within the society.

Audit in the Post NEP Era

From the early 1970s with the launching of the NEP until perhaps the mid-1980s when the government was forced to redress the NEP due to the occurrence of the 1985-86 economic recession, the one word perhaps best able to describe the audit practice was its apparent "neglect" by political executives. During this period, with the MACPA thriving and the presence of the audit section in the Companies Act, it appears that the nation's leaders saw no further need to focus on the audit system. Examination of what took place within the audit arena whereby the accounting statutory body MIA was left inactive leading to a number of negative repercussions demonstrates a lack of concern for ensuring that the audit and related areas should function appropriately by those parties involved in their administration. This could possibly be due to the direct access to internal financial information and to the corporations' directors by those who were from the government side who now also assumed the role of shareholders. Such access subverted any strong demand for a truly functional audit and related matters. The direct and indirect access to information apparently reduced a potential for agency problems except for those deemed to be outsiders.[31] But when these outsiders were mainly speculative investors, they appeared to show that they "accepted" information asymmetries.

The authorities might also have failed to improve upon the audit function due to the fact that they did not want accounting practitioners to make their life unnecessarily difficult given the "underhand" acts that they committed (or had to commit) to ensure the goals of NEP (and/or "their own") were fulfilled at "whatever" price. This very point was made clear by the leader of Aliran, the NGO for "freedom, justice and solidarity" in Malaysia, Chandra Muzaffar when he tried to explain the reluctance of national leaders to take action against those responsible for corrupt activities (Chandra, 1989, p. 99).[32] He wrote: "To expose their misdemeanors would be to expose the New Economic Policy's not so subtly concealed agenda of creating Malay capitalists, whatever the costs and the consequences. Ethics have to be set aside for the time being - so it has been argued in certain official circles - to facilitate the rapid growth of a Malay capitalist class." Overall, audit in Malaysia during the NEP era was in an unstable and unsatisfactory state. Unfortunately, the situation did not really improve even after the NEP came to an unofficial end in 1985. Although this time period saw the revival of the MIA in 1987 and the Companies Act 1965 heavily amended in 1985 resulting in additional duties and responsibilities for accountants and auditors, the audit transformation might be safely said to be superficial. Specifically, the actions of MIA in the regulatory field and the implementation of the auditors' ROC reporting duty under the amended Companies Act were below expectations. And yet there did not seem to be any decisive efforts on the part of those with the power and authority to see that these were improved.[33]

It is a fact that for auditing to reach its potential, transparency in conduct, and a situation in which those making decisions can be held accountable, is required. All these requirements did not fit the Malaysian environment as succinctly described in mid-1997 by the Editorial to the NST (7 June 1997):

- At the pace of its economic growth, Malaysia, too will feel the vice of corruption sooner or later. Like others before it, this country will also try to look the other way, and do as much as it can to avoid rocking the economic boat. Like their Asian peers, politicians will trust to the moral superiority of a few good men to keep the others in line. And there is always the argument against washing dirty linen in public, the stubborn loyalty of politicians to their compatriots, and an equally obstinate belief that corruption is confined to an indiscreet minority. In politics, hard choices require courage and often pose uncertain risks - which is why politicians will try to postpone them until their hands are forced. The instinct of self-preservation will usually urge politicians to control the damage done by disclosures of corruption, rather than attempt to root it out. (Emphasis added.)

SOLUTIONS AND RECOMMENDATIONS

There were six reasons (in italics) disclosed by the Editorial as to why corruption could be considered to have gone unhampered, and as disclosed by the Anti-Corruption Agency, corruption had been on the rise over the last 20 years and tougher punishments were needed (New Sunday Times, 8 June 1997). The people could not perhaps expect much from their accountants and auditors when their elected leaders did not seem to think that it was their responsibility to ensure that their "compatriots" were really conducting themselves with integrity. For one reason or another, leaders acted with much leniency ensuring cases of corruption were swept under the carpet, and the auditors who might have incurred audit failures could expect in turn that they would be able to go scot-free every time a business collapsed and financial scandal erupted.[34] Specifically, in Malaysia, the MIA although it was revived in 1987, was not expected to emerge as a strong accounting body able to play the required role in confronting cases of corruption, nepotism and patron-clientelism that had been plaguing the country for many decades but particularly in the few years prior to the onset of the Asian Financial Crisis in 1997. In short, it was in the interest of certain sections in the Malaysian society to see a malfunctioning audit marked by an incapable accounting professional body and a weak enforcement of a company law section on auditor's reporting duty to ROC. Therefore, while the MIA council members appeared to be ineffective and those overseeing the audit related sections of amended Companies Act had failed to play their role, others with the power to make corrections had not translated their words into actions.

This failure by the power elite to take the appropriate actions could also be traced to the case of the MIA-MACPA rivalry and that of the enforcement of Malaysian Accounting Standards Board (MASB) standards. Details of these two cases may be found in Azham (2002). See also Susela (1999). Briefly, on the former, the series of public disagreements between leaders of the MIA and MACPA had failed to force the authorities to make a stance as to which body they saw as the leader of the nation's accounting profession (Malaysian Business, 16 Aug. 1988, p. 19; Malaysian Business, 1 Aug. 1996, p. 1). As for the latter, the establishment of the MASB by the government in mid-1997 to take over from the MIA the responsibility of setting accounting standards had failed in ensuring that it was equipped with the power of enforcement – though early on in 1994 (The Malaysian Accountant, June 1994, pp. 14-15) and later in the following year the then Finance Minister in his 1996 budget speech (NST, 28 Oct. 1995) did mention such a need. The failure to act accordingly could only mean that those with power were not really serious in seeing the emergence of a well-respected accounting profession and high quality financial reports. For what appears to be an act of "too little too late" coming from the authorities, just several months before the country was dragged into the quagmire of the Asian Financial Crisis 1997-98, the ROC was reported to have sent its few officers scurrying around the country to check audit working papers of audit firms (Business Times, 21 Feb. 1997). The fact that this activity by the ROC which had never been conducted before (as found in an interview with the Companies' Registrar himself) happened to coincide with the efforts conducted by yours truly (to interview personalities such as the former finance minister Tun Daim Zainuddin and the Companies' Registrar) had led yours truly to conclude that there was more to this action of the ROC than what met the eye. These accountants were supposed to complete their task at the end of the year. However, there did not appear to be any reported news on the outcome of their operation till later during the following year.[35] In the interview conducted with the Companies' Registrar, he stated that the investigations had uncovered that some of the complaints that he received from various parties including shareholders on the "correctness of accounts" and "quality of auditing" were found to be valid. Furthermore, he said that it had been found that the MIA "had not carried out the task of regulating its members to the ROC's satisfaction". Capitalism per se does not require external audit. This is especially the case when the capitalism one refers to is the cooperative, insider or crony type (see Kunio, 1988). The so-called independent audit is an antithesis to such economy.

Thus, in Malaysia, one may find evidence where what may be considered a cornerstone for external audit, is downplayed by those who should know better. In an interview which took place in 1988, Datuk Mohamad of the audit firm Hanafiah, Raslan and Mohamad (HRM) mentioned what took place in 1964, "when all the large accountancy practices in the country were owned and dominated by foreigners" (Malaysian Business, 16 Aug. 1988, p. 13): "The late Tun Razak (who was then the deputy prime minister and later prime minister) called the three of us [he and his two colleagues] in one day and said: 'Why don't you guys set up a local auditing firm? At least try. If you can't make it, we'll take you back'." Next he was quoted as saying: "It was a difficult decision to make.... [b]ut we were lucky to receive a lot of assistance from Tun Razak. Right from the beginning, big clients like the National Electricity Board (NEB), the Police Cooperative, the Social Welfare Department and many government-related statutory bodies had their accounts audited by us." When the 1970s arrived with the government playing a much bigger role in the economy, HRM being the only "Bumiputra accounting firm" around was hired to audit the burgeoning number of public enterprises and other government entities. Note also that when it concerned the local Chinese auditors, the MIA's official journal, Akauntan Nasional (Dec. 1990, p. 18), had reported how some MIA members "with small practice" were having difficulty with the newly issued MIA Code of Ethics related to the need for auditors to be independent. As a result, the chairman of the MIA's Ethics Committee, Khoo Eng Choo, noted the following (Akauntan Nasional, Dec. 1990, p. 18): "The Committee is more concerned with the auditors of public listed companies rather than with auditors of family companies."

All in all, in the absence of widespread stock ownership and less than a free market to allocate resources, monitoring of management operations can perhaps be provided by other methods which differ from external audits. Probably in Malaysia that has always been the case – though to what extent such monitoring is done professionally is anyone's guess. Thus, by the time the nation experienced the damage brought about by the Asian Financial Crisis 1997-98, audit in Malaysia could hardly be regarded as an intrinsic and constitutive component of the government of economic life. In other words, its presence to a good extent was devoid of meaning. Not surprisingly, the nation's audit arena was filled with lost hope and utter neglect. Just another story of the triumph of hope over experience that Malaysians are so used to.

FUTURE RESEARCH DIRECTIONS

Although there have been numerous studies such as those by Enthoven (1977, 1973) on the role of accounting in economic development and others such as the effect of international transfer of accounting skills (Seidler, 1967; Needles, 1976), accounting is constantly seen as a technical activity which provides financial information for economic development. The scholarly works are invariably normative and are deemed located in the functionalist paradigm. Thus, they fail to examine how accounting is very much a reflection of the society it is located in. There always appears to be a lack of attention to developing countries' socio-economic factors which impact upon accounting resulting in/to suggestions that the transfer of Western accounting technologies and ideas would be unproblematic and undeniably and automatically beneficial to these countries - though experience time and again appears to prove otherwise.

The use of the theory of political economy in this chapter in explaining the rationale for auditing in Malaysia should help address the issue of lack of accounting studies in developing countries where accounting is regarded as a part of the wider socio-economic and political context. In other words, in the very notion of accounting propagated by Burchell et al. (1985) where the accounting processes and institutions are not so much influenced by the wider social, economic and political environments as "inter-twined" with them, and thus, as proposed by Hopper and Powell (1985, p. 93), need to be studied together. The Malaysian audit story covering a period of the first forty years after independence in 1957, has provided evidence of the character of auditing as a social activity within a specific network of changeable social relations. It is embedded in its social, economic and political context. Time and again, factors surrounding audit have had an impact on the audit process itself. Audit in Malaysia therefore cannot be interpreted simply as a technical phenomenon residing outside the social domain.[36]

Within the context of audits, new forms of risks, such as cyber security risks, are emerging. This also contributes to the argument that as much focus should not be placed on mandatory audit firm rotation and that greater focus should be accorded to non-audit services which constitute threats to audit independence, as well as emerging risks such as cyber security risks - and also risks which emerge as a result of changes and fluctuations to the economy, namely currency risks.

CONCLUSION

From a practice originating as a consequence of the need perceived by the national leaders in the late 1950s and 1960s to maintain the status quo in the nation's modern economy, following the launching of the NEP in early 1970s, the function of auditing in the Malaysian society was in most cases devoid of any essence of mission; instead, it was created, shaped and changed by the pressures which gave rise to its development over time. The role that it served was intertwined in the contexts in which it operated. As has been noted by Hopper et al. (1987), accounting development has been implicated in broader ideological and political struggles in the society.

The basic structural purpose of the audit in Malaysia as presented in several authoritative sources such as Company Law is really nothing more than to provide the "image" of a modern economy to attract investments from overseas. It is a kind of representation that is not supported by reality on the basis of much of the nation's history after independence. Specifically, the changes occurring in the audit system since the first half of 1980s onwards were more ephemeral than real, structural rather than in-depth. In other words, pressure for change was related directly to the creation of the modern audit infrastructure, and not to the need for its effective and appropriate administration in the Malaysian social environment. This is perhaps understandable since very little actually changed in the manner that political and economic power were distributed among members of Malaysian society and in the context of the so-called change from a predominantly command-economic system in the 1970s to a more capital-market economic system in the late 1980s and beyond.

All in all, it appears that the process of auditing was affected by certain groups who possessed special interests. These parties had made it certain for audit to operate in congruence with their expectations and objectives. If changes were to take place, they would be mobilised in the pursuit of their vested interests. Armstrong (1985, 1987), Hopper et al. (1987), Lehman and Tinker (1987), Loft (1986), Miller and O'Leary (1987) to mention a few have stressed this very point. Notwithstanding their rhetoric, it may safely be said that they had little interest in seeing changes in the status quo. As Rohwer (1995, p. 281) in his acclaimed work on the rising of East Asian nations had noted, "... elites do not normally reform themselves or do things to threaten their own position". Overall, audit in Malaysia prior to the onset of the Asian Financial Crisis 1997/98 was in an uncertain and unsatisfactory state – similar to those found in other Asian countries such as the Philippines (Dyball & Valcarcel, 1999) and Japan (Sakagami et al., 1999). It was clearly influenced by the broader context in which it was embedded. It was the result of historical events which, on the face of vested interests and distinctive social, economic and political attributes, had failed to ensure that its existence in recent years would really make a huge difference to the pre-existing arrangement which emerged in the early 1970s with the launching of the NEP.

Corporate and financial collapses such as that of Enron and Lehman Brothers, as well as the recent 2008/2009 global Financial Crises, not only highlight the need for more effective corporate governance mechanisms, which will be facilitated through Corporate Social Responsibility, but also serve to re inforce the role and importance of external audits – particularly in concentrated ownership and family structured systems – a feature which is prevalent in South and East Asian countries. The need for focus on such a role, as well as regulatory incentives which have recently been introduced by the Basel Committee on Banking Supervision, is evidenced by efforts being taken to implement such reforms, which include Basel III Leverage and Supplementary Leverage Ratios – notably in jurisdictions such as China, India and Pakistan. However, in respect of efforts aimed at promoting and focusing on audits, more work is needed in this area – particularly with regards to family owned and concentrated ownership systems and structures.

Against these observations, it needs to be added, that whilst more efforts are required in the field of audits, family owned structures, as well as several jurisdictions in Asia weathered the recent Financial Crises better than certain other more developed economies. This can only serve to highlight the more devastating consequences of financial crises in dispersed ownership structures and capital market based economies, and hence the need for focus on more effective audits and corporate governance mechanisms in such economies. In this regard, Corporate Social Responsibility serves a fundamental and pivotal role, not only as a corporate governance mechanism, but also in facilitating greater accountability to wider stakeholders whose scope extends beyond that of the traditional principal agent theory. Where greater focus is accorded to audits, and they are effectively implemented as they should be, and where stakeholders are engaged in Corporate Social Responsibility, as they should be, the audit expectations gap should be mitigated.

REFERENCES

Abu-Hassan, K. (1986). *Public Accounting and the Accounting Profession in Malaysia*. Paper presented at the Universiti Utara Malaysia's Professional Lecture Series, October, Universiti Utara Malaysia, Jitra.

Ahmad-Noordin, Z. (1981). Proposal for the Establishment of A National Institute of Public Finance and Accountancy. *The Malaysian Accountant*, *2*(1), 25–28.

Ahmad-Noordin, Z. (1986). Value for Money Audits - The Practical Aspect. In *Proceedings for the MIA and MACPA jointly organised 5th ASEAN Federation of Accountants Conference*.

Aliran. (1981a). *Aliran Speaks: Being a Collection of Aliran's Views on Various Social Issues From August 1977 to September 1981*. Aliran.

Aliran (1981b). *Corruption*. Aliran.

Aliran. (1988). *Issues of the Mahathir Years*. Aliran.

Armstrong, P. (1985). Changing Management Control Strategies: The Role of Competition Between Accountancy and Other Organizational Professions. *Accounting, Organizations and Society*, *10*(2), 129–148. doi:10.1016/0361-3682(85)90012-1

Armstrong, P. (1987). The Rise of Accounting Controls in British Capitalist Enterprises. *Accounting, Organizations and Society*, *12*(5), 415–436.

ASEAN Accounting Research Unit. (1992). The Auditing Framework in ASEAN. School of Accounting and Business Research Centre, Nanyang Technological University, Singapore.

Azham, M. A. (1994). *Accountability in the Audit Profession in Malaysia*. Kuala Lumpur: University of Malaya Press.

Azham, M. A. (2002). *Ethnicity, Foreign Investments and Strong Pragmatic Government: Towards Interpreting Accounting Progress in Malaysia*. Paper presented at the Universiti Teknologi MARA organised Conference on Financial Reporting: Issues in the 21st Century, Shah Alam.

Bass, J. R. (1973). *Malaysian Politics, 1968-1970: Crisis and Response*. (Unpublished PhD Thesis). University of California, Berkeley, CA.

Brennan, M. (1985). Class, Politics and Race in Modern Malaysia. In R. Higgott & R. Robison (Eds.), *Southeast Asia: Essays in the Political Economy of Structural Change* (pp. 93–127). London: Routledge and Kegan Paul.

Briston, R. J. (1978). The Evolution of Accounting in Developing Countries. *The International Journal of Accounting*, *14*(1), 105–120.

Bruce, S. W. (1988). *Certified Public Accountants: A Profession in Crisis*. (Unpublished PhD Thesis). Claremont Graduate School.

Burchell, S., Clubb, C., & Hopwood, A. G. (1985). Accounting in its Social Context: Towards a History of Value Added in the United Kingdom. *Accounting, Organizations and Society*, *10*(4), 381–413. doi:10.1016/0361-3682(85)90002-9

Burchell, S., Clubb, C., Hopwood, A. G., Hughes, J., & Nahapiet, J. (1980). The Roles of Accounting in Organizations and Society. *Accounting, Organizations and Society*, *5*(1), 5–27. doi:10.1016/0361-3682(80)90017-3

Carnegie, G. D., & Napier, C. J. (1996). Critical and Interpretive Histories: Insights into Accounting's Present and Future Through Its Past. *Accounting, Auditing & Accountability Journal*, *9*(3), 7–39. doi:10.1108/09513579610121956

Central Bank. (1987). *The Role of External Auditors in the Supervision of Financial Institutions in Malaysia*. Kuala Lumpur: SEACEN.

Chan, P., & Horii, K. (1986). *Impact of the New Economic Policy on the Malaysian Economy: With Special Reference to Ownership and Control*. Tokyo: Institute of Developing Economies.

Chandra, M. (1989). *Challenges and Choices in Malaysian Politics and Society*. Penang: Aliran.

Chee, S. H. (1971). *Sociocultural Pluralism and Political Change: The Dilemmas of the Bimodal Society in Malaya*. (Unpublished PhD Thesis). University of Pittsburgh.

Choo, K. E. (1991). *'Trust Me' Approach of Professional Accountants vs 'Show Me' Attitude of the Public Towards Professional Ethics*. Paper presented at the MIA and MACPA jointly organised 7th National Accountants Conference, Kuala Lumpur.

Committee on International Accounting Operation and Education. 1976-78, of the American Accounting Association. (1978). Accounting Education and the Third World. American Accounting Association.

Cooper, D., & Sherer, M. J. (1984). The Value of Corporate Accounting Reports: Arguments for a Political Economy of Accounting. *Accounting, Organizations and Society*, *9*(3/4), 207–232. doi:10.1016/0361-3682(84)90008-4

Dahl, R. A. (1967). *Pluralist Economy in the United States*. Rand McNally.

DiGabriele, J., & Ojo, M. (2013). Objectivity and independence: The Dual Roles of External Auditors and Forensic Accountants. *Journal of Forensic and Investigative Accounting, 6*(2).

Djojohadikusomo, S. (1968/69). Trade and Aid in South-East Asia, Vol. 1: Malaysia and Singapore. University of Malaya Co-op, Kuala Lumpur.

Dyball, M. C., & Valcarcel, L. J. (1999). The "Rational" and "Traditional": The Regulation of Accounting in the Philippines. *Accounting, Auditing & Accountability Journal*, *12*(3), 303–327. doi:10.1108/09513579910277384

Dye, T. R. (1986). *Who's Running America?* (4th ed.). Prentice-Hall.

Edwards, C. B. (1975). *Protection, Profits and Policy: An Analysis of Industrialization in Malaysia.* (Unpublished PhD Thesis). University of East Anglia.

Enthoven, A. J. H. (1973). *Accountancy and Economic Development Policy*. Amsterdam: North-Holland Publishing Company.

Enthoven, A. J. H. (1977). *Accountancy Systems in Third World Economies*. Amsterdam: North-Holland Publishing Company.

Flint, D. (1983). The Scope for Auditing Research. In *Discussion Papers of Symposium on Auditing Research*. The University of Glasgow Press.

Friedland, J. (1989, November 9). A Call to Account. *Far Eastern Economic Review*, 70-5.

Gale, B. (1985). *Politics and Business: A Study of Multi-Purpose Holdings Berhad*. Petaling Jaya: Eastern Universities Press.

Gomez, E. T. (1990). *Politics in Business: UMNO's Corporate Investments*. Petaling Jaya: Forum Enterprise.

Gomez, E. T. (1994). *Political Business: Corporate Involvement of Malaysian Political Parties*. Townsville, Queensland: Centre for South East Asian Studies, James Cook University.

Gomez, E. T. (1997). The Economics and Politics of Privatization in Malaysia. *Journal of the Asia Pacific Economy*, *2*(2), 178–200. doi:10.1080/13547869708724616

Gul, F. (1983). *History and Development of Accounting Education in Malaysia*. Singapore: The Regional Institute of Higher Education and Development.

Hagiwara, Y. (1972). Political Culture and Communalism in West Malaysia. *The Developing Economies*, *10*(3), 250–266. doi:10.1111/j.1746-1049.1972.tb00281.x

Hai, G. J. (1970/71). Recent Legislation on the Profession of Accountancy in Malaysia and Singapore. *The Accounting Journal*, *1*(1), 25–36.

Hanafiah, N. (1990). *Ethical Standards in the Accounting Profession*. Paper presented at the Universiti Utara Malaysia and Petronas jointly organised Seminar on Management Ethics, Kuala Lumpur.

Hara, F. (1991). Malaysia's New Economic Policy and The Chinese Business Community. *The Developing Economies*, *29*(4), 350–370. doi:10.1111/j.1746-1049.1991.tb01040.x

Hirschman, C. (1971). Ownership and Control in the Manufacturing Sector of West Malaysia. *UMBC Economic Review*, *7*(1), 20–39.

Hirschman, C. (1983). Ownership and Control in the Manufacturing Sector of West Malaysia. In D. Lim (Ed.), *Further Readings on Malaysian Economic Development* (pp. 209–220). Kuala Lumpur: Oxford University Press.

Hopper, T., & Powell, A. (1985). Making Sense of Research into the Organizational and Social Aspects of Management Accounting: A Review of its Underlying Assumptions. *Journal of Management Studies*, *22*(5), 429–465. doi:10.1111/j.1467-6486.1985.tb00007.x

Hopper, T. M., Storey, J., & Willmott, H. (1987). Accounting for Accounting Towards the Development of a Dialectical View. *Accounting, Organizations and Society*, *12*(5), 437–456. doi:10.1016/0361-3682(87)90030-4

Hopwood, A. G. (1987). The Archeology of Accounting Systems. *Accounting, Organizations and Society*, *12*(3), 207–234. doi:10.1016/0361-3682(87)90038-9

Horii, K. (1991). Disintegration of the Colonial Economic Legacies and Social Restructuring in Malaysia. *The Developing Economies*, *24*(4), 281–313.

Hui, L. M. (1983). The Ownership and Control of Large Corporations in Malaysia: The Role of Chinese Businessmen. In L. Y. C. Lim & L. A. P. Gosling (Eds.), *The Chinese in Southeast Asia: Ethnicity and Economic Activity* (Vol. I, pp. 275–315). Maruzen Asia, Singapore.

Hui, L. M. (1988). Contradictions in the Development of Malay Capital: State, Accumulation and Legitimation. In J. G. Taylor & A. Turton (Eds.), *Sociology of 'Developing Societies' Southeast Asia* (pp. 19–32). London: Macmillan Education Ltd. doi:10.1007/978-1-349-19568-8_2

Humphrey, C., Moizer, P., & Turley, S. (1992). The Audit Expectations Gap - Plus Ca Change, Plus C'est La Meme Chose? *Critical Perspectives on Accounting*, *3*(2), 137–161. doi:10.1016/1045-2354(92)90008-F

Ismail, M. S. (1994). The Role of Public Sector in the Malaysian Economy. In National Institute of Public Administration Malaysia (Ed.), Malaysian Development Experience: Changes and Challenges. INTAN.

Jacob, R. (1992). Can You Trust That Audit? *Fortune*, *18*(November), 91–94.

Jesudason, J. V. (1989). Ethnicity and the Economy: The State, Chinese Business, and Multinationals in Malaysia. Oxford University Press.

Johnson, T. J., & Caygill, M. (1971). The Development of Accounting Links in the Commonwealth. *Accounting and Business Review*, *1*(2), 155–173. doi:10.1080/00014788.1971.9728562

Jomo, K. S. (1986). *A Question of Class: Capital, the State, and Uneven Development in Malaya*. Singapore: Oxford University Press.

Jomo, K. S. (Ed.). (1995). *Privatizing Malaysia: Rents, Rhetoric, Realities*. Oxford, UK: Westview Press.

Junid, S. (1980). *British Industrial Investments in Malaysia, 1963-1971*. Kuala Lumpur: Oxford University Press.

Kennedy, J. (1993). *A History of Malaya* (3rd ed.). Kuala Lumpur: S. Abdul Majeed and Co.

Koon, T. Y. (1994). *Employee Fraud in Malaysia: A Case Study*. (Unpublished PhD Thesis). University of London.

Kuala Lumpur Stock Exchange and Malaysian Strategic Consultancy Sdn. Bhd. (Eds.). (1992). Malaysia The Rising Star: Business and Investment Opportunities and Challenges Towards 2020. KLSE and MSC Sdn. Bhd.

Kunio, Y. (1988). *The Rise of Ersatz Capitalism in South-East Asia*. Oxford University Press.

Lehman, C., & Tinker, A. (1987). The 'Real' Cultural Significance of Accounts. *Accounting, Organizations and Society*, *12*(5), 503–522.

Leigh, M. (1992). Politics, Bureaucracy, and Business in Malaysia: Realigning the Eternal Triangle. In A. J. MacIntyre & K. Jayasuriya (Eds.), *The Dynamics of Economic Policy Reform in South-East Asia and the South-West Pacific* (pp. 115–123). Singapore: Oxford University Press.

Leong, H. K. (1988). *Indegenizing the State: The New Economic Policy and the Bumiputera State in Peninsular Malaysia*. (Unpublished PhD Thesis). Ohio State University.

Liang, F. S. (1989). How Old is the Auditing Profession in Singapore? *Singapore Accountant*, *5*(7), 9–10.

Lim, D. (1973). *Economic Growth and Development in West Malaysia*. Oxford University Press.

Limlingan, V. S. (1986). *The Overseas Chinese in ASEAN: Business Strategies and Management Practices*. Manila: Vita Development Corporation.

Limlingan, V. S. (1994). *The Visible Hand and the Developing Economy: Essays on Management in Southeast Asia* (2nd ed.). Manila: De La Salle University Press.

Linderberg, M. M. (1973). *Foreign and Domestic Investment in the Pioneer Industry Program, Malaysia 19651970, Political, Economic, and Social Impacts*. (Unpublished PhD Thesis). University of Southern California.

Loft, A. (1986). Towards a Critical Understanding of Accounting: The Case of Cost Accounting in the U.K., 1914-1925. *Accounting, Organizations and Society*, *11*(2), 137–169. doi:10.1016/0361-3682(86)90028-0

Means, G. P. (1986). Ethnic Preference Policies in Malaysia. In N. Nevitte & C. H. Kennedy (Eds.), *Ethnic Preference and Public Policy in Developing Societies* (pp. 95–118). Boulder, CO: Lynne Reinner Publishers, Inc.

Megat, A. R. (1979). *Future of the Accountancy Profession in Malaysia*. Paper presented at the MACPA 21st Anniversary Seminar, Kuala Lumpur.

Miller, P., & O'Leary, T. (1987). Accounting and the Construction of the Governable Person. *Accounting, Organizations and Society*, *12*(3), 235–265. doi:10.1016/0361-3682(87)90039-0

Mohd.-Ariff, Y. (1993). *Securities Commission: Regulator of the Capital Market*. Paper presented at the 9th National Accountants' Conference, Kuala Lumpur.

Mohd.-Salleh, M. (1989). *The Equity Structure of Listed Companies*. Paper presented at the Persatuan Sains Sosial Malaysia and Institut Pengajian Tinggi, Universiti Malaya jointly organised New Economic Policy and Its Future conference, Universiti Malaya.

Mohd.-Salleh, M. (1993). The Malaysian Capital Market: New Rules of the Game. *Capital Markets Review*, *1*(1), 1–21.

Mohd.-Sheriff, M.-K. (1992). Economic Outlook and Privatization Trends Towards 2020. In Kuala Lumpur Stock Exchange and Malaysian Strategic Consultancy Sdn. Bhd. (Eds.), Malaysia The Rising Star: Business and Investment Opportunities and Challenges Towards 2020. KLSE and MSC Sdn. Bhd.

National Operations Council. (1969). *The May 13 Tragedy: A Report*. National Operation Council.

Needles, B. E. Jr. (1976). Implementing a Framework for the International Transfer of Accounting Technology. *The International Journal of Accounting*, *12*(1), 45–62.

Ojo, M. (2005). *The External Auditor's Role in Bank Regulation and Supervision: Helping the Regulator Avoid Regulatory Capture*. Paper presented at the 2006 Institute for Business and Finance Research Conference, Costa Rica.

Ojo, M. (2006). *The Role of External Auditors and International Accounting Bodies in Financial Regulation and Supervision*. Paper presented at the 2006 SASE (Society for the Advancement of Socio Economics) Conference in Trier.

Ojo, M. (2006). *Audit Independence: Its Importance to the External Auditor's Role in Banking Regulation and Supervision*. Paper presented at the 2006 Institute for Business and Finance Research Conference, Costa Rica.

Ojo, M. (2006). Avoiding Another Enron: The Role of the External Auditor in Financial Regulation and Supervision. In *Global Auditing: Concepts and Concerns*. ICFAI University Press.

Ojo, M. (2008). *The Role of the External Auditor in Bank and Supervision: A Comparative Analysis Between the UK, Germany, Italy and the USA* (PhD Thesis). Oxford Brookes University.

Ojo, M. (2010). The Role of the IASB and Auditing Standards in the Aftermath of the 2008/2009 Financial Crisis. European Law Journal, 16(5).

Ojo, M. (2013). Recovering from the Global Financial Crisis: Achieving Financial Stability in Times of Uncertainty. Business Experts Press.

Ojo, M. (2014a). *Role of External Auditors in Corporate Governance and Financial Reporting*. Kindle Books and Amazon Publications.

Ojo, M. (2014b). *The Adoption of International Financial Reporting Standards and Basel III Requirements: A Justification for the Role of Audits?*. Paper presented at the International Conference on New Trends in Business, Management, and Social Sciences, Marina Bay Sands, Singapore

Ojo, M. (2014c). *Role of External Auditors in Corporate Governance and Financial Reporting: Capital and Liquidity Requirements, and the Finance Theory*. Academic Press.

Ong, B. K. (1987). Market Manipulation and the Securities Industry Act 1983. *The Malaysian Accountant*, 2(4), 25–31.

Onn, F. C. (1989). *Malaysian Corporate Economy Restructuring: Progress Since 1970*. Paper presented at the Persatuan Sains Sosial Malaysia and Institut Pengajian Tinggi, Universiti Malaya jointly organized New Economic Policy and Its Future Conference, Universiti Malaya.

Parker, W. C. Jr. (1973). *Communications and the May 13th Crisis: A Psychocultural Interpretation*. Kuala Lumpur: University Malaya Press.

Peng, K. K. (1979). *Dependence and the Malaysian Economy*. (Unpublished Master Thesis). Universiti Sains Malaysia.

Peng, K. K. (1983). *The Malaysian Economy*. Kuala Lumpur: Sdn. Bhd.

Peng, O. C. (1989). *Auditor's Report - Where Lies its Values?* Paper presented at the MIA and MACPA jointly organised 5th National Accountants Conference, Kuala Lumpur.

Phenix, P. (1986, April). Directors, Shareholders and Auditors Under the Companies Act 1965 - As Amended. The Malaysian Accountant, 7-16.

Pillai, P. N. (1984). *Companies and Securities Handbook - Singapore & Malaysia*. Singapore: Butterworths.

Puthucheary, J. (1960). *Ownership and Control in the Malayan Economy*. Eastern Universities Press Ltd.

Ram, G. S. (1985). *Criminal Law and Commercial Crimes*. Paper presented at the HRM Fighting Financial Fraud, Kuala Lumpur.

Redha, A. (1985). *Capital Accumulation and the State in Malaysia. Ilmu Masyarakat, 8,*1–27.

Rohwer, J. (1995). *Asia Rising: How History's Biggest Middle Class Will Change the World*. Singapore: Butterworth Heinemann Asia.

Sakagami, M., Yoshimi, H., & Okano, H. (1999). Japanese Accounting Profession in Transition. *Accounting, Auditing & Accountability Journal, 12*(3), 340–357. doi:10.1108/09513579910277401

Samuels, J. M., & Piper, A. G. (1985). *International Accounting: A Survey*. London: Croom Helm.

Saruwatari, K. (1991). Malaysia's Localization Policy and its Impact on British-Owned Enterprises. *The Developing Economies, 24*(4), 371–386.

Schlossstein, S. (1991). *Asia's New Little Dragons: The Dynamic Emergence of Indonesia, Thailand and Malaysia*. Chicago: Contemporary Books.

Seidler, L. J. (1967). *The Function of Accounting in Economic Development - Turkey as a Case Study*. London: Frederick and Prager Publishers.

Shing, G. Y. Y. (1981). The Audit License. *The Malaysian Accountant, 2*(2), 32–33.

Siang, L. K. (1982). *Malaysia in the Dangerous 80s*. Petaling Jaya: Democratic Action Party.

Siang, L. K. (1986). *Malaysia: The Crisis of Identity*. Petaling Jaya: Democratic Action Party.

Sikka, P., Willmott, H. C., & Lowe, T. (1989). Guardians of Knowledge and Public Interest: Evidence and Issues of Accountability in the UK Accountancy Profession. *Accounting, Auditing & Accountability Journal, 2*(2), 47–71. doi:10.1108/09513578910132286

Sum, H. L. C., & Wishart, D. A. (1989). Commercial Law. In A. Krishnan (Ed.), *Survey of Malaysian Law* (pp. 113–124). Kuala Lumpur: Malayan Law Journal Sdn. Bhd.

Susela, S. D. (1999). 'Interests' and Accounting Standard Setting in Malaysia. *Accounting, Auditing & Accountability Journal, 12*(3), 357–387. doi:10.1108/09513579910277410

Syed, H. A. (1984). Social Relations: The Ethnic and Class Factors. In H. A. Syed (Ed.), *Ethnicity, Class and Development in Malaysia* (pp. 13–31). Kuala Lumpur: Malaysian Science Social Association.

Tay, J. S. W. (1994). Malaysia. In T. E. Cooke & R. H. Parker (Eds.), *Financial Reporting in the West Pacific Rim* (pp. 231–264). London: Routledge.

Teik, G. C. (1971). The May Thirteenth Incident and Democracy in Malaysia. Oxford University Press.

Tinker, A. M. (1980). Towards a Political Economy of Accounting: An Empirical Illustration of the Cambridge Controversies. *Accounting, Organizations and Society*, *5*(1), 147–160. doi:10.1016/0361-3682(80)90031-8

Tong, T. L., & Ann, C. T. (1996, April). Non-Disclosure in the Abridged Profit and Loss Accounts of Malaysian Listed Corporations. The Malaysian Accountant, 2-5.

Tong, T. L., Zainal, A. K., & Wah, C. P. (1989). *Information Needs of Users and Voluntary Disclosure Practices of Malaysian Listed Corporations*. Paper presented at the International Accounting Seminar on Accounting Trends, Issues and Challenges, Universiti Pertanian Malaysia.

Vreeland, N., Dana, G. B., Hurwitz, G. B., Just, P., Moeller, P. V., & Shinn, R. S. (1976). *Area Handbook for Malaysia* (3rd ed.). Washington, DC: U.S. Government Printing Office.

Wai, T. T. (1982). *Income Distribution and Determination in West Malaysia*. Oxford University Press.

Walton, P. (1986). The Export of British Accounting Legislation to Commonwealth Countries. *Accounting and Business Review*, *16*(64), 353–357.

Willmott, H. C. (1985). Setting Accounting Standards in the UK: The Emergence of Private Accounting Bodies and Their Role in the Regulation of Public Accounting Practice. In W. Streeck & P. Schmitter (Eds.), *Private Interest Government: Beyond Market and State*. London: Sage.

Willmott, H. C. (1991). The Auditing Game: A Question of Ownership and Control. *Critical Perspectives on Accounting*, *2*(1), 109–121. doi:10.1016/1045-2354(91)90021-5

Woon, T. K. (1982). The Role of the Malaysian State in the Restructuring of Employment. Jurnal Ekonomi Malaysia, 6, 32-62.

Woon, T. K., & Kam, W. P. (1989). *Restructuring of Employment*. Paper presented at the Persatuan Sains Sosial Malaysia organised National Economic Policy and Its Future seminar, Kuala Lumpur.

Yan, L. S. (1994). The Malaysian Economy, 1957-91: An Overview. In National Institute of Public Administration Malaysia (Ed.), Malaysian Development Experience: Changes and Challenges. INTAN.

Yun, H. A. (1984). Capitalist Development, Class and Race. In H. A. Syed (Ed.), *Ethnicity, Class and Development in Malaysia* (pp. 296–328). Kuala Lumpur: Malaysian Science Social Association.

Zainal-Aznam, Y. (1991). Distributional Policies and Programmes: The Malaysian Experience. In L. K. Hock & S. Nagaraj (Eds.), *The Malaysian Economy Beyond 1990: International and Domestic Perspectives* (pp. 343–379). Persatuan Ekonomi Malaysia, Kuala Lumpur.

Zainal-Aznam, Y. (1994). Growth and Equity in Malaysia. In National Institute of Public Administration Malaysia (Ed.), Malaysian Development Experience: Changes and Challenges. INTAN.

ENDNOTES

1 See remarks made by the then chairman of the Securities Commission (SC) (The Malaysian Accountant, Oct/Dec 1993, p. 15), the Finance Minister (Akauntan Nasional, Sept. 1989, pp. 21-23; Aug. 1990, p. 26; Oct. 1990, pp. 20-21) and those by Tun Ismail Ali, the former Governor of Central Bank and the chairman of the Bumiputra trust agency, Permodalan Nasional Berhad (PNB), and several listed companies (The Malaysian Accountant, July-Sept 1988, p. 18).

2 Just before the Companies Act 1965 came into force, in 1965, the audit firm Peat, Marwick, Mitchell & Co. located in Kuala Lumpur was sued by plaintiffs who were shareholders of a company - Kiwi Dry Cleaners Ltd. - at the High Court of Malaya (Civil Suit No. 324 of 1965 Kuala Lumpur). See (1967) 1 MLJ 87. (MLJ stands for Malayan Law Journal.)

3 Hereafter referred to as NST.

4 For example, as noted Malaysian Medical Council chairman Professor Datuk Dr Mahmood Mohd Noor, "[t]he number of medical negligence or malpractice suits in Malaysia is relatively few but the cases filed over the last two years were more than the average for the previous five years" (NST, 29 Dec. 1994). As a result, it is reported that the Law Ministry is now looking into ways to introduce limits on the amount of money a plaintiff can claim (NST, 29 Dec. 1993).

5 This view of his was however different to that of the former, for Oh Chong Peng (1989) did say that some amount of pressure for change had been dispensed by regulatory authorities like the Capital Issues Committee (which was replaced by the Securities Commission in 1992) and the Central Bank.

6 Deloitte Touche Tohmatsu was criticized by a Hong Kong inspector over audits it conducted for a group of companies which were under criminal investigation (International Accounting Bulletin, 8 Nov 1993, p. 1). The firm was alleged to have committed audit failure leading to the publication of misleading financial statements. In Singapore, the collapse of Pan-El, a property, salvage and hotel group, resulted in an unprecedented three-day closure of the Kuala Lumpur and Singapore stock exchanges in December 1985, the demise of six broking firms and the trial of three key figures in the Pan-El Group on charges ranging from criminal breach of trust to share forgery (NST, 6 June 1988). The uproar over the alleged failure of the auditors to conduct proper audits was brought to public attention in late 1986 when the Singapore Minister of Finance mentioned in his speech in Parliament that there was "an inexplicable audit failure" in the Pan-El affair. The following year, the investigation undertaken by the Singapore Society of Accountants (SSA) culminated with Coopers & Lybrand publicly reprimanded for the quality of its audit work. As for South Korea, in 1993, the country's Securities Supervisory Board (SSB), which regulates the nation's audit practice, issued warnings to seven of South Korea's audit firms for their alleged audit negligence (International Accounting Bulletin, 17 Jan. 1994, p. 4). This warning took place after SSB conducted a quality review of auditing practice of selected firms. Out of the seven firms warned, four were affiliates of the Big Six (now Big Four). Finally, in the case of India, as a result of the loss of US$1.5 billion through a securities fraud involving banks and mutual funds, the auditors were criticized by a Joint Parliamentary Committee (JPC) set up by the Parliament to investigate the case (International Accounting Bulletin, 14 March 1994, p. 3). Not surprisingly, the Reserve Bank of India (RBI) in 1993 dropped from its list of auditors for 1992/3 about 20 audit firms which acted as auditors for the institutions involved during the 1991/2 fiscal year (International Accounting Bulletin, 21 June

1993, p. 2). These firms which included all the Big Six were ordered to take a one year "period of rest".

7 For South Korea, in December 1991, alleged failure of the auditors to uncover significant liabilities of now bankrupt companies had led to the investors filing the first ever lawsuit against the auditors (International Accounting Bulletin, Feb. 1992, p. 3). As for Singapore, in 1988, the former shareholders of Pan-El sued its group auditor, Coopers & Lybrand, for US$105 million (NST, 6 June 1988). It perhaps needs to be noted too that early on in December 1987, a former partner of another accounting firm, acting as auditor for a number of Pan-El's subsidiaries, pleaded guilty to a criminal charge brought against him for issuing a misleading audit report. He was sentenced to two months in jail and fined for S$10,000.

8 Note that Dahl (1967) defines power and conflict as the ability to impose one's will upon another and the existence of more than one interest, respectively.

9 Dye (1986) argues that a cohesive "power elite" exercise authority over a variety of institutions. This elite is comprised of a small group of dominant, authoritative individuals or entities. The elite functions through, among other things, interlocking directorships, interlocking institutional experiences and similar social backgrounds. However, instead of a single power elite, Dye says that a society may have different groups of individuals or entities which exercise power in its various sectors. Thus, leadership or authority is dispersed. More importantly perhaps it is not unusual for these elites to be in conflict with each other.

10 Previously in the Federation of Malaya, company law was governed by the Companies Ordinance 1946, whilst in the State of Singapore, it was governed by the Straits Settlements Ordinance 1940. The Sarawak Companies Ordinance was similar to the North Borneo Companies Ordinance, which was based on Hong Kong companies legislation which in turn was modelled from the English Companies Act of 1929.

11 Note however that in the Parliamentary Debates (Vol. II, no. 8, Col. 1558 and dated 9 Aug. 1965), it was stated by the then Minister of Commerce and Industry, Dr. Lim Swee Aun, that the committee with the responsibility to draft the Companies Bill (whose chairman came from the ministry of commerce and industry and with the assistance of John Finemore, a Colombo Plan draftsman from Australia) had considered not only the present legislation in force in the UK, Australia, India and New Zealand but also the draft code prepared for Ghana by Professor Gower and the reports presented in the UK by the committees chaired by Lord Cohen and Lord Jenkins.

12 The MIA president mentioned in 1987 that the power to issue audit and liquidator licenses had been delegated in accordance with Section 8(7) of the Companies Act 1965, to a committee in the finance ministry (The Malaysian Accountant, Oct-Dec 1987, p. 10). He did not say however when this committee had actually started its operation.

13 The public and registered members are those with accounting bachelor or post-graduate diploma degrees from local higher institutions or accounting professional qualifications from MIA's recognized local and overseas accounting bodies. To become a member, he or she also needed to have three to five years relevant experience in public accounting firms for public accountants and in commerce/industry/public sector entity for registered accountants. (Five years are the rule. But it will be shortened to four years for those with High School Certificate and to three years for those graduating with degrees or diploma from local higher institutions.) The recognized accounting bodies (as listed in the Accountants Act's First Schedule) are the Chartered Institutes of Scotland, England and Wales, Ireland, Australia, Canada and India; the Societies of Accountants of Australia

and New Zealand; the Association of Certified Accountants (UK); the Institute of Cost and Management Accountants (UK); and Malaysian Association of Certified Public Accountants (MACPA). As for the licensed accountants, they do not have MIA recognized accounting qualifications but are allowed to practice for either one of the following two reasons: they are already in operation as accountants, tax-consultants or tax advisers prior to the passing of the Accountants Act in 1967; the finance minister has granted them limited approval to act as company auditor under Section 8(6) of the Companies Act 1965.

14 The Act however with regard to a tax consultant or a tax adviser has a provision allowing him or her to practice or hold him/herself out as one when he or she has the authority to do so as granted by any other law that is enforced within the country.

15 As defined by Peng (1979, p. 193) to be the ratio between net fixed investment and net profits.

16 The unofficial estimate of the total dead however was as high as six or seven hundred. The riots took place in the aftermath of the May 1969 general election when the Chinese-dominated opposition parties registered impressive gains at the polls. They celebrated their victory by taunting the Malays on Malay areas of Kuala Lumpur. The Malays in turn organized counter demonstrations which moved into Chinese quarters. With insults exchanged on the streets, rioting ensued (see Bass, 1973; Parker, 1973; Chee, 1971; Teik, 1971; and National Operations Council, 1969).

17 He was among the first few Bumiputra sent to Australia under the Colombo Plan to study Accounting (Business Times, 17 Aug. 1989). He qualified as a Chartered Accountant in 1960 after five years with Price Waterhouse in Melbourne. Upon his retirement in 1989, he took over the business of the audit firm Baharom-Jasani (Business Times, 17 Aug. 1989). In 1991, it was reported (The Star, 10 July 1991) that Shamsir Jasani & Co, the seventh largest accounting firm in the country, had 130 staff and was backed by Grant Thornton International.

18 See set of untitled bounded documents in the MIA library, stamped on its first page as "Confidential" and dated 1 October 1988 and which appears to have been forwarded to the then Finance Minister by the MIA Council to gain his approval for the various amendments suggested for the Accountants Act 1967. Hereinafter, it will be referred to as the "MIA 1988 Bounded Document".

19 From both the documented sources and interviews, a variety of answers is found as to why the MIA limited itself to play a "registering role" for two decades (see Azham, 2002).

20 Note that this remark was probably made in response to the criticism made by the then Central Bank's Governor, Tan Sri Jaafar Hussein, towards the MACPA leadership (see The Malaysian Accountant, July 1986, p. 6). Note also that an interviewee who had been involved with the MACPA investigation committee for several years mentioned that the MACPA could be stricter in punishing errant members.

21 It is notable that the 1981, 1982 and 1984 Annual Reports of MACPA mentioned the various efforts conducted by the MACPA in confronting the issue of unregistered accountants. The MACPA 1984 Annual Report for example, mentioned that the MACPA had sent a memorandum to the Accountant-General who was the MIA president. Next it stated (p. 22): "We now await his action against persons identified in our memorandum as violating the provisions of the Accountants Act 1967." Apparently, he did not do anything that could make a difference. This should not perhaps be surprising due to the fact that these accountants were needed in the then fast growing economy which was facing severe shortage of qualified accountants (see Committee on International Accounting Operation and Education, 1976-78, of the American Accounting Association, 1978, p. 39; Ahmad Noordin, 1981, p. 25).

22 Perhaps nothing else could describe the appalling state of audit during this period than the case of Bank Rakyat which was illustrated in a 1979 Parliamentary White Paper. In summary, Bank Rakyat was established in 1950. By 1975, it had expanded its paid up capita to over RM 15 million and membership comprised of over twenty three thousands individuals and just over 1000 cooperative societies. It faced acute financial problems from 1973 which resulted in it being rescued by the government in 1977. The parliamentary paper revealed widespread corrupt activities by parties inside the bank and those related to it, including the external auditor, the audit firm Kassim Chan & Co. And yet the auditor appeared to have escaped without censure or penalty. An opposition MP Lim Kit Siang in a speech in the Parliament in June 1979 argued (Siang, 1982, p. 266): "In other countries, such negligence and conflict of interest could have resulted in professional action being taken against the firms of auditors, and I want to know what action the Government has taken against Kassim Chan & Co. for its professional negligence and conflict of interest, leading to such colossal losses". He also claimed (p. 265) that the role played by the auditor in the "Great Bank Rakyat Betrayal" was one of the "sorriest episodes" of all. From an interview conducted with one of the leaders of the MACPA, it was found that except for the MACPA which suspended the membership of the audit partner in charge for "three months", it appeared that (as far as he knew it) the government authorities in the form of for example, the Attorney General or the police had taken no action against the auditor as a consequence. Even the Ministry of Finance had failed to withdraw his audit licence. As for the MIA that did not even have the right machinery in place in the form of investigative and disciplinary committees, there was nothing to be expected of it. In fact, in the MIA 1967-1987 Annual Report, this very auditor had been listed as an MIA council member since 1972. In other words, when the Bank Rakyat case became public and he was named in the Parliamentary White Paper for failing to do a proper audit and lacking independence, not only did he not face any sanctions from the MIA, but he also continued to act as a council member of the MIA, as if nothing had happened!

23 That of the equity requirements on investment in most business enterprises: 30 percent equity in a business enterprise for Bumiputra, 40 percent for other Malaysians and 30 percent foreigners.

24 In terms of the number of companies listed, the increase was from 321 listed in 1992 to over 500 companies by the end of 1995. At the end of 1993, the market value of the KLSE had also jumped to RM 620 billion - an increase of 152 percent from the RM 246 billion recorded at the end of the previous year (NST, 14 May 1994). In 1993 too, the total volume and turnover rose to 108 billion units valued at RM 387 billion, which exceeded the combined volume and turnover for the past 20 years! In 1994, the International Finance Corporation, an affiliate of the World Bank, posted in the Internet that the KLSE's market capitalization as at November 1993 was US$175 billions - the second biggest after Hong Kong among 22 emerging markets capitalization. It is perhaps important to note that paralleling these numerical advances, the government during the same period had embarked on a number of steps related to the nation's securities market – a continuation of those taken in the last half of 1980s. These included requiring the formation of audit committee for listed companies (Akauntan Nasional, Nov/Dec. 1993, p. 26), the setting up Securities Commission (SC) (Yusof, 1993; Mohd.-Salleh, 1993), both in 1993, and the upgrading of penalties for any breach of the KLSE listing requirements from public reprimands and suspension of trading to fines of up to RM 100,000 (NST, 30 Sept. 1994) in the following year. Finally, in 1995, the government unveiled an 18-point liberalizing package for the capital market with local and international objectives.

25 The merger proposal was rejected on 17 June, 1985. Reason given was that there was no need for the merged body (the MICA) as there was already an accounting body in the country entrusted with all the required tasks to spearhead the accounting profession in the form of the MIA (MIA Annual Report, 1967-87, p. 11). The interviews had however found that there was no "outright" rejection by the government. See Azham (2002).

26 In other words, the MIA was supposed to be a full-fledged accounting professional body. In the following year however, in Parliament, at a time when the media was having a field day reporting on the public quarrels between the leaders of the MIA and the MACPA (see Azham, 2002), his deputy made remarks which were not encouraging at all to those in the MIA. He said that the MIA should continue to oversee the MACPA and other professional accounting bodies (The Star, 12 Oct. 1988; Business Times, 12 Oct. 1988). Both bodies he claimed had different functions and responsibilities. He also said that through the Accountants Act 1967, the MIA was set up to monitor, regulate and coordinate the accounting profession for the purpose of safeguarding public interest and ensuring high professional standards. The MIA in short was to act as mere supervisory and coordinating body for the rest of accounting professional bodies in the country.

27 The apparent exceptions took place in two cases: one in 1992 when the MIA president was reported to have said that the MIA had found from its recent investigation involving 40 accountants that there were auditors who had failed to issue proper audit report (NST, 12 Apr. 1992). The other was in 1993 under the headline "MIA Warning to Errant Members" (NST, 28 Jan. 1993). However on closer inspection, the story involved members of MIA who colluded with unqualified accountants. Thus, this story was nothing new. It is because on this very subject of collusion between members and the so-called unqualified accountants, the MIA over the years was fond of issuing numerous statements to the media making one warning after another that stern action would be taken against its members with really no news as to whether the actions in fact, had been taken. See The Malay Mail (4 Feb. 1988; 26 Feb. 1992) and NST (17 Sept. 1988; 31 Jan. 1991).

28 The MIA in contrast to the MACPA did not divulge the types of disciplinary action taken against the members in its annual reports. Why it did not find fit to clearly spell what these actions were appears to be one of those questions whose answers are anyone's guess.

29 The excuse for no disciplinary actions taken in 1989 was this as appeared in the MIA 1989 Annual Report (p. 13): Dato' Shamsir Omar who was sitting in the disciplinary committee left the council (and thus the committee too) due to his retirement from his position as the then Accountant-General. As for the year 1990, the excuse as found in the MIA 1990 Annual Report (p. 13) was this: shortage of manpower "especially" with the resignation of the Institute's legal officer.

30 Remarks made by the newly appointed finance minister (Akauntan Nasional, Sept/Oct 1991, p. 23; The Malaysian Accountant, June 1992, p. 18) and the MIA itself (ASEAN Accounting Research Unit, 1992, p. 75; MIA 1992 Annual Report, p.16) provided evidence of the fact that the country was facing a shortage problem of qualified accountants/auditors. In the NST (12 Apr. 1991), the following was also stated: "A Malaysian Institute of Accountants (MIA) document says the shortage of auditors and tax consultants is very acute. While there are over 172,000 companies registered with the Registrar of Companies, there are only about 600 approved company auditors." But the MIA from the time when it was activated had kept on shifting the date as to when it would start organizing the professional examinations! And when the examination was finally set up in 1996, the MIA did not provide a real alternative or an actual additional avenue for locals wishing to qualify as accountants because it was a combined effort of both the MIA and the CACA (Akauntan

Nasional, Oct. 1995, p. 4). The collaborative exam structure was exactly the same as the UK based qualification which had been offered in the country for decades. The difference between the two examinations was that students now had the option of sitting for the UK or Malaysian law variant papers.

31 For information on the audit expectations gap, see Ojo (2007). General Literature on the Audit Expectations Gap: Journal of Forensic Accounting Volume VIII, Numbers 1 & 2 January – December 2007. First appeared online in 2006. See also Practical Training and the Audit Expectations Gap: The Case of Accounting Undergraduates of Universiti Utara Malaysia (June 2007) Journal of Financial Reporting and Accounting 01/2008; 6(1):55-74, Emerald Publications

32 Note that Chandra Muzaffar and Aliran appear to be well versed in this subject matter. Check for example Aliran (1981a, Chapter Three), Aliran (1981b), Aliran (1988a, Chapter Four) and Chandra (1989, pp. 47-56). For more on the same subject, please check also the following: The speeches made by Lim Kit Siang on 25 October 1977, 27 October 1975 and 14 July 1971 which appear in Siang (1978); the section entitled "On a Clean, Efficient and Democratic Government" in Siang (1986); and finally Schlossstein (1991, Chapter Four).

33 This could be because of the fact that by the late 1980s and early 1990s, even after a significant proportion of the economy had been transferred - under the so-called privatization exercise - from the government to the private sector resulting to what was proclaimed to be a strong accounting profession, what appears to be the case was that much of the private sector was still in the hands of those associated closely with the government sector (see Gomez, 1997; Jomo, 1995). This section of the private sector may even be considered as an "extension" of the government sector where reigning politicians and their political parties had for years been deeply involved in the business sector (see Gomez, 1994, 1990; Leigh, 1992; Leong, 1988, Chapter Six; and Gale, 1985). There was merely a superficial rearrangement of wealth and thus power among the few in the society. It is also notable that when it concerned the listing of a number of privatized entities at the KLSE, the percentage of shares offered for sale did not exceed thirty percent of the total shares (Mohd.-Sheriff, 1992): MAS, 30 percent; MISC, 17 percent; STM, 23.9 percent; and TNB, 22.8 percent. As a result, partial divestment of equity of government-owned entities provided a means whereby, the government was still in the case of these companies, their major shareholder. This very fact is not surprising since the local corporate scene was filled with individuals or companies owning at least 51 percent of the shares of the so-called public companies including those listed on the KLSE. So, even in the 1990s when the NEP era was supposed to have come to an end, the NST (30 May 1994) reported that more than two-thirds of the 335 companies on the main board and all of the 92 on the second board were controlled either by one or a few shareholders with more than 51 percent of the shares. This domination was not illegal since the KLSE listing rules required no more than a public float of 25 percent of the total shares issued. As a result, the listed companies still remained private companies (Mohd.-Salleh, 1989). They were public and listed only in names. Many of the listed companies were labelled by chairman of the Malaysian Institute of Economic Research (MIER), Datuk Dr. Kamal Salih, as "private-owned public company" (NST, 21 August 1991). Most shares were still held by insiders - family members, friends, clan members and others known personally to the companies' founders. And when it concerned privatized entities including those listed on the KLSE, the shareholders were other government entities. Therefore, on the whole, the "principal-agent" dichotomy did not exist or was at best blurred in the Malaysian context. Even though more and more companies were formed from the 1970s onwards, many of

these were "companies" merely in name - leading to various distressful conducts perpetrated by majority shareholders who also managed their daily affairs. The unsavory acts of these companies included the tendency to flout the law (Ram, 1985; Azham, 2002) and the reluctance to disclose much (Tong et al., 1989; Tong and Ann, 1996; Tay, 1994; Jaafar, 1992). Thus, the need for a truly functional audit was still not as acute as would have been expected if indeed a new political economic context had emerged after the two recessions in the 1980s. In fact, it appears that a weak audit profession that devoted more attention to promotional aspects than regulation suited certain parties, notwithstanding the rhetoric by a few among the power elite stressing from time to time the need for improvements in practice, stricter enforcement of rules and regulations, etc.

34 Perhaps a good case in point is the "BMF Affair" that took place in the first half of 1980s that led to the loss of around US$1 billion and the death of the (internal) auditor who investigated the case. Koon (1994) in her study of the BMF Affair pointed out what the government appeared to have done "to prevent" its public disclosure. On pages 194-95 of her thesis, she listed down the "systematic cover-up of the case from the Malaysian public" ranging from the denial made by the BBMB of the extent of its subsidiary's (BMF) involvement in the Carrian Group in September 1982 to the creation of a limited Committee of Inquiry by the government after rejecting public demand for a Royal Commission in January 1984 and finally to the government's reluctance to publish the report of the Committee of Inquiry in 1986. Later, due to public's demand for publication, only 2,000 copies were published at the price of RM 250 which was beyond the reach of average Malaysians! With all this in the background, it is perhaps not surprising to find that HRM as the auditor of the parent body BBMB was "quietly" replaced soon after by another auditor. This apparently was the worst that could happen to an auditor whose audit opinion in its audit reports was the opposite of the stance taken by the Committee of Inquiry which disclosed that both audited financial statements of BMF and BBMB did not give a true and fair view of the state of affairs of BBMB and the Group as at 31 December 1981 (Siang, 1986, p. 36). This revelation of what took place in the "private sector" may be added to those that came straight from those in the know in the arena of government operation where the leaders had repeatedly proclaimed the need for clean government and stiff actions against corrupt acts. The then deputy accountant-general (Akauntan Nasional, Jan. 1990, p. 19), noted that the government's reaction had been indifferent towards accounting as a tool for effectiveness and efficiency. And from the former auditor-general, Tan Sri Ahmad Noordin, the following was his remark when he was discussing value for money audits in government operations (Ahmad-Noordin, 1986, p. 47):

We have accordingly amended or rather we had the Audit Act amended to ensure that the Auditor-General has the necessary power within the law to carry out this value for money audit as I mentioned just now. What seemed to be the constraint when I was there was that as value for money or performance audit penetrates into the activities of governments, there was a natural tendency for authorities having the power to approve staff for the Audit Office to make it difficult for the Audit Office to get the necessary skills and manpower to carry out this work.

Thus, it may safely be said that the debilitating atmosphere in the audit arena in the post-NEP era had been deliberate and intended to deflect attention from creating a "culture of accountability" or full public disclosure, because interested parties did not want to face the unnecessary "complication" of explaining themselves to anyone in their pursuit of gaining economic ascendancy. This is stated by Belkaoui (1974, as reported by Samuels and Piper, 1985, p. 141): a class elite in many developing countries are interested in maintaining secrecy, thus, the financial reporting system was purposely made to be weak so that it was easy for this elite to maintain secrecy for their own gain.

35 Perhaps it was because at that time Malaysia was getting bogged down by the Asian Financial Crisis? So, there was no need for additional bad news that could only make the economy worse off? It perhaps needs to be noted that on the eve of the Asian Financial Crisis, just a few months after the operation had begun, the NST (8 July 1997) did file a report on remarks coming from the domestic trade and consumer affairs minister that there were five cases of auditors obstructing the ROC officers in conducting their inspection which to that date numbered to 123 audit firms. He also mentioned that the southern branch of the MIA had sent out circulars asking its members not to co-operate with the ROC should their firms be called for inspection. He therefore warned/ advised the auditors to co-operate with the ROC or face legal action.

36 For influences and the impact of risk in auditing and financial regulation, and those changes likely to impact the future of auditing, see Ojo M (2009) 'The Growing Importance of Risk in Regulation Journal of Risk Finance http://www.emeraldinsight.com/doi/abs/10.1108/15265941011043639 Vol.11 Iss: 3, pp.249 - 267

Chapter 7
Investigating the Relationship between Foreign Direct Investment and Corporate Social Responsibility:
Central Bank Independence and Inflation

Marianne Ojo
North-West University, South Africa

Olusegun Felix Ayadi
Texas Southern University, USA

ABSTRACT

Should regulatory incentives which incorporate the lowering of environmental and labor standards, generate life threatening and environmental repercussions, as well as those resulting in moral hazard and excessive risk taking levels, be encouraged? This chapter not only investigates whether central bank independence is positively correlated with inflation, but also highlights other variables which could impact the relationship between Corporate Social Responsibility and Foreign Direct Investment. It will highlight why a continuous need for updating of data is necessary given the inability to capture data specific variables and why the introduction of complementary standards would serve to bolster measures aimed at promoting financial stability and encouraging investors – rather than incentives aimed at diluting such standards. In so doing contributes to previous and current literature on the topic – by way of reference to investigations and studies which have revealed concerns in the ability to adequately capture data – particularly in light of the recent 2008/2009 Financial Crisis.

DOI: 10.4018/978-1-5225-0305-7.ch007

INTRODUCTION

The recent introduction of Enhanced Supplementary Leverage Ratios in several jurisdictions, despite arguments related to the burdensome nature of requirements and conditions attached to their implementation, as well as competitive advantages or disadvantages, not only underlies the importance of these regulations in aiming to avert disastrous consequences which could arise where systemically relevant institutions are threatened, but also highlights the importance of sending appropriate signals to foreign investors that the jurisdiction is relatively stable in terms of financial stability and regulatory measures.

The OECD Guidelines highlight the fact that:

- The ability of multinational enterprises to promote sustainable development, is greatly enhanced when trade and investment are conducted within the context of open, competitive and appropriately regulated markets (OECD, 2008).

Why should standards which have the potential to facilitate the realization of CSR goals and objectives be relaxed as a means of accommodating and attracting foreign investment?

Should cost benefit considerations apply where such standards are so crucial to the realization of CSR goals? Should economic and profit considerations supersede those relating to ethical, and legal obligations?

Does this necessarily mean that jurisdictions with less stringent standards – such as those pertaining to Basel III Leverage and Supplementary Leverage Ratios, have greater potential to attract foreign investment than those jurisdictions which have imposed more stringent requirements? (Ojo, 2014, 2015)

A financial environment which operates with the optimal level of regulatory requirements, which are crucial in facilitating a business environment built on trust, confidence – such that investors are able to rely on information being generated by the management and directors of an enterprise or business, as well as an environment which facilitates transparency, disclosure, should generally constitute incentives for investors to be attracted to such an environment. Further, as rightly, indicated in OECD Guidelines, a competitive market environment, should also serve as an engine which fosters growth and development.

Why is it then the case that foreign direct investment in certain jurisdictions does not necessarily translate to propellers of growth and development in such jurisdictions – whether these are developed, emerging or developing economies?

Whilst UNCTAD statistics reveal dramatic growth in certain jurisdictions, this cannot be said of others.[1]

One plausible reason can only be that certain jurisdictions have failed to consider the benefits of fully implementing or complying with regulatory, environmental or ethical standards, or are encouraging investment incentives which whilst aimed at encouraging growth and development, are not necessarily facilitating the generation of benefits which full implementation of certain regulatory and ethical standards would have facilitated.

It is definitely a trade game where you either implement the standards at a level such that costs of such implementation are minimal – whilst compromising certain Corporate Social Responsibility goals. Further, the environment within which such standards are supposed to be implemented may be negatively influenced by political, institutional and legal impediments, such that it warrants little effort to fully implement or even introduce such standards. In other words, profits dominate the firm or MNEs' corporate goals and objectives given such negative external influences.

According to UNCTAD (2014),

- Investment incentives mostly focus on economic performance objectives, less on sustainable development. Incentives are widely used by governments as a policy instrument for attracting investment, despite persistent criticism that they are economically inefficient and lead to misallocations of public funds. To address these concerns, investment incentives schemes could be more closely aligned with the SDGs (Sustainable Development Goals).

The following incentives have been highlighted by UNCTAD as constituting means of attracting foreign investment (UNCTAD, 2014):

- Financial Incentives
- Fiscal Incentives
- Regulatory Incentives

Regulatory incentives, namely those which include the "lowering of environmental, health, safety or labor standards, as well as temporary or permanent exemption from compliance with applicable standards", will constitute greater focus of this chapter.

As well as responding to issues and concerns related to whether standards which have the potential to facilitate the realization of CSR goals and objectives should be relaxed as a means of accommodating and attracting foreign investment, whether cost benefit considerations should apply where such standards are so crucial to the realization of CSR goals, and whether economic and profit considerations should supersede those relating to ethical, and legal obligations, this chapter also aims to highlight why foreign direct investment in certain jurisdictions does not necessarily translate to propellers of growth and development, with the expected results in such jurisdictions – as is the case with other jurisdictions. It will attempt to address many of these questions by way of reference to other variables which may impact financial growth and development - variables such as inflation, external factors such as political influences on economic decisions and the importance of corporate governance and institutional frameworks aimed at ensuring that vital regulations and standards are complied with and effectively enforced.

BACKGROUND AND LITERATURE REVIEW (CONCEPTUAL, THEORETICAL AND EMPIRICAL FRAMEWORKS)

In order to illustrate the impact of political interference on monetary and economic policies, as well as financial development in certain economies, reference will be made to the literature and empirical analyses relating to central bank independence and financial development. This will serve to consolidate the argument that other variables, namely inflation, can impact corporate social responsibility and goals, where political factors impact economic and monetary policies and decisions.

Central Bank Independence

Central Bank Independence (CBI) is often cited as prescription to assure price stability in an economy. Cross-country empirical studies especially in industrial economies suggest a negative relationship between CBI and inflation. According to Hayo and Hefeker (2002), Central Bank Independence is neither necessary nor sufficient for reaching monetary stability.

In relation to the debate on whether Central Bank Independence is evidential of low inflation, several theories have been propounded:

High CBI and Low Inflation?

The following three theories have been put forward by Eijffinger & Haan (1996):

- The public-choice theory[2] whereby Buchanam and Wagner (1977) examine concepts of Keynesian economics.
- Sargent-Wallace (1981) theory
- Time-inconsistency theory problem of monetary policy as explained by Kydland and Prescott (1977), Calvo (1978) and Barro and Gordon (1983).

Based on the summary of empirical studies carried out by Cukierman et al. (1992) and Berger et al. (2001), they conclude that among industrial countries, legal CBI index is negatively correlated with inflation but TOR (turnover of central bank governors) has no correlation with inflation. They also conclude that among developing countries, legal CBI index is not correlated with inflation but TOR is significantly related to inflation.

The following five measures and indicators of financial development and financial systems are highlighted by Beck et al. (2000):

- DMCD: Ratio of deposit money banks assets to central bank assets
- LLGDP: Ratio of liquid liabilities to GDP[3]
- CBGDP: Ratio of central bank assets to GDP
- DMGDP: Ratio of deposit money banks assets to GDP
- INF: Inflation index $[\pi/(1 + \pi)]$

The following data, figures and tables reflect annual data collected between the period 1970 and 2003 and are based on the five above mentioned indicators.

Table 1. Data descriptive statistics

	INF	DMCD	LLGDP	CBGDP	DMGDP
Mean	0.159	0.605	0.210	0.120	0.153
Standard Deviation	0.104	0.169	0.069	0.075	0.058
Skewness	0.963	0.106	-0.076	0.220	0.483
Kurtosis	2.898	2.267	2.032	2.472	2.062
Jarque-Bera Statistic	5.269	0.824	1.361	0.668	2.568

Table 2. Data correlation matrix

	INF	DMCD	LLGDP	CBGDP	DMGDP
INF	1.000	-0.455	0.143	0.518	-0.027
DMCD		1.000	-0.306	-0.892	-0.155
LLGDP			1.000	0.516	0.903
CBGDP				1.000	0.417
DMGDP					1.000

Table 3. Unit root test results

	INF	DMCD	LLGDP	CBGDP	DMGDP
SERIES IN LEVELS					
ADF Statistic	-3.140	-1.415	-1.775	-1.446	-1.261
KPSS Statistic	0.171	0.382***	0.196	0.460***	0.194
FIRST DIFFERENCE OF SERIES					
ADF Statistic	-5.910*	-6.114*	-4.979*	-4.185*	-4.500*
KPSS Statistic	0.5000**	0.229	0.153	0.261	0.115

Table 4. Johansen Bivariate Co integration test results

λi	H0	H1	λ-max statistic	H0	H1	λ-trace statistic
(a) INFLATION AND DMCD 0.507 0.048	r = 0 r ≤ 1	r = 1 r = 2	22.647** 1.562	r = 0 r ≤ 1	r = 1 r = 2	24.209** 1.562
(b) INFLATION AND LLGDP 0.359	r = 0	r = 1	14.225	r = 0	r = 1	17.952**
0.110	r ≤ 1	r = 2	3.727	r ≤ 1	r = 2	3.727
(c) INFLATION AND LLGDP 0.380	r = 0	r = 1	15.303**	r = 0	r = 1	18.351**
0.091	r ≤ 1	r = 2	3.048	r ≤ 1	r = 2	3.048
(d) INFLATION AND DMGDP 0.325	r = 0	r = 1	12.566	r = 0	r = 1	15.082
0.076	r ≤ 1	r = 2	2.516	r ≤ 1	r = 2	2.516

SUMMARY OF RESULTS (1)

Based on ADF unit-root test, in which all the time series data are integrated of order 1,
The Johansen cointegration results show:

- INF and DMCD are cointegrated
- INF and LLGDP are cointegrated
- INF and CBGDP are cointegrated
- INF and DMGDP are not cointegrated

SUMMARY OF RESULTS (2)

Inflation is negatively correlated with DMCD and DMGDP
Inflation is positively correlated with LLGDP and CBGDP

Interpretation of Results

There is a long-run relationship between the level of financial development and inflation. The level of financial development is more appropriate than the existing indices of central bank independence. It is not logical to assume that all developing countries are homogenous in terms of the role and influence of central banks on price stability.

Issues, Controversies, Problems

Adequately Accounting for Data and Capturing of Data Following the 2008/2009 Financial Crisis

According to Beck, Demirguc-Kunt, and Levi (2010):

- While the previous indicators measure the liability side of financial intermediaries' balance sheets, indicators of the asset side capture credit allocation, one of the most important functions of financial intermediaries. Private credit by deposit money banks and other financial institutions to GDP is the ratio of claims on the private sector by deposit money banks and other financial institutions to GDP. It is a standard indicator in the finance and growth literature; countries with higher levels of private credit to GDP have been shown to grow faster and experience faster rates of poverty reduction. A somewhat narrower indicator—limited to deposit money banks—is private credit by deposit money banks to GDP.

Beck et al also add that whilst the data figures for the period ending 2007 do not fully capture the recent crisis, indicators of banking efficiency, profitability, and stability match the trends in the boom period leading up to the recent global financial crisis (Beck, Demirguc-Kunt, & Levi, 2010). Further, they make the following observations (Beck, Demirguc-Kunt, & Levi, 2010):

- That the lower margins for traditional lines of business and the search for higher returns were possible only through high-risk taking, especially in high-income countries.
- Integration into global financial markets has also increased, though the driving forces have differed for different income groups.
- While the increase in international lending and bond issues has been concentrated in high-income countries, low- and lower middle-income countries have benefited from higher remittance flows.

The following section hence makes reference to present and previous literature on variables impacting financial development, foreign direct investment and corporate social responsibility, as a means of highlighting and addressing gaps which may arise from inadequately accounting for data – as well as highlighting the importance of effective corporate governance mechanisms in realizing corporate social goals.

SOLUTIONS AND RECOMMENDATIONS

Relationship between Foreign Direct Investment (FDI) and Corporate Social Responsibility (CSR)

Drawing on investigations carried out by Fortanier and Van Wijk (2010) - based on the analysis of three sub Saharan countries and in which it is ascertained by them that that MNEs crowd out local firms from the labour market by hiring their best-trained employees and where it is implied that human capital development in the hotel sector will not be driven by FDI, Kolk and Tulder (2010) conclude on this basis and are of the opinion that "well-developed institutions - in this case via training and education systems, are a prerequisite for positive effects from FDI" and that further, country-of-origin aspects were considered by Auger, Devinney, Louviere and Burke (2010), in terms of the products included in their study as well as consumers from six different countries.

Based on studies undertaken by Goyal (2006) and Kolk and van Tulder, (2010) they conclude that there has been a correlation between increases in CSR and increases in FDI since the 1990s.

However, as reflected by recent UNCTAD reports (2014), whilst positive effects of FDI are evidenced in certain countries, this cannot be said of others. Based on conclusions derived from Kolk and Tulder, as regards their opinions on training and education systems being pre requisites for positive effects from FDI, an argument can be made for the need to distinguish between those jurisdictions which are well equipped with the adequately balanced institutional, legal, and governance frameworks and those without such frameworks as constituting a basis for evaluating and analyzing the effects of FDI. In this respect, and drawing on Carroll's pyramid of Corporate Social Responsibility (DiGabriele & Ojo, 2016), training and education cannot constitute the sole pre requisites, particularly in jurisdictions with underperforming institutional structures, for determining the positive effects of FDI. As highlighted in the Chapter "Corporate Social Responsibility and Foreign Direct Investment: Engaging Innovation, Auditors and Stakeholders in Corporate Social Responsibility" (2016), compliance with laws, business principles and codes of conduct, without doubt, constitutes the most fundamental and strategic level of the pyramid since goals and objectives attributed to other levels of the pyramid, namely longer term goals of sustainability, and goals relating to nutritional, water and rural development, will not be realised to their maximum potential where compliance with regulations and other related laws and principles are not effectively implemented and enforced.

Further Empirical Studies on the Relationship between Corporate Social Responsibility and Foreign Direct Investment

Based on results derived by Gonzalez Perez, Riegler and Riegler (2011), as regards the relationship between Corporate Social Responsibility and Foreign Direct Investment, investigations of which incorporated "two different approaches for the empirical examination of the relationship between FDI and CSR", such approaches in their opinion denoting and implying a significantly correlated relationship between the variables of interest (Perez, Riegler, & Riegler, 2011):

- It was concluded that the first approach implied a correlation between a CSR index and FDI, while the second approach suggests that FDI in Colombia is environmentally responsible because it reduces its negative externalities on CO2 emissions.
- Further, they add that the first approach, whilst having the advantage of being more general, was also disadvantageous in the sense of ignoring any specific effects of the relationship and that even though the second approach provided deeper insight into the specific relationship between the variables, was limited in the sense that it only takes into account the actual results.

FUTURE RESEARCH DIRECTIONS

Challenges involving private sector investment in the public sector, as well as efforts aimed at consolidating regional and international standards – particularly in matters of environmental matters, reducing pollution and dangerous chemical emissions continue to constitute focal points and whilst progress is being made in certain jurisdictions, evidence exists to support the fact that many developing economies still suffer from environmental consequences resulting from failures of their governments to implement and enforce required environmental standards and effective corporate governance mechanisms.

CONCLUSION

Should regulatory incentives, namely those which include the "lowering of environmental, health, safety or labor standards, as well as temporary or permanent exemption from compliance with applicable standards" be encouraged where such incentives generate behavior which not only has life threatening and environmental repercussions, but also results in moral hazard and excessive risk taking levels? Given efforts being undertaken to address systemic risks, with particular reference to: recently introduced Enhanced Supplementary Leverage Ratios; as well as their applicability to systemically relevant institutions; the need to adequately balance interests of wider stakeholders;

The consideration of more damaging consequences of a major disruption to financial stability, as well as the need to implement reliable complements to present financial indicators, should take precedence over a dilution of standards which would only encourage reckless behavior emanating from the desire to place profit maximizing priorities at the fore.

The literature review concludes that legal CBI index is negatively correlated with inflation but TOR (turnover of central bank governors) has no correlation with inflation. It is also concluded that among developing countries, legal CBI index is not correlated with inflation but TOR is significantly related to inflation.

As reflected from the investigation and results from the data incorporated into this chapter, it is not logical to assume that all developing countries are homogenous in terms of the role and influence of central banks on price stability. Further, certain data may not adequately capture specific effects which exist between variables and such data need to be continuously adjusted to reflect actual results. In order to ensure that corporate social responsibility goals and objectives are maximally realized, more effective corporate governance mechanisms, standards and effective compliance and enforcement mechanisms should be in place. Training and education cannot constitute the sole pre requisites for determining the positive effects of FDI – particularly in those jurisdictions where political influences are of such impact that economic policies, legal and institutional frameworks are affected and environmental repercussions emanate as a result of such external social and political factors.

REFERENCES

Barro, R. J., & Gordon, D. B. (1983). Rules, discretion and reputation in a model of monetary policy. *Journal of Monetary Economics*, *12*(1), 123–125. doi:10.1016/0304-3932(83)90051-X

Beck, T., Demirgüç-Kunt, A., & Levine, R. (2000). A New Database on Financial Development and Structure. *World Bank Economic Review, 14*, 597-605.

Beck, T., Demirgüç-Kunt, A., & Levine, R. (2009). *Financial Institutions and Markets across Countries and over Time: Data and Analysis*. Policy Research Working Paper 4943. World Bank.

Beck, T., Demirgüç-Kunt, A., & Levine, R. (2010). Financial Institutions and Markets across Countries and over Time: The Updated Financial Development and Structure Database. *The World Bank Economic Review*, *24*(1), 77–92. doi:10.1093/wber/lhp016

Berger, H., de Haan, J., & Eijffinger, S. (2001). Central Bank Independence: An Update of Theory and Evidence. *Journal of Economic Surveys*, *15*, 3–40.

Calvo, G. A. (1978). On the Time Consistency of Optimal Policy in a Monetary Economy. *Econometrica*, *46*(6), 1411-1428. Retrieved from http://www.jstor.org/stable/1913836

Cukierman, A. (1992). *Central Bank Strategy, Credibility, and Independence*. Cambridge, MA: MIT Press.

DiGabriele, J. A., & Ojo, M. (2016). *Corporate Social Responsibility and Foreign Direct Investment: Engaging Innovation*. Auditors and Stakeholders in Corporate Social Responsibility.

Fortanier, F., & Van Wijk, J. (2010). Sustainable tourism industry development in sub Saharan Africa: Consequences of foreign hotels for local employment. *International Business Review*.

Gonzalez Perez, M., Riegler, S., & Riegler, F. (2011). *Foreign Direct Investment (FDI) and Social Responsibility Networks (SRN) in Colombia*. Academic Press.

Goyal, A. (2006). Corporate Social Responsibility as a Signalling Device for Foreign Direct Investment. *International Journal of the Economics of Business*, *13*(1), 145–163. doi:10.1080/13571510500520077

Hayo, B., & Hefeker, C. (2002). Reconsidering Central Bank Independence. *European Journal of Political Economy, Elsevier*, *18*(4), 653–674. doi:10.1016/S0176-2680(02)00113-1

Kolk, A. & Van Tulder, R. (2010). International Business, Corporate Social Responsibility and Sustainable Development. *International Business Review, 19*(1).

Kydland, F., & Prescott, E. (1977). Rules Rather than Discretion: The Inconsistency of Optimal Plans. *Journal of Political Economy*, *85*(3), 473–490. doi:10.1086/260580

Levine, R. (2005). Finance and Growth: Theory and Evidence. In P. Aghion & S. Durlauf (Eds.), *Handbook of Economic Growth*. Amsterdam: North Holland.

Loayza, N., & Ranciere, R. (2006). Financial Development, Financial Fragility, and Growth. *Journal of Money, Credit and Banking*, *38*(4), 1051–1076. doi:10.1353/mcb.2006.0060

Lucas, R. E., & Sargent, T. J. (1981). Rational Expectations and Econometric Practice. University of Minnesota Press.

Ojo, M. (2014). *Credit Risk Measurement, Leverage Ratios and Basel III*. Paper presented at the Third International Conference on Credit Analysis and Risk Management.

Ojo, M. (2015a). Implementing Basel III Through the Capital Requirements Directive (CRD) IV: Leverage Ratios and Capital Adequacy Requirements. *Journal of Business Law and Ethics, 3*(1).

Ojo, M. (2015b). *The Unintended Consequences and Challenges of the Basel III Leverage Ratio: Supplementary Leverage Ratios*. Academic Press.

Otero, J., & Manuel, R. (2006). Inflation Before and After Central Bank Independence: The Case of Colombia. *Journal of Development Economics, Elsevier*, *79*(1), 168–182. doi:10.1016/j.jdeveco.2004.12.005

Shearman & Sterling LLP. (2014). *Enhanced Leverage Ratios for UK Financial Institutions*. Author.

UNCTAD. (2014). World Investment Report 2014: Investing in the SDGs: An Action Plan. United Nations.

ENDNOTES

1 "Europe, traditionally the largest FDI recipient region, is at less than one third of its 2007 inflows and one fourth of its outflows. The United States and the European Union (EU) saw their combined share of global FDI inflows decline from well over 50 per cent pre-crisis to 30 per cent in 2013." See UNCTAD, "World Investment Report 2014: Investing in the SDGs: An Action Plan" see page x

2 "*Democracy in Deficit* paved the way in economics in endogenizing the role of government in discussions of macroeconomic theory and policy. The basic discovery was that Keynesian economics had a bias toward deficits in terms of political self-interest. That is, at the margin politicians preferred easy choices to hard ones, and this meant lower taxes and higher spending. Thus, what-

ever the merits of Keynesian economics in using government fiscal policy to "balance" the forces of inflation and deflation and employment and unemployment in an economy, its application in a democratic setting had severe problems of incentive compatibility; that is, there was a bias toward deficit finance. And, of course, there is no need to reiterate here the evidence in the United States and elsewhere for the correctness of the Buchanan insight on Keynesian economics." See J M. Buchanan and R E. Wagner, *Democracy in Deficit: The Political Legacy of Lord Keynes* (New York: Academic Press, 1977), volume 8 in the series.

3 "Liquid liabilities to GDP is a traditional indicator of financial depth. It is the ratio of currency plus demand and interest-bearing liabilities of banks and other financial intermediaries to GDP." See T Beck, A Demirguc-Kunt,and R Levine (2010) Financial Institutions and Markets across Countries and over Time: The Updated Financial Development and Structure Database. The World Bank Economic Review, Vol. 24, No. 1,pp. 77–92 doi:10.1093/wber/lhp016 Advance Access Publication January 11, 2010 Published by Oxford University Press on behalf of the International Bank for Reconstruction and Development

Section 4

Recent Global Developments Impacting the Global Economy

As illustrated by recent global developments, which namely include, falling oil prices, the need for alternative sources of more environmentally friendly sources of renewable energy, is accentuated by the fact that the oil and gas industries are currently impacting the global economy in more negative than positive respects. Hence, sometimes economies may be compelled to re think their inclination towards more economically oriented objectives and responsibilities.

Chapter 8
Corporate Social Responsibility and Financial Development:
Promoting Global Economic Development

Genevieve Dupont
American University of Paris, France

Marianne Ojo
North-West University, South Africa

James Rossi
University of Greenwich, UK

ABSTRACT

This chapter not only attempts to identify those variables which govern and impact the relationship and interplay between Corporate Social Responsibility and Foreign Direct Investment, but illustrate the conditions under which such variables are likely to be most susceptible to change and fluctuations – as well as consequences that are likely to be generated as a result of such fluctuations. In so doing it also contributes to the literature in highlighting why greater focus and priority should be accorded to Foreign Direct Investment and Corporate Social Responsibility, as tools for poverty alleviation. Further, as well as accentuating, under the conclusion section, why the UK Government strategy for building more plants after Hinkley Point, implies that the UK would not reap all benefits of the Project, the chapter expansiates on contributory factors which have resulted in the decision of the UK Government to delay its decision on the Hinkley Point Project. Contributory factors, which include among a notable few, the need for flexible generating capacity was also cited, since renewable energy cannot be easily converted at Hinkley Point.

DOI: 10.4018/978-1-5225-0305-7.ch008

INTRODUCTION

According to recent IMF reports (Hayden, 2015:1),[1] it was highlighted that between 2004 and 2013, Latin America "recorded impressive growth and strong progress on a range of social issues." Identified factors of economic growth were considered to have resulted from a combination of "high commodity prices and economic management", coupled with "progressive social policies". Recent reports however, present a very uncertain and uneven projection for 2015 and the years ahead owing to various factors which not only include and result from slowing down of growth in emerging economies, but also a fall in commodity prices which have resulted from the economics and dynamics currently taking place in several emerging economies.

The World Economic Outlook (2015) highlights and accentuates the fact that "prospects in emerging markets and developing economies vary across countries and regions." However, the uncertainty which clouds the present global landscape in relation to growth and development, particularly for 2015 is considered to be a combination of factors which is attributed to the weakened growth evidenced in the last quarters of 2015, with growth for emerging and developing economies forecasted to decline from 4.6 percent in 2014 to 4.0 percent in 2015 (see Hayden, 2015:1).[2]

Maurice Obstfeld, the IMF Economic Counsellor and Director of the Research Department, attributes recent developments to a combination of "at least three powerful forces", namely:

- China's economic transformation—away from export- and investment-led growth and manufacturing, in favor of a greater focus on consumption and services;
- Second, and related, the fall in commodity prices; and third,
- The anticipated increase in U.S. interest rates, which in his view, is likely to have global consequences, as well as contribute to current uncertainties.

Current Uncertainties

Whilst it is widely anticipated that the United States (the Federal Reserve) will raise interest rates, before the end of 2016, other jurisdictions such as the United Kingdom are having to lower interest rates. Such a move has not only generated greater uncertainty, but is also a consequence of the EU Referendum and the result of the Brexit vote which took place on the 23rd June 2016.

The EU Referendum has had far reaching implications, so far, on the UK economy - even such repercussions are considered to be short term. As well as the fall in value of the pound, which dipped to its lowest levels (against the dollar) - since 1985, in the immediate aftermath of the EU Referendum, further repercussions were to emerge - subsequently. Consequences of the lower pound include: Higher import prices, higher inflation, but on a more positive note, lower export prices (good for exports).

Higher inflation, as well a slowdown in economic activity also prompted speculations of low interest rates. Banking, airline, property shares were generally affected as reflected during early trading returns on UK government bonds - reported to be at lowest ever levels. Even though shares were temporarily down, the share results were not as bad as was expected. The uncertainty was also attributable to concerns relating to whether the economy was undergoing/would undergo prolonged recovery or whether such recovery would be temporary. There is also a need to balance medium term with undue prolonged uncertainty. As of the 30th of June, a week after the Referendum, shares appeared to have recovered and the reaction of markets, as well as representing a shift from perceived risky capital markets to less risky safe havens (gold, money markets), it was hoped, signaled a sign of positive investment for the economy. However, further repercussions of the June 2016 Brexit vote were to emerge a month later. On the 26th July 2016, NatWest and the Royal Bank of Scotland (RBS), signaled that they would charge customers for holding deposits - even though this was considered to be targeted at business customers as it was also realized that such a move could result in bank runs, the hoarding of cash, or even worse, switching to other competitors. Following the slowdown in economic activity, following the Brexit vote, it was anticipated that the encouragement of businesses to put their cash into greater use (rather than just sitting in bank accounts) would inject a necessary boost to the economy. As well as the possibility of negative interest rates, it was also anticipated that following the release of the Report on the GDP for the second quarter, in the months leading to the end of June, the Governor of the Bank of England would announce a cut in interest rates on the 4th August 2016, a drop from its current base rate of 0.5%. The Report on the GDP Growth in the three months to the end of June, which recorded a growth of about 0.6%, and more positive than expected, was however primarily related to the pre Referendum period (prior to the 23rd June). On the 28th July, Lloyds Bank's announcement that it would cut a further 3000 jobs - in addition to previously announced figures of 9,000, as well as the closure of 200 branches, was not only considered to be a consequence of cost cutting initiatives, but also a further consequence of Brexit: namely, lower interest rates being introduced and persisting owing to Brexit uncertainty, as well as profits resulting therefrom.

BACKGROUND AND LITERATURE REVIEW

The observations relate to recent trends in the global growth, in addition to slowed growth forecast for emerging economies. Falling commodity prices, as well as uncertainties hovering around interest rate hikes may be contrasted with the observations in Figure 1.

Given the recent global turmoil and uncertainties surrounding corporate governance in matters relating to transparency and disclosure, bribery and corruption, as well as political disturbances in various regions across the globe, it would be well worth placing greater focus on the alleviation of poverty in all economies – advanced, emerging and developing economies.

Further, since governance persistently constitutes major challenges, particularly for developing economies, tackling poverty and promoting entrepreneurship programs and schemes, as a means of resource generation and wealth creation should be accorded greater priority within the Corporate Social Responsibility model. This is not to say that corporate governance initiatives should be abandoned or watered down. Corporate governance continually constitutes a very vital aspect and concept which should take priorities within the corporate governance model.

The encouragement and engagement of the general public as vital stakeholders in the Corporate Social Responsibility process - with goals and objectives centered around "Project: Avoid Waste" and the promotion of environmental objectives and initiatives would be relatively easy to achieve once the public is educated as regards the level and seriousness of addressing such issues - as well as their impact as vital stakeholders in the process.

The signing of online petitions - as well as the completion of online forms and hard copies distributed on streets to customers and the general public, comprise various modes whereby the direct engagement of such stakeholders can be facilitated as vital tools aimed at promoting the compliance and enforcement of vital corporate governance goals and mechanisms.

Figure 1. International prices of oil, coal, and natural gas, 2006–2012 (Indexed January 2000=100)
Sources: *IMF World Economic Outlook (WEO), U.S. Energy Information Administration (EIA), and the Organisation for Economic Co-operation and Development (OECD).*
Note: *Coal price is average of quarterly U.S. import prices (EIA) and quarterly OECD import price (IEA/OECD). Natural gas price is average of the monthly U.S. import and export prices (EIA); these prices are weighted averages for LNG and pipeline natural gas. Crude oil price is average of Brent, Dubai, and WTI monthly prices (WEO/Primary Commodities Price System). Gasoline price is monthly New York Harbor conventional gasoline spot price (EIA). Diesel price is monthly Los Angeles ultra-low sulfur CARB diesel spot price (EIA). Gasoline and diesel prices are then averaged.*

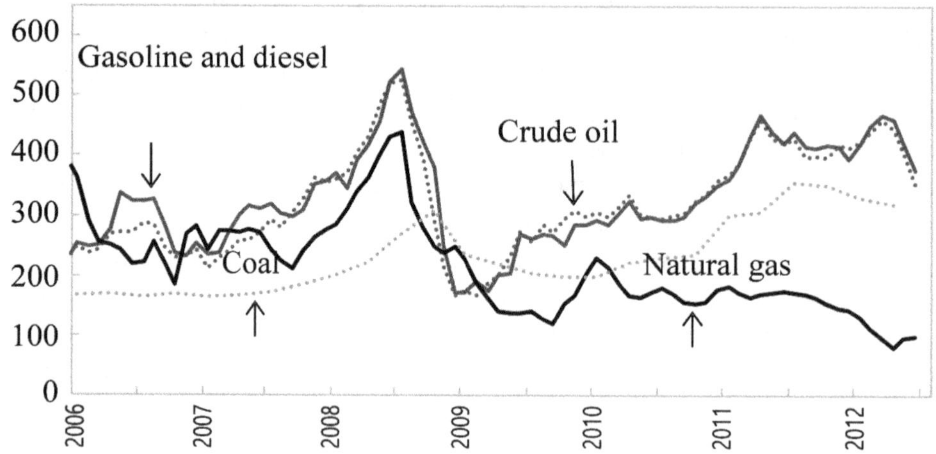

Corporations such as Amazon and supermarket chains have been able to address the environmental and recycling/waste issues raised by customers through the input of customer opinions - be it through online questionnaires provided via Amazon websites or forms which are completed by customers (as well as customer complaint locations (customer service desks) located at local supermarkets and grocery stores. Such vital means of collection of information also constitute the first phase of the E Commerce process - which has witnessed the rapid rise of the Internet and other processes involving mobile banking.

The corporate governance model requires that such data be treated with utmost confidentiality - both in respect of the challenges, concerns confronting customers, ways and suggestions whereby such concerns could be addressed, as well as means whereby data of highest confidentiality, namely sensitive customer details and data could be accorded protection without being compromised. It is also vital to underline the importance of such stakeholder involvement in mitigating information asymmetries, as well as reducing transaction costs. Whilst concerns have been raised regarding packaging waste by several E Commerce enterprises, such concerns also need to be balanced against the importance of adequate protection to avoid products getting damaged during the delivery process.

Whilst the internet revolution and mobile banking has resulted in job losses for many, it could also serve the good of the less privileged, namely, those with less mobility and access in travelling to the nearest banks - having lost their local branches, and having no internet facilities at home.

Innovativeness and the rise of E Commerce has also witnessed the generation of new and uprising, budding entrepreneurs who have been able to make very positive contributions to their communities through the creation of websites, mobile apps, companies which assist restaurants who usually throw away large quantities of nutritional products in donating such to the homeless - as well as those on the lower income earning classification.

The creation of food banks, as well as agencies whose aim primarily consists in donating furniture and other home and electrical appliances which are still in very good condition, to charities, businesses, as well those families in need of such products - and without any cost - as long as they are able to collect these and bear responsibility for the transportation of these items to their final destination, has also resulted in less waste being generated at the local dumps, and income generating professions and resources for those involved.

Hence whilst the rise of the Internet and mobile banking has resulted in job losses and branch closures, new and innovative forms of technology are also arising - with entrepreneurs being created and less waste being generated through the donations of supermarket chains, restaurants, and used furniture outlets/businesses, which "recycle" such products whilst creating jobs and resources in the process.

Post offices, also whilst being victims of the Internet revolution, are benefiting from bank closures - by serving as substitutes and replacements for such banks. However, more needs to be done for those without access to replacements for local bank branch closures

Corporate Social Responsibility and Corporate Social Accountability

As well as the determination of appropriate channels through which grants, schemes and funds for environmental and poverty alleviating causes should be facilitated, it is also vital to ensure that such grants and funds are allocated to the appropriate individuals. This ideally being by reason of merit, commitment and passion towards such social goals and objectives – such that funds are not misused, misappropriated or allocated to non-qualifying individuals as is the case with the allocation of numerous government contracts – particularly in jurisdiction with ineffective corporate governance controls and mechanisms.

In this respect it is also noteworthy and important to distinguish three phases of the screening process through which individuals are awarded the grants or awards to fund their chosen causes. Such phases are as follows:

1. Pre-screening phase
2. Screening phase
3. Post Screening phase

The Pre-Screening Phase

This embraces those checks and safeguards which are in place to ensure that grants are awarded to individuals on the basis of merit – and not merely by social or family associations. From this perspective, application forms are of importance since such connections can be easily ascertained through the stipulation of certain criteria which need to be fulfilled in order for individuals to qualify for such awards. Further, background and independent checks – as well as investigations should be undertaken as a precautionary measure since competence for such awards is a subjective quality which cannot be determined solely on the basis of one factor. Whilst links with the awarders of the grant or the philanthropist enterprise, certainly do not justify the award of a grant, other factors may override and justify the merits of such an individual for the award.

The Screening Phase

This ideally should involve a practical demonstration of the candidate's ability and suitability for the grant – as applied for, through the pre-screening phase/s. The phase usually takes the form of interviews whereby the candidate can visibly present ideas or demonstrate his/her commitment to the project.

Having passed both of the above phases, the candidate should unconditionally be certified as competent and qualified to undertake the designated objectives – as well as be eligible for the award.

The Post Screening Phase

This phase should be aimed at providing qualified candidates with the tools, expertise, as well as resources required to fulfil their goals and objectives. In other to bolster their incentives annual awards such as "Entrepreneur or Innovator of the Year", in the form of monetary or trophy recognition could be granted to deserving winners. Further this stage and phase should be specifically aimed towards continued development of the skills and expertise required by qualified candidates to meet their goals and objectives.

Accountability from this perspective can be defined on the basis of the awarding enterprise' ability to justify their selection criteria, as well as their choice of candidates, on the basis of the results achieved – namely, the attainment of the desired goals and objectives. Where such a goal is not accomplished – either by reason of failure to support such candidates professionally, or through the diversion and misappropriation of funds for other causes or to other pockets, then lack of accountability can be ascertained.

The results of an investment in projects should be evidenced not just locally – but impact many lives as well as contribute towards encouraging other projects of a similar nature. Such is the attribute of entrepreneurship schemes which not only add value to the individual involved – but also serves as a means of creating other successful entrepreneurs and visibly improving the quality of life of the locality involved. A successful project is evidenced by the outcome – namely, the impact of such a project locally – as well as globally.

Penalty Clause Provisions

Grants and awards for projects aimed at alleviating poverty and promoting environmental causes should be treated as binding agreements and contracts and as such, any party failing to uphold commitments and obligations aimed at fulfilling the stipulated goals and objectives of the project should commensurably, depending on the nature and severity – consequential upon such withdrawal, be penalized for doing so.

Individual circumstances will vary, depending amongst other factors, on the length and period of time expected to fulfil project obligations, the amount awarded, amounts already expended by individual parties, as well as the stage of the completion process before obligatory commitments and/or obstacles were presented. Attribution and apportionment of culpability to fulfil such obligations will also be dependent on individual situations – hence clarity is required within the contract in stipulating concisely and clearly, the stated and expected goals, objectives and desired outcomes of the project.

As precautionary measures to avoid possible disruptions to the completion of such projects, arrangements should be in place to instigate or facilitate negotiations where signals are apparent from either party that progress is being obstructed.

Amounts awarded under penalty clauses should also take into consideration time, energy and expenditure which has been expended on the project – as well as consequential loss for not completing such projects. In the case of the awarding enterprise, opportunity costs of not having designated the project to another competent candidate may be considered.

ISSUES, CONTROVERSIES, PROBLEMS

Explanations for Recent Trends

Dynamics considered to be different from the 2008/2009 Financial Crisis, primarily center around that unlike those factors which are considered contributory to the Crisis, namely, a failure of the system and structure of financial regulation in several jurisdictions, as well as other events which resulted from the sub-prime markets, shadow banking operations, and which to a large extent has been addressed by Basel III and other capital and securities markets regulations,

It is evident that the above mentioned dynamics differ from those highlighted under the introductory section. Whilst the 2008/2009 also comprised of a combination of factors which predominantly featured systemic risks posed by the collapse of systemically relevant financial institutions and also a degree of information asymmetries and uncertainty, the present forecasts appear to be attributed to the latter.

Oil prices, it appears, are currently being determined by other factors which exclude more than merely the economics of demand and supply – factors such as political factors, inclusively of the de-stabilization of the Middle East and recent ongoing tensions in Syria which have also contributed to a rallying of prices and volatility with oil prices.

Whilst it is hoped that prices will rise in the near future, consequences of low and falling commodity prices – and particularly oil, signify continued and persistent low level of revenues for many oil firms. This is particularly worrying for those corporations who have resorted to hedging as a means of cover and have to service their debts. It is feared that unless these firms have continued access to, or granted the required hedging, they may be compelled to cut back on drilling, further worsening revenue inflows, and potential result in job cuts, as well as liquidation or filing for bankruptcy.

As highlighted in the World Economic Outlook Report (2015),

The prospect of rising U.S. interest rates and a stronger dollar has already contributed to higher financing costs for some borrowers, including emerging and developing economies. And while the growth slowdown in China is so far in line with forecasts, its cross-border repercussions appear larger than previously envisaged, including through weaker commodity prices and reduced imports.

Table 1 illustrates IMF forecasts and projections for the period 2014 to 2016.

SOLUTIONS AND RECOMMENDATIONS

In addition to structural reforms highlighted,[3] the importance of international and regional cooperation as means of resolving current political tensions, which have contributed to an extent, to volatile prices, should not be ignored. Effective negotiation and communication are paramount to achieving such coop-

Table 1. Latest IMF projections

Global growth likely to be weaker this year than last, with improving prospects in the advanced economies but a fifth year of slowing in emerging markets.
(percent change)

		Projections		Difference from July 2015 WEO update[1]	
	2014	2015	2016	2015	2016
World Ouput	3.4	3.1	3.6	-0.2	-0.2
Advanced Economies	1.8	2.0	2.2	-0.1	-0.2
United States	2.4	2.6	2.8	0.1	-0.2
Euro Area	0.9	1.5	1.6	0.0	-0.1
Germany	1.6	1.5	1.6	-0.1	-0.1
France	0.2	1.2	1.5	0.0	0.0
Italy	-0.4	0.8	1.3	0.1	0.1
Spain	1.4	3.1	2.5	0.0	0.0
Japan	-0.1	0.6	1.0	-0.2	-0.2
United Kingdom	3.0	2.5	2.2	0.1	0.0
Canada	2.4	1.0	1.7	-0.5	-0.4
Other Advanced Economies	2.8	2.3	2.7	-0.4	-0.4
Emerging Market and Developing Economies	4.6	4.0	4.5	-0.2	-0.2
Commonwealth of Independent States	1.0	-2.7	0.5	-0.5	-0.7
Russia	0.6	-3.8	-0.6	-0.4	-0.8
Excluding Russia	1.9	-0.1	2.8	-0.8	-0.5
Emerging and Developing Asia	6.8	6.5	6.4	-0.1	0.0
China	7.3	6.8	6.3	0.0	0.0
India	7.3	7.3	7.5	-0.2	0.0
ASEAN-5[2]	4.6	4.6	4.9	-0.1	-0.2
Emerging and Developing Europe	2.8	3.0	3.0	0.1	0.1
Latin America and the Caribbean	1.3	-0.3	0.8	-0.8	-0.9
Brazil	0.1	-3.0	-1.0	-1.5	-1.7
Mexico	2.1	2.3	2.8	-0.1	-0.2
Middle East, North Africa, Afghanistan, and Pakistan	2.7	2.5	3.9	-0.1	0.1
Saudi Arabia	3.5	3.4	2.2	0.6	-0.2
Sub-Saharan Africa	5.0	3.8	4.3	-0.6	-0.8
Nigeria	6.3	4.0	4.3	-0.5	-0.7
South Africa	1.5	1.4	1.3	-0.6	-0.8
Low-Income Developing Countries	6.0	4.8	5.8	-0.3	-0.4

Source: IMF, World Economic Outlook, October 2015
[1]Difference based on rounded figures for July 2015 WEO Update
[2]Indonesia, Malaysia, Philippines, Thailand, and Vietnam

eration and consensus which is not just merely adequate to the agreement of surface or general issues, but targeted at addressing deep rooted conflicts which have historical or economic origins.

Success has been achieved with the implementation of major capital, liquidity regulations, and leverage ratios – as evidenced by Basel III, across major advanced economies where complex and diverse structures of financial regulation persist. There should be no reason why complexities and indifferences cannot be negotiated upon to arrive at a favorable and consensual result. Perhaps the current political tensions, have built up over such a long period, with devastating economic, religious and environmental impacts, that the situation is more complex than merely harmonizing and effectively implementing capital and leverage ratios.

One thing is however certain. As is the case with the implementation of reforms, standards or regulations, a phase in period is required for involved parties to adjust to new requirements, rules and reforms. It may take some time, however, desired results can be achieved if the correct blueprint and ground is laid before subsequent negotiations are commenced and implementation of agreements and reforms take place.

FUTURE RESEARCH DIRECTIONS

Focusing on Poverty Alleviation as a Means of Contributing to Global Growth and Development

It is evident that local initiatives provide significant incentives for foreign direct investment. Whist environmental incentives and goals targeted at reducing carbon emissions may not be very popular with many foreign investors and multinational enterprises at the moment, greater focus and initiatives should be undertaken to engage locals within the Corporate Social Responsibility model – in addition to greater priority being accorded to goals aimed at reducing poverty.

Further UNCTAD proposes a range of initiatives,[4] including entrepreneurship, which are aimed at "increasing the absorptive capacity" of local economies, as a means of maximizing the benefits of private investment entering SDG sectors and these are as follows:

- Firstly, revolving around increasing involvement of local entrepreneurs; micro, small and medium-sized firms; and smallholders, in the case of agricultural investment.
- Secondly, governments can increase the domestic skills base not only as an enabler for private investment, but also to increase the transfer of benefits to local economies.
- Thirdly, local enterprise development and upgrading can be further encouraged through the widening and deepening of SDG-oriented linkages programs. Technology dissemination and knowledge sharing between firms is key to technological development, for instance of new technologies that would result in green growth.

Investing in New Technologies Which Promote Green Growth

The approval of the Hinkley Point Nuclear Power station in Somerset by EDF Energy on the 28th July 2016, and the same day decision by the UK Government to delay its decision in response to this, could be considered by many observers to be quite understandable - given the prevailing economic conditions - as well the current UK government budget deficit. Having been instigated and initiated by the previous government, the current government was under pressure to consider cost implications - as well as other industries and concerns which are also pivotal to the UK economy.

Problems highlighted from the results of the UK Referendum include, namely the disconnect between Westminster and communities - communities which exclude London (namely, the rest of England - as well as Wales). Particularly those communities who had lost mining industries recently, had high unemployment rates. There was a realization of the growing need to engage with changing communities - as well as the wider public and stakeholders as a whole. The importance of Welsh steel production to the British economy is not only evidenced by the fact that Tata Steel contributes about £200 million in wages to the Welsh economy, but also the fact that 400,000 people are employed at Port Talbot.

Following the EU Referendum in the UK, Tata Steel placed the sale of its bidding process on hold - as well as efforts to secure a credible buyer and viable long term recovery solution to ongoing problems.

The approval of the nuclear station at Hinkley Point Somerset, is not only estimated to cost around 18 billion, making it the most expensive and largest power plant in the world, but is anticipated would provide around 7% of the UK's electricity supply.

Other alternative sources of energy are however considered to include carbon capture storage (lower carbon alternatives), as well as renewable energy.

In addition to the cost of £29.7 billion in top-up payments, a £92 m/wh cost over the 35-year life of the plant is estimated - more than double the present cost. Further issues also relate to:

1. Environmental concerns
2. Technical risks arising from untested vital technical components
3. The fact that price guarantee circumvents EU state aid and competition riles - thus effectively making the Project illegal;
4. Likelihood of higher energy bills - given current experience which EDF projects are encountering (also involving delays in implementation and the spiraling of costs beyond predicted budget and estimate).

The Government, hence was considered wise in requesting more time to reconsider the policy and project and in its delay of a decision till Autumn.

CONCLUSION

Essential to effective communication and negotiations is disclosure, transparency and the intention to make agreements work between all parties involved. This chapter has attempted to provide an explanation for the recent trends in economic activities in emerging economies, as well as addressing how gaps in corporate social goals can be achieved as a means of sustainable development and restoring global growth.

The chapter has highlighted why economic objectives, alone, namely profit maximizing goals, cannot on its own achieve meaningful realization of corporate social objectives aimed at fostering growth and development. Close collaboration aimed at achieving a consensus on international agreements, as well as effective compliance with, and enforcement of, codes and agreement, are also vital to securing the future – in matters relating to economic, social and environmental issues.

Whist environmental incentives and goals targeted at reducing carbon emissions may not be very popular with many foreign investors and multinational enterprises at the moment, greater focus and initiatives should be undertaken to engage locals within the Corporate Social Responsibility model – in addition to greater priority being accorded to goals aimed at reducing poverty and furthering environmental initiatives.

Further, the Government strategy for building more plants after Hinkley Point, implies that the UK would not reap all benefits of the project. The need for flexible generating capacity was also cited, since renewable energy cannot be easily converted at Hinkley Point.

Where Investment with Other Partners and Allies Also Increases Uncertainty and Risks

The fact that the Hinkley Point Project is a joint project between France, China and the United Kingdom - with China contributing a third of the funds, whilst EDF approved of funding on the 28th July 2016, may also have raised doubts and the need to be cautious - in view of the global economic environment - particularly with the global slowdown and consideration of matters of national interest and security. Further, the Government strategy for building more plants after Hinkley Point, implies that the UK would not reap all benefits of the Project. The need for flexible generating capacity was also cited, since renewable energy cannot be easily converted at Hinkley Point. Even though economic benefits are to be reaped from the Hinkley Point Project, through the creation of jobs, the long term environmental consequences, costs, and risks involved, currently appear to outweigh its economic benefits.

Investing in New Technologies which facilitate environmental goals and promote the awareness of innovativeness which is aimed at poverty reduction, rather than technology which merely results in job losses and detrimental consequences for the environment and its locals, should be accorded greater attention and focus.

REFERENCES

Coady, D., Gillingham, R., Ossowski, R., Piotrowski, J., Tareq, S., & Tyson, J. (2010). *Petroleum product subsidies: Costly, inequitable, and rising*. IMF Staff Position Note No. 10/05. Washington, DC: International Monetary Fund. Available at http://www.imf.org/external/pubs/ft/spn/2010/spn1005.pdf

Ebert, S., Metschies, G. P., Schmid, D., & Wagner, A. (2009). International Fuel Prices 2009 (6th ed.). Eschborn: Deutsche Gesellschaft für Technische Zusammenarbeit.

Fofana, I., Chitiga, M., & Mabugu, R. (2009). Oil Prices and the South African Economy: A Macro-Meso-Micro Analysis. *Energy Policy*, *37*(December), 5509–5518. doi:10.1016/j.enpol.2009.08.030

Gupta, S., Verhoeven, M., Gillingham, R., Schiller, C., Mansoor, A., & Cordoba, J. P. (2000). *Equity and Efficiency in the Reform of Price Subsidies: A Guide for Policymakers*. Washington, DC: International Monetary Fund.

Hayden, J. (2015, September). Under Pressure. *Finance & Development*.

Institute for Fiscal Studies (IFS). (2012). *Tax and Benefit Tables*. Available at www.ifs.org.uk/fiscalFacts/taxTables

International Monetary Fund. (2013). *Energy Subsidy Reform: Lessons and Implications*. Author.

International Monetary Fund. (2015). World Economic Outlook "Uncertainty, Complex Forces Weigh on Global Growth. *IMF Survey. International Monetary Fund*, *6*(October). Retrieved from http://www.imf.org/external/pubs/ft/survey/so/2015/res100615a.htm

Nielsen, L. (2009). *Global Relative Poverty*. IMF Working Paper. Office of Internal Audit and Inspection, IMF.

UNCTAD. (2009). *The Role of International Investment Agreements in Attracting Foreign Direct Investment to Developing Countries.* New York: United Nations.

UNCTAD. (2010). *Most-Favoured-Nation Treatment.* New York: United Nations.

UNCTAD. (2011a). *Local Production of Pharmaceuticals and Related Technology Transfer: A Series of Case Studies by the UNCTAD Secretariat.* New York: United Nations.

UNCTAD. (2011b). *Foreign Direct Investment in LDCs: Lessons Learned from the Decade 2001–2010 and the Way Forward.* New York: United Nations.

UNCTAD. (2011c). *Investment and Enterprise Responsibility Review.* New York: United Nations.

UNCTAD. (2011d). *Development-led globalization: Towards sustainable and inclusive development paths. Report of the Secretary-General of UNCTAD to UNCTAD XIII.* United Nations.

UNCTAD. (2012). *Investment Policy Framework for Sustainable Development: Towards a New Generation of Investment Policies (IPFSD).* New York: United Nations.

UNCTAD. (2013a). *Investment Policy Review: Bangladesh.* New York: United Nations.

UNCTAD. (2013b). *Economic Development in Africa Report 2013: Intra-African Trade – Unlocking Private Sector Dynamism.* New York: United Nations.

UNCTAD. (2013c). *The Least Development Countries Report 2013: Growth with Employment for Inclusive and Sustainable Development.* New York: United Nations.

UNCTAD. (2014). *Skill Development in the Bangladesh Garments Industry: the Role of TNCs.* New York: United Nations.

UNCTAD. (2014). *Investing in the SDGs: An action plan.* United Nations.

ENDNOTES

1. See Remarks by Jeffrey Hayden, Editor Finance & Development
2. The IMF's *World Economic Outlook* (*WEO*) also "foresees lower global growth compared to last year, with modest pickup in advanced economies and a slowing in emerging markets, primarily reflecting weakness in some large emerging economies and oil-exporting countries - with global real GDP being forecast to grow at only 3.1 percent this year – in comparison to recorded growth of 3.4 in 2014. Growth is expected to rebound to 3.6 percent next year."
3. Including measures aimed at "strengthening labor force participation, facilitate labor market adjustment, tackle legacy debt overhang, and lower barriers to entry in product markets, especially in services."
4. See UNCTAD, UNCTAD Report 2014, *Investing in the SDGs: An Action Plan* page 177. "A range of policy tools is available to increase absorptive capacity, including the promotion and facilitation of entrepreneurship, support to technology development, human resource and skills development, business development services and promotion of business linkages."

Chapter 9
Foreign Direct Investment as a Tool for Poverty Alleviation

James Rossi
University of Greenwich, UK

Genevieve Dupont
American University of Paris, France

ABSTRACT

It has been argued that "Absolute poverty can be alleviated if at least two conditions are met. First, economic growth must occur—or mean income must rise—on a sustained basis. Second, economic growth must be neutral with respect to income distribution or reduce income inequality." By way of reference to current and previous literature on economic development, this chapter aims to investigate the relationship between poverty, economic growth, and income distribution, as a means of mitigating gaps in the literature on the topic, as well as contributing to the literature of Foreign Direct Investment as a tool for poverty alleviation.

INTRODUCTION

The absence of public support for subsidy reform partly reflects a lack of confidence in the ability of governments to reallocate the resulting budgetary savings to benefit the broader population, as well as concerns that vulnerable groups will not be protected. This is particularly challenging in oil-exporting countries, where subsidies are seen as a mechanism to distribute the benefits of natural resource endowments to their populations; in addition, these countries typically lack capacity to administer targeted social programs. Governments are also often concerned about the inflationary effects of higher domestic energy prices and their adverse impact on the international competitiveness of domestic producers. Furthermore, subsidy reform can be complex when it involves efforts to reduce inefficiencies and production costs, as is often the case for the electricity sector. (IMF, 2013:5).

DOI: 10.4018/978-1-5225-0305-7.ch009

It has been argued (Jenkins, 2005:540) that one of the shortcomings of the current Corporate Social Responsibility model arises from its failure to accord greater focus and emphasis on poverty alleviation – which in part, is limited and attributed to the priority with which business and economic objectives are endowed. Herein lies the role of multinational enterprises in engaging the Government, wider stakeholders in designing effective social programs which not only constitute part of its corporate social goals and objectives, but can also be effectively enforced and complied with, through international codes and agreements.

It is also apparent from the investigated cases of subsidy reforms that opposition to such reforms arise primarily as a result of the inability of certain governments to effectively allocate designated resources in the manner deemed appropriate. Hence since issues appear to be more affiliated with domestic governance and local enforcement mechanisms, international and supranational entities may constitute more effective mechanisms for effectively enforcing and complying with related agreements, codes and standards. Further, as illustrated in chapter two, greater or equal status should be accorded to legal and ethical objectives, as embodied within Carroll's pyramid of Corporate Social Responsibility when such status is compared to that which is accorded to economic objectives.

As well as highlighting the advantages and disadvantages of energy subsidies as a means of identifying those areas of concerns and how they can be addressed, this chapter is aimed at proposing means whereby stakeholders and particularly wider stakeholders, the Government and multinational enterprises, can be effectively engaged in Corporate Social Responsibility as a tool for designing more effective social programs which are aimed at implementing successful subsidy reforms.

BACKGROUND AND LITERATURE REVIEW

Conceptual Framework

Subsidies are defined by the International Monetary Fund, as comprising of two elements, namely (IMF, 2013:6):

- Consumer subsidies
- Producer subsidies

Further, consumer subsidies are considered to arise "where the prices paid by consumers, including both firms (intermediate consumption) and households (final consumption), are below a benchmark price", whilst producer subsidies arise "when prices received by suppliers are above this benchmark." (IMF, 2013:6)

As well as growth and economic impacts of energy subsidies, environmental and social costs are also associated with such subsidies. Other disadvantages attributed to energy subsidies include the following (IMF, 2013:15-19):[1]

- Subsidies can discourage investment in the energy sector. Low and subsidized prices for energy can result in lower profits or outright losses for producers, making it difficult for SOEs to expand energy production and unattractive for the private sector to invest both in the short and long term.

- Subsidies cause overconsumption of petroleum products, coal, and natural gas, and reduce incentives for investment in energy efficiency and renewable energy. Such over-consumption in turn, aggravates global warming and worsens local pollution. High levels of vehicle traffic that are encouraged by subsidized fuels also have negative externalities in the form of traffic congestion and higher rates of accidents and road damage.
- The losses incurred by electricity suppliers due to subsidized prices have severely constrained their ability to invest in new electricity capacity and improve service quality.
- Deficient electricity infrastructure and shortages dampen economic growth and weaken competitiveness.
- Subsidies can crowd out growth-enhancing public spending. Some countries spend more on energy subsidies than on public health and education.
- Subsidies diminish the competitiveness of the private sector over the longer term.
- Subsidies create incentives for smuggling.

The need for effective and successful subsidy reforms is therefore apparent given the aforementioned disadvantages associated with energy subsidies. Such reforms where effectively implemented, confer the benefits of mitigating competitive disadvantages associated with energy subsidies as well as liberating resources which have been tied up as a result of such subsidies (see Fofana et al: 2009).

Table 1 provides a summary of results from subsidy reforms undertaken across several jurisdictions.

Issues, Controversies, Problems

It is argued that (Khan:2000):

Absolute poverty can be alleviated if at least two conditions are met. First, economic growth must occur—or mean income must rise—on a sustained basis. Second, economic growth must be neutral with respect to income distribution or reduce income inequality. Generally, poverty cannot be reduced if economic growth does not occur. In fact, the persistent poverty of a substantial portion of the population can dampen the prospects for economic growth (Ravallion & Datt, 1999).[2]

As highlighted under previous chapters, corporate social responsibility can be defined as:

- A model of extended corporate governance whereby those in control of the firm have responsibilities that range from the fulfillment of their fiduciary duties owed towards the owners (principal) to the fulfillment of analogous fiduciary duties owed towards all the firm's stakeholders.

Further, the engagement of stakeholders as proposed under the model, as well as

the engagement of stakeholders at appropriate stages, as well as the incorporation of applicable and most suitable forms of rules during such phases of the mediation process between agents and stakeholders, such that flexibility is facilitated in the process to allow for contingencies whilst also compelling effective enforcement and compliance mechanisms, corporate social responsibility should be fostered through the outcomes emanating from better, focused planning, control, decision making, as well as more effective accountability, compliance and enforcement mechanisms, (Ojo, Forthcoming)

Table 1. Summary of country energy subsidy reform episodes

Region/Country	Energy product	Reform episode	Reform outcome	Reform impact	IMF-supported program during the reform episode	Conditionality on energy subsidy reform
CEE-CIS						
Turkey	Fuel	1998	Successful	SOEs turned from net loss to net profitability	Yes	Yes
Armenia	Electricity	Mid-1990s	Successful	Electricity sector financial deficit declined from 22 percent of GDP in 1994 to zero after 2004	Yes	Yes
Turkey	Electricity	1980s	Successful	Generated additional revenues for maintenance	Yes	Yes
Poland	Coal	1990–1998	Unsuccessful	n.a.	Yes	Yes
	Coal	1998	Successful	The industry became financially viable and achieved substantial reduction in government transfer	No	
Emerging and Developing Asia						
Indonesia	Fuel	1997	Unsuccessful	n.a.	Yes	Yes
	Fuel	2003	Unsuccessful	n.a.	No	
	Fuel	2005	Partially successful	Subsidies declined from 3.5 percent of GDP in 2005 to 1.9 percent in 2006	No	
	Fuel	2008	Partially successful	Subsidies declined from 2.8 percent of GDP in 2008 to 0.8 percent in 2009	No	
Philippines	Fuel	1996	Successful	0.1+ percent of GDP	Yes	Yes
Philippines	Electricity	2001	Successful	Subsidies declined from 1.5 percent of GDP in 2004 to zero in 2006	No	
LAC						
Brazil	Fuel	Early 1990s–2001	Successful	From 0.8 percent of GDP in subsidies in mid-1990s to revenue generating since 2002	Yes	Yes
Chile	Fuel	Early 1990s	Successful	n.a.	No	
Peru	Fuel	2010	Partially successful	0.1 percent of GDP	No	
Brazil	Electricity	1993–2003	Successful	0.7 percent of GDP	Yes	Yes
Mexico	Electricity	1999/2001/2002	Unsuccessful	n.a.	Yes	No
MENA						
Iran	Fuel	2010	Partially successful	Growth in the consumption of petroleum products initially stabilized	No	
Mauritania	Fuel	2008	Unsuccessful	n.a.	Yes	No
	Fuel	2011	Partially successful	Subsidies declined from 2 percent of GDP in 2011 to close to zero in 2012	Yes	Yes
Yemen	Fuel	2005	Partially successful	Subsidies declined from 8.7 percent of GDP in 2005 to 8.1 percent in 2006	No	
	Fuel	2010	Partially successful	Subsidies declined from 8.2 percent of GDP in 2010 to 7.4 percent in 2011	Yes	Yes
Sub-Saharan Africa						
Ghana	Fuel	2005	Partially successful	50 percent price increase on average	No	
Namibia	Fuel	1997	Partially successful	0.1+ percent of GDP	No	
Niger	Fuel	2011	Partially successful	0.9 percent of GDP	No	
Nigeria	Fuel	2011–12	Partially successful	Subsidies declined from 4.7 percent of GDP in 2011 to 3.6 percent in 2012	No	
South Africa	Fuel	1950s	Successful	Successfully avoided subsidies and secured supply	No	
Kenya	Electricity	Mid-1990s	Successful	Subsidies declined from 1.5 percent of GDP in 2001 to zero in 2008	Yes	Yes
Uganda	Electricity	1999	Successful	2.1 percent of GDP	Yes	Yes

Source: IMF staff.

Note: n.a.=not applicable.

Note: CEE-CIS=Central and Eastern Europe and Commonwealth of Independent States, LAC=Latin America and Caribbean, S.S. Africa=Sub-Saharan Africa, and MENA=Middle East and North Africa.

Source: IMF, ENERGY SUBSIDY REFORM: LESSONS AND IMPLICATIONS at page 22

Of all the identified barriers to successful subsidy reforms, the focus of attention, for purposes aimed at realizing the aims and objectives of this chapter will be obstacles to communication between stakeholders, the Government and multinational enterprises, namely informational asymmetries which may arise between these groups. In aiming to facilitate communication, this section will consider, based on the case study undertaken in association with Table 1, the identified barriers to communication between stakeholders and governments as a means of addressing how multinational enterprises can be more effectively engaged in the communication process to address such obstacles and challenges.

The identified obstacles which were identified as having contributed to the implementation of successful subsidy reforms are as follows (IMF, 2013: 23 and 24):

- Lack of information regarding the magnitude and shortcomings of subsidies.
- Lack of government credibility and administrative capacity.
- Concerns regarding the adverse impact on the poor.
- Concerns regarding the adverse impact on inflation, international competitiveness, and volatility of domestic energy prices.
- Opposition from specific interest groups benefiting from the status quo.
- Weak macro-economic conditions.

Philanthropic Responsibilities as Means of Promoting Environmental Goals: As Well as Objectives Aimed at Reducing Poverty

Biofuel and renewable energy programs and funding should be encouraged and funded by philanthropist enterprises as this would not only contribute towards job creation possibilities and the discovery of entrepreneurs, but would also serve as a value added tool in contributing to the quality of life for locals – as well as environmental sustainable goals.

Such funds should be channeled through mechanisms which would ensure that the highest degree of accountability procedures and safeguards are in place. Whilst charities and non-governmental organizations constitute examples of such organizations through which these funds can be facilitated, appropriate internal corporate governance mechanisms should also be in place to enforce the ultimate goals of alleviating poverty and promoting a healthier environment. Herein also lies a role for corporate social responsibility reports – as well as continuous and progressive reporting which is aimed at highlighting improvements and developments in the lives and localities of beneficiaries of philanthropic programs – as well as impacts of such programs on the development of such individuals and localities.

Chapter eight has already highlighted how Corporate Social Responsibility and Corporate Social Accountability can be fostered. As highlighted under the chapter,

- As well as the determination of appropriate channels through which grants, schemes and funds for environmental and poverty alleviating causes should be facilitated, it is also vital to ensure that such grants and funds are allocated to the appropriate individuals. This ideally being by reason of merit, commitment and passion towards such social goals and objectives – such that funds are not misused, misappropriated or allocated to non-qualifying individuals as is the case with the allocation of numerous government contracts – particularly in jurisdiction with ineffective corporate governance controls and mechanisms.

SOLUTIONS AND RECOMMENDATIONS

Engaging Stakeholders, the Government and Multinational Enterprises in Corporate Social Responsibility: Designing More Effective Social Programs as a Means of Implementing Successful Subsidy Reforms

In order to facilitate communication between governments, multinational enterprises and stakeholders, it is evident that clarity of reform policies, an education of the public and users of such information as regards the adverse impacts of energy subsidies and an appreciation of the reasons constituting the need for subsidy reforms, that is training programs, need to be in place.

Clarity of longer term plan objectives, embodied in a "comprehensive reform plan" which evaluates the impact of reforms, as well as the importance of effective planning have been demonstrated from results of the studies undertaken in Table 1 (see IMF, 2013: 25 and 26):

To facilitate effective dialogue between the parties involved and the stakeholders, it is always beneficial to engage stakeholders in consultation exercises (Gupta, Verhoeven, Schiller, Mansoor & Cordoba, 2000; Sacconi, n.d.) to provide a feedback, as well as inform on what is to be expected on the part of all parties involved, hence mitigating information and implementation gaps (Ojo, Forthcoming).

Further information asymmetries can be mitigated between stakeholders, governments and enterprises, where Corporate Social Responsibility reports are provided with clarity, transparency and accuracy of information.

Governance continually constitutes a major problem in the public's sceptism and confidence of some governments' inability to efficiently allocate resources in a manner which is equitable across diverse income levels. It is for this very reason that the involvement of multinational enterprises in the dialogue and stakeholder engagement process is essential as a means of fostering greater accountability, as well as implementing more safeguards in the form of corporate governance mechanisms.

The need to reduce carbon emissions, as well as other greenhouse gases which contribute to environmental pollution should not be viewed so negatively by multinational enterprises, as constituting more costs than benefits - such that it clouds the positive attributes of Corporate Social Responsibility.

Where multinational enterprises and corporations, cannot be trusted to deliver their promises, in respect of environmental agreements, as well as their products, then legislative and judicial branches may well serve their purposes. For this very reason, the importance of legislation, codes of conduct, standards and ethics, well supersede economic and profit making objectives. The imposition of fines and sanctions should serve as an effective deterrent such that multinational enterprises and corporations are not only reminded of their obligations to the environment, but also safety and health repercussions which accrue to affected wider stakeholders where there is failure to comply with standards and obligations to which such corporations have pledged (or should have pledged) their allegiance.

FUTURE RESEARCH DIRECTIONS

The internet has revolutionized E commerce and in turn, multinational enterprises on such a large scale that cyber security issues continually constitute concerns which are put forward by many multi-national enterprises. As well as physical controls, namely the segregation of duties which introduce a degree of accountability into the financial reporting process, the design, marketing stages of many products, also warrant the same degree of scrutiny and focus. For such reasons robust internal controls need to be in place, as well as substantive and control testing procedures (tests of control), which need to be undertaken by independent and objective experts – and at adequately scheduled periodic intervals.

This applies to the auditing of financial statements, as well as other financial reports, such that such statements and reports which are generated, can be relied upon with credibility by investors and wider stakeholders. In the same regard, products and design need to be tested for any possible defects which not only constitute environmental hazard, but also occupational and safety concerns. There are likely to be cases where human error is attributable to a defective design – such that the repercussions for the environment, those directly affected (customers and suppliers particularly) and wider stakeholders cannot be quantified. In this respect, it is hard to imagine how corporations are willing to take risks in appeasing and rectifying such damage – which not only embraces monetary, but also reputational costs and potential long term damage to a very vital asset of the corporation – trust and goodwill.

CONCLUSION

How can governments "reallocate resulting budgetary savings" to the benefit the broader population and wider stakeholders, and how can concerns that vulnerable groups will not be protected, be addressed? Through the engagement of multinational enterprises, as far as is applicable, in effective consultations and dialogue between all involved parties. Such concerns being more founded in those jurisdictions where gaps are significantly lacking as regards matters of effective enforcement, compliance, and corporate governance mechanisms. Effective communication requires communication of clear purposes, objectives, both on a short and longer term, as well as effective planning to effectively execute designs and strategies. For these reasons, all relevant and involved stakeholders should be effectively engaged at applicable phases of planning, control and decision making to ensure that energy savings and reforms are allocated and implemented in such a way that the most vulnerable[3] stakeholders, particularly the poor are accounted to, and that poverty alleviation goals are realized. In addition to a comprehensive reform plan, "appropriately phased and sequenced price increases" are recommended in successfully implementing and realizing the benefits of a successful reform program (see IMF 2013, pages 25 and 28).

Whilst savings from subsidy reforms can be better targeted and reallocated in a more efficient and equitable manner to the benefit of the vulnerable or most vulnerable, a greater form of poverty alleviation lies herein: ensuring that existing and future generations benefit from, and inherit a reasonable quality of life through less carbon emissions and gradual reduction of greenhouse gases.

REFERENCES

Coady, D., Gillingham, R., Ossowski, R., Piotrowski, J., Tareq, S., & Tyson, J. (2010). *Petroleum Product Subsidies: Costly, Inequitable, and Rising*. IMF Staff Position Note No. 10/05. Washington, DC: International Monetary Fund. Available at http://www.imf.org/external/pubs/ft/spn/2010/spn1005.pdf

Ebert, S., Metschies, G. P., Schmid, D., & Wagner, A. (2009). International Fuel Prices 2009 (6th ed.). Eschborn: Deutsche Gesellschaft für Technische Zusammenarbeit.

Fofana, I., Chitiga, M., & Mabugu, R. (2009). Oil Prices and the South African Economy: A Macro-Meso-Micro Analysis. *Energy Policy*, *37*(December), 5509–5518. doi:10.1016/j.enpol.2009.08.030

Gupta, S., Verhoeven, M., Gillingham, R., Schiller, C., Mansoor, A., & Cordoba, J. P. (2000). *Equity and Efficiency in the Reform of Price Subsidies: A Guide for Policymakers*. Washington, DC: International Monetary Fund.

IMF. (2013). *Energy Subsidy Reform: Lessons and Implications*. IMF.

Institute for Fiscal Studies (IFS). (2012). *Tax and Benefit Tables*. Available at www.ifs.org.uk/fiscalFacts/taxTables

Jenkins, R. (2005). Globalization, Corporate Social Responsibility and Poverty. *International Affairs*, *81*(3), 525–540. doi:10.1111/j.1468-2346.2005.00467.x

Khan, M. H. (2000). Rural Poverty in Developing Countries. *Finance & Development, 37*. Retrieved from http://www.imf.org/external/pubs/ft/fandd/2000/12/khan.htm

Ojo, M. (forthcoming). E Commerce As a Tool For Resource Expansion: Postal Partnerships, Data Protection Legislation and the Mitigation of Implementation Gaps. *IGI Global Publications*.

Parry, I. W. H. (2011). How Much Should Highway Fuels Be Taxed? In U.S. Energy Tax Policy. Cambridge, UK: Cambridge University Press.

Parry, I. W. H., & Small, K. A. (2005). Does Britain or the United States Have the Right Gasoline Tax? *The American Economic Review*, *95*(4), 1276–1289. doi:10.1257/0002828054825510

Parry, I. W. H., & Strand, J. (2011). *International Fuel Tax Assessment: An Application to Chile*. IMF Working Paper No. 11/168. Washington, DC: International Monetary Fund. Available at http://www.imf.org/external/pubs/ft/wp/2011/wp11168.pdf

Sacconi, L. (2004). *Corporate Social Responsibility (CSR) as a Model of 'Extended' Corporate Governance: An Explanation Based on the Economic Theories of Social Contract*. Reputation and Reciprocal Conformism.

ENDNOTES

1 "Electricity subsidies in sub-Saharan Africa (SSA) are substantial and primarily reflect high costs of production".

2 "Rural poverty accounts for nearly 63 percent of poverty worldwide, reaching 90 percent in China and Bangladesh and between 65 and 90 percent in sub-Saharan Africa. (Exceptions to this pattern are seen in several Latin American countries in which poverty is concentrated in urban areas.) In almost all countries, the conditions—in terms of personal consumption and access to education, health care, potable water and sanitation, housing, transport, and communications—faced by the rural poor are far worse than those faced by the urban poor."

3 It is highlighted that "given the high share of benefits that accrues to upper-income groups, the inefficiencies that subsidies create in resource allocation, and in some countries the large share of the expatriate population, energy subsidies are a much less effective policy instrument for distributing wealth than other public spending programs".

APPENDIX 1

Figure 1. International prices of oil, coal, and natural gas, 2006–2012 (Indexed January 2000=100)
Sources: IMF World Economic Outlook (WEO), U.S. Energy Information Administration (EIA), and theOrganisation for Economic Co-operation and Development (OECD).
Note: Coal price is average of quarterly U.S. import prices (EIA) and quarterly OECD import price (IEA/OECD). Natural gas price is average of the monthly U.S. import and export prices (EIA); these prices are weighted averages for LNG and pipeline natural gas. Crude oil price is average of Brent, Dubai, and WTI monthly prices (WEO/Primary Commodities Price System). Gasoline price is monthly New York Harbor conventional gasoline spot price (EIA). Diesel price is monthly Los Angeles ultra-low sulfur CARB diesel spot price (EIA). Gasoline and diesel prices are then averaged.
Source: IMF, ENERGY SUBSIDY REFORM: LESSONS AND IMPLICATIONS page 4

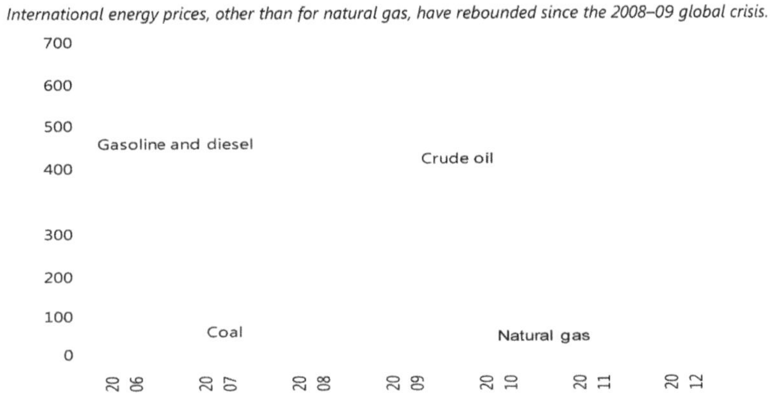

APPENDIX 2

- Countries in *Emerging and Developing Asia* were responsible for over 20 percent of global energy subsidies. They amounted to nearly 1 percent of regional GDP or 4 percent of total government revenues, with petroleum products and electricity accounting for nearly 90 percent of subsidies. Energy subsidies exceeded 3 percent of GDP in four countries (Bangladesh, Brunei, Indonesia, and Pakistan).
- The *Central and Eastern Europe and CIS* accounted for about 15 percent of global energy subsidies, including the highest share (at nearly 36 percent) of global natural gas subsidies. Energy subsidies amounted to over 1½ percent of regional GDP or 4½ percent of total government revenues, with natural gas and electricity accounting for about 95 percent. They exceeded 5 percent of GDP in four countries (Kyrgyz Republic, Turkmenistan, Ukraine, and Uzbekistan).
- The *Latin America and Caribbean* made up over 7½ percent of global energy subsidies (approximately ½ percent of regional GDP or 2 percent of total government revenues), with petroleum subsidies accounting for nearly 65 percent. Energy subsidies exceeded 5 percent of GDP in two countries (Ecuador and Venezuela).
- **Sub-Saharan Africa** accounted for about 4 percent of global energy subsidies. Energy subsidies amounted to 1½ percent of regional GDP or 5½ percent of total government revenues, with elec-

Figure 2. Pre-tax energy subsidies by region, 2011

Sources: Staff estimates, Organisation for Economic Co-operation and Development, International Energy Agency, Deutsche Gesellschaft für Internationale Zusammenarbeit, IMF World Economic Outlook, and World Bank.

Note: Adv.=Advanced, CEE-CIS=Central and Eastern Europe and Commonwealth of Independent States, LAC=Latin America and Caribbean, S.S. Africa=Sub-Saharan Africa, MENA=Middle East and North Africa, and E.D. Asia=Emerging and Developing Asia.

[1]Data for electricity are for the most recent year available. Subsides in percent of GDP and revenues are calculated as identified subsidies divided by regional GDP and revenues, respectively.

Source: IMF, ENERGY SUBSIDY REFORM: LESSONS AND IMPLICATIONS page 11

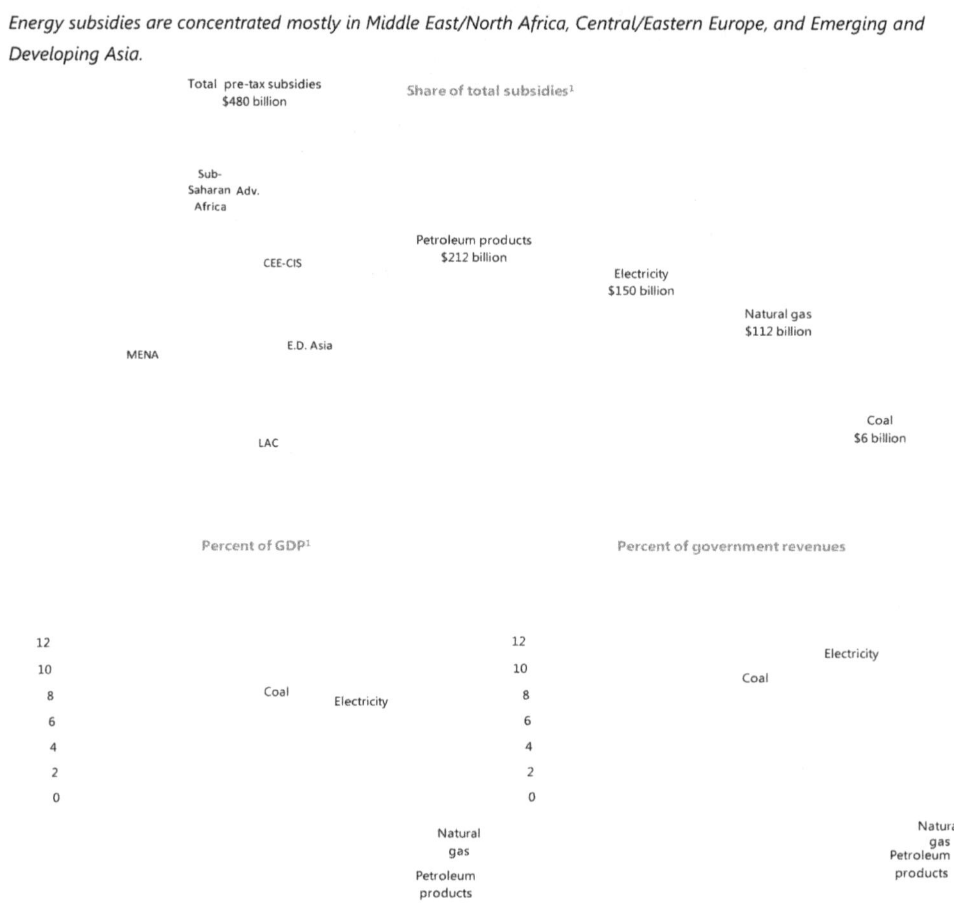

tricity subsidies accounting for over 70 percent. Total subsidies exceeded 4 percent of GDP in three countries (Mozambique, Zambia, and Zimbabwe).

- The only **advanced economy** where energy subsidies were a non-negligible share of GDP was Taiwan Province of China at 0.3 percent of GDP (electricity).

Source of Table: IMF, ENERGY SUBSIDY REFORM: LESSONS AND IMPLICATIONS Page 22
"The findings from the country studies identified in Table 1 are complemented with the insights from additional country studies conducted previously by the IMF and others, including Gupta and others (2000); Coady and others (2006); IMF (2008b); Coady and others (2010); Global Subsidies Initiative (2010); the UNEP (2002 and 2008); World Bank (2010); Vagliasindi (2012); and Arze del Granado,

Figure 3. Pre-tax petroleum subsidies among petroleum importing and exporting countries, 2011
Sources: Staff estimates, Organisation for Economic Co-operation and Development, International Energy Agency, Deutsche Gesellschaft für Internationale Zusammenarbeit, IMF World Economic Outlook, and World Bank.
Note: CEE-CIS=Central and Eastern Europe and Commonwealth of Independent States, LAC=Latin America and Caribbean, MENA=Middle East and North Africa, and E.D. Asia=Emerging and Developing Asia. Subsidies in percent of GDP are calculated as identified subsidies divided by regional GDP. Number of countries in each category indicated in parentheses.
Source: IMF ENERGY SUBSIDY REFORM: LESSONS AND IMPLICATIONS Page 12

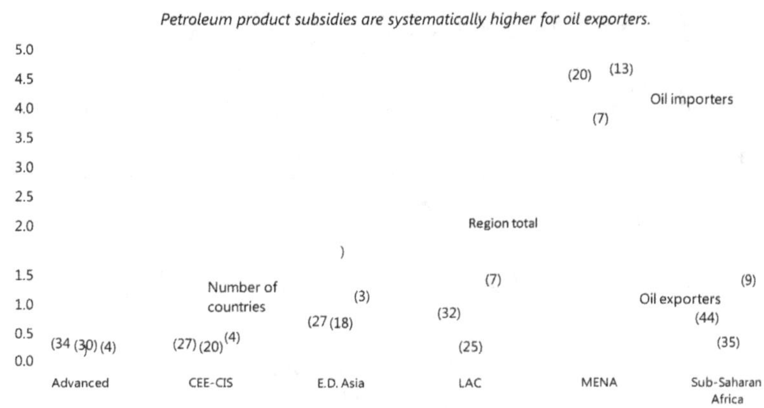

Coady, and Gillingham (2012). They also draw on lessons from technical assistance reports on energy subsidies undertaken by the Fiscal Affairs Department."

"Appendix Table 2 summarizes some estimates of motor fuel taxes to correct for these externalities that have been conducted for the United States, the United Kingdom, and Chile. The corrective tax estimate for Chile is higher, reflecting a combination of elevated local emission rates and a high incidence of pedestrian deaths and traffic congestion."

Table 2. Corrective Motor Fuel Taxes, selected countries (cents per liter, 2011 dollars)

	Gasoline (cars)			Diesel (trucks)	
	United States	United Kingdom	Chile	United States	Chile
Total	36	42	71	37	62
Contribution of:					
local pollution	3	4	18	10	16
carbon	6	5	6	6	6
congestion	15	26	19	10	16
accidents	12	8	28	3	12
noise	0	0	0	2	1
road damage	0	0	0	6	12

Scurces: IFS (2012), Parry (2011), Parry and Strand (2012), and Parry and Small (2005).
Nctes: The above studies estimate corrective diesel fuel taxes for the United States and Chile, but not for the United Kingdom.

Source: IMF, ENERGY SUBSIDY REFORM: LESSONS AND IMPLICATIONS at page 44

Chapter 10
Promoting Foreign Direct Investment:
Corporate Social Responsibility as Signaling Device and Tool for Corporate Governance

Jose J Haspa DeLarosiere
Universidad EAFIT, Colombia

Maria DiGabriele
New York University, USA

ABSTRACT

If audits serve as formidable internal monitoring tools which facilitate corporate governance, and Corporate Social Responsibility has been proven to serve as "an extension of corporate governance", as well as a signaling device, are both tools not instrumental in promoting Foreign Direct Investment? Through an analysis and evaluation of the literature relating to audits and Corporate Social Responsibility, this chapter aims to investigate the above claim and question on how Corporate Social Responsibility, as "an extension of corporate governance", as well as a signaling mechanism, could facilitate and promote Foreign Direct Investment.

INTRODUCTION

The role of the emerging and BRICS economies in propelling global growth, as well as determining and forecasting the direction of stock markets, is increasingly becoming apparent. This change in the previous trend which was previously dictated by the state of the United States economy, also presents a source of concern given apparent uncertainty and political tensions between certain leading economies and the United States. In addition to the leading and pivoting role assumed by China, the influence and impact of oil prices on stock markets has been witnessed and observed with increased interest since the end of October 2014. The importance of financial disclosure and transparency in leading market economies –

DOI: 10.4018/978-1-5225-0305-7.ch010

particularly for institutional investors has continually and persistently been brought to the fore. Owing to concerns of steep drops in the Dow and persistent uncertainty about the future and not the current state of the United States economy, on the 24th August 2015, a massive sell-out was instigated following a dip of about 1000 points.[1] This being attributed not only to dipping commodities such as oil prices, but primarily in response to observations that prognosis on China's growth was weaker than forecasted, as well as concerns about extent of cover ups about actual state of China's economy.

The vital question remains the extent to which BRICS are able to sustain the expected momentum as propellers of growth and Foreign Direct Investment – at a global level - as merely opposed to a regional level. Furthermore, was the massive sell out which followed in response to the Dow's loss, an over-reaction to China's stock market figures and the fact that expected prognosis about growth, particularly within China's manufacturing sector, may not be as robust as initially anticipated? Or is a combination of other factors such as uncertainty over the hike in interest rates by the Fed Reserve, as well as policy responses by other central banks attributable to the panic?

Is a slow down or bust period approaching in China or the BRICS economies – particularly having experienced a boom cycle whereby China was able to resist the pressures encountered by many other advanced economies following the Financial Crisis of 2008? Such bust cycle periods having been evidenced in the Asian Financial Crisis of 1997 and then a decade later when the 2008 Global Financial Crisis was preceded by a boom period in the housing markets?

This chapter aims to contribute to the literature on how Corporate Social Responsibility, as "an extension of corporate governance" (Sacconi, 2004:6), as well as a signaling mechanism (Goyal, 2006:4), can facilitate and promote Foreign Direct Investment.

Background and Literature Review

In addition to UNCTAD reports following post 2012 decline – with inflows rising 9 per cent in 2013, to $1.45 trillion, and projections, that FDI flows could rise to $1.6 trillion in 2014, $1.7 trillion in 2015 and $1.8 trillion in 2016, with relatively larger increases in developed countries, the following key observations were also made (UNCTAD, 2014):

- FDI flows to developed countries increased by 9 per cent to $566 billion, leaving them at 39 per cent of global flows, while those to developing economies reached a new high of $778 billion, or 54 per cent of the total.
- FDI outflows from developing countries also reaching record levels with developing and transition economies together investing $553 billion, or 39 per cent of global FDI outflows, compared with only 12 per cent at the beginning of the 2000s.
- Megaregional groupings' impact on global FDI – with Asia-Pacific Economic Cooperation (APEC) remaining the largest regional economic cooperation grouping, with 54 per cent of global inflows.
- The poorest countries are becoming less and less dependent on extractive industry investment and natural resources – with manufacturing and services now make up about 90 per cent of the value of announced projects both in Africa and in LDCs.

The highlighted observations (above) can be contrasted with the following observations provided by Goyal (2006:2):

The economic size and potential growth of a developing country are the major determinants of the foreign capital it attracts. There is intense competition to attract FDI. Liberalization, incentives such as lower tax rates, and investment targeting are among the measures governments are taking. After the East Asian crisis, FDI has been recognized as a more stable component offoreign inflows. But the developing country share of FDI has never recovered its peak share of 44% reached in 1997, and aggregate FDI has continued to be below the dollar 1.4 trillion reached in 2000. However, UNCTAD, based on its surveys, expects FDI to rise again in 2004 and a renewed surge to follow in the next few years, especially in the services sector. There are signs that this is materializing.

According to 2014 UNCTAD data and figures, at regional level (UNCTAD, 2014):

- FDI inflows to Africa rose by 4 per cent to $57 billion, driven by international and regional market-seeking and infrastructure investments with expectations for sustained growth of an emerging middle class being cited as contributory factors in the attraction of FDI in consumer-oriented industries: including food, IT, tourism, finance and retail. The overall increase was driven by the Eastern and Southern African sub-regions, as others saw falling investments. In Southern Africa flows almost doubled to $13 billion, mainly due to record-high flows to South Africa and Mozambique. In both countries, infrastructure was the main attraction, with investments in the gas sector in Mozambique also playing a role. In East Africa, FDI increased by 15 per cent to $6.2 billion as a result of rising flows to Ethiopia and Kenya. Kenya is becoming a favored business hub, not only for oil and gas exploration but also for manufacturing and transport. Intra-African investments are increasing, led by South African, Kenyan, and Nigerian TNCs.
- With total FDI inflows of $426 billion in 2013, developing Asia accounted for nearly 30 per cent of the global total and remained the world's number one recipient region. Whilst FDI inflows to East Asia is reported to have risen by 2 per cent to $221 billion, inflows to South-East Asia is also recorded to have increased by 7 per cent to $125 billion. Inflows to South Asia rose by 10 per cent to $36 billion in 2013 - the largest recipient of FDI in the sub region, being India. Most notable are reports of FDI flows to West Asia having decreased in 2013 by 9 per cent to $44 billion – with failure to recover for the fifth consecutive year.
- Elsewhere, uneven growth in FDI was reported for Latin America and the Caribbean. Whilst flows to Central America and the Caribbean (excluding offshore financial centers) are reported to have increased by 64 per cent to $49 billion, and FDI outflows from Latin America and the Caribbean (excluding offshore financial centers) are reported to have declined by 31 per cent to $33 billion, a slight decline was reported in relation to Brazil - a slight decline by 2 per cent, despite a reported 86 per cent increase in flows to the primary sector. FDI in Chile and Argentina are also reported to have declined by 29 per cent and 25 per cent to $20 billion and $9 billion, respectively, due to lower inflows in the mining sector. [2]

Further evidence of persistent regional tensions and political uncertainties as being contributory to holding back investors – even though differences are reported between countries (UNCTAD, 2014:xx) are currently being witnessed in recent news and stock market reports – impacted by declining oil prices and the difficulties encountered by BRICS in sustaining the forecasted acceleration of growth.

Timokhina (n.d.)h ighlights the role and vital importance assumed by BRICS - as well as the resilience of China through the recent global financial economic crisis:

Brazil, Russia, India, China and South Africa – so-called BRICS countries became significant capital exporters in the last 20 years. Abbreviation "BRIC" appeared in 2001, when it was suggested that by 2050 aggregate GDP of these countries will exceed the corresponding indicator of the developed economies, and South Africa joined the group in 2011.

China's strategic role – not only as a vital propeller and accelerator of global growth, but also its influence in its "economic role to promote Africa's development" is highlighted (Timokhina, n.d.).

Goyal (2006) argues that CSR works as a form of signaling and that since it reduces the returns from non-cooperative strategies it implements an efficient equilibrium.[3] In capital markets where so much uncertainty and asymmetric information is involved, reliable signaling mechanisms in the form of audits also serve as vital corporate governance mechanisms.

ISSUES, CONTROVERSIES, PROBLEMS

The Significance and Impact of Reliable Signaling Mechanisms in Capital and Stock Market Economies

Recent stock market crashes end of August 2015[4] at the New York Stock Exchange, are not only indicative of panic and loss of investor confidence, but also a huge degree of uncertainty hovering over the markets. Amidst very high volume trading on the NYSE and explanations of a possible market correction, the consolation that trading markets worldwide were also affected by the crash in China's stock markets, and based on the dynamics which were in operation with major Financial Crises in the two previous decades, it was concluded and predicted that a rebound in the stock markets would take place.

A rebound in the stock markets did take place – however temporarily. Even though the NYSE closed on the 24th August 2015 with a loss of 588 points, following an initially devastating drop to 1000 points in the first few minutes of the opening bell, there was a temporary rebound the following day. Following a move by the Chinese central bank to lower interest rates, a measure prompted by the stock market crash, following the "Black Monday" in China, stocks in Wall Street and other major stock markets temporarily rebounded as evidenced from data generated across global stock markets. However the Dow ended the day, 25th August 2015, with a loss of 205 points. Based on the previous trading figures from the previous five days,[5] an aggregate loss of 1850 points was recorded and a 3000 point drop in three months from the all-time high which was registered on the 19th May 2015.

Issues impacting loss of investor confidence in the Chinese stock markets can certainly be attributed to the lack of transparency in the markets, uncertainty, the reliability of accounting data emanating from the markets and consequently, how to adequately price shares and stocks. Even though the "stock market correction" which occurred on the 24th August 2015 in the NYSE was considered by many analysts and some investors as an inevitable and anticipated event which was also widely considered necessary within the NYSE, the massive sell off, panic, and surprise – even to traders, could also be explained by the differences in operating dynamics when compared with the 1997 Asian Financial Crisis and the 2008 Global Financial Crisis. In comparison to the 2008 Financial Crisis where financial structural issues within the banking system and regulatory issues were contributory, massive regulatory reforms have been operating since then to bolster Tier One capital as well as other measures implemented following Basel III reforms. The extent of the surprise could also partially be explained by the fact that the Chinese economy, in contrast to its counterparts and other leading economies, had maintained resilience through the 2008 Financial Crisis – having weathered the storms and turbulence of the recent Financial Crisis which culminated in September 2008.

The uncertainty of data emanating from China was not the only factor which was contributory to the Dow's plunge. As highlighted, falling commodity prices in oil, as well as uncertainty surrounding interest rate hikes, all played a role in the massive stock market sell off in the week beginning 24th August. This happening despite the fact that the build up to China's slow down had been evident for months. Such expectancy is also reflected in the distinction between the fundamentals of the US economy and present occurrences in Wall Street.

The current reasonably healthy state of the United States economy – as evidenced by relatively low unemployment rates, low interest rates, lower household debt was highlighted.

Even though uncertainty currently hovers over global stock markets, it is argued by many analysts that there should be no cause for concerns – particularly based on results from previous stock market crashes and financial crises. Whether the present situation will draw similar and comparable repercussions remains to be seen. Present concerns are certainly justified – not only given the slow-down in the BRICS anticipated growth – and the consequent big worries emanating from these emerging markets, but also worries over oil and oil exporting countries. Oil was not the only commodity affected in the Dow's plunge, but also other commodities such as gold and silver – so-called safe haven for investors. Certainly China's role as a major player and its impact and 15% assumption of the world economy, places global markets in a very vulnerable and volatile situation where its economy is affected – as demonstrated by recent events. The dynamics have certainly changed over the years. Policy responses by major economies will certainly play crucial roles in addressing the present stock market uncertainties.

The present situation with global financial markets is further compounded by the fact that many governments cannot lower interest rates than the present levels. Hopefully the worst fears surrounding the extent of the slow-down in the emerging economies will not materialize. Is the market melt-down over yet? Can the emerging economies sustain their expected momentum? It will be interesting to see what unfolds in the months to come – particularly the policy response of the Fed Reserve in September 2015. Whilst the United States economic fundamentals remain solid – or relatively robust, and the high likelihood that Federal Reserve will not raise interest rates in September 2015 persists,[6] policy responses from leading economies still justify the concerns and volatile reactions in the markets.

Maybe the recent events[7] at Wall Street and the "correction" may be just what is needed to bring many investors, analysts, and traders to the reality of what should be expected and be better prepared to deal with asset bubbles.

SOLUTIONS AND RECOMMENDATIONS

As highlighted by Ojo (n.d.), the crucial factors fueling panics and sudden crashes, frequently boils down to information asymmetries, extent of uncertainty, and lack of transparency and disclosure of vital financial data. Improving Foreign Direct Investment, will therefore require increased transparency, disclosure of financial information and data as a means of addressing information asymmetries between the principal and the agent. Further, with broader stakeholders who fall within the scope and ambit of the stakeholder theory, such asymmetries can be mitigated as proposed by Sacconi (2004) under his model of Corporate Social Responsibility as a tool of extended corporate governance.

According to Sacconi (2004:6), corporate social responsibility can be defined as:

a model of extended corporate governance whereby those in control of the firm have responsibilities that range from the fulfillment of their fiduciary duties owed towards the owners (principal) to the fulfillment of analogous fiduciary duties owed towards all the firm's stakeholders."

The engagement of stakeholders as proposed under the model, as well as

the engagement of stakeholders at appropriate stages, as well as the incorporation of applicable and most suitable forms of rules during such phases of the mediation process between agents and stakeholders, such that flexibility is facilitated in the process to allow for contingencies whilst also compelling effective enforcement and compliance mechanisms, corporate social responsibility should be fostered through the outcomes emanating from better, focused planning, control, decision making, as well as more effective accountability, compliance and enforcement mechanisms, (Ojo, 2016)

would considerably address information asymmetries between the principal and investors – whether such investors fall within the scope of the traditional principal agent theory or whether they fall under the broader stakeholder theory.

FUTURE RESEARCH DIRECTIONS

In order to address information asymmetries which contribute to considerable uncertainty, lack of transparency and disclosure in financial markets, considerable measures are being undertaken to enhance audit quality – particularly aspects relating to the provision of certain categories of non-audit services, pursuant to the Sarbanes Oxley Act – which was implemented in 2002, in the aftermath of Enron. The provision of such categories of non-audit services by audit firms, being considered to impair auditors' independence and objectivity. However it has also been argued that the provision of non-audit services by audit firms contributes to knowledge spill overs which are acquired where an audit firm has acquired certain knowledge and skills – as a result of the provision of such non audit services and that such spillovers result in savings and cost reductions which would not otherwise be acquired by engaging a different audit firm. The engagement of a different firm implying that more costs would be employed in such a firm's acquisition of new knowledge. It is therefore also argued that greater focus should revolve around the proportion of non-audit fees generated by an audit firm – in relation to the audit fees earned.

Where such a proportion of non-audit fees in relation to audit fees is considerably high, then it can reasonably be inferred that undue reliance is being placed by the audit firm on its client and hence, greater likelihood that the audit firm's objectivity and independence is likely to be compromised.

In addition to above arguments, and lack of concrete empirical data and research to support the claims that the provision of non-audit services by an audit firm, are detrimental to the extent that such firm's objectivity and independence are compromised, a focus on audit quality has been propounded.

Similar arguments which apply to the provision of non-audit services can be related to another factor which is considered to affect and impair auditors' independence and objectivity, namely, mandatory rotation of audit firms. Whilst a failure to rotate its auditors within an acceptable and stipulated time period is attributable to many corporate collapses, as well as facilitating an environment where creative accounting practices which distort the reliability and relevance of accounting information are practised, it is also argued that an appropriate balance needs to be struck such that auditors are not so frequently rotated that knowledge has to be re-learned by new audit firm – to the detriment and cost disadvantage of the client corporate firm. Whilst ten years, appears to be a growing consensus for the period of mandatory audit rotation, particularly in Europe, other jurisdictions are not of the same opinion.

In various jurisdictions such as South Africa and Malaysia, partial mandatory audit firm rotation is considered a more flexible and feasible option.

As a result of the need for consensus, on a global level, in matters relating to factors which impair audit objectivity and independence, particularly the issue of mandatory audit firm rotation, such factors also contributing to audit quality and the relevance, accuracy and reliability of accounting information generated through financial statements, further efforts aimed at arriving on such a global consensus are required.

CONCLUSION

Whilst lack of transparency, disclosure of financial and accounting information have been proven to contribute to information asymmetries, uncertainty and panics in financial markets, it also needs to be highlighted that accuracy, reliability and relevance of accounting information is of paramount importance – such that this vital information can be reasonably relied upon by investors.

For these reasons, the focus on audit quality, as well as the importance of audits as vital signaling mechanisms, continue to constitute significant areas – both in terms of Corporate Social Responsibility, as well as factors which determine and influence Foreign Direct Investment in matters of uncertainty and forecasted growth in financial global markets.

As highlighted under the literature review, maybe the recent events at Wall Street and the "correction" may be just what is needed to bring many investors, analysts, and traders to the reality of what should be expected and be better prepared to deal with asset bubbles. It is certainly the case that a great deal of uncertainty persists as regards the actual pace of economic growth in emerging economies, as well as the degree of reliability to be placed on financial data and accounting information in certain economies.

Recent events in global financial markets – particularly with January 2016 heralding a very volatile start to the year, indicate that issues relating to doubts and uncertainty surrounding financial information and the actual pace of global growth are not just temporary one-off events. With the Dow having plunged by more than 300 points to -364.8 during the second week of January 2016[8] – and with all three major indices (the Dow Industrial, S& P 500 and NASDAQ) going into correction zones – and the S&P 500 reaching its lowest level since September 2015, the volatility resonating around and within financial markets is certainly not solely restricted to the United States, but also to other major European. Asian financial markets and other leading economies, who have witnessed plunges during the first months of 2016.

The falling oil prices - as well as the response undertaken by OPEC and oil cartels, China's growth and that of other emerging economies, certainly constitute vital areas of attention during 2016. So is the response undertaken in the areas of monetary policy – and also measures aimed at bolstering audit quality and facilitating financial transparency and disclosure.

REFERENCES

Annual Report on the OECD Guidelines for Multinational Enterprises 2010 Corporate Responsibility: Reinforcing a Unique Instrument. (2010). OECD Publishing.

Annual Report on the OECD Guidelines for Multinational Enterprises 2014 Responsible Business Conduct by Sector. (2015). OECD Publishing.

Blowfield, M. (2005). Corporate Social Responsibility: Reinventing the Meaning of Development? *International Affairs, 81*(3), 515–524. doi:10.1111/j.1468-2346.2005.00466.x

Carney, M. (2016). The Turn of the Year. Text of the Peston Lecture by Mr Mark Carney, Governor of the Bank of England and Chairman of the Financial Stability Board, at the Queen Mary University of London, London, UK.

Draghi, M. (2016). *How Domestic Economic Strength Can Prevail over Global Weakness*. Keynote speech by Mr Mario Draghi, President of the European Central Bank, at the Deutsche Börse Group New Year's reception 2016, Eschborn.

Emerging Market Economics. (2002). *Pro-poor Investment: Maximizing the Contribution of Investment and Business to Poverty Reduction, Report to the Department for International Development*. London: DFID.

Gore, C. (2000). The Rise and Fall of the Washington Consensus as a Paradigm for Developing Countries. *World Development, 28*(5), 789–804.

Goyal, A. (2006). Corporate Social Responsibility as a Signaling Device for Foreign Direct Investment. *International Journal of the Economics of Business, 13*(1), 145–163. doi:10.1080/13571510500520077

Kolk, A., & van Tulder, R. (2010). International Business, Corporate Social Responsibility and Sustainable Development. *International Business Review, 19*(2), 119–125.

OECD. (2011). *OECD Guidelines for Multinational Enterprises*. OECD Publishing. doi:10.1787/9789264115415-en

Ojo, M. (2014). *Why the Traditional Principal Agent Theory May No Longer Apply to Concentrated Ownership Systems and Structures*. Paper presented at the Third International Conference on Humanities, Economics and Geography, Abu Dhabi. doi:10.15208/beh.2013.16

Ojo, M. (2015). Audits, Audit Quality and Signaling Mechanisms: Concentrated Ownership Structures. *American Research Journal of Humanities and Social Sciences, 1*(2). Retrieved from www.arjonline.org

Ojo, M. (2016a). E Commerce As a Tool For Resource Expansion: Postal Partnerships. *Data Protection Legislation and the Mitigation of Implementation Gaps. IGI Global Publications.*

Ojo, M. (2016b). *Regulating Stock Market Crashes and Information Uncertainty: A Matter of Regulatory Style and Structure?*. Forthcoming.

Restoy, F. (2016). The Organisation of Financial Supervision. Speech by Mr Fernando Restoy, Deputy Governor of the Bank of Spain, participating in the presentation of the "Guide to the Spanish Financial System" (Guía del Sistema Financiero Español), compiled by AFI (Analistas Financieros Internacionales) and sponsored by Funcas (Fundación de las Cajas de Ahorros), Madrid, Spain.

Sacconi, L. (2004). *Corporate Social Responsibility (CSR) as a Model of 'Extended' Corporate Governance: An Explanation Based on the Economic Theories of Social Contract.* Reputation and Reciprocal Conformism.

Timokhina, O. (2014). *Chinese Foreign Direct Investment in Africa in Corporate Social Responsibility Context.* Maastricht School of Management Working Paper No. 2014/29.

UNCTAD. (2014). *Investing in the SDGs: An Action Plan.* UNCTAD.

ENDNOTES

1 A plunge of about 1078 points (-1078) at the beginning of the day – which ended with a recovery of about 700 points by the end of the day.

2 "Flows to Peru also decreased, by 17 per cent to $10 billion. In contrast, FDI flows to Colombia increased by 8 per cent to $17 billion, largely due to cross-border M&As in the electricity and banking industries." See ibid at page xx

3 A Goyal (2006), "Corporate Social Responsibility as a Signaling Device for Foreign Direct Investment", at page 4
It is also added that "CSR may serve as a credible signal of a firm's type. Although the country prefers the cooperative strategy it opts for the non-cooperative one if that is the dominating strategy for the firm, but signaling expenditure can change the payoffs to the firm, so that cooperation becomes its dominant strategy. This binding to cooperation makes the efficient equilibrium possible. The accommodating firm has the capacity to design credible signals of its type if it has a longer-term commitment to a business plan, since it is then willing to amortize its signaling expenditure over a longer period." Ibid at page 6

4 24th August 2015

5 With losses of 163, 358, 531, 588 and 205 points

6 On the 31st August 2015, Dow capped worst month in five years – dropping 15 points that day to end August with the worst monthly percentage since 2010. In August 2015, Dow lost 6+% of its value. The following day, the 1st September 2015, China's worst manufacturing results in 3 years sent Dow plunging down at 400+ points (-467) amidst revelation of reports. On the 17th September, interest rates were retained unchanged by the Federal Reserve. Fed Reserve said that rates would remain near zero because present global developments may restrain economic activity.

7 As of the 7th January 2016, shares experienced steep plunges and dives following a continuation of incidents attributed to a slowdown of China's economy – as well as plunging oil prices which reached their lowest levels in 12 years. Following announcements by Chinese regulators that they would "pull the plug on circuit breakers" which had been implemented seven days before, US investors were engaged in massive sell offs which were also triggered by the fear of resulting losses which could occur if swift action to sell was not undertaken before stocks stopped trading. The Dow and shares on the NYSE not only witnessed a 2.4% drop – but also impacts of the global slowdown – which were experienced in other major financial markets around the world.

8 The 13th January 2016

Section 5

A Focus on Statistical and Empirical Aspects of Corporate Social Responsibility, Foreign Direct Investment, and the Need for Mitigation of Audit Expectation Gaps

Chapter 11
Foreign Direct Investment in China:
Its Impact on Economic Growth (Revisited)

Agya Atabani Adi
Federal University Wukari, Nigeria

James A. Rossi
University of Greenwich, UK

ABSTRACT

In accounting for the gaps in the literature between the period 2011 and 2016, more recent literature – particularly empirical related studies on the topic have been consulted to consolidate on the paper "Foreign Direct Investment in China: Its Sectoral and Aggregate Impact on Economic Growth". As highlighted by Wei (2013), it is important to recognize and acknowledge that the relationship between FDI and employment is affected by many variables, such as growth of the national population, increased exports, and growth of the domestic economy. Furthermore, as illustrated by Iamsiraroj and Doucouliagos (2015), whilst positive and negative effects may be demonstrated in relation to economic growth, in some countries, no effects can be deduced as regards the relationship between economic growth and FDI in certain other countries. This chapter also aims to accentuate the need for greater focus on environmental issues - as well as poverty alleviation - than is currently the case within the sphere and framework of Carroll's pyramid of Corporate Social Responsibility.

INTRODUCTION

As well as the consideration of other objectives which will be introduced towards the end of this section, this chapter is aimed at highlighting why corporate governance mechanisms such as audits are assuming an ever increasing role in mitigating information gaps resulting from lack of investor confidence and growing mistrust, as well as the mitigation of information asymmetries and uncertainties which have the potential to generate shocks, panics and turmoils in financial markets.

DOI: 10.4018/978-1-5225-0305-7.ch011

According to Agrawal and Khan (2011:71,72):

FDI is an important factor in the globalization process as it intensifies the interaction between states, regions and firms. Growing international flows of portfolio and direct investment, international trade are all parts of this process. Globalization offers an unprecedented opportunity for developing countries to achieve faster economic growth through trade and investment. In the period 1970s, international trade grew more rapidly than FDI, and thus international trade was by far than most other important international economic activities. This situation changed dramatically in the middle of the 1980s, when world FDI started to increase sharply. In this period, the world FDI has increased its importance by transferring technologies and establishing marketing and procuring networks for efficient production and sales internationally (Shujiro Urata, 1998). The large increase in the volume of FDI during the past two decades provides a strong incentive for research on this phenomenon.

After the global financial crisis, the status and importance of Asian economies have increased a lot because of their more than expected resilience to financial crisis. Asian economies are expanding rapidly and their growing clout can be felt from the fact that out of top 5 economies of the world (in terms of GDP by PPP) 3 are Asian. Asia, with the exception of Japan, South Korea, Hong Kong and Singapore, is currently undergoing rapid growth and industrialization spearheaded by China and India - the two fastest growing major economies in the world.

However, recent global trends, reports and developments reveal a slowing down in the pace of growth – as well as anticipated growth in the emerging economies – and notably, China. Whilst many factors are contributory to such developments, it is also vital to consider corporate governance related aspects which may have contributed to the quality of financial reporting and the reliability of financial reporting instruments and financial data in China.

It is recently acknowledged that the level of accuracy of financial data constitutes a huge matter of concern for financial investors in global markets and this has also been evidenced by the recent volatility in leading global financial markets.

Whilst the value relevance of accounting information and data in capital markets of selected jurisdictions constitutes the focus of investigation and analysis in another publication (Ojo, 2016), this chapter will briefly consider the importance of accounting information for investors – as well as Foreign Direct Investment in many emerging economies.

This chapter also aims to analyze and consolidate on the findings of Adi and Ogbole (2013) in relation to their paper "Foreign Direct Investment in China: Its Sectoral and Aggregate Impact on Economic Growth".

Since the results from their studies are based on data analysis which spans a period of 2005 to 2010, this chapter also aims to mitigate the gaps in the literature by way of reference and consultation to more recent research on the topic. The chapter will also illustrate why environmental concerns and poverty alleviation still constitute vital areas in need of redress and greater focus within the framework of Carroll's pyramid of Corporate Social Responsibility.

MAIN FOCUS OF THE CHAPTER

Background to the Study: Theoretical and Empirical Review

Whilst many studies on the topic and in the literature highlight the positive effects of economic growth on Foreign Direct Investment, there are also controversial and refuting results which dispute the validity that economic growth has positive effects for Foreign Direct Investment.

Iamsiraroj and Doucouliagos (2015) highlight and demonstrate that "there is a robust positive correlation between growth and FDI" – however further studies are also cited as having reached controversial conclusions.

As well as incorporating meta-regression analysis into their study, they applied it to 946 estimates from 140 empirical studies.

Furthermore, they highlight the fact that the positive effects between growth and FDI are more visible – even if slightly, with developing countries than is the case with other countries.

According to Iamsiraroj and Doucouliagos (2015),

Studies which demonstrate positive correlation between growth and FDI, "empirical studies which find that economic growth is an incentive for FDI inflows" include those carried out by Al Nasser 2010; Jiménez 2011; Kandil 2011; Mohamed & Sidiropoulos 2010). They also add that (pages 5 and 6):

There are several reasons why foreign investors might prefer faster growing markets. For example, cost efficiency of production and the realization of economies of scale and scope in production are closely linked with market size (Blonigen et al. 2007; Filippaios et al. 2003; Greenaway et al. 2007; Vernon 1966; Wang & Swain 1995). Other things equal, a growing market can be attractive to FDI because of the likelihood that a larger market will enable a more efficient scale of production through the realization of economies of scale (Agosin & Machado, 2007; Carstensen & Toubal, 2004). That is, growth is a measure and signal of market demand and market demand attracts FDI.

The importance of favorable prospects for market growth as a means of facilitating long-term commitment by foreign investors, is also highlighted.

Other studies which accentuate a negative correlation, that is negative effects of economic growth on FDI, are as follows (Iamsiraroj & Doucouliagos (2015:7):

Studies by Buchanan et al. (2012), Jensen (2003), and Wint and Williams (2002) – which all find a significantly negative impact of economic growth in attracting FDI in developing countries.

One explanation for such empirical results, according to Iamsiraroj and Doucouliagos (2015) is that it is a measurement artifact.

More importantly, it is demonstrated that whilst positive and negative effects may be demonstrated in relation to economic growth, in some countries, no effects can be deduced as regards the relationship between economic growth and Foreign Direct Investment. Iamsiraroj and Doucouliagos (2015) add, with reference to (Akinlo, 2004), that "in Africa, extractive FDI is located in several mineral-rich countries, where market size and growth rate are not the key motivation for FDI" (Akinlo, 2004) – and that consequently, in such cases, economic growth and FDI will be unrelated.

According to the OECD (2000:3):

Because of its size, China's "open door policy" launched twenty years ago constitutes a unique and vast laboratory for the study of major structural changes in China and the world economy. It also provides an opportunity to test the benefits and the shortcomings of the economic policies which have been followed by the Chinese authorities and identify the improvements that could be brought about to increase the economic positive fall-outs of Chinese economic reforms.

In its study, the OECD (2000:4) also remarks that:

Despite shortcomings in available data, the synthesis note clearly shows that FDI has brought substantial and definite changes in China's external and internal economic structure. In fact the findings of the study are amazingly consistent with economic theory and existing economic literature. They confirm the complexity and diversity of China's economic situation and the broad ramifications of Chinese economic reforms.

Zhang (n.d.) also uses data from over a period of 1992 to 2004 to analyze the impact of FDI inflows on China's income growth. His results appeared to illustrate that "positive growth effects seems to rise over time in coastal than inland areas." He also adds that FDI seemed to contribute to China's economic growth through direct effects, such as facilitating productivity and promoting imports, and positive externality effects – such as facilitating transition and diffusing technology (page 13). He concludes that the effects of foreign invested enterprises on the Chinese economy appeared to increase with FDI inflows between the period of 1992 and 2004, and that such effects appeared to be more prominent in coastal areas than in the inland region (page 13).

In attempting to answer the question revolving round the core research streams that have evolved around the phenomenon of FDI to China (Fetscherin, Voss, & Gugler: 236), Fetscherin, Voss, and Gugler, amongst other criteria and factors, employ:

An interdisciplinary historiographic bibliometric citation analysis to reveal patterns in the analyses of research about FDI to China (Garfield,1963; Small,1974; Moedetal.,1985) and relate their findings to the four main streams of research in international business as identified by Dunning and Lundan (2008a). These are: (1) the motives and determinants of FDI; (2) 'inside' the multinational enterprise (MNE); (3) the impact of MNE activities; and (4) policy implications for the host country.

In their opinion, they consequently expand on work by Peng, Lu, Shenkar, and Wang (2001), Li and Tsui (2002) and Quer, Claver, and Rienda (2007) by analyzing a very large sample of literature on FDI to China in an objectified manner and in close relationship to the foundations of international business research, rather than management studies (see Fetscherin, Voss, & Gugler: 236).

In comparing the pace of growth between India and China, Agrawal and Khan (2011:72) remark:

India and China have experienced rapid economic growth in recent years. The growth, in part, is attributed to the adoption of liberal trade policies by each country in 1990's, and the consequent surge in the flows of foreign capital to both these countries. China and India, as the two largest developing countries in the world, have been both enjoying fast economic growth since the 1990s. China seems to *be performing better. In 1975, China was at par with India in GDP, yet 33% lower in its GDP per capita ($146 versus $220). But over the years China developed more rapidly than India and surpassed India in terms of GDP per capita in 1984.*

What's more phenomenal, however, is the difference in their FDI performance. China has been able to attract more FDI than India, both in terms of net inflow and as % of GDP, from the beginning. Over the past decade, China has established itself as the top recipient of foreign direct investment (FDI) among developing countries. The World Prospectus Survey 2010-2012, released by the United Nations Conference on Trade and Development (UNCTAD), showed that China has once again retained title of the world's most important FDI destination.

They also highlight the significance of "knowing what the effect of FDI on their growth is". Having considered the controversial results relating to the positive and negative effects of economic growth on FDI, it is interesting to discover that their findings and results revealed the following (see Agrawal & Khan, 2011:76):

- Confirmation that FDI promotes economic growth, and further provides an estimate that 1% increase in FDI would result in 0.07% increase in GDP of China and 0.02% increase in GDP of India.
- That China's growth is more affected by FDI than India's growth and FDI is not as much significant as other variables to predict growth.
- The study also provides possible reasons behind China's great show of FDI and the lessons India should learn from China for better utilization of FDI.
- That majority of the foreign investors prefer China over India for investment opportunities as China has a bigger market size than India, offers easy accessibility to export market, government incentives, developed infrastructure, cost-effectiveness, and macro-economic climate – even though India on the other hand has talented management system, rule of law, transparent system of work, cultural affinity and regulatory environment.

In investigating the impact of FDI on employment in China, Wei (2013), highlights the importance of recognizing and acknowledging that the relationship between FDI and employment is affected by many variables, such as growth of the national population, increased exports, and growth of the domestic economy. As a result these variables were taken into consideration for the study, and then data analysis was also undertaken to determine whether FDI was helpful in the creation of more job opportunities for the Chinese economy in general, the magnitude of this impact, and the impact of FDI on employment in China's primary, secondary, and tertiary sectors (see Wei, 2013:7).

In order to determine the relationship between FDI and employment in China's overall economy, 8 predictor variables are used by Wei (see page 20), namely: FDI, total wages, consumption, government spending, investment, net exports, interest rates for deposits, and interest rates for loans – further, the data employed spanned over the period 1985 to 2011. The overall results of the study indicated the following (Wei, 2013: 52, 53):

- FDI did not reveal a significant relationship with employment - however, taking the autoregressive error structure into consideration, the interest rates for loans has a stronger effect on employment.

- The FDI used in the primary sector has a significant positive effect on employment and that for the secondary sector, the effect of FDI on employment is not significant, while GDP has a large positive effect on employment.
- It was also recommended that the Chinese government could choose to expand the four components of GDP for the secondary sector (see page 52).
- That for the tertiary sector, the effect of total wages is not significant, while FDI has a negative effect on employment and GDP has a positive effect on employment, with FDI's negative effect bigger than GDP's positive effect.

The differentiation of stock markets in China is also acknowledged to be necessary and essential to the determination of value relevance of accounting information in such markets. In distinguishing the A share only firms and the AB share firms, it is added that "these two types of companies also differ in monitoring function performed by independent auditors and that although A-share companies are mostly audited by domestic CPAs, AB-share companies normally hire international accounting firms (the now big Four) to audit their IAS-based financial statements in addition to domestic auditors responsible for Chinese GAAP statements (see page 13).

Chen, Chen and Su also add that "since auditors play an important role in the quality of financial reporting and international CPA firms are of better perceived reputation, they believe that the double monitoring performed by international and domestic auditors in AB[1] companies is another factor contributing to higher quality financial reporting and therefore more relevant accounting information in the market (Chen, Chen & Su, 1999:13)." Further, they are of the opinion that:

whilst A-share companies only follow Chinese GAAP in preparing financial statements, companies that also issue B-share to foreign investors are required to publish both Chinese GAAP-based and IAS-based financial reports. In addition, AB-share companies are also required to disclose the break-down details of the reconciliation discrepancy. Since IAS-based financial statements are, on average, less subject to managers' manipulations (Chen et al.1999), the magnitude of the reconciliation discrepancy is likely to be interpreted by investors as an indication of the quality of Chinese GAAP-based financial statements (Chen, Chen & Su, 1999:13).

Value relevance of accounting information is hence not only determined by whether the market is an A share only company or firm, or whether it is an AB share company, but also based on the level of stock liquidity operating across the market. In this respect, Chen at al (2001:7) also emphasize the importance of distinguishing between institutional[2] and individual holdings – and that "although individual and institutional holdings constitute a company's total tradable shares as in other stock markets, individual investors generate most of the trading volume in the Chinese market."

Value relevance of accounting information is hence a very important issue – not just from the perspective of Foreign Direct Investment and the reliability and relevance of financial and accounting information for investors – whether institutional of individual, but also in matters of Corporate Social Responsibility and financial reporting. This being of crucial importance given the need to enhance the quality and presentation of financial information, the need for comparability and consistency as a means of enhancing the relevance and reliability of financial information. This issue of reconciliation discrepancy hence constitutes a matter in need of urgent redress in capital markets.

Consequently the Enron case in the United States also revealed the flaws in the interpretation of GAAP. In the case (see page 26),[3] it was highlighted that "Enron's accounting was misleading to users and that specifically, the accounting risks for Enron were too high to be considered acceptable or presented fairly. To make them acceptable, adjustments would have been necessary to the reported estimates. Accounting risks should have been reduced to an acceptable level (as suggested by ISA 540) so that the reported numbers were more reliable."

RESEARCH METHODOLOGY

According to Adi and Ogbole (2013:24), In spite of positive benefits of FDI, many scholars have argued that it exerts some negative effect on economic growth in some sectors of the economy, and hence they decided to empirically investigate this latter argument using time series data drawn from three sectors of the Chinese economy (1995 to 2010), namely; primary (natural resources); secondary (manufacturing) and tertiary (service).

- The Douglas' production function forms the theoretical model/framework on which the econometric model used in their study is based. The production function assumes two factor inputs as follows:
  Y= A f (KαLβ) where Y is the total output of the economy;
  L is the Labour utilized in production process;
  K is the capital. A is the technology/total factor productivity.

Their model specification is as follows:

Model specification

Log Yt = β0 + β1log Capt + β2log Labt + μt .... (1)

where Log Yt is the log of real GDP; log Capt is the log of Capital stock at time t; and β2log Labt is the log of Labour used at time t.

They used the augmented Cob-Douglas' production function (a modified form of equation 1), with FDI included as one of the factor inputs by splitting capital into FDI and domestic investment (Dinv.) Equation (1) is thus modified as (see Adi & Ogbole, 2013:26):

Log Yt = β0 + β1log Dinvt + β2log FDIt + β3log Labt +μt....... (2)

LogDinvt is the log of domestic investment at time t
LogFDIt is the log of Foreign Direct Investment at time t
LogLabt is the Labour used at time t.

As well as re-iterating their de-aggregation of economic activity as with the case of Clark (1940) and Fisher (1939), into primary, secondary and tertiary sectors and control domestic investment and labour in order to determine the effect of FDI on each of these sectors (see Adi & Ogbole page 27), they also modify equation (2) as follows:

$$\text{Log Yt} = \gamma 0 + \gamma 1\text{logFDItpri} + \gamma\ 2\text{logFDItsec} + \gamma\ 3\text{logFDItter} + \mu t \ldots\ldots \quad (3)$$

where: Log Yt = log of Real GDP; logFDItpri = log of FDI in primary industry; FDItsec = log of FDI in secondary industry; FDItter = log of FDI in tertiary; $\gamma 1$, $\gamma 2$ and $\gamma 3$ = elasticity in primary, secondary and tertiary industries respectively; $\gamma 0$ = Intercept; μt = Disturbance term (Error term) (which includes other explanatory variables such as domestic investment, fixed capital investment, Educational level, Government policy, labor, technology etc.); and t = Data collected at time t.

Data Description

Other statistics used are as follows (see page 27):

Annual Time series data (from annual FDI utilized in 21 sectors of China's economy) was used but grouped into the national industrial classification in China (primary, secondary and tertiary). The data are in millions of US Dollars. The traditional approach of homogeneity of FDI was assumed and hence the quality of FDI was not ascertained. Domestic capital formation was used as proxy for domestic investment and number of employed persons per 10,000 persons as proxy for labor.

RECOMMENDATIONS AND FUTURE DIRECTIONS

Recommendations cited in their study include:

1. FDI attracting economic policies with greater attention to the secondary and tertiary sectors of the economy;
2. FDI attracting economic policies should pay more emphasis on the secondary sector at the early stage of such policies as this sector exerts growth enhancing spillover effects on other sectors and industries is the economy;
3. Economic policies that de-emphasize FDI into the primary sector as this may exert negative influence on economics growth;
4. Human resource capacity building economic policies that would take advantage of technology transfers and managerial skills acquisition occasioned by such FDI, more so that some corporations technically deprive the host economies ready access to their advance technologies.

Based on their findings, the following were recommended:

1. FDI attracting macroeconomic policies should be formulated to attract FDI as it spurs economic growth, at least the aggregate level.
2. Though FDI should be attracted to both the secondary and tertiary sectors, to spur economic growth, yet emphasis should be on the secondary sector (at the early stage of FDI policy) as it has spillover effect on other industries in the economy through it wider array of economic linkages;

3. FDI inflow into the primary sector should not be encouraged due to its negative growth effect on the industry;
4. Government policy should adequately focus on human resource development through transfers of advanced technological know-how, superior managerial and marketing skills from the foreign corporations.

To the above recommendations, the following considerations must also be mentioned as being in need of redress. When should economic policies and economic objectives take subordinate roles to the implementation of regulations, standards which are aimed at compelling compliance with environmental standards, rules and regulations? As demonstrated by recent global events and falling oil and gas prices, the impact of such a slump in prices, economically, may be more apparent in oil exporting countries than oil importing countries – however, environmental repercussions of continued consumption of oil and gas – in huge quantities, particularly encouraged and fueled by prevailing low prices, and evidenced by higher carbon emissions, generate far reaching consequences which are not only measured monetarily, but also in terms of potential life threatening and toxic emissions.

Environmental Issues and Their Relation with Corporate Social Responsibility and Foreign Direct Investment Continue to Constitute Areas Which Should be Focal Points and in Need of Attention

As highlighted by (Fetscherin, Voss, & Gugler: 243):

Areas that currently underdeveloped and offer opportunities for international business scholars to explore come to light. It is proposed that the following themes need further attention, namely: FDI and environmental issues; FDI and corporate social responsibility; FDI and social impacts; FDI and institutional transformation in China; and FDI and the growth of the Chinese MNE. Inward FDI to developing countries is often accused for negatively impacting the host country by exploiting low environmental standards to shift polluting production processes from countries where these are prohibited (He, 2006; Cole & Elliott, 2005). Further, after relocating polluting facilities, MNEs could engage in institutional spillover and seek to secure an institutional environment that is favorable for them. China has a track record of environmental incidences and low practical environmental standards despite having a written book law (Ross, 1998).

The extent to which environmental regulation can be and has been shaped and exploited in China by MNEs is therefore an important research topic. In particular, MNEs seek to exploit their technological superiority while need to ensure that their product quality and standards are comparable globally. From this perspective MNEs should have a self-interest in supporting and enforcing strict environmental regulation. Environmental issues have gained new momentum with the advancement of greenhouse gas measurements and the global debate on climate change.

As already highlighted in the volume, and with particular regards to the chapters on poverty alleviation and according to World Bank reports (World Bank, 2002:63), private investment in Sustainable Forest Management (SFM) is not only attracting a lot of attention because of the magnitude of funds being invested and diverted towards this industry and sector, but also because of the opportunities it provides for developing countries.

Private sector actors and contributors who have been identified to have an influence on the forest sector, include (Toppinen et al, 2014: 65):

- Large multinational companies
- Local companies of varying sizes
- Individual private investors (such as conservation investments by philanthropists)
- Community or cooperative enterprises which implement sustainable forest management; and
- Small scale forest owners

Further, as regards accountability and corporate governance measures in this sector, focus is considered to continually "shifting towards placing more emphasis on environmental and social sustainability of the industry", not only because of opportunities being provided for emerging economies such as Brazil, Russia, India and China, but also because of the scale and opportunities for investments in such countries, the current challenges being encountered by investors, as well as limited research on MNE's foreign investment in China.

CONCLUSION

As a means of accounting for the gaps in the literature between the period 2011 and 2016, further more recent literature – and particularly empirical related studies on the topic have been consulted. As highlighted by Wei (2013), it is important to recognize and acknowledge that the relationship between FDI and employment is affected by many variables, such as growth of the national population, increased exports, and growth of the domestic economy.

More importantly, it has recently been demonstrated by Iamsiraroj and Doucouliagos (2015) that whilst positive and negative effects may be illlustrated in relation to economic growth, with respect to certain countries, no effects can be deduced as regards the relationship between economic growth and Foreign Direct Investment – with regards to other countries.

When should economic policies and economic objectives take subordinate roles to the implementation of regulations, standards which are aimed at compelling compliance with environmental standards, rules and regulations? Perhaps the need to implement and effectively enforce auditing and regulatory standards will serve as a necessary and compelling impetus and trigger which will pave the way for the implementation and enforcement of environmental standards. As demonstrated by recent global events, economic objectives and policies may be compelled to take subordinate positions where a matters of national interest are at stake, and where certain economic policies and practices serve as a deterrent to foreign investors whose interests are better served by greater demonstration of transparency and financial reporting within the corporate process.

REFERENCES

Adi, A. A., & Ogbole, F. O. (2013). *Foreign Direct Investment in China: Its Sectoral and Aggregate Impact on Economic Growth*. MPRA Paper No. 62166. Retrieved from http://mpra.ub.uni-muenchen.de/62166/

Agosin, M. R., & Machado, R. (2007). Openness and the international allocation of foreign direct investment. *The Journal of Development Studies*, *43*(7), 1234–1247. doi:10.1080/00220380701526410

Agrawal, G., & Khan, M. (2011). Impact of FDI on GDP: A Comparative Study of China and India. *International Journal of Business and Management, 6*(10). doi:10.5539/ijbm.v6n10p71

Akinlo, A. E. (2004). Foreign direct investment and growth in Nigeria: An empirical investigation. *Journal of Policy Modeling*, *26*(5), 627–639. doi:10.1016/j.jpolmod.2004.04.011

Al Nasser, O. M. (2010). How does foreign direct investment affect economic growth? The role of local conditions. *Latin American Business Review*, *11*(2), 111–139. doi:10.1080/10978526.2010.486715

Blonigen, B. A., Davies, R. B., Waddell, G. R., & Naughton, H. T. (2007). FDI in space: Spatial autoregressive relationships in foreign direct investment. *European Economic Review*, *51*(5), 1303–1325. doi:10.1016/j.euroecorev.2006.08.006

Chandana, C., & Peter, N. (2006). *Economic Reforms, Foreign Direct Investment and its Economic Effects in India.* Kiel Working Paper No. 1272.

Chen, et al.. (1999). *Is Accounting Information Value Relevant in the Emerging Chinese Stock Market?* Academic Press.

Chen, , Chen, S., & Su, X. (2001). Is Accounting Information Value-Relevant in the Emerging Chinese Stock Market? *Journal of International Accounting, Auditing & Taxation, 10*(1), 1–22. doi:10.1016/S1061-9518(01)00033-7

Christopher E. (2007). The FDI – Employment Link in a Globalizing World: The Case of Argentina, Brazil and Mexico. Employment Analysis Unit, Employment Strategy Department, Employment Strategy Papers.

Clark, C. (1940). *The Conditions of Economics Press*. London: Macmillian.

Edward, M. G., & Erika, W. (2001), Foreign Direct Investment in China: Effects on Growth and Economic Performance. In Achieving High Growth: Experience of Transitional Economies in East Asia. Oxford University Press.

Fetscherin, M., Voss, H., & Gugler, P. (2010). 30 Years of foreign direct investment to China: An interdisciplinary literature review. *International Business Review*, *19*(3), 235–246. doi:10.1016/j.ibusrev.2009.12.002

Findlay, R. (1978). Relative Backwardness, Direct Foreign Investment and the Transfer of Technology: A Simple Dynamic Model. *The Quarterly Journal of Economics*, *92*(1), 1–13. doi:10.2307/1885996

Fisher, A. G. B. (1939). Production, Primary, Secondary and Tertiary. *The Economic Record*, *15*(1), 24–38. doi:10.1111/j.1475-4932.1939.tb01015.x

Greenaway, D., Sapsford, D., & Pfaffenzeller, S. (2007). Foreign direct investment, economic performance and trade liberalisation. *World Economy*, *30*(2), 197–210. doi:10.1111/j.1467-9701.2007.00887.x

Hirschman, A. (1958). *The Strategy of Economic Development*. New Haven, CT: Yale University Press.

Iamsiraroj, S., & Doucouliagos, H. (2015). *Does Growth Attract FDI?* Discussion Paper No. 2015-18. Retrieved from http://www.economics-ejournal.org/economics/discussionpapers/2015-18http://www.economics-ejournal.org/economics/journalarticles/2015-19

IFRS. (2013). *IASB issues Discussion Paper on Conceptual Framework*. IFRS.

IFRS. (2014). *Fairness of Reporting, Acceptable Accounting Risk and the IASB's Conceptual Framework Review: Insights from the Enron Trial*. IFRS.

Iršová, Z., & Havránek, T. (2013). Determinants of horizontal spillovers from FDI: Evidence from a large meta-analysis. *World Development*, *42*, 1–15. doi:10.1016/j.worlddev.2012.07.001

James, L., & Kam, K. (2006). China's FDI-income growth nexus. *The 17th Annual Conference of the Association for Chinese Economic Studies*. Victoria University.

Jensen, N. M. (2003). Democratic governance and multinational corporations: Political regimes and inflows of foreign direct investment. *International Organization*, *57*(3), 587–616. doi:10.1017/S0020818303573040

Jiang, J., & Masaru, L. (2010). *How does FDI Affect the Regional Economic Growth in China? Evidence from Sub-regions and Industries of the Jiangxi Province, P.R. China*. IDEC, Hiroshima University Discussion Paper.

Jiménez, A. (2011). Political risk as a determinant of Southern European FDI in neighboring developing countries. *Emerging Markets Finance and Trade*, *47*(4), 59–74. doi:10.2753/REE1540-496X470404

Kandil, M. (2011). Financial flows to developing and advanced countries: Determinants and implications. *International Journal of Development Issues*, *10*(1), 60–91. doi:10.1108/14468951111123337

Laura, A. (2003). Foreign Direct Investment and Growth: Does the Sector Matter. Harvard Business School.

Lipsey, R. E. (2002). *Home and Host Country Effects of FDI*. National Bureau for Economic Research, Working Paper No. 92939.

Low, L. (2005). *Foreign Investment in Guangdong: Effects on Economic, Growth and Regional Distribution Determinants*. Hong Kong Baptist University.

Nadia, D. (2006). *Does the Worldwide Shift of FDI from Manufacturing to Services Accelerate Economic Growth - a GMM estimation study*. The Graduate Center, CUNY.

Nicole, M., & Sandra, P. (2005). *FDI Impact on Growth: Spatial Evidence from China*. Academic Press.

Nicole, M., & Sandra, P. (2007). FDI in Chinese Cities: Spillovers and Impact on Growth. The World Economy Journal Compilation, 837-862.

OECD. (2000). *Main determinants and impacts of foreign direct investment on China's economy*. Working papers on international investment Number 2000/4. OECD.

OECD-ILO. (2008). *The impact of Foreign Direct Investment on Wages and Working Conditions Conference On Corporate Social Responsibility Employment and Industrial Relations: Promoting Responsible Business Conduct in a Globalizing Economy*. OECD.

Toppinen, A., Zhang, Y., Hansen, E., Kurki, K. & Li, N. (2014). Role of Corporate Responsibility: Insights From Three Forest Industry Multinationals Investing in China. *Journal of Small Business Management*.

UNCTAD. (1999). *Trends in international investment agreements: An Overview*. UNCTAD.

UNCTAD. (2012). *World Investment Report 2012: Towards a new generation of investment policies*. Geneva: United Nations.

Vincent, P., & Andrea, A. (2004). *Private sector development*. World Bank Group Vice President note 273.

Wan, X. (2010). A Literature Review on the Relationship between Foreign Direct Investment and Economic Growth. *International Business Research, 3*(1).

Wang, J. Y., & Blomstrom, M. (1992). Foreign Investment and Technology Transfer: A Simple Model. *European Economic Review*, 36.

Wei, Y. (2013). *The effect of FDI on employment in China*. Graduate Theses and Dissertations. Paper 13379.

Wen, M. (2003). FDI, Regional Geographical and Market Conditions, and Regional Development: A Panel Study on China. Division of Economics. *RSPAS, ANU, 15*(7), 1–28.

Whalley, J., & Xian, X. (2006). *China's FDI and Non-FDI Economies and the Sustainability of Future High Chinese Growth*. National Bureau Economics Research Working Papers.

Wooster, R. B., & Diebel, D. S. (2010). Productivity spillovers from foreign direct investment in developing countries: A meta-regression analysis. *Review of Development Economics, 14*(3), 640–655. doi:10.1111/j.1467-9361.2010.00579.x

World Bank. (2002). *Engaging the Private Sector in Forest Sector Development.* Retrieved from http://siteresources.worldbank.org/EXTFORSOUBOOK/Resources/02-FSB-Ch02.pdf

World Bank. (2013). *How We Classify Countries.* Retrieved from http://data.worldbank.org/about/country-and-lending-groups

Zhang, K. (2001). How Does FDI Affect Economic Growth in China? *Economics of Transition*, 1-23.

Zhang, K. (n.d.). *Foreign Direct Investment and Economic Growth in China: A Panel Data Study For 1992 -2004*. Academic Press.

Zhang. (2006). *Foreign Direct Investment and Economic Growth in China*. WTO China and Asian Economics held at International University of Business and Economics (UIBC), Beijing, China.

ENDNOTES

1 They argue that the mere existence of the dual-GAAP reporting system in AB companies, along with the disclosure of the reconciliation discrepancy, is a sufficient motivational factor which makes it more likely for AB-share companies to produce higher quality accounting information than A share companies with a one-GAAP reporting system. Also see Chen et al (2001:8).

2 Institutional shareholders in China and distinguished from institutional shareholders from the West. In this regard Chen et al add that "While institutional shareholders in China may hold a large percentage of company's stock, their ability to trade is severely restricted by the government policy and trading rules in China. The institution-held shares can only be transferred to other institutions with approvals from the government. The transfer price is based on negotiations rather than the market price. Consequently, a higher percentage of individual holdings may indicate a more active market, and it is through an active market that stock prices have the potential to fully reflect public information including accounting information." See Chen et al, 2001:7

3 See Fairness of Reporting, Acceptable Accounting Risk and the IASB's Conceptual Framework Review: Insights from the Enron Trial

Chapter 12
The Audit Expectations Gap: Mitigating Information Asymmetries and Corporate Social Responsibility as a Signaling Device

Marianne Ojo
North-West University, South Africa

Teck Heang Lee
Universiti Tunku Abdul Rahman, Malaysia

Azham Ali
Universiti Utara Malaysia, Malaysia

Rosli Mohamad
Universiti Utara Malaysia, Malaysia

Nor Zalina Mohamad Yusof
Universiti Utara Malaysia, Malaysia

ABSTRACT

Corporate Social Responsibility necessitates effective engagement of stakeholders and investors – both at local and international levels. As well as demonstrating that changes in perceptions do not warrant an internship program as a means of reducing the audit expectations gap as misperceptions are still found among respondents on issues of auditing after the completion of the internship program, this chapter will seek to demonstrate why Corporate Social Responsibility endeavors which focus on the mitigation of information asymmetries between the management of an enterprise and local and international investors, also translates to effective corporate social responsibility reporting – in the sense that the engagement of stakeholders - facilitated primarily through legal and ethical responsibilities, ultimately results in the realization of economic and philanthropic responsibilities. From an economic perspective, the mitigation of information asymmetries and systemic risks, without doubt, constitutes the most important of rationales or other objectives that could be presented.

DOI: 10.4018/978-1-5225-0305-7.ch012

INTRODUCTION

As highlighted through this volume, Corporate Social Responsibility necessitates effective engagement of stakeholders and investors – both at local and international levels. Where Corporate Social Responsibilities are fulfilled, and responsibilities and goals within the sphere of Carroll's pyramid of Corporate Social Responsibility are realized, such that the engagement of stakeholders is facilitated primarily through legal and ethical responsibilities, and ultimately through economic and philanthropic responsibilities then Foreign Direct Investment is expected to yield the benefits which accrue to the economy as well those which should materialize through formidable corporate social responsibility reporting.

The issue of "audit expectation gap (AEG)" has been very significant to the accounting profession since the mid-1970s and continues to be debated on until today. In the 1970s and 1980s, massive corporate failures resulted in the accounting profession being severely criticized by the public. For example, in 1973, Equity Funding – an insurance firm based in Los Angeles - collapsed when computer-based fraud was discovered. In May 1982, Drysdale Government Securities collapsed followed by Penn Square Bank two months later. In 1985, the $340 million fraud in ESM Government Securities became the largest securities fraud case ever to come before a US federal court at that time. Auditors were then forced to battle with legal suits taken against them. Meanwhile, the mounting list of corporate failures and abuses, alleged audit failures, and lawsuits against prominent accounting firms generated concern outside the profession which subsequently prompted/resulted in the House Subcommittee on Oversight and Investigations of the Committee on Energy and Commerce conducting a hearing or congressional investigation of the profession, which was chaired by John Dingell, ("Management Accounting", 1985). In defense, the profession defined the concept of AEG and focused public criticism on that concept.

The AEG refers to the difference between what the public and other financial statement users perceive auditors' responsibilities to be and what auditors believe their responsibilities to entail (Marteens & McEnroe, 2001). It is assumed that auditors and users of financial statements have a different perception of the term "external audit" (De Beelde et al., n.d.). Reiter and Williams (n.d) are of the view that the expectations gap refers to the public's expectation that companies with "unqualified" audit opinion, hence a true and fair view of the financial statements, should be free of financial fraud and short-term risks of business failure. These misconceptions of the public feed the legal liability crisis facing the accounting profession (Maccarone, 1993 as cited by Koh & Woo, 1998). Power (1993) called it an institutional process/ referred to it as institutional processes of "blame allocation". Litigation, press comments, internal inquiries are among the methods of allocating the blame.

The US accounting profession also responded to the scandals and criticism by appointing the Commission on Auditors' Responsibilities (the Cohen commission) in 1974 and in 1978. The Cohen Report concluded that there was an "expectations gap" between what auditors did and what the public expected of them. And then in 1986 the Anderson Committee issued its report, Restructuring Professional Standards to Achieve Professional Excellence in a Changing Environment, in response to concerns over the profession's ability to serve public interest and retain public confidence. In 1987 The National Commission on Fraudulent Financial Reporting (popularly known as the Treadway Commission) reported on how fraudulent financial management could be reduced and how auditors could reduce the "expectations gap" between themselves and the public (Mousselli, 2005). This was followed by the ASB's release, in 1988, of nine "expectation gap" standards (SAS no. 53 through 61) which were intended to reduce the gap between what the informed public perceived auditors to be responsible for and what auditors regarded their own responsibilities to be. However, those standards have not succeeded in reducing the gap (Martens & McEnroe, 1991).

The profession is of the view that, in general, the public believes that auditors should take on more responsibilities in detecting fraud, illegal acts, and material misstatements and to improve communication about the nature and the results of audits including giving early warnings about the possibility of business failure (Guy & Sullivan, 1988). Nine new standards are believed to address these issues. These standards cover four broad categories namely: improving external communication, detecting fraud and illegal acts, making audit more effective, and improving internal communication. The new standards also introduce a new auditor's report (Kolins, 1988). However, the public regards auditors as having a duty to society to be responsible for the independent certification/verification of financial statements. One crucial way in which SAS Nos 56-61 fails to express the audit duty and, hence, fails to reduce the expectations gap, relates to auditors' responsibilities with regard to illegal acts by clients (Martens & McEnroe, 1991).

Therefore, despite the profession's efforts to address the issue of AEG, the gap still exists. As mentioned by the SEC's Chief Accountant Michael Sutton, there are five "erroneous/mistaken ideas/perceptions" held by some accountants; one of it being "auditors have closed the expectation gap". Even the new auditing standards on fraud cannot be expected to totally close the gap (Steinberg, 1997). This is supported by Sikka et al.'s (1998) contention that due to social conflict, the meaning of social practices, such as audits, is subject to continuous challenges and (re)negotiations and the gap between competing meanings of audit cannot be eliminated. And so, in 2002, the profession was back in the spotlight following another series of corporate collapses that made history in the US. As noted by Eden et al. (2003), criticism against auditors is renewed with every public corporation's failure and each financial loss the public bears. The firm Arthur Andersen went into demise because of its association with Enron, even though the verdict of obstruction of justice against the firm was overturned in 2005 by the US Supreme Court (Moussalli, 2005). The crisis then led to the enactment of the Sarbanes-Oxley Act 2002 that is said to be "the most sweeping reform ever to affect the accounting profession" (Castellano, 2002). As a result, accounting firms are now regulated entities.

Those corporate crises led to new expectations and accountability requirements, hence, creating this so-called expectation gap. An expectation gap is detrimental to the auditing profession as highlighted by Limperg (1933) (cited in Porter & Gowthorpe, 2001):

If auditors fail to identify society's expectations of them, or to recognize the extent to which they meet (or, more pertinently, fail to meet) those expectations, then not only will they be subject to criticism and litigation but also, if the failure persists, society's confidence in the audit function will be undermined and the audit function, and the auditing profession, will be perceived to have no value (p.5)

In view of the detrimental effect of AEG to the auditing profession, various methods have been suggested in the literature to reduce the AEG. Education is one of the methods often recommended by researchers and practitioners as a means of reducing the AEG (Gramling et al., 2006). However, little is known about the effect of practical experience such as internship programs on the AEG.

Purpose of the Study

The purposes of this study are:

1. To conduct a survey on students' view on issues pertaining to auditors and the audit process; the role of auditors; the groups to whom auditors should be responsible; possible prohibitions and regulations; and how successful auditors are at particular activities.

2. To determine whether there is a significant difference in students' view before and after their completion of the internship program.

Motivation and Significance

This study is carried out because of the importance of both issues, AEG and internship, not only to the accounting profession but also to academics. In Malaysia, accounting internship programs are becoming more important and as noted by Minai et al. (2005), it is a requirement in all public universities in Malaysia. In fact, one of the key recommendations made in the Wan Zahid Higher Education Report1 is for the industrial internship to be made compulsory under the planned national education policy (The Star, 29 April 2006). Industrial internships lasting at least six months are aimed at increasing employment prospects and giving graduates a holistic education. This recommendation has been made despite claims made by few (for example, see Lim, 2006) that industrial training is just a waste of time. Prior to this, the Malaysian Employers' Federation (MEF) made suggestions to the Government in response to the maelstrom surrounding jobless graduates, one of them being to make practical training or internship compulsory (Lim, 2006). The MEF was of the view that the root of the problem of joblessness was founded in the current education system which did not cater to the private sector employers' requirements that offered 90% of the total job opportunities in Malaysia (Utusan Malaysia, 9 September 2004). This is consistent with a proposition made by Kranacher (2006) that one of the several ways to ensure that the public's expectations – that all accountants are competent and ethical – are met is to require internship as part of the education process. Practical experience is seen as an ideal way of exposing students to professional issues. In Universiti Utara Malaysia (UUM), a six month internship program is compulsory for all accounting students. Starting 2006, under UUM's collaboration with AIESEC, students are given opportunities to do their internship training overseas.

On the other hand, the series of corporate collapses in the US in the year 2002 again highlighted the existence of AEG. The audit function, which has been criticized for more than 30 years now, has never been as poor as it is today (Eden et al., 2003). And, as Berardino (former CEO of Anderson Worldwide) put it, following the bankruptcy of Enron and the demise of Arthur Andersen, "… a fundamental crisis of confidence, of understanding" (Frontline Bigger than Enron, n.d.). Donald T. Nicolaisen, Chief Accountant of the SEC recognised that there was still an expectation gap surrounding the auditor's responsibility for detecting fraud and called for the gap to be addressed ("In the Public Interest", 2005). Similarly in Malaysia, most of the auditors cited "the audit expectation gap" and "auditors independence" as their major concerns (Mohamed and Muhamad Sori, 2002). Therefore, there is a need to see/investigate how this crisis can be dealt with in Malaysia (There is a need to investigate/deal with this crisis in Malaysia) especially considering the evidence given by Lee and Palaniappan (2006); Fadzly and Ahmad (2004) and Kasim and Mohd Hanafi (2005) that indicate a wide expectation gap and misconceptions about audit in Malaysia.

Finally, despite the importance of internship programs, no study has been undertaken to examine the effect of practical experience or internships in reducing AEG. Studies on AEG mostly concentrate on the impact of audit education. Previous research done in Malaysia investigate the effect of audit education in reducing AEG (Kasim & Mohd Hanafi, 2005) and the benefits of internship to students (Minai et al., 2005). Pierce and Kilcommins (1996) suggest that although education can make a significant contribution to narrowing the expectation gap, there is a need to supplement it with other measures. Therefore, this study seeks to provide evidence of another way of educating public on audit, which is through internship program.

BACKGROUND AND LITERATURE REVIEW

Audit Expectation Gap

Definitions of the Expectations Gap

The issue revolving round the expectations gap debate relates to the different and inconsistent meanings attributed to the definition of an audit by users of financial statements, the public and the audit profession. The "expectations gap" is the difference between what the public and users of financial statements perceive the role of an audit to be and what the audit profession claim is expected of them during the conduct of an audit. As mentioned in the introduction, this definition is preferred as it is important to distinguish between the audit profession's expectations of an audit on the one hand, and the auditor's perception of an audit on the other hand. Apart from users of financial statements and the general public, an auditor may also perceive a somewhat different interpretation or worse still, fail to comply with the standards set by the audit profession.

According to Pierce and Kilcommins (1995/96), the audit expectations gap is when external auditors' understanding of their role and duties is com-pared against the expectations of user groups and the general public. Liggio (1974) defined the audit expectations gap as the difference between the levels of expected performance as interpreted by the independent accountant and the user of financial statements. These definitions use external auditors as their bench mark rather than the audit profession. The use of the audit profession as bench mark would provide a less subjective element and help narrow the expectations gap. In this sense it would be a preferred definition and would also provide a more stable element of the expectations gap – as the audit profession's expectations are more well-defined than individual auditors' expectations. Reference by Liggio to "users of financial statements," as opposed to members of the general public, however, pro-vides opportunity to narrow the expectations gap as it is obviously more feasible to educate users of financial information (via general meetings etc) than it is to educate members of the general public. This will be discussed in detail later.

The Cohen Commission in 1978 considered whether a gap might exist between what the public expected and what auditors could reasonably expect to accomplish. As rightly stated by Porter (1993, page 50), many definitions have failed to mention the possibility of sub-standard performance by auditors. Even though Porter highlights the importance of considering the *full extent* of the audit expectations gap which can be done by comparing society's expectations of auditors against the perceived performance of auditors, an *easier* comparison can be achieved through an analysis of the more objective components of the expectations gap.

The subjective components of the expectations gap could be made "more objective" by considering and analyzing each component and measures which could be taken to reduce the expectations gap created by each of these components. Unreasonable expectations from the public could be transformed to reasonable expectations of users of financial statements (since it is more feasible to educate users of financial information and since not all members of the public use financial information). After measures have been taken to eliminate the expectations gap relating to the components, a comparison of the reason-able expectations of users of financial statements against what the audit profession expect can then be made. This would provide for a more objective and stable analysis of the expectations gap.

Components of the Expectations Gap

Some commentators have attributed the expectations gap to users' confusion, widespread misunderstanding, ignorance and/or lack of education (Sikka et al, 2003:2). Porter (1993: 50) analyses the total expectations gap into three separate components; namely, sub-standard performance (16%), deficient standards (50%) and unreasonable expectations (34%). As seen from these components, deficient standards component is the most objective component whilst unreasonable expectations and sub-standard performance are the subjective components. Even though unreasonable expectations are subjective, it still constitutes a significant proportion of the expectations gap and cannot be ignored.

Sub standard performance should also not be ignored even though it constitutes just 16% of the expectations gap. After all possible measures have been taken to reduce this component it could be ignored. The sub standard performance element is a problem arising from individual auditors, deficient standards stemming from the audit profession whilst unreasonable expectations emanate from the public. An analysis of the individual components of the expectations gap this way helps to know and understand better how to deal with and reduce these problems creating the expectations gap. In particular, it pro-vides knowledge as to where more efforts should be concentrated namely, the reforms of auditing standards (since this constitutes half the problem).

The expectations gap is an issue for auditors as a greater "expectations gap" would lead to lower credibility, earning potential and prestige associated with their work (Sikka et al, 2003:1). It is also an issue for the public and investors in particular since wealth creation and political stability in a capitalist economy depends significantly on confidence and accountability and external audit is supposed to provide such confidence and accountability (Sikka et al, 2003:1).

Is it Possible to Eliminate the Expectations Gap?

The nature of the components of the expectations gap make it difficult to eliminate.[1] Perceived performance of auditors is an element which is difficult to measure and changes constantly. It is possible to substantially reduce but not totally eliminate.

A number of suggestions have been put forward as a means of narrowing the expectations gap. These include an expanded audit report which offers scope to inform users of what auditors actually do; broadening the role and responsibility of auditors in the areas of fraud, illegal acts and strengthening the perceived independence of auditors (Pierce & Kilcommins, p 3).

The implementation of auditing education has been suggested by Pierce & Kilcommins (p 3) as a means of reducing the expectation gap. According to them, audit education would surely help reduce the expectations gap but would not on its own be sufficient to solve the problem of expectations gap as other components of the expectations gap exist. Audit education would partly solve the problem of unreasonable expectations but not address deficient standards and sub-standard performance. Porter (1993) also adds that in order for audit education to be effective, society should be educated on duties which may reasonably be expected of auditors.

The MacDonald Commission expressed their opinion that audit education was unlikely to be effective in reducing the gap since it concluded that for the most part, public expectations were reasonable and achievable (Pierce & Kilcommins, p 3).

Sikka et al (2003) also argue that he expectations gap can be addressed by the audit profession widening the responsibilities of auditors. Even if new standards were implemented, the issue of enforcement is another matter which needs to be addressed.. As a result, enforcement and audit liability measures are also required.

Elements of the user misunderstanding gap investigated in the study by Pierce and Kilcommins include (i) Duties; (ii) Ethical and legislative framework (iii) Liability (iv) Audit report. The duties' component consists of fraud and error and many commentators have found the expectations gap to be widest in relation to detection and reporting of fraud (Pierce & Kilcommins). The second element, the ethical and legislative framework included issues such as auditor independence, auditor appointment and audit regulation (Pierce & Kilcommins). In relation to auditor liability, Gloeck and de Jager argue that the *Caparo* case added a liability gap to the expectations gap since the public does not know to whom the auditor is liable.

However, it could also be said that the substandard performance component of the expectations gap already embraces the liability gap as auditors are encouraged to underperform – especially where no economic incentives exist for them to owe a duty of care to third party stakeholders.

Historical Background of the Expectations Gap

The origins of auditing date back to Greek, Egyptian and earlier civilizations and whilst there was the emergence of large manufacturing organizations in the eighteenth century, the usual association between audits and fraud detection remained (Sikka et al, 2003). Towards the end of the nineteenth century, a more prominent accountancy profession associated audits with fraud detection even though there was opposition by those who argued that it was unreasonable to expect the auditor to expose fraudulent acts (Sikka et al, 2003). Lawrence Dicksee's text-book is often considered to be the first major auditing text-book and his original book which was published in 1892 stated clearly that the scope of an audit included namely, the detection of fraud, technical errors, and errors of principle. He also stated that the detection of fraud was a most important portion of the auditor's duties and that the whole duty of the auditor was to ascertain the exact state of the client's affairs on a certain date (see page 6). However, other authors such as Robertson and Montgomery argued on the contrary and considered the detection of fraud to be a secondary audit objective (see Sikka et al p 12).

Humphrey et al noted that the position adopted by the profession in Britain during the twentieth century played down any suggestion that auditors had responsibility linked to fraud apart from that which arose from the need to confirm the truth and fairness of financial statements (Humphrey, Moizer & Turley, p55). Chandler et al (1993) reviewed the development of audit objectives between 1840 and 1940 and concluded that the primary objective in relation to public companies between 1830 and 1860 was the verification of financial statements and that more emphasis was put on fraud detection in the late nineteenth century. They also added that the primary audit objective reverted back to financial statements verification in the early part of the twentieth century. However, according to some, in the early part of the twentieth century, fraud detection continued to be regarded as a major audit objective (see Sikka et al, p 13).

According to Brown (1962), the confusion over audit objectives was finally resolved after 1940 and fraud detection was generally accepted to be a secondary objective. However, the objectives of auditing have not been adjusted to conform with operational processes of auditing (Power, 1997: p 21). For example, selective sampling would have corresponded to a primary objective of financial statements verification whilst 100% testing would correspond with the detection of fraud (Power, 1997: p 21).

One important difference between mid-to-late Victorian England and more recent times is the presence or lack of presence of audit expectations (Eu-Jin & Cobbin, 2005).

According to Eu-Jin and P. Cobbin (2005):

- Victorian England is seen as a time of evolution and formulation of expectations and whilst gaps existed in the nineteenth century, they were mainly to do with inconsistencies and not expectations. The differing inconsistent expectations between the judiciary and the auditing profession is illustrated in the landmark cases of *London and General Bank (No 2)* [1895] and *Kingston Cotton Mill (No 2)* [1896] in which the UK Court of Appeal delivered two significant judgements:
    - **London and General Bank (No2)[1895] (Eu-Jin & Cobbin, 2005):** This case concerned the adequacy of security on bank loans, whether shareholders had been deceived as to the condition of the company, whether dividends had been paid out of capital and not available profits. The first instance decision had been against the defendants (the auditor). However in the Appeal Court, LJ Lindley overturned the previous court's decision. His opinion on the auditor's duty is as follows: "...the duty of an auditor is to convey information not to arouse inquiry and although an auditor might infer from an unusual statement that something was seriously wrong, it by no means followed that ordinary people would have their suspicions aroused" (Eu-Jin & Cobbin, 2005). Lindley also stated that it was not the auditor's duty to guarantee the books showing the true position of the company's affairs or to guarantee that the balance-sheet was accurate.
    - **Kingston Cotton Mill (No 2) [1895]:** The first instance decision involved the auditor relying on managers' certificates without the auditor conducting a physical observation of the inventory or taking steps to confirm valuation. In that decision, Vaughan Williams found that the auditors and directors were liable for dividends paid from non-existent profits. However dam-ages sought against them in respect of consequent insolvency on the basis of tort was denied. There was a lot of concern by the audit profession following this decision and the validity of managers' certificates was also called into question. However Lopes in the Appeal Court over-turned the decision in his famous judgement: "It is the duty of an auditor to bring to bear on the work he has to perform that skill, care and caution which a reasonably competent, careful and cautious auditor would use. What is reasonable skill, care and caution must depend on the particular circumstances of each case. An auditor is not bound to be a detective or as was said to approach his work with suspicion or with a foregone conclusion that there is something wrong. He is a watchdog but not a blood-hound. He is justified in believing tried servants of the company in whom confidence is placed by the company."

These two cases were the foundations of certain auditing standards which focused on the accepted fraud and error objectives and placed the nature of the audit on center stage. Apart from establishing that the auditor was not expected to fish out every fraud it established the use reason-able care and skill in his handling of relevant books and records. However, the fact that *London and General Bank (No 2)* [1895] and *Kingston Cotton Mill (No 2)* [1896] confirmed the "reasonableness" test did not completely remove any concern created due to the subjective nature of the reasonableness test.

During the early years of the twentieth century, fraud detection as an audit objective came to be replaced by the objective of checking that the appropriate accounting standards had been adopted and correctly used in constructing financial statements (Sikka et al, p 13). Between 1940 and 1970, fraud detection seemed to be regarded as a secondary audit objective even though this move had not been approved by the Companies Acts of 1948 and 1967.

The re-emergence of fraud detection as an audit objective occurred during the Thatcher administration and was also strongly highlighted during the mid- 1970s property and secondary banking crisis (Sikka et al, p13). In 1985, a working party of the Institute of Chartered Accountants in England and Wales (ICAEW) was established to consider the matter relating to auditors' responsibilities in relation to fraud (Power, p 23). This was prompted as a result of criticisms about the audit function following the col-lapse of Johnson Matthey Bankers (Power, p 23). The collapse of Johnson Matthey Bankers in 1984 also brought about questions on regulation of financial markets and the government being unhappy with the role of auditors, wanted to impose upon auditors a duty to report fraud to the Bank of England even without the knowledge of the client organization (Sikka et al p 16). In response to this, the Institute of Chartered Accountants in England and Wales argued against Lord Justice Bingham's recommendations for an imposition of statutory duty. The working party of the Institute of Chartered Accountants in England and Wales suggested instead that companies should be required by statute to maintain adequate systems of internal control (Power, p 23). Problems which could threaten the auditor client relation-ship, duty of confidentiality were mentioned and these issues though apparent seemed more important than the protection of the public's interests.

- It took another three years for the Institute of Chartered Accountants in England and Wales to issue draft guidance on the auditor's responsibility for detecting fraud and other irregularities. This document was amended further and published as a full operational guideline in February 1990. Management responsibility for setting-up adequate systems of internal controls is high-lighted but auditors are reminded to plan the audit to provide a "reasonable expectation" of detecting material misstatements. "Materiality" has been interpreted in professional guidance as the degree of tolerable or acceptable error in financial statements but like the term "reasonable expectation" it is not specified beyond this. It is important that further clarification in relation to these terms are provided as the question to whether auditors have a responsibility to detect fraud depends on the interpretation of these terms. The guidance document does not deny the auditor's duty to detect fraud – however, it qualifies this duty by the "reasonable expectation" term. (see Power, p 23)

Materiality

The International Standard on Auditing (ISA UK and Ireland) 320 establishes standards and pro-vides guidance on the concept of materiality and how this relates to audit risk. The concept of "materiality" is defined in the International Accounting Standards Board's "Framework for the Preparation and Presentation of Financial Statements" as follows:

Information is material if its omission or misstatement could influence the economic decisions of users taken on the basis of the financial statements. Materiality depends on the size of the item or error judged in the particular circumstances of its omission or misstatement. Thus, materiality provides a threshold or cut-off point rather than being a primary qualitative characteristic which information must have if it is to be useful.

The problem with this definition revolves round the word "judged". The assessment of materiality is based on professional judgement (ISA UK and Ireland 320. 4).

In planning the audit, the auditor establishes an acceptable level of materiality in order to detect quantitatively material misstatements (ISA UK and Ireland 320. 5). In addition, both the amount (quantity) and nature (quality) of misstatements need to be considered (ISA UK and Ireland 320. 5).

The auditor also needs to consider the possibility of misstatements of relatively small amounts which could cumulatively have a material effect on the financial statements (ISA UK and Ireland 320.6). An error could be potentially material if it is repeated each month for a particular month end procedure statements (ISA UK and Ireland 320.6). Materiality at both the entire financial statement level and in relation to classes of transactions, account balances and disclosures also need to be considered (ISA UK and Ireland 320.7). Legal and regulatory requirements may also affect materiality (ISA UK and Ireland 320.7).

From the above definition and standard, it can be seen that a lot of subjective issues affect the concept of materiality. Legal and regulatory issues which may affect materiality need to be more clearly defined and an error estimate given by the Auditing Practices Board. A lot of matters left to be judged by the individual auditor should be also be determined and clearly set out in the standards.

"Material significance" is defined by ISA (UK and Ireland) 250 Section B:

A matter or group of matters is normally of material significance to a regulator's function when, due either to its nature or its potential financial impact, it is likely of itself to require investigation by the regulator. (ASB Bank, n.d.)

Whilst judgement is also required by the auditor in determining whether a matter is or likely to be of material significance, material significance does not have the same meaning as materiality in the context of financial audit (ISA, UK & Ireland, 250. 62). A particular event which may have little impact on the financial statements of an entity may be of a nature or type that is likely to change the perception of the regulator (ISA, UK & Ireland, 250. 62).

ISA (UK and Ireland) 240: The Auditor's Responsibility to Consider Fraud in an Audit of Financial Statements

In carrying out the above function, the auditor is expected to maintain a sceptic attitude through-out the audit despite the fact that his past experience with the entity about the honesty and integrity of management (ISA, UK & Ireland 250. 24). The auditor also con-siders reports from the deposit taker's compliance department, legal department and money laundering reporting officer with reviews under-taken by third parties such as reports prepared under section 166 of the Financial Services and Markets Act 2000 (ISA, UK & Ireland, 250. 42).

Examining the Social Framework of the Audit

Sikka et al have argued that meanings of the audit are determined by particular social arrangements which are always subject to change and as a result it is difficult for the audit to have a fixed meaning (Sikka et al, p 5). However it will be argued that even though social and global changes have shaped the role of the auditor and hence the role of an audit, some components within the definition of an audit can still be considered as fixed. The advent of technology, internal control systems have definitely transformed the environment within which an audit operates. Periodical surveys should be carried out in the general public to ascertain what many perceive to be the role of an auditor. These surveys should be carried out only after the public has been sufficiently educated about the role of the audit. After this draft proposals should be made whereby public is still involved is invited to submit their ideas or challenge any proposals. The draft proposals on the definition of an audit should be a more acceptable definition by popular consensus – as realized through the opinions received from surveys carried out on the public. There should be an objective component within the definition of an audit which would be the public's reasonable expectations. These expectations could be deemed reasonable as public would already have been educated about the role of auditors, nature of audits before a survey is carried out to find out what the public want from an audit.

The subjective component definition of an audit would be revised from time to time – depending on social, environmental changes. The objective component would also be revised from time to time based on periodical surveys. In the absence of an imposition of statutory duty on auditors, the fraud and error detection role of an auditor seems to be a role which should become a primary audit objective – as this would help bring about some form of accountability. Of course, the auditor cannot be expected to sniff out every form of fraud – only material ones. The cases of Enron and Parmalat certainly involved huge amounts of money which are deemed significant and material from a subjective or an objective point of view. Why were the auditors involved not able to detect such material amounts?

In the absence of appropriate audit liability measures, there are no incentives to deter the external auditor from such gross misconduct. The re-instatement of fraud detection (and also error detection) as a primary audit objective which constitutes a fixed component definition of an audit (as the public has every right to expect this duty from the auditor – provided issues relate to material fraud) would certainly help bring some form of accountability within the audit profession.

FRAUD AND ERROR DETECTION ROLE OF AN AUDIT

The meaning attributed by users of financial statements as regarding the definition of an audit cannot be fixed but elements within the definition of what constitutes an audit can. Such components within the definition of an audit include the fraud and error role.[2]

The role of fraud and error detection is one which is encouraged. If the public (and more specifically, users of financial statements) were educated about this role, it would be deemed to be a reasonable expectation. Surveys should be conducted frequently to determine if this role is one which is perceived by the greater part of users of financial information as that which is the role of the auditor.

Users of financial information should also be made aware that the fraud and error role is applicable to *material* misstatements. The role of the auditor in verifying financial statements and pro-viding an opinion in relation to those statements is one which relies greatly on the subjective professional judgment as to materiality.

MAIN FOCUS OF THE CHAPTER

Research Design

Methods of Data Collection

A four-page questionnaire was distributed to UUM's Bachelor of Accounting students before they left for internship and after they finished the program. The questionnaires were adapted and modified from Ferguson et al. (2000). Part 1 sought to solicit students' view, before and after internship program, about auditors and auditing process; part 2 was based on the role of auditors; part 3 asked questions that related to the groups to whom auditors should be responsible; part 4 was based on propositions relating to possible prohibitions and regulations; part 5 asked students' views on how successful auditors were at particular activities; and finally part 6 was based on students' demographic information. A seven-point Likert scale was used in the questionnaire with a "7" indicating "strongly agree" and a "1" indicating "strongly disagree".

As the basic concept of an expectation gap concerns differences in opinions, the use of a questionnaire survey provides some justification as a research approach. Variation in the familiarity with the audit function is not really a problem as the purpose of the study is to identify where different perceptions about auditing exist, not the validity or authority of particular perceptions (Humphrey et al., 1993).

Data Analysis

As the study is a non-hypothetical deductive survey by nature, the main analysis is on statistical significance of one of the central tendency attributes, which is the mean of responses given by the students before and after the completion of the internship program. Paired t-tests were used to examine the significance or otherwise apparent differences of the students' view before and after the internship program of each of the question asked on 5 different parts as mentioned above. T tests were also used to determine the overall existence of each part (i.e. Section I-V) of the questionnaire.

FINDINGS AND DISCUSSION

Demographic of Respondents

There were 117 respondents who responded to the survey. The demographic details are shown in Table 1. 91 of the respondents are Malay, 22 are Chinese, 2 are Indian and 2 for other races. 7 of the respondents had undertaken audit work experience for a period of 6 months or less prior to the internship program. In view of the fact that the number of respondents with audit work experience was limited to 6% and that the period of work experience for most these respondents was less than 6 months, no significant difference should therefore be expected from their responses as compared to those without audit work experience.

Table 1. Analysis of demographic data

	Frequency	Percent
Race		
Malay	91	77.8
Chinese	22	18.8
Indian	2	1.7
Other	2	1.7
Total	117	100
Gender		
Male	11	9.4
Female	106	90.6
Total	117	100
Prior working experience in audit industry		
No	110	94
Yes	7	6
Total	117	100
Period of experience		
Less than 3 months	3	43
3-6 months	4	57
Total	7	100

Views about Auditors and the Audit Process

Section I of Table 2 shows the responses to 13 statements on views about auditors and the audit process. A mean value of greater than "4" was deduced from 11 statements based on responses of the respondents prior to the internship program. This implies that respondents agree to these 11 statements. Conversely, a mean value of less than "4" indicates that respondents prior to internship program disagree that: i) an audit is of very little benefit to a company (Q6); and ii) Auditors do not understand the problems of business (Q8). The disagreements relating to these statements imply that respondents acknowledge the values of auditing and the ability of auditors to understand the problems of a business. The possible reason for such responses could be due to the fact that respondents have gained sufficient knowledge from the auditing education in the university in order for them to recognize the value of auditing and the fundamental audit process prior to the internship program.

As shown in Section I of Table 2, respondents responded differently after the completion of the internship program with respect to 9 of the 13 statements. Significant differences are found on statements 2, 3, 4, 6, 7, 8, 9, 10 and 12. Overall, the results reveal that the internship program has influenced the perceptions of the respondents significantly in relation to the views of auditors and the audit process. The significant changes in perceptions are evidenced by the T-test showed in Section I of Table 3. [t (104)=2.638, p=0.10].

The nature of the changes in perceptions prior to and after the internship program can be analyzed through the T-Statistic in Section I of Table 2. A positive T-Statistic in statements 2, 8, 9, 10 and 12

Table 2. Pre-post changes in students' views

Question	Pre	Post	T-Statistic
Section 1: Views about auditors and the audit process			
1	5.15	4.98	1.413
2	5.08	4.79	2.315**
3	4.48	4.98	-3.298***
4	4.04	4.32	-1.898*
5	4.17	4.33	-1.435
6	3.02	3.45	2.631***
7	4.63	4.93	-2.158**
8	3.31	3.00	2.131**
9	5.21	4.56	4.485****
10	5.54	5.14	3.487****
11	5.34	5.18	1.324
12	5.23	4.98	2.143**
13	5.44	5.33	1.000
Section II: View about auditors' roles			
1	5.91	5.89	0.159
2	5.26	5.56	-2.254**
3	4.61	4.97	-2.866***
4	4.58	4.82	-1.58
5	4.94	4.99	-0.325
6	5.24	5.3	-0.467
7	4.92	5.12	-1.586
8	5.13	5.23	-0.911
9	5.07	5.27	-1.785*
10	5.31	5.51	-1.669*
Section III: Views about groups to whom auditors should be responsible			
1	5.33	5.4	-0.493
2	4.79	4.85	-0.377
3	5.23	5.27	-0.24
4	4.82	4.85	-0.217
Section IV: Views about possible prohibitions and regulations on audit firms			
1	5.21	5.31	-0.622
2	3.67	3.8	-0.73
3	4.47	4.79	-1.989**
4	4.16	4.54	-2.933***
5	4.6	4.96	-2.913***
6	5.26	5.42	-1.469
7	5.1	5.13	-0.212

continued on following page

Table 2. Continued

Question	Pre	Post	T-Statistic
8	4.77	4.84	-0.59
9	4.71	4.82	-0.914
Section V: Views about how successful auditors are at Particular activities			
1	5.31	5.22	0.699
2	5.4	5.18	1.858
3	5.64	5.83	-1.652
4	5.34	5.25	0.728
5	5.31	5.06	1.928*
6	5.18	5.04	0.908
7	5.26	5.22	0.282
8	5.77	5.48	2.466**
9	5.47	5.2	1.685*
10	6.03	5.89	1.202
11	5.66	5.55	0.819
12	5.56	5.56	0.000
13	5.48	5.44	0.26
14	5.8	5.79	0.061
15	5.93	5.63	1.959*
16	5.33	5.16	1.149
17	5.41	5.05	2.396**
18	5.84	5.78	0.386
19	5.74	5.55	1.3

* Significant at 1% significance level, **Significance at 5% significance leve1, *** Significant at 10% significance level

indicates that there is a significant change in perceptions where respondents rated these statements at a lower rate after the completion of the internship program as compared to their responses prior to the internship program. These statements are: i) Too much is expected of auditors by the investing community (Q2); ii) auditors do not understand the problems of business (Q8); iii) auditors provide significant protection against fraud (Q9); iv) auditors should be identifying ways to improve management efficiency (Q10); and v) audit committees comprising non executive directors should improve auditor independence (Q12). On the contrary, a negative T-Statistic was found in 4 of the statements that showed significant differences in responses after the completion of the internship program. They are: i) auditors are too concerned with keeping company management happy (Q3); ii) the audit process is seriously weakened by imprecise auditing standards (Q4); iii) an audit is of very little benefit to a company (Q5); and iv) audits generally take too long to complete (Q7).

The manner of change in perceptions of the respondents implied that respondents had gained supplementary knowledge in addition to the auditing knowledge acquired from the university which allowed them to exercise their judgment more critically in evaluating the statements. This is evidenced by a greater or lesser extent of agreement by the respondents in relation to these questions. Of special interest are Q6, Q7 and Q8.

Table 3.

Section I						
	Perception of the students		**N**	**Mean**	**Std. Deviation**	**Std. Error Mean**
Index	Prior internship program		117	4.6762	0.49917	0.04871
	After internship program		117	4.5267	0.51918	0.05067
Independent Samples Test						
		t	**df**	**Sig. (2-t tailed)**	**Mean Difference**	**Std. Error Difference**
Index	Equal variances assumed	2.638	104	0.10	0.1495	0.5666
Section II						
	Perception of the students		**N**	**Mean**	**Std. Deviation**	**Std. Error Mean**
Index	Prior internship program		117	5.0904	0.70424	0.06567
	After internship program		117	5.2730	0.79077	0.07374
Independent Samples Test						
		t	**df**	**Sig. (2-t tailed)**	**Mean Difference**	**Std. Error Difference**
Index	Equal variances assumed	2.213	114	0.029	0.18261	0.08253
Section III						
	Perception of the students		**N**	**Mean**	**Std. Deviation**	**Std. Error Mean**
Index	Prior internship program		117	5.0431	0.99579	0.09246
	After internship program		117	5.0927	0.5070	0.08827
Independent Samples Test						
		t	**df**	**Sig. (2-t tailed)**	**Mean Difference**	**Std. Error Difference**
Index	Equal variances assumed	-0.400	115	0.690	-0.04957	0.12390
Section IV						
	Perception of the students		**N**	**Mean**	**Std. Deviation**	**Std. Error Mean**
Index	Prior internship program		117	4.7040	0.68869	0.06658
	After internship program		117	4.8712	0.68869	0.06658
Independent Samples Test						
		t	**df**	**Sig. (2-t tailed)**	**Mean Difference**	**Std. Error Difference**
Index	Equal variances assumed	2.544	106	0.012	0.16719	0.06571
Section V						
	Perception of the students		**N**	**Mean**	**Std. Deviation**	**Std. Error Mean**
Index	Prior internship program		117	5.6101	0.66697	0.06916
	After internship program		117	5.4556	0.68030	0.07054
Independent Samples Test						
		t	**df**	**Sig. (2-t tailed)**	**Mean Difference**	**Std. Error Difference**
Index	Equal variances assumed	1.876	92	0.064	0.15450	0.08236

The mean of 3.02 indicates that respondents prior to the internship program disagreed that an audit is of little benefit to a company (Q6). Significantly different responses were found with respect to this statement after completion of the internship program. The mean of the responses increased to 3.45.

The increase in mean implies that respondents disagree with this statement to a lesser extent and such responses may be due to the practical experience gained from the internship program which allows them to have a more realistic view on the actual contribution of an audit to a company.

Likewise, the mean for the statement Q(7): audits generally take too long to complete increased from 4.63 to 4.93. The internship program allowed the respondents to evaluate this statement more reliably as they were likely to experience an actual audit assignment during the period of internship. As such, they are in a better position to express their opinion on this statement. The increase in mean implies that respondents agree to a greater extent that an audit takes too long to complete. This result is likely to indicate that respondents acknowledge a longer time is needed in order for auditors to perform a good quality audit assignment.

In contrast, the mean for Q(8): auditors do not understand the problems of business, decreased from 3.31 to 3.00. This implies that respondents disagree to a greater extent with regard to this statement. The reason for respondents evaluating this statement differently may be due to the opportunity of being in contact with auditors during the period of internship which allowed them to have a closer observation of auditors' abilities and competence in performing their duties. As a consequence, more credible and reliable evaluation of this statement could be given after the completion of the internship program. The results indicate that respondents agree that auditors are capable of understanding the problems of businesses.

Views about Auditors' Roles

Section II of Table 2 presents the responses on two issues; namely, i) the aspects of what the auditor's role should be with respect to clients' audited financial statements; and ii) the aspects on what the auditor's role should be with respect to the audited firm. The results reveal that a mean value of greater than "4" was found for both prior to and after the internship program. This implies that respondents are of the opinion that these are the present responsibilities of auditors in connection to the financial statements and the audited firm.

The present statutory requirement based on Section 174 of the Companies Act 1965 in Malaysia requires auditors to i) report to the members of the company on the accounts; ii) ensure timely submission of the audit report by the company; iii) express an opinion on the truth and fairness of the financial statements; and iv) ensure compliance with the requirements of the Company Act 1965 and the applicable "approved accounting standards". The "approved accounting standards" are those standards that are issued or approved by the Malaysian Accounting Standards Board (MASB). Under Section 174 (8) of the Companies Act 1965, auditors are required to report to the Registrar on any breach or non-compliance of any provision of the Companies Act 1965. Auditors are required to follow the Malaysian Approved Standards on Auditing (MASA) during the conduct of their audits. Any breach of, or failure to comply with MASA could be considered as conduct discreditable to the profession, and this could lead to disciplinary action against the auditors involved.

With effect from 30 September 2004, the Malaysian Institute of Accountants (MIA) implemented the Anti-Money Laundering Act 2001 (the AMLA, 2001). The AMLA (2001) requires auditors, accountants and company secretaries who are members of the MIA to report suspicious transactions of their clients to the Financial Intelligence Unit in the Bank Negara (Central Bank of Malaysia). In addition, Section 50 of the Securities Industry Act 1983 stipulates that auditors are required to report to the Securities Commission (SC) on any irregularities that are found during the course of the audit which may jeopardise the funds or property of the shareholders.

A review of the present statutory requirements in Malaysia shows that only 6 statements represent the current existing duties of auditors in Malaysia. These are: i) auditors should ensure that audited financial statements comply with Generally Accepted Accounting Principles (Q1); ii) auditors should ensure that audited financial statements are consistent with conventional accounting practices (Q2); iii) auditors should ensure that audited financial statements contain no significant deliberate distortions (Q3); iv) auditors should ensure that audited financial statements contain no significant accidental errors (Q4); v) auditors should ensure the appropriate regulatory authorities have been informed of any significant malpractice; and vi) auditors should ensure the balance sheet provides a fair valuation of the company. Statements 5, 6, 7, and 8 are currently not statutory requirements for auditors in Malaysia.

The mean values of "4" for respondents prior to and after the internship program shows that respondents failed to recognize that the duties stated in statements 5, 6, 7, and 8 are not presently required of auditors in Malaysia. These duties are: i) auditors should ensure that all significant fraud is detected (Q5); ii) auditors should ensure that a satisfactory system of internal controls is being operated (Q6); iii) auditors should ensure that the future viability of the company is not in doubt (Q7); and iv) auditors should ensure that the company is being run efficiently (Q8). According to the MASA, the management of the companies should be responsible for these duties instead of the auditors.

The findings also show that respondents responded significantly differently with respect to the four statements after completion of the internship program. They are: i) auditors should ensure that the audited financial statements are consistent with conventional accounting practices (Q2); ii) auditors should ensure that the audited financial statements contain no significant deliberate distortions (Q3); iii) auditors should ensure that the appropriate regulatory authorities have been informed of any significant malpractice (Q9); and iv) auditors should ensure that the balance sheet provides a fair valuation of the company (Q10). The change in perceptions after the completion of the internship program with regards to Q2 (mean from 5.26 to 5.56), Q2 (mean from 4.61 to 4.97), Q9 (mean from 5.07 to 5.27) and Q10 (mean from 5.31 to 5.51) indicated that the internship program had strengthened the knowledge of respondents with respect to the duties of auditors required by statutes in Malaysia. The T-test shows in Section II of Table 3. [t (114)=2.213, p=0.029] shows that overall, there is a significant difference in opinions in relation to auditors' roles prior to and after completion of the internship program.

SOLUTIONS AND RECOMMENDATIONS

Views about Groups to Whom Auditors Should be Responsible

This section elicits the opinions of respondents in respect of the parties whom auditors should be responsible to if a company's financial statements are significantly misstated and the audit report does not disclose the company's true position regarding the misstatement. Arens et al. (2006) point out that, auditors can be liable to their clients and under certain circumstances to parties other than their clients under the common law and the statutory law in Malaysia.

When auditors fail to carry out their duties competently, legal actions can be taken against them by various parties. Gramling et al. (1996) claim that under the common law and law of tort, auditors may be responsible to parties in privity (e.g. audit client), primary beneficiaries (e.g. a lender requiring an audit before providing financing), foreseen and limited classes (e.g. parties entitled to receive an audit report in fulfillment of some business transaction; shareholders and bondholders are not included), and foreseeable parties (e.g. investors).

Legal action can also be taken against auditors in Malaysia for violating the Securities Commission (Amendment) Act 2003 and Companies Act 1965. Under Section 57 of the Securities Commission (Amendment) Act 2003, any third party who purchased securities described in the registration statement may sue the auditor for material misrepresentation or omission in audited financial statements included in the registration statement. In addition, under Section 46 of the Companies Act 1965, auditors are liable to pay compensation to persons who purchase shares or debentures on the faith of the prospectus (authorized by auditors) for any loss sustained by reason of untrue statements or willful non-disclosure of any matter which is material (Arens et al., 2006).

The results in Section III of Table 2 (the mean value of greater than "4") show that prior to the internship program, respondents held auditors to be responsible to:

1. Existing holders (Q1);
2. Potential shareholders (Q2);
3. Existing creditors (Q3); and
4. Potential creditors (Q4).

Consistently, the results show that respondents held auditors to be responsible to the same parties after the completion of internship program. This is indicated by the mean value of greater than "4". Evidenced in Section III of Table 3 [t(115)=-0.400, p=0.690], there were no significant changes in the overall opinions among respondents prior to and after the completion of the internship program with respect to the parties to whom auditors should be responsible to.

The findings reveal that, the formal audit education given to the respondents in the university prior to the internship program had failed to educate the respondents that the potential shareholders and potential creditors were not considered as foreseeable parties mentioned above. The internship program had also failed to notify the respondents with regards to whom auditors should be liable for.

Overall, the results suggested that despite the formal audit education in the university and the practical experience gained from the internship program, respondents held auditors to be responsible to the groups of people who are currently not acknowledged under the common law and statutory law in Malaysia. This in turn also indicated an unreasonable expectation among respondents of the auditors on this issue.

Views about Possible Prohibitions and Regulations on Audit Firms

Section IV of Table 2 presents the responses of eight propositions related to the prohibitions and regulations that should be placed on an audit firm, and one statement about the profit-making motive of the audit firm. The results show that respondents prior to the internship program, agreed to all the prohibitions in statements 1, 3, 4, 5, 6, 7, 8 and 9 imposed on the audit firms except for the provision of management advisory services to its audit clients. Respondents responded in a similar way after they had completed their internship program as they agreed to all prohibitions imposed on the audit firms except for the provision of management advisory services. However, significant difference was found with respect to statements 3, 4 and 5 indicating that respondent agreed to these statements to a greater extent.

Under Section 10(a) of the Accountants Act 1967, the MIA is empowered to establish a code of conduct for the inculcation of sound professional practice and for the prevention of illegal dishonorable practices by members. This code of conduct, called MIA By-Laws (On Professional Ethics, Conduct, and Practice), consists of general statements of ideal conduct or specific rules that define unacceptable behavior. MIA members are required to observe the standards of professional conduct and refrain from committing unprofessional conduct which includes, but is not confined to, any act or default likely to bring discredit to the members, the Institute, or the accounting profession.

Under the MIA By-Laws, auditors are not explicitly prohibited from any activities as prescribed in statements 1 to 9 (except for statement 1). However, recommendations have been made to promote and strengthen auditor independence. For example, even though the code of conduct in MIA By-Law section 290 does not prohibit the provision of management advisory services to the audit client; auditors are however, advised in relation to their financial dependency on those management advisory services- that these should not jeopardize their professional independence while performing audit services for the clients.

The significant difference in responses after the completion of the internship program found in statements 3, 4 and 5 suggests that respondents agree to a greater extent that: i) primary objective of auditors should be providing quality auditing services instead of maximizing auditors wealth; ii) auditors should not be financially over dependent on one audit client as this is likely to create threats to the independence of the audit firm; and iii) audit rotation is essential. As shown in Section IV of Table 3 [t(106)=2.544, p=0.012], overall there are significant changes in opinions among respondents prior to and after the completion of the internship program with respect to the propositions related to prohibitions and regulations on an audit firm.

The results of the section reveal that respondents are of the opinion that regulations are needed for audit firms. Generally respondents agreed to most of the propositions of the prohibitions and regulations prior the internship program. A greater extent of agreement (increase in mean value) to the prohibitions and regulations were found among respondents after the completion of internship program. Such responses are likely to suggest that after gaining the working experience in an audit firm, respondents may not find the present regulations sufficient in maintaining the professionalism required in the auditing profession in Malaysia. As such, further regulations are needed to strengthen the audit practice in Malaysia.

Views about How Successful Auditors are at Particular Activities

An evaluation of the auditors' performance is shown in Section V of Table 2. The purpose of this section is to elicit the perceptions of respondents with regards to 19 performance attributes of the auditors. The results presented in Section V of Tables 2 show that respondents perceive auditors as having performed well on all 19 activities. This is evidenced by the mean value of greater than "4" from the responses. Consistently, respondents were also satisfied with the performance of auditors after they had completed their internship program. This is also indicated by the mean value of greater than "4" as shown in Section V of Table 2.

As shown in Section V of Table 3 [t(92)=1.876, p=0.064], significant differences were found from the overall responses of the 19 performance attributes even though the respondents were overall satisfied with the performance of the auditors after the completion of the internship program. Significant differences were found to exist between 5 performance attributes, namely: i) predicting future (Q5); ii) detecting errors and irregularities (Q8); iii) preventing errors and irregularities (Q9); iv) reporting truthfully(Q15); and v) limiting their own legal responsibility (Q17).

The results in Section V of Table 2 also reveal that a positive T Statistic was found with respect to all of the 5 performance attributes. This indicates that respondents had rated the performance attributes at a low rate after they had completed their internship program. This likely to suggest that respondents had gained a more realistic view of the competence of auditors. For example, based on the competition market auditors may find it difficult to report truthfully as they are financially dependent on audit clients. Moreover, as auditors faced significant increase in criticism and litigation in the present auditing environment, limiting their legal responsibility could also be unlikely. In addition, in order to be competitive in the audit market, auditors might have to compromise audit quality. Thus, in view of the current situation of the audit profession in Malaysia, auditors were likely to be evaluated at a lower rate by the respondents after the completion of the internship program. This indeed also reflected the realignment of the idealistic view of the respondents prior to the internship program to a more realistic view of the auditors after the internship program was completed.

In addition, respondents rated the performance of auditors at a lower rate and this could likely be explained by the fact that auditors are currently not required by statute to perform the duties of predicting the future viability of the company, and preventing and detecting of errors and irregularities of audited companies. As such, auditors may not have focused on these duties in the course of the audit. As a result, respondents may not have been impressed by auditors' performance on these duties as per their observation during the internship program. Therefore, a low rate was awarded in respect of these activities.

IMPLICATION ON AUDIT EXPECTATION GAP

Research, for example Mohamed and Muhamad Sori (2002), Fadzly and Ahmad (2004), and Lee and Palaniappan (2006), confirmed the existence of an AEG in Malaysia. The existence of the gap is due to different perceptions between the public (including clients) and auditors with respect to the actual roles of auditors; the services provided by auditors; and issues on auditors' independence (Mohamed and Muhamad Sori, 2002). A wide gap was found regarding auditors' responsibilities in fraud detection and prevention, preparation of financial statements and accounting records, and in internal controls (Fadzly and Ahmad, 2004). The analysis of the AEG in Lee and Palaniappan (2006) indicated the existence of unreasonable expectation on the part of users; deficient standards of auditing in Malaysia; and deficient performance of auditors

An AEG is detrimental to the auditing profession as it affects the perceived value of auditing and the reputation of auditors (Wa and Selva, 1993). Education has been prescribed as a means of reducing the AEG (Monroe and Woodliff, 1993; Gramling et al,.1996; and Kasim and MohdHanafi, 2005).However; no study has yet been conducted to examine the effect of internship program on the AEG. Hence, this study aims to provide such contribution to auditing literature. Significant changes in perceptions were found in this study with respect to auditing issues after the completion of an internship program. This section intends to discuss the implications of these changes in perceptions on the AEG.

Significant changes were found after the completion of an internship program on the perceptions of the respondents with respect to: i) issues about auditors and the auditing process (Section I); ii) role that should be played by auditors (Section II); iii) prohibitions and regulation on an audit firm (Section IV); and iv) competency of auditors on various activities (Section V).An analysis of the results shows an internship program may have the following implications on the AEG:

1. Respondents, after the internship program, held auditors to be responsible for fraud prevention and detection; guaranteeing the viability of the business; and efficiency of the internal control. These duties are not currently required under Malaysian statutory law. Lee and Palaniappan (2006) assert that duties, for example, related to the prevention and detection of fraud and errors are regarded as unreasonable expectation of auditors. Hence, this implies that misperceptions of the actual role of auditors are still found among respondents even where they have completed an internship program in an audit firm.
2. Respondents held auditors to be liable to potential shareholders and creditors after the completion of the internship program. This in turn indicated the existence of an expectation gap as it extended the actual scope of auditors' liabilities. Such responses were also likely to explain the phenomenon of the increase in the number of litigation cases against the audit profession in the past decades.
3. Respondents agreed to a greater extent after the completion of an internship program on the prohibition and regulation of auditors. Such responses are likely to cause an expectation gap as it is unlikely for auditors to agree on the imposition of higher prohibitions and regulations against them.
4. Respondents recognized the competence of auditors in various activities to a greater extent after the completion of the internship program. The increased recognition of the competence of auditors after the internship program could imply that the deficient performance gap found in Lee and Palaniappan (2006) may be reduced through an internship program. The possible reason for better evaluation of auditors' performance may be due to fact that respondents could have gained a better insight into the performance of auditors during the internship period.

Identifying Contributory Factors to the Audit Expectations Gap (AEG) as a means of Enhancing Corporate Social Responsibility and Financial Reporting

As well as the engagement of stakeholders in the financial reporting process, it is vital to ensure that communication between management of an enterprise and stakeholders (wider stakeholders inclusively) is facilitated in such a way that information asymmetries are optimally mitigated.

Factors which are usually contributory to such information asymmetries between management, investors and users of financial information include the following:

- Lack of verifiability of values (confirmatory and predictive values) within the financial statements
- Lack of disclosure of items – and particularly material items within financial statements
- Lack of transparency or accessibility to vital information such as is necessary to assist investors or users of financial information in the decision making process
- Lack of comparability and consistency of items such as to facilitate understandability, informed judgements and reliable predictions

Recent initiatives of the IASB and the FASB aimed at addressing the above issues include the provision of more useful information to users through new disclosure requirements. With respect to IFRS adoption, the facilitation of convergence between IFRS and US GAAP has constituted top priority – particularly in respect of IFRS 16 (Leases). Issues identified with the previous Leases Standard, IAS 17 Leases, included namely the following:

The absence of information about leases on the balance sheet meant that investors and analysts did not have a complete picture of the financial position of a company, and were unable to properly compare companies that borrow to buy assets with those that lease assets, without making adjustments.

Application of previous lease accounting requirements did not necessitate the reporting of many leasing transactions. Further, listed companies using IFRS or US GAAP, it is further highlighted (see IFRS, 2016: page 3), disclosed almost US$3 trillion of off balance sheet lease commitments in 2014.

Prioritizing the Pyramid of Corporate Social Responsibility

Prioritizing the Pyramid of Corporate Social Responsibility Based on Importance of Responsibilities

As resonated throughout this volume, assigning the order of priority to responsibilities within the pyramid of Corporate Social Responsibility, such priorities comprising of economic, legal, ethical and philanthropic responsibilities, is not so straightforward given the interdependency of such responsibilities on each other. In particular, the importance role assumed by philanthropic responsibilities as a means of poverty alleviation has also been highlighted.

Another way of assigning the order of priority to levels within the CSR pyramid consists of evaluating the levels based on the objective of mitigating information asymmetries – a crucial and important means of enhancing the role of Corporate Social Responsibility as a reliable signaling device for users of financial information – and particularly, investors.

Prioritizing the Pyramid of Corporate Social Responsibility Based on the Need to Mitigate Information Asymmetries, as well Facilitate Enhanced Corporate Financial Reporting Procedures

An important question to be asked is which level of the CSR pyramid would at most, facilitate the objective of mitigating information asymmetries, namely, the most vital and effective mode of achieving and formulating effective corporate governance mechanisms. In this respect, the most obvious response to this would be through legislation, and then ethical codes, principles etc – all aimed at facilitating ethical responsibilities (which could be regarded as embracing a narrower scope than those aimed at facilitating legal responsibilities).

Legal and ethical responsibilities are not only considered means whereby the goal of mitigating information asymmetries can be achieved, but also ultimately achieving the firm's economic responsibility and primary objective of profit maximization – without which the secondary goal of realizing philanthropic objectives cannot be achieved.

Hence the order of importance can be said to commence with legal responsibilities (compliance with effective legislation), followed by ethical responsibilities (compliance with ethical codes etc), then economic responsibilities, and then philanthropic responsibilities.

In this sense the order of priority is assigned on the basis that the most important is the most effective means whereby the ultimate goal can be realized. Without effective corporate governance mechanisms, the firm may not realize even its primary goal of profit maximization.

Prioritizing the Pyramid of Corporate Social Responsibility Based on the Need to Achieve Other Aims and Objectives

(Namely the primary goal of profit maximization, and the secondary goal of philanthropic responsibilities and poverty alleviation – the secondary goal also serving as an avenue in job creation – as well as other worthy causes).

From an economic perspective, and from the view of the rationale for rules, regulations – particularly financial regulations, the mitigation of information asymmetries and systemic risks, without doubt constitutes the most important of rationales or other objectives that could be presented.

Ultimately, the various levels of the CSR pyramid are crucial and symbiotic to one another and the goal of corporate social responsibility should also embrace as fore objective, the aim of communicating effectively and understandably financial information to users of such information, as well as investor, such that they can assess not only the performance of the enterprise, but also evaluate and identify channels through which the enterprise's funds are being diverted.

FUTURE RESEARCH DIRECTIONS

No conclusive findings on the effect of an internship program on the AEG are evidenced in the discussions. This is because the internship program failed to correct some of the misperceptions of an audit. This also implies that an internship program is unlikely to be used as a method of eliminating the AEG although better recognition of auditors' competence was found among respondents after the completion of an internship program. However, an internship program may be used to complement audit education in a university as it enables students to have a better insight into the actual duties and performance of auditors.

The results show there is a significant change in perceptions among students after the internship program. However, changes in perceptions do not warrant an internship program as a means of reducing the audit expectations gap as misperceptions are still found among respondents on issues of auditing after the completion of the internship program. Nevertheless, an internship program can still be used to complement audit education in a university as it is an ideal way to expose students to professional issues and enables them to have a better insight of the actual performance and duties of auditors.

CONCLUSION

Increased litigation and criticism of the auditor has left little room for doubt that auditors are facing a liability and credibility crisis (Russell, 1986). Lim (1993) and Woolf (1985) assert that the blame should not entirely be placed on the auditors as the nature and objectives of auditing are perceived differently between the public and auditors. These differences in perceptions have created the existence of the audit expectation gap. Audit expectation gap is critical to the auditing profession because the greater the expectation gap, the lower the credibility, earning potential and prestige associated with the work of auditors. Hence, effective methods in reducing the gap are in dire need.

The audit profession believes that the expectation gap could be reduced over time through education. Studies have been carried out overseas and in Malaysia to determine the effect of education in narrowing the audit expectation gap. Extending the knowledge, this paper investigates whether academic internship program could reduce the audit expectation gap in Malaysia. To achieve this objective, a research instrument adopted and modified from Ferguson et al. (2000) was administered on 117 UUM's students before and after an internship program.

The results show there is a significant change in perceptions among students after the internship program, as regards auditors and the audit process, the role of auditors, possible prohibitions and regulations, and how successful auditors are at particular activities. However the changes in perceptions do not warrant an internship program as a means of reducing the audit expectation gap. This is because misperceptions/misconceptions were still found among respondents on auditing issues after the completion of the internship program. However, an internship program could still be used to complement the formal audit education in a university as it is an ideal way of exposing students to professional issues and enables students to have a better insight into the actual performance and duties of auditors.

The identification and confirmation of funds towards environmental and philanthropic causes do not only serve as sources of useful information to users and investors, but also signals or indication that the firm's funds may be used to fund negatively associated projects or are being diverted into unaccountable channels.

Hence the role of Corporate Social Responsibility as an effective and formidable signaling device is enhanced where the mitigation of information asymmetries between management, users of financial information and investors is facilitated – and namely, through mitigating the audit expectations gap (AEG).

This chapter has sought to demonstrate why Corporate Social Responsibility endeavors which focus on the mitigation of information asymmetries between the management of an enterprise and local and international investors, also translates to effective corporate social responsibility reporting – in the sense that the engagement of stakeholders - facilitated primarily through legal and ethical responsibilities, ultimately results in the realization of economic and philanthropic responsibilities.

From an economic perspective, and from the view of the rationale for rules, regulations – particularly financial regulations, the mitigation of information asymmetries and systemic risks, without doubt constitutes the most important of rationales or other objectives that could be presented. This chapter has further highlighted how the levels of hierarchy within the pyramid of Corporate Social Responsibility can be redefined.

REFERENCES

Beck, G. W. (1974). *Public Accountants in Australia – Their Social Role*. Melbourne: Australian Accounting Research Foundation.

Benau, M. A. G., Humphrey, C., Moizer, P., & Turley, S. (1993). Auditing Expectations and Performance in Spain and Britain: A Comparative Analysis. *The International Journal of Accounting*, *28*, 281–307.

Best, P. J., Buckby, S., & Tan, C. (2001). Evidence of the Audit Expectation Gap in Singapore. *Managerial Auditing Journal*, *16*(3), 134–144. doi:10.1108/02686900110385579

Brown, R. E. (1962). Changing Audit Objectives and Techniques. *Accounting Review*, *37*, 696–703.

Castellano, J. G. (2002). *Chair's Corner*. AICPA. Available at http://www.aicpa.org/pubs/cpaltr/sept2002/chair.htm

Chandler, R. A., Edwards, J. R., & Anderson, M. (1993). Changing perceptions of the role of the company auditor: 1840 – 1940. *Accounting and Business Review*, *23*(Autumn), 443–459. doi:10.1080/00014788.1993.9729890

Cohen Commission : Commission on Auditors' Responsibilities. (1978). AICPA.

Darnill, A. (1992, March). The Profession and the Public. Singapore Accountant, 23-25.

De Beelde, I., Cooreman, S., & Leydens, H. (n.d.). *Expectation of Users of Financial Information with Regard to the Tasks Carried Out by Auditors*. University of Ghent. Available at: www.fetew.ugent.be/fac/research/WP/Papers/wp_99_75.pdf

Dicksee, L. (1892). *Auditing: A Practical Manual for Auditors*. Academic Press.

Eden, Y., Ovadia, A., & Zuckerman, B. A. (2003, May). Rethinking Sarbanes-Oxley: Why the Act Doesn't Serve the Interests of the Industry or the Markets. CMA Management, 32-35.

Epstein, M., & Geiger, M. (1994). Investor Views of Audit Assurance: Recent Evidence of the Expectation Gap. *Journal of Accountancy*, *177*(1), 60–66.

Eu-Jin, T., & Cobbin, P. (2005). *A Re Visitation of the 'Audit Expectations Gap': Judicial and Practitioner Views on the Role of the Auditor in late-Victorian England.* Academic Press.

Fadzly, A. N., & Ahmad, Z. (2004). Audit Expectation Gap – The Case of Malaysia. *Managerial Auditing Journal*, *19*(7), 897–915. doi:10.1108/02686900410549420

Ferguson, C. B., Richardson, G. D., & Wines, G. (2000). Audit Education and Training: The Effect of Formal Studies and Work Experience. *Accounting Horizons*, *14*(2), 137–167. doi:10.2308/acch.2000.14.2.137

Frank, E. K., Lowe, D. J., & Smith, J. K. (2001). The Expectation Gap: Perceptual Differences between Auditors, Jurors and Students. *Managerial Auditing Journal*, *16*(3), 145149. doi:10.1108/02686900110385588

Frontline: Bigger than Enron: Accounting Lesson. (n.d.). Available at http://www.pbs.org/wgbh/pages/frontline/shows/regulation/lessons/

Gramling, A., Schatxberg, J., & Wallace, A. (1996, Spring). The Role of Undergraduate Auditing Coursework in Reducing Audit Expectation Gap. *Issues in Accounting Education*, 131–146.

Guy, D. M., & Sullivan, J. D. (1988, April). The Expectation Gap Auditing Standards. *Journal of Accountancy*, 36–44.

Humphrey, C., Moizer, P., & Turley, S. (1993). The Audit Expectations Gap in Britain: An Empirical Investigation. *Accounting and Business Review*, *23*(sup1), 395–411. doi:10.1080/00014788.1993.9729907

IFRS. (2016). *IFRS 16 Leases, Project Summary and Feedback Statement January 2016*. IFRS.

Kasim, M. A., & Mohd-Hanafi, S. R. (2005). *An Empirical Study on the Effect of Undergraduate Auditing Course in Reducing Audit Expectation Gap at Universiti Tenaga Nasional (UNITEN)*. Paper presented at the AAAA Conference, Kuala Lumpur, Malaysia

Koh, H., & Woo, W. (1998). The Expectation Gap in Auditing. *Managerial Auditing Journal*, *13*(3), 147–154. doi:10.1108/02686909810208038

Kolins, W. (1988). *The New Auditing Standards*. The Financial Manager.

Kranacher, M.-J. (2006, April). Regulating the Accounting Profession: What Distinguishes a CPA from an Accountant? *The CPA Journal*. Available online at http://www.cpajournal.com/

Lee, T., & Palaniappan, A. (2006). *Audit Expectation Gap: An Empirical Study in Malaysia*. Paper presented in The Malaysian Finance Association's 8th Annual Conference at University Malaysia Sabah, Kota Kinabalu.

Liggio, C. (1974). The Expectation Gap: The Accountant's Waterloo. *Journal of Contemporary Business*, *3*, 27–44.

Lim, H. (1993). Address by the ICPAS President, Mr Lim Hock San, at the ICPAS' 30th Anniversary Dinner held at the Neptune Theatre Restaurant on 6 March 1993. *Singapore Accountant*, *9*, 9.

Lim, J. (2006, April 9). When Practical Training Falls Short. New Strait Times.

Lowe, D. J. (1994). The Expectation Gap in the Legal System: Perception Differences between Auditors and Judges. *Journal of Applied Business Research*, *10*(Summer), 39–44.

Management Accounting. (1985). Accountants Must Clean Up Their Act – Rep. John Dingell Speaks Out. Author.

Martens, S. C., & McEnroe, J. E. (1991). Inter-professional Struggles over Definition: Lawyers, Accountants and Illegal Acts. *Critical Perspectives on Accounting*, *2*(4), 375–384. doi:10.1016/1045-2354(91)90009-3

Minai, B., Mustapha, M., & Saleh, A. (2005). *An Empirical Investigation of Perceived Benefits of Practical Training Using Factor Analysis*. Paper presented at the 6th Asian Academy of Management Conference, Perak, Malaysia.

Mohamed, S., & Muhamad Sori, Z. (2002, January). Audit Expectation Gap – The Malaysian Experience. *The Chartered Secretary*, 12-15.

Monroe, G. S., & Woodliff, D. R. (1993). The Effect of Education on the Audit Expectation Gap. *Accounting and Finance*, *33*(May), 61–78. doi:10.1111/j.1467-629X.1993.tb00195.x

Moussalli, S. (2005). Accounting for the Journal's First 100 Years: A Timeline From 1905 to 2005. *Journal of Accountancy*. Available at: http://www.aicpa.org/pubs/jofa/oct2005/index.htm

Pierce, B., & Kilcommins, M. (1996). *The Audit Expectation Gap: The Role of Auditing Education*. DCUBS Research Paper Series, No. 13. DCUBS Dublin. Available at: http://www.dcu.ie/dcubs/research_papers/index.shtml

Porter, B. (1993). An Empirical Study of the Audit Expectation-Performance Gap. *Accounting and Business Review*, *24*(93), 49–68. doi:10.1080/00014788.1993.9729463

Porter, B., & Gowthorpe, C. (2001). *The Audit Expectation-Performance Gap: Some New Evidence from the United Kingdom*. Paper presented at the National Auditing Conference, Leicester, UK.

Porter, B., Simon, J., & Hatherly, D. (2005). *Principles of External Auditing*. John Wiley & Sons, Ltd.

Power, M. (1993). *The Politics of Financial Auditing*. Oxford, UK: The Political Quarterly Publishing Co. Ltd.

Power, M. (1997). *The Audit Society*. Oxford, UK: University Press.

Russell, G. (1986). All Eyes on Accountants. *Time*, *21*(April), 58.

Sikka, P., Puxty, A., Willmott, H., & Cooper, C. (1998). The Impossibility of Eliminating the Expectation Gap: Some Theory and Evidence. *Critical Perspectives on Accounting*, *9*(3), 299330. doi:10.1006/cpac.1997.0159

Steinberg, R. B., & Walker, D. E. (1997). The AICPA National Conference on SEC Developments. *The CPA Journal, 47*.

Turner, L. (2006, March). In the Public Interest: Regulating with a Customer Focus. *The CPA Journal*. Available online at http://www.cpajournal.com/

Utusan Malaysia. (2004, September 9). *MEF: Sistem Pendidikan Negara Gagal*. Author.

Wa, J., & Selva, M. (1993). *The Audit Expectation Gap in Hong Kong*. Paper presented to Fifth Annual Conference of Accounting Academics, Hong Kong.

Woolf, E. (1985, April). We Must Stern the Tide of Litigation. The Accountant, 1819.

Yoshimi, H. (n.d.). *Audit Expectation Gap in Japan: A Comparative Analysis with Britain*. Discussion Paper Series A, No.28. Faculty of Economics, Hokkaido University.

ENDNOTES

1 P. Sikka et al argue that due to social conflict the meaning of social practices continually face challenges and the gap between competing meanings of audit cannot be eliminated.

2 The auditor's role in relation to fraud detection has been concluded to be the critical component of the Audit Expectations Gap, according to most studies researching the nature of the gap.

Section 6

The Need to Place Stringent and Effective Regulations before Economic Considerations

Chapter 13
Enhancing Regulatory, Financial, Fiscal Investment Incentives as a Means of Promoting Foreign Direct Investment

Jon Edwards
Oxford University, UK & Goethe University, Germany

Sarah Newton
Kent University, UK

ABSTRACT

According to UNCTAD, regulatory incentives, which include "lowering of environmental, health, safety or labor standards; temporary or permanent exemption from compliance with applicable standards; stabilization clauses guaranteeing that existing regulations will not be amended to the detriment of investors", in addition to financial incentives, are considered "less important policy tools for attracting and benefiting from Foreign Direct Investment." Whilst survey results, also illustrate that fiscal incentives are the most important type for attracting and benefiting from foreign investment, it is also highlighted that certain scenarios exist whereby investment incentives could be regarded as "compensation for information asymmetries between the investor and the host government, as well as for deficiencies in the investment climate, such as weak infrastructure, underdeveloped human resources." This chapter not only explores how environmental incentives can serve as means of attracting investment, but also contributes to the literature on how their effectiveness could be enhanced.

DOI: 10.4018/978-1-5225-0305-7.ch013

INTRODUCTION

Investment Incentives as a Means of Promoting Environmental Incentives

Investment incentives can be used to attract or retain FDI in a particular host country (locational incentives). In such cases, they can be perceived as compensation for information asymmetries between the investor and the host government, as well as for deficiencies in the investment climate, such as weak infrastructure, underdeveloped human resources and administrative constraints (UNCTAD, 2014:109).

Based on UNCTAD reports, foreign investment is attracting greater interest from the tourism and extractive sectors – contrasted with manufacturing industries which are considered to have been "negatively affected by erosion of trade preferences" (UNCTAD, 2014)[1]

There are notable differences between the benefits conferred by the tourism and extractive sectors. Whilst the tourism industry is able to stimulate initiatives and incentives which generate environmental awareness, as well as organized programs and activities that draw greater attention and focus to the devastating consequences of water, air and land pollution – all of which destroy natural habitats and areas of potential natural beauty, the extractive industry on the other hand, needs to observe balances derived from generating and refining natural resources as a means of promoting economic development and growth, as well as the potential consequences of the over-exploitation and depletion of such resources.

These arguments provide justification for the encouragement of measures aimed at promotion the adoption and use of biofuels, renewable energy such as solar and wind energy, which whilst generating valuable resources as a means of wealth creation, do not deplete such resources to threatening and alarming levels. Further these measures also contribute to ensuring a healthier and less polluted environment.

In this respect, the detrimental cycles and consequences triggered and resulting from air, land and water pollution also need to be highlighted. Whilst the generation of products and energy from natural mineral resources, in some cases, generate less devastating consequences, that is, the depletion of such non-renewable resources, other forms of mineral extraction deplete such resources, as well as pollute the environment with such magnitude which is difficult to quantify in terms of economic and environmental costs – causing further damage to aquatic life, avarian or land organisms.

However, it also needs to be emphasized that certain regions attract tourism,[2] as well as extraction generated incomes owing to their ability to adequately manage such resources – through the implementation, compliance with and effective enforcement of relevant and appropriate environmental standards, corporate governance mechanisms and structures.

This chapter is aimed at highlighting why environmental, regulatory, safety and labor standards should not necessarily be diluted. It also contributes to the literature by highlighting and recommending how and why governance structures require efficient accountability structures which are able to operate effectively and independently from political interference in order to ensure that appropriate policy responses are administered in times of crisis and temporary setbacks.

Wisdom was once asked:

"What is the secret of ageless, timeless beauty?
Such as that of the mountains and hills...
Old yet full of wonder?..............................."

And in response, Wisdom said:

Renewed and renewable energy
Renewed and renewable strength
Retention of originality from source
Unpolluted and undisturbed
And of course, fulfilment of the intended purpose for its creation.

(Original quote - Anonymous)

BACKGROUND AND LITERATURE REVIEW

Financial, Fiscal and Regulatory Incentives: Conceptual Framework and Definitions

Figure 2 (UNCTAD, 2014:110) [3] presents major types of incentives which include financial, fiscal and regulatory incentives

According to UNCTAD (2014; see also page 96) and based on this table, the following definitions are attributed to financial, fiscal and regulatory incentives:

Figure 1. Industries with encouraging prospects for FDI attraction: jurisdictional basis
Source: UNCTAD, 2014 page 28

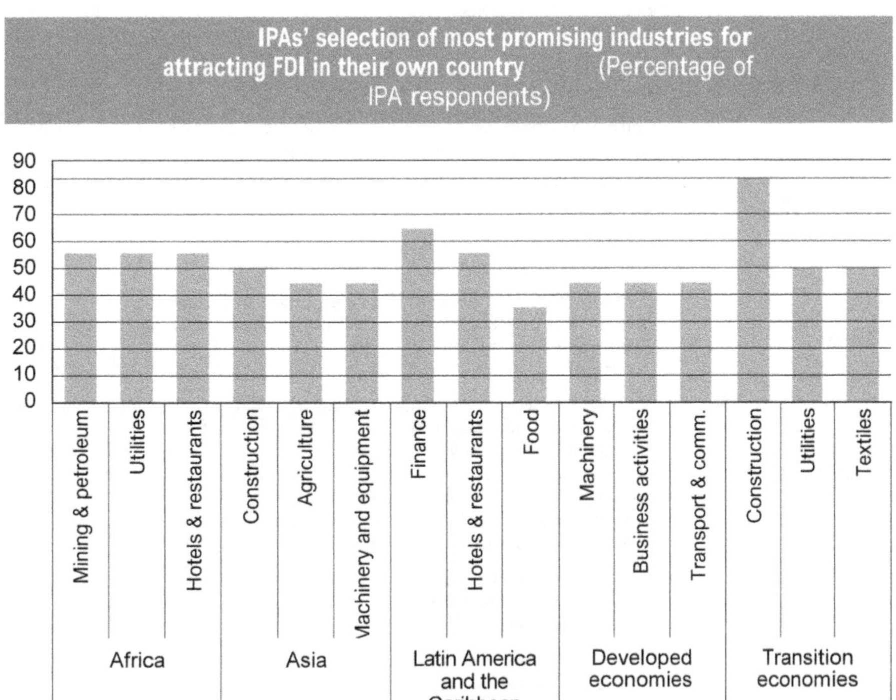

Source: UNCTAD survey.

Note: Based on responses from 80 IPAs. Aggregated by region or economic grouping to which resp

Figure 2. Investment incentives by type and mechanism
Source: Based on UNCTAD (2004).

	Financial incentives
Investment grants	"Direct subsidies" to cover (part of) capital, production or marketing costs in relation to an investment project
Subsidized credits and credit guarantees	Subsidized loans Loan guarantees Guaranteed export credits
Government insurance at preferential rates, publicly funded venture capital participating in investments involving high commercial risks	Government insurance at preferential rates, usually available to cover certain types of risks (such as exchange rate volatility, currency devaluation and non-commercial risks such as expropriation and political turmoil), often provided through an international agency
	Fiscal incentives
Profit-based	Reduction of the standard corporate income tax rate or profit tax rate, tax holiday
Capital-investment-based	Accelerated depreciation, investment and reinvestment allowances
Labour-based	Reduction in social security contribution Deductions from taxable earnings based on the number of employees or other labour-related expenditures
Sales-based	Corporate income tax reductions based on total sales
Import-based	Duty exemptions on capital goods, equipment or raw materials, parts and inputs related to the production process Tax credits for duties paid on imported materials or supplies
Export-based	Export tax exemptions, duty drawbacks and preferential tax treatment of income from exports Income tax reduction for special foreign-exchange-earning activities or for manufactured exports Tax credits on domestic sales in return for export performance, income tax credits on net local content of exports Deduction of overseas expenditures and capital allowance for export industries
Based on other particular expenses	Corporate income tax deduction based on, for example, expenditures relating to marketing and promotional activities
Value added based	Corporate income tax reductions or credits based on the net local content of outputs Income tax credits based on net value earned
Reduction of taxes for expatriates	Tax relief to help reduce personal tax liability and reduce income tax and social security contribution
	Other incentives (including regulatory incentives)
Regulatory incentives	Lowering of environmental, health, safety or labour standards Temporary or permanent exemption from compliance with applicable standards Stabilization clauses guaranteeing that existing regulations will not be amended to the detriment of investors
Subsidized services (in kind)	Subsidized dedicated infrastructure: electricity, water, telecommunication, transportation or designated infrastructure at less than commercial price Subsidized services, including assistance in identifying sources of finance, implementing and managing projects and carrying out pre-investment studies; information on markets, availability of raw materials and supply of infrastructure; advice on production processes and marketing techniques; assistance with training and retraining; and technical facilities for developing know-how or improving quality control
Market privileges	Preferential government contracts Closing the market to further entry or the granting of monopoly rights Protection from import competition
Foreign exchange privileges	Special exchange rates Special foreign debt-to-equity conversion rates Elimination of exchange risks on foreign loans Concessions of foreign exchange credits for export earnings Special concessions on repatriation of earnings and capital

Financial incentives include:

- Investment grants
- Subsidized credits and credit guarantees
- Government insurance at preferential rates, publicly funded venture capital participating in investments involving high commercial risks

Fiscal incentives may be:

- Profit based
- Capital investment based
- Labor based
- Sales based
- Import based
- Export based
- Based on other particular expenses
- Value added based
- As well as reduction of taxes for expatriates

Regulatory incentives include:

- Lowering of environmental, health, safety or labor standards
- Temporary or permanent exemption from compliance with applicable standards
- Stabilization clauses guaranteeing that existing regulations will not be amended to the detriment of investors

Does the lowering of health, labor or safety standards justify intended benefits to be derived from attracting foreign investors – even where such initiatives are intended to create jobs?

Should other measures inclusive of entrepreneurship programs aimed at value and job creation not be encouraged? Ultimately, environmental and safety costs of lowering regulatory standards may exceed those benefits intended to be generated – particularly in respect of long term and irreparable damages.

A clear impediment to the successful implementation of regulations and standards, has consistently presented itself in the form of lack of effective enforcement mechanisms. Enforcement is defined by the OECD as "actions taken by organs of the state such as the securities regulator, public prosecutor, company registrar etc, as well as by institutions exercising devolved authority such as self-regulatory organizations (SRO), as well as procedures for shareholders/stakeholders to seek redress. Effective enforcement requires the availability of effective, proportionate and dissuasive sanctions in the event of non-compliance (OECD, 2007:11)."[4]

The importance of enforcement and corporate governance mechanisms such as accountability, transparency and disclosure is hereby considered in the following section. Further mechanisms which should have been effectively implemented in response to the recent Financial Crisis will be considered by way of reference to impediments of such mechanisms.

MAIN FOCUS OF THE CHAPTER

Issues, Controversies, Problems

Should environmental or regulatory standards be lowered in a bid to promote Foreign Direct Investment? This volume has also sought to emphasize the importance of independence from political structures, with reference to Central Bank Independence, in matters relating to fiscal and monetary policy setting and decision making structures and organs. The following section highlights measures being undertaken to safeguard government and politically prone structures, namely State Owned Enterprises (SOEs).

As well as highlighting the importance of governance of state owned enterprises (SOEs) being carried out in a transparent and accountable manner, the 2014 OECD SOE Guidelines accentuates other governance criteria, most notably, which include the following (see page 7):[5]

- That the ownership entity should be held accountable to representative bodies such as the Parliament and have clearly defined relationships with relevant public bodies, including the state supreme audit institutions.
- Setting and monitoring the implementation of broad mandates and objectives for SOEs, including financial targets, capital structure objectives and risk tolerance levels;
- Setting up reporting systems that allow the ownership entity to regularly monitor, audit and assess SOE performance, and monitor their compliance with applicable corporate governance standards;
- Developing a disclosure policy for SOEs that identifies what information should be publicly disclosed, the appropriate channels for disclosure, and procedures for ensuring quality of information.
- When permitted by the legal system and the state's level of ownership, maintaining continuous dialogue with external auditors and specific state control organs.

The importance of accountability, the supreme role held by Parliament – that is legislature, as well as ensuring that legislation is interpreted by courts in such a manner, which whilst deviating from the original intent of the legislator, accords with what is considered fair and equitable – based on current practices and developments, has constituted the subject of contentious debates. Whilst it is argued by some that legislation needs to be interpreted strictly and rigidly in accordance with the spirit and intent of the legislator – even where this may result in absurdity (the literal rule of statutory interpretation), flexibility, it is also argued by others, should be introduced – to the extent that it does not result into a practice whereby judges "make and unmake" the law. Making and unmaking the law, understandably, also encouraging prospects whereby an abuse of powers occurs – as well as gradual blurring of a separation of powers.

As illustrated by the afore mentioned requirements and guidelines, audits and auditors assume vital roles in corporate financial reporting, communication, monitoring procedures, transparency, disclosure and verification of information. In relation to controls and accuracy of information, the importance of the quality of information made public to investors is distinguished based on the premises and consequences of the impacts of releasing adverse and negative information on stock markets. Whilst it is vital to ensure that accurate, reliable, relevant information, amongst other desirable attributes of accounting information, is released – such that investors can reasonably rely upon such information, greater caution as regards the manner of release of accurate information should be exercised - where such information is not exactly positive information.

As evidenced by recent panics in global stock markets, uncertainty about quality of information, as well as adverse financial reports have such devastating effects – which have been proven in some previous similar occurrences of panics and stock market crashes to have generated undue concerns. Whilst certain panics and crashes have origins that are linked to stock market corrections, such temporary disturbances resulting from the dissemination of adverse information are to be distinguished from adverse information based on uncertainty that has resulted from persistent and long term based cover ups of the real crux of the matter.

As is the case with the need for effective mechanisms and special resolution regimes designed to enable central banks fulfil their roles as lender of last resort – such that this role is facilitated for a limited time without being made public – in averting potential bank runs which have devastating systemic consequences, there is also need for caution of release of information within global financial markets. This being the case even where such information is deemed accurate, reliable and relevant. In this sense, the importance of appropriate policy responses designed to calm potentially or non-potentially devastating investment news cannot be over emphasized. Neither can flexibility or time – which is afforded to central banks and other organs and institutions designed to address the impacts of the release of potentially devastation information.

In this respect audits and auditors have a central function in arrangements with central banks, financial and investment institutions and authorities in communicating timely, accurate and complete information. Appropriate flows of information, dialogues and communication between all parties involved is also vital since timely, accurate and complete communication of information on the part of one party does not serve to avert a crisis where a key link in the communication process fails to respond appropriately and in a timely fashion. This has been demonstrated with arrangements involving single financial regulators – as evidenced by the recent 2008/2009 Financial Crisis – resulting in a restructuring of financial regulation.[6]

According to the OECD Report to G20 Finance Ministers and Central Bank Governors (2015:37),

The corporate governance framework should recognize the rights of stakeholders established by law or through mutual agreements and encourage active co-operation between corporations and stakeholders in creating wealth, jobs, and the sustainability of financially sound enterprises.

The importance of respecting rights of stakeholders, which are "often established by law (e.g. labor, business, commercial, environmental, and insolvency laws) or by contractual relations", is also highlighted in the Report (OECD, 2015: 37). Further, it is re-iterated that "stakeholders and other interested parties, including creditors and competitors, should have access to efficient redress through unbiased legal or arbitration processes when they consider that their rights have been violated" (OECD, 2015:22).

In matters relating to stakeholder relations and political engagements, the following points have also been emphasized (OECD, 2014:10):

- The boards of SOEs should be required to develop, implement and communicate compliance programs for internal codes of ethics. These codes of ethics should be based on country norms, in conformity with international commitments and apply to the company and its subsidiaries.
- SOEs should not be used as vehicles for financing political activities. SOEs themselves should normally not make political campaign contributions.

As regards transparency and disclosure, state owned enterprises are required to comply with the same standards and rigor – as is the case with listed companies and such standards include the following (OECD, 2014:11):

- SOEs should develop efficient internal audit procedures and establish an internal audit function that is monitored by and reports directly to the board and to the audit committee or the equivalent company organ.
- SOEs should also be subject to an annual independent external audit based on internationally recognized standards. Specific state control procedures do not substitute for an independent external audit.

SOLUTIONS AND RECOMMENDATIONS

The recent panics and crashes which occurred in Wall Street will also require a re-think in the engagement of expertise – such as those provided by auditors, in furnishing effective communication in matters relating to the manner and timing of release of vital information – given potentially devastating economic consequences resulting from such a release. This being applicable to cases where temporary crashes have occurred – based on unfounded panics. Whilst stock market corrections are indeed necessary, and do indeed serve as warning signs and red flags, frequencies and origins of such panics need to be mitigated and also addressed.

The conclusive chapter of this volume 'Decentralization and the Evolution of Common Law" further consolidates on how financial experts can be engaged in the legislative process – such that greater accountability is fostered, as well as delivering more efficient and equitable outcomes based on resource allocation and efficiency.

Suggested Areas for Future Research

Whilst other chapters have focused primarily on Corporate Social Responsibility, this chapter has focused on Foreign Direct Investment.

Furthering Initiatives Aimed at Fostering the Destruction of Resources, Environment and Sources of Livelihoods in Areas Such as the Amazonian Forests.

Focal Point: The Kayapo

Difficulties and challenges of one of the Amazonian tribes, the Kayapo, not only consist of possible threats to their means of livelihood, the loss of their lands and homes – as well as resources, but also the struggle for survival. More comprehensively, the following evidence, based on reports (BBC, 2014), highlights the trends which have contributed to continued and recent campaigns to preserve their means of livelihood:

- Forced migrations into rainforests as a result of invasions
- Loss of land and habitat
- Diseases resulting from the invasion and intrusion of land and habitat

The Kayapo tribe, gained global attention, as well as some benefits from investments in the 1980s and were able to collaborate with successful projects – such as those which involved the Body Shop – as well as their endeavors with logging partnerships ("logging of species on their lands") through third party representatives.

However, such initiatives which attracted a lot a global and media attention – and which fostered their environmental campaigns and initiatives, were hindered through subsequent legislation which prohibited such logging partnerships, as well as shortcomings and allegations directed at the government - which has been criticized for failing to intervene in protecting the interests of the Kayapo tribe.

The following highlights the plight of the tribe since 2008 – a period since which it is reported, that six Kayapo leaders, have been killed:

- In 1989, the Kararao Dam Project, was denied funding from the World Bank. The Project, which comprised of a proposal to create a series of six hydroelectric dams within their territory had threatened to devastate their way of life. The proposal would not only have flooded around 8,300 square miles, but would also have resulted in the displacement of entire communities – as well as the destruction of a substantial proportion of land which formed the basis of their subsistence. Further, it is reported, fish stocks, deprived of migratory routes, would have been depleted and huge areas of untouched rainforest would have been destroyed (BBC, 2014).
- In May 2008, almost 20 years after their successful Kararao Dam Protest, the Kayapo were confronted with the prospect of damming once again – mainly in the form of the proposal of a huge hydroelectric dam (the Belo Monte Dam) spanning the Xingu River (a southern tributary of the Amazon) and which threatened their homes and environment once again. It was estimated that this would not only result in the world's third largest hydroelectric dam affecting an estimated 10,000 indigenous peoples, but also many ribeirinhos, small farmers and rural settlers in the proposed area (BBC, 2014).

Challenges to be Addressed

Now in June 2016, the Kayapo tribe are still confronted with ongoing disputes in their battle to preserve their means of livelihood. Addressing powerful and corrupt business interests, as well as organized crime and political affiliations, coupled with failures of communication between the tribe and the more modern world in which in its government is situated, has not only resulted in at least 50 people being killed recently whilst trying to protect their land from loggers in the Amazon forests, but also witnessed Brazil's indigenous tribes being pressured for their land and resources. It is also recently reported that about 5000 square meters of land have been depleted through the illegal cut and exported timber trade industry.

Hence addressing such illegal and corrupt corporate interests, as well as the problem of contact with modern Brazil constitutes a challenge in the Kayapo tribe's race for survival.

CONCLUSION

It should be re called that salient vital lessons drawn from the recent Financial Crisis do not necessarily focus on governments' inability to implement effective structures of regulation, but the inability of such arrangements to respond timely, and effectively owing to communication problems and the level of expertise operating at required levels, as well as involved, in responding to such moments of crisis. There are certain areas which the central bank remains endowed and equipped with, in addressing certain policy measures and responses – than could be reasonably expected of an independent financial agency.

This chapter has highlighted why environmental, regulatory, safety and labor standards should not necessarily be diluted. As well as contributing to the literature by highlighting and recommending how and why governance structures require efficient accountability structures which are able to operate effectively and independently from political interference, it also draws attention to how environmental incentives can be generated as an alternative means in generating and encouraging tourism, entrepreneurship, innovation in fostering growth and development. Further, audits and auditors can address the need to "compensate for information asymmetries between the investor and the host government."

Ultimately, Foreign Direct Investment should constitute a symbiotic relationship between the parties involved – such that beneficial economic objectives to derived therefrom, economic objectives such as job creation, value creation and knowledge generating resources, as well as technological and innovative advancement initiatives, are fostered.

Legislation prohibiting the logging partnerships between the Kayapo tribe and their outside investors should also have foreseen the detrimental consequences of such legislation. Where such logging partnerships are symbiotic to the extent that environmental interests constitute core and primary concern – such interests being pivotal to a party's means of subsistence, livelihood and survival, then other interests – economic, or otherwise should assume secondary importance.

Where economic benefits are also accentuated, and objectives aimed at promoting such goals constitute focal points, they should also serve as incentives which should deter non-compliance with regional, national and international agreements. Furthermore, given the emphasis and focus directed at such economic and symbiotic benefits, these should also serve as a deterrence to efforts aimed at lowering regulatory standards – particularly those which would result in a watering down of valuable principles, goals and objectives, which are aimed at preserving the environment and fostering compliance with environmental standards.

Economic benefits to be derived from Foreign Direct Investment engagements, partnerships, and collaborations, should constitute a solid basis whereby parties involved are encouraged and incentivized to enter into such arrangements – and not to be regarded as burdensome arrangements which would result in unnecessary and unproductive lowering of regulatory standards which could signal adverse consequences for the environment.

REFERENCES

ADBI. (2009). *Demand for Infrastructure Financing in Asia 2010–2020. ADBI Internal Report*. Tokyo: ADBI.

FSB (Financial Stability Board). (2008). *Enhancing Market and Institutional Resilience*. Retrieved from www.financialstability-board.org

High Level Task Force on Innovative International Financing for Health Systems. (2009). More *Money for Health, and More Health for the Money*. Author.

OECD. (2007). *Methodology For Assessing the Implementation of the OECD Principles of Corporate Governance*. OECD.

OECD. (2009a). *Private Sector Participation in Water Infrastructure*. Paris: OECD.

OECD. (2009b). *The Financial Crisis: Reform and Exit Strategies*. Retrieved from http://www.oecd.org/daf/ca/corporategovernanceandthefinancialcrisis.htm

OECD. (2009c). *Business Ethics and OECD Principles: What Can Be Done to Avoid Another Crisis*. OECD.

OECD. (2011). *Enhancing the Role of the Boards of Directors of State Owned Enterprises*. Retrieved from http://www.oecd.org/daf/ca/boardpracticesincentivesandgoverningrisks.htm

OECD. (2012). *Strategic Transport Infrastructure Needs to 2030*. Paris: OECD.

OECD. (2014). *Guidelines On Corporate Governance Of State-Owned Enterprises*. OECD.

OECD. (2015). *Guidelines On Corporate Governance Of State-Owned Enterprises*. OECD.

UNCTAD. (2014). *World Investment Report 2014: Investing in the SDGs, An Action Plan*. UNCTAD.

ENDNOTES

1 UNCTAD, 2014 at page x. "Mineral extraction and downstream-related activities, business and finance, and tourism are the main target industries for FDI in SIDS. Tourism is attracting increasing interest by foreign investors, while manufacturing industries – such as apparel and processed fish – that used to be a non-negligible target for FDI, have been negatively affected by erosion of trade preferences." See UNCTAD, 2014 at page xxii

2 "African IPAs expect further investments in the extractive and utilities industries, while Latin American IPAs emphasize finance and tourism services. Asian IPAs refer to positive prospects in construction, agriculture and machinery. " See UNCTAD, 2014 at page 27

3 "Mineral extraction and downstream related activities, tourism, business and finance, constitute the main target industries for Foreign Direct Investment."

4 Further, as well as adding that "enforcement might not be effective if, for example, rights of enforcement reside only with a regulator or company registrar who may not have the right incentives or resources to enforce the law", it is also highlighted that enforcement can also be undertaken through effective means of redress for shareholders/stakeholders.

5 See more recent version, OECD, OECD Guidelines on Corporate Governance of State-Owned Enterprises: 2015 Edition © OECD at page 32 which highlights that "In developing and updating the State's ownership policy, governments should make appropriate use of public consultation. As well as effective and early use of public consultation can be instrumental in facilitating acceptance of the ownership policy by market participants and key stakeholders, the development of the ownership policy can also involve consultations with all concerned government entities, for example relevant legislative or parliamentary committees, the state audit institution, as well as relevant ministries and regulators."

6 As evidenced by the tripartite arrangement between the UK's Financial Services Authority, Bank of England and HM Treasury – in the aftermath of the Northern Rock Crisis.

Chapter 14
Corporate Social Responsibility: A Manifestation in FDI

Chandra Sekhar Patro
GVP College of Engineering (Autonomous), India

K. Madhu Kishore Raghunath
GVP College of Engineering (Autonomous), India

ABSTRACT

There is a famous saying "With Great Power Comes Great Responsibility" and speaking of this in terms of a country's financial position Foreign Direct Investment (FDI) can be considered as a power and CSR as a share of responsibility. Generally the unfurling of CSR is a riveted and intrigued corner of developing country like India. Every business entity is willing to take up more responsibility as it is given lot of respect from various international agencies in the form of FDI and most of the organizations are realizing that more business heights will imply sustained development for social progress. Social innovation is the output derived when FDI and CSR come together leading to development of a nation in various facets. The purpose of the study is to articulate the impact of FDI on CSR activities in Indian context and to analyze the importance of how both FDI and CSR are interdependent and complement each other in various facets, not forgetting the fact that it's high time for Indian economy to boost up its CSR activities keeping in view the subsequent flow of investments.

INTRODUCTION

In recent years, the term Corporate Social Responsibility (CSR) has emerged as an inclusive and global concept to embrace corporate social responsibility, responsiveness, and the entire spectrum of socially beneficial activities of businesses (Archie, 1991). The focus on social performance emphasizes the concern for corporate action and accomplishment in the social sphere. With a performance perspective, it is clear that firms must formulate and implement social goals and programs as well as integrate ethical sensitivity into all decision making, policies, and actions with a results focus.

DOI: 10.4018/978-1-5225-0305-7.ch014

When a section of people were quizzed, regarding *what do they know about Corporate Social Responsibility (CSR)?* Most of them replied that it was something that companies have to deal with. The second question was *what do they generally expect from companies as CSR?* Well, it's a fact that before someone is asked a question, we should have some knowledge about the given question and its solution. So, let's see what is understood by the concept of corporate social responsibility.

CORPORATE SOCIAL RESPONSIBILITY (CSR)

"Corporate social responsibility also referred to as corporate conscience, corporate citizenship or responsible business is a form of corporate self-regulation integrated into a business model where as a part of CSR companies goes beyond profit motive concept and engages in actions that appear to further some social good, beyond the interests of the firm and that which is required by law also. CSR aims to embrace responsibility for corporate actions and to encourage a positive impact on the environment and stakeholders including consumers, employees, investors, communities, and others."

"What does it mean for a corporation to be socially responsible? Academics and practitioners have been striving to establish an agreed-upon definition of this concept for 30 years." Now articulating about the evolution of CSR in 1960, Keith Davis suggested that social responsibility refers "to business decisions and actions taken for reasons at least partially beyond the firm's direct economic or technical interest." At about the same time(Eells and Walton, 1961), argued that CSR refers to the "problems that arise when corporate enterprise casts its shadow on the social scene, and the ethical principles that ought to govern the relationship between the corporation and society."

Today, one cannot pick up a newspaper, magazine or journal without encountering some discussion of the issue, some recent or innovative example of what business is thinking or doing about CSR, or some new conference that is being held in Specific journals, news magazines, books, dictionaries, encyclopedias, and websites.The acronym "CSR" (Corporate Social Responsibility) became popular in the 1960s and has remained a term used indiscriminately by many to cover legal and moral responsibility more narrowly construed.

Observers increasingly note that corporate social responsibility has become a mainstream business activity. Firms are investing ever more resources in public goods provision and many companies reduce negative externalities below levels required by law. More than half of Fortune Global 250 firms now provide regular public statements exclusively discussing CSR, and approximately 10 percent of S&P 100 companies report in detail on CSR activities(Kotler and Lee, 2004a; Baskin and Gordon, 2005). More than one third of large firms have voluntary external certifications for social and environmental standards, and nearly 11 percent of professionally managed US investment was certified as socially responsible. It is estimated that US and European markets have over 2 trillion USD and 300 billion EURO in certifies socially responsible assets. Firms such as IBM, General Motors or Microsoft even inform potential employees about their CSR efforts(Turban and Greening, 1997).

Definitions of CSR

1. The *European Commission* (EC)defines CSR as "the responsibility of enterprises for their impacts on society". To completely meet their social responsibility, enterprises "should have in place a

process to integrate social, environmental, ethical human rights and consumer concerns into their business operations and core strategy in close collaboration with their stakeholders".

2. The *World Business Council for Sustainable Development* (WBCSD) defines CSR as "the continuing commitment by business to contribute to economic development while improving the quality of life of the workforce and their families as well as of the community and society at large."
3. According to the UNIDO, "Corporate social responsibility is a management concept whereby companies integrate social and environmental concerns in their business operations and interactions with their stakeholders.

From the above definitions, it is clear that:

1. The CSR approach is holistic and integrated with the core business strategy for addressing social and environmental impacts of businesses.
2. CSR needs to address the well-being of all stakeholders and not just the company's shareholders.
3. Philanthropic activities are only a part of CSR, which otherwise constitutes a much larger set of activities entailing strategic business benefits.

Since corporate social responsibility and sustainability are so closely entwined, it can be said that corporate social responsibility and sustainability is a company's commitment to its stakeholders to conduct business in an economically, socially and environmentally sustainable manner that is transparent and ethical(Singh & Verma, 2014).

FACETS OF CORPORATE SOCIAL RESPONSIBILITY

For Corporate Social Responsibility (CSR) to be accepted by a conscientious business person, it should be framed in such a way that the entire range of business responsibilities is embraced (Carroll, 1991). All these kinds of responsibilities have always existed to some extent, but it has only been in recent years that ethical and philanthropic functions have taken a significant place.

The figure.1 depicts the facets of total Corporate Social Responsibility (CSR) which constitutes of four kinds of social responsibilities. And each of these four categories namely, economic responsibilities,

Figure 1. Facets of corporate social responsibility

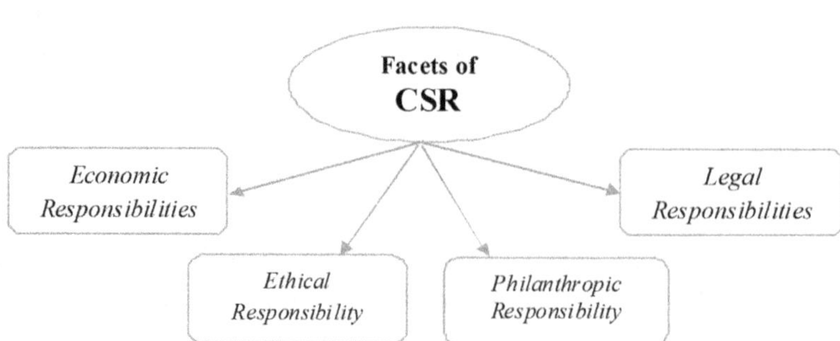

legal responsibilities, ethical responsibilities, and philanthropic responsibilities requires close consideration in the business.

- **Economic Responsibilities:** Historically, business organizations were created as economic entities designed to provide goods and services to societal members. The profit motive was established as the primary incentive for entrepreneurship. Before it was anything else, business organization was the basic economic unit in our society. As such, its principal role was to produce goods and services that consumers needed and wanted and to make an acceptable profit in the process. At some point the idea of the profit motive got transformed into a notion of maximum profits, and this has been an enduring value ever since.
- **Legal Responsibilities:** Society has not only sanctioned business to operate according to the profit motive; at the same time business is expected to comply with the laws and regulations promulgated by federal, state, and local governments as the ground rules under which business must operate. As a partial fulfillment of the "social contract" between business and society firms are expected to pursue their economic missions within the framework of the law. Legal responsibilities reflect a view of "codified ethics" in the sense that they embody basic notions of fair operations as established by our lawmakers. They are depicted as the next layer on the pyramid to portray their historical development, but they are appropriately seen as coexisting with economic responsibilities as fundamental precepts of the free enterprise system.
- **Ethical Responsibilities:** Although economic and legal responsibilities embody ethical norms about fairness and justice, ethical responsibilities embrace those activities and practices that are expected or prohibited by societal members even though they are not codified into law. Ethical responsibilities embody those standards, norms, or expectations that reflect a concern for what consumers, employees, shareholders, and the community regard as fair, just, or in keeping with the respect or protection of stakeholders' moral rights.
- **Philanthropic Responsibilities:** Philanthropy encompasses those corporate actions that are in response to society's expectation that businesses be good corporate citizens. This includes actively engaging in acts or programs to promote human welfare or goodwill. Examples of philanthropy include business contributions to financial resources or executive time, such as contributions to the arts, education, or the community. A loaned-executive program that provides leadership for a community's United Way campaign is one illustration of philanthropy.

PRINCIPLES OF CORPORATE SOCIAL RESPONSIBILITY (CSR)

Because of the uncertainty surrounding the nature of CSR activity it is difficult to define CSR and to be certain about any such activity. It is therefore imperative to be able to identify such activity and we take the view that there are three basic principles which together comprise all CSR activity (Stephanie, 2015). These activities are referred as follows:

- **Sustainability:** The principle of sustainability assumes that corporate success and social well-being are interdependent and that the long-term interests of an organization are best served by improving its economic, socio-cultural, and environmental/energy practices, also known as the three pillars of sustainability. As a responsible corporation, we respect the interests of our stakeholders (shareholders, employees, customers, suppliers, and the wider community) and we actively seek out opportunities to improve the environment and to contribute to the well-being of the communities in which we do business.

- **Accountability:** This is concerned with an organization recognizing that its actions affect the external environment, and therefore assuming responsibility for the effects of its actions. This concept therefore implies a quantification of the effects of actions taken, both internal to the organization and externally. More specifically the concept implies a reporting of those quantifications to all parties affected by those actions. This implies a reporting to external stakeholders of the effects of actions taken by the organization and how they are affecting stakeholders. This concept therefore implies recognition that the organization is part of a wider societal network and has responsibilities to that entire network rather than just to the owners of the organization.
- **Transparency:** Transparency, as a principle, means that the external impact of the actions of the organization can be ascertained from that organization's reporting and pertinent facts are not disguised within that reporting. Thus all the effects of the actions of the organization, including external impacts, should be apparent to all from using the information provided by the organization's reporting mechanisms. Transparency is of particular importance to external users of such information as these users lack the background details and knowledge available to internal users of such information. Transparency therefore can be seen to follow from the other two principles and equally can be seen to be a part of the process of recognition of responsibility on the part of the organization for the external effects of its actions and equally part of the process of transferring power to external stakeholders.

Why are Companies Engaged in CSR?

Companies that are socially responsible in making profits also contribute to some, although obviously not all, aspects of social development. Every company should not be expected to be involved in every aspect of social development. That would be ludicrous and unnecessarily restrictive. But for a firm to be involved in some aspects, both within the firm and on the outside will make its products and services (for example, financial services) more attractive to consumers as a whole, therefore making the company more profitable. There will be increased costs to implement CSR, but the benefits are likely to far outweigh the costs (Hopkins, 2003).

Corporate social responsibility is not a new issue. The social responsibility of business was not widely considered to be a significant problem from Adam Smith's time to the Great Depression. But since the 1930s, and increasingly since the 1960s, social responsibility has become an important issue not only for business but in the theory and practice of law, politics and economics (Hopkins, 2007). The need to address questions of low living standards, exploitation, poverty, unemployment and how to promote social development in general, has to date been almost entirely the preserve of governments. Clearly, they will continue to have a, if not the, major role to play in this area. But, increasingly in the future, the promotion of social development issues must also be one of partnership between government and private and non-governmental actors and, in particular, the corporate sector (Hopkins, 2004).

Corporate social responsibility (CSR) is not a weapon that should be embraced by every organization; CSR is a way for companies to benefit themselves while also benefiting society. When CSR is defined to the uninitiated, we typically get many reactions which are worth watching, but then on a serious note CSR has proven to be an Asset to the companies embracing it (Reeves, 2012).

If a question is put forth why Corporate Social Responsibility (CSR) is influential, the following would answer the question.

- **Economic Development:** Economic development is a policy intervention endeavor with aims of economic and social well-being of people, economic growth is a phenomenon of market productivity and rise in GDP.
- **Brand Competitiveness:** In view of heavy competition prevailing among companies, to enhance their brand competiveness companies do involve in CSR activities which multiple their brand competitiveness.
- **Financial Implication**: Expectations of society are changing from day to day, which impacts the profits of a company and every company is financially implicated through its act toward society, today customers expect not just a product from the company but they think it has a role to play towards society, upon which customers prefer to make purchase decision.
- **Customer and Employee Engagement:** Customer and Employee interaction is only possible when employees come down to understand the customer needs which again are possible only through CSR where they can understand the problem and come up with a solution.
- **Build Long-Term Employee, Consumer and Citizen Trust:** Ultimate goal of perpetual succession of a company can be achieved only when there is a consensus between employees, customers and citizens, hence CSR provides a platform.
- **Enhances Goodwill and Organizational Health:** CSR activities indirectly contribute towards the development of Goodwill and Organizational health.
- **Corporate Citizenship:** The extent to which businesses are socially responsible for meeting legal, ethical and economic responsibilities placed on them by shareholders. The aim is for businesses to create higher standards of living and quality of life in the communities in which they operate, while still preserving profitability for stakeholders.
- **Mitigates Social Evils:** The contribution of companies towards the society not only just helps in improving the society but also plays a major role in eradicating the many of social evils prevailing in the business.
- **Balance of Responsibility and Power:** CSR is the best platform where they get an opportunity to balance their power and responsibility. Generally every company will have some responsibility towards society on par with its power and only when they balance both of them hand in hand, business organizations succeed.
- **Superiority of Prevention over Cure:** It is always good to be proactive in all areas and when it comes to CSR, companies must adopt some form of CSR so as to prevent themselves from losing the race.

Corporate Social Responsibility (CSR) in Today's' Generation

The CSR debate has largely revolved around the conduct of multinational corporations (MNEs) and other large private companies which, due to their size, have the ability to significantly influence domestic and international policy and the communities in which they operate (Kercher, 2007). CSR supporters argue that the efficient functioning of global markets depends on socially responsible business conduct.

There are a number of factors relevant to the current CSR debate (Kercher, 2007) including:

- Globalization and the proliferation of cross-border trade by MNEs resulting in an increasing awareness of CSR practices relating to areas such as human rights, environmental protection, health and safety and anti-corruption;
- Organizations, such as the UN, the Organization for Economic Co-operation and Development (OECD) and the International Labor Organization (ILO), have developed compacts, declarations, guidelines, principles and other instruments that outline norms for acceptable corporate conduct;
- Access to information and media enables the public to be more informed and to easily monitor corporate activities;
- Consumers and investors are demonstrating increased interest in supporting responsible business practices and are demanding more information as to how companies address risks and opportunities relating to social and environmental issues;
- Recent high profile corporate collapses have contributed to public mistrust and the demand for improved corporate governance, accountability and transparency;
- Commonality of expectations by citizens of various countries with regard to minimum standards corporations should achieve in relation to social and environmental issues, regardless of the jurisdiction in which the corporation operates; and
- Increasing awareness of the inadequacy of current regulations and legislation with regard to CSR matters and the regulation of MNEs.

Now-a-days it is seen that consumers are avoiding what they see (rightly or wrongly) as socially irresponsible products or the products of companies that have allegedly not acted in society's best interest (Hopkins, 2004). Enterprises have noted that social responsibility is good for business for, and from, each of the many end-users within which they trade and operate. These are: their shareholders and potential investors; managers; employees; customers; business partners and contractors or suppliers; the natural environment; and the communities within which they operate, including national governments. Such azimuths are now commonly known as an enterprise's stakeholders (Hopkins, 2003).

EXAMPLES OF CSR IN INDIA

As per (India Briefing, 2012), below are few of the many companies along with their CSR activities:

Tata Group

Tata Group in India has a range of CSR projects, most of which are community improvement programs. For example, it is a leading provider of maternal and child health services, family planning, and has provided 98 percent immunization in Jamshedpur. The company also endorses sports as a way of life. It has established a football academy, archery academy, and promotes sports among employees (India Briefing, 2012). It offers healthcare services all over the country with programs like rural health development. Tata Group also has an organized relief program in case of natural disasters, including long-term treatment and rebuilding efforts. It did laudable work during the Gujarat earthquakes and Orissa floods. It also supports education, with over 500 schools, and also is a benefactor of the arts and culture. It has done abundant work in improving the environment and local populations around its industries.

Aptech

Aptech a leading education player with a global presence that has played a broad and continued role in encouraging and nurturing education throughout the country since its inception. As a global player with complete solutions-providing capabilities, Aptech has a long history of participating in community activities. It has, in association with leading NGOs, provided computers at schools, education to the deprived, and training and awareness-camps (India Briefing, 2012).

Infosys

Infosys is aggressively involved in a variety of community growth programs. In 1996, the company created the Infosys Foundation as a not-for-profit trust to which it contributes up to 1 percent of profits after tax every year. Moreover, the Education and Research Department at Infosys also works with employee volunteers on community development projects. The management team at Infosys continues to set examples in the area of corporate citizenship and has involved itself vigorously in key national bodies (India Briefing, 2012). They have taken initiatives to work in the areas of research and education, community service, rural outreach programs, employment, healthcare for the poor, education, arts and culture, and welfare activities undertaken by the Infosys Foundation.

Mahindra and Mahindra

At Mahindra & Mahindra, the K.C. Mahindra Education Trust was established in 1953 with the purpose of promoting education. Its vision is to renovate the lives of people in India through education and financial assistance across age groups and across income strata. The K.C. Mahindra Education Trust undertakes a number of education plans, which make a difference to the lives of worthy students. The Trust has provided more than Rs.7.5 crore in the form of grants, scholarships and loans. It promotes education mostly by the way of scholarships (India Briefing, 2012).

Table 1. Industry-wise segregation of major CSR activities undertaken by firms

Industry	Health	Education	Community Development/ Rural Development	Environment	Total
Oil & Gas	23.50%	35.29%	29.41%	11.76%	100%
Automobile	40.00%	10.00%	40%	10%	100%
Consumer Durables	24.76%	21.34%	15.25%	28.75%	100%
Iron & Steel	35.29%	23.53%	35.29%	5.88%	100%
Banking & Financial Services	8.57%	20.00%	48.57%	35%	100%
Power	10.00%	10.00%	45%	35%	100%
Infrastructure	8.35%	30.55%	44.44%	16.66%	100%
Cement	22.20%	25.00%	29%	23.8%	100%
Paper &Pulp	19.90%	24.10%	18%	38%	100%
Pharmaceutical	30.00%	28.00%	22.00%	20.00%	100%

Source: Calculated by the author from the annual reports of the top 100 firms

FOREIGN DIRECT INVESTMENT (FDI)

One key feature of liberalization has been greater openness to foreign direct investment (FDI) as a means of acquiring technologies, skills and access to international markets, and of entering dynamic trade and production systems internal to multinational enterprises. One of the most striking developments during the last two decades is the spectacular growth of FDI in the global economic landscape. This unprecedented growth of global FDI in 1990 around the world has made FDI aspect an important and vital component of development strategy in both developed and developing nations and policies are designed in order to stimulate inward flows. In-fact FDI provides a win to win situation to the host and the home countries. Both countries are directly interested in investing FDI, because they benefit a lot from such type of investment (Mundra, Mundra, & Singh, 2013).

The 'home' countries want to take the advantage of the vast markets opened by industrial growth. On the other hand the 'host' countries want to acquire technological and managerial skills and supplement domestic savings and foreign exchange. Moreover, the paucity of all types of resources viz., financial, capital, entrepreneurship, technological know-how, skills and practices, access to markets abroad in their economic development, developing nations accepted FDI as a sole visible panacea for all their scarcities. Further, the integration of global financial markets paves ways to this explosive growth of FDI around the globe (Lall & Narula, 2004).

There is hardly a facet of the Indian psyche that the concept of 'foreign' has not permeated. This term, connoting modernization, international brands and acquisitions by MNCs in popular imagination, has acquired renewed significance after the reforms initiated by the Indian Government in 1991. Contrary to the grand narrative 'opening of flood-gates idea' of 1991, what took place was a gradual process of changes in policies on investment in certain sub-sections of the Indian economy (Singh, 2005). It is furthermore described as a source and of course enabler of economic development, modernization, and employment generation, whereby the overall benefits (dependent on the policies of the host government), triggers technology spillovers, assists human capital formation, contributes to international trade integration and particularly exports, helps create a more competitive business environment, enhances enterprise development, increases total factor productivity and, more generally, improves the efficiency of resource use.

Definitions of FDI

FDI is a process whereby residents of one country (source country) acquire ownership of assets for the purpose of controlling the production and distribution and other activities.

- IMF's Balance of Payment manual defines "FDI as an investment that is made to acquire lasting interest in an enterprise operating in an economy other than that of an investor, the investor's purpose being to have voice in the management of the enterprise."
- The United Nations (1999) World investment Report(UNICTAD) defines "FDI as an investment having involving long term relationship and reflecting a lasting interest and control of resident entity in one economy in an enterprise resident in an economy other that of the foreign direct investor."

HISTORY OF FDI

The historical background of FDI in India can be traced back with the establishment of East India Company of Britain. British capital came to India during the colonial era of Britain in India. However, researchers could not portray the complete history of FDI pouring in India due to lack of abundant and authentic data. Before independence major amount of FDI came from the British companies. British companies setup their units in mining sector and in those sectors that suits their own economic and business interest (Malhotra, 2014).

After Second World War, Japanese companies entered Indian market and enhanced their trade with India, yet U.K. remained the most dominant investor in India. Further, after Independence issues relating to foreign capital, operations of MNCs, gained attention of the policy makers. Keeping in mind the national interests the policy makers designed the FDI policy which aims FDI as a medium for acquiring advanced technology and to mobilize foreign exchange resources. The first Prime Minister of India considered foreign investment as "necessary" not only to supplement domestic capital but also to secure scientific, technical, and industrial knowledge and capital equipment's. With time and as per economic and political regimes there have been changes in the FDI policy too (Khan & Khan, 2015).

The industrial policy of 1965, allowed MNCs to venture through technical collaboration in India. However, the country faced two severe catastrophes in the form of foreign exchange and financial resource mobilization during the second five year plan (1956-61). Therefore, the government adopted a liberal attitude by allowing more frequent equity participation to foreign enterprises, and to accept equity capital in technical collaborations. The government also provides many incentives such as tax concessions, simplification of licensing procedures and de- reserving some industries such as drugs, aluminum, heavy electrical equipment's, fertilizers, etc., in order to further boost the FDI inflows in the country.

According to Khan & Khan (2015) the liberal attitude of government towards foreign capital lures investors from other advanced countries like USA, Japan, and Germany, etc. But due to significant outflow of foreign reserves in the form of remittances of dividends, profits, royalties etc., the government has to adopt stringent foreign policy in 1970s. During this period the government adopted a selective and highly restrictive foreign policy as far as foreign capital, type of FDI and ownerships of foreign companies was concerned. Government setup Foreign Investment Board and enacted Foreign Exchange Regulation Act in order to regulate flow of foreign capital and FDI flow to India.

Table 2. In-flow of FDI in India

Year	Mid 1948	Mar 1964	Mar 1974	Mar 1980	Mar 1990	Mar 2000	Mar 2010	Mar 2014
Amount of FDI	256	565.5	916	933.2	2705	18486	123378	147518
Cumulative increase	256	821.5	1737.5	2670.7	5375.7	23861.7	147239.7	294757.7

Source: Calculated by the author from the reports

Figure 2. FDI growth in India

The inflow of Foreign Direct Investments increases with the attractiveness of the country, due to the following factors in different proportions depending on the industry and the country:

- large GDP and market potential
- advanced know-how
- skilled work-force;
- low labor cost and wages;
- low taxation;
- lower environmental protection;
- high tariff protection;
- favorable laws and public incentives;
- Intentional and professional territorial marketing.

ADVANTAGES OF FDI

The main advantages of FDI (ConnectUS, n.d.) include the following:

- **Economic Development Stimulation:** Foreign direct investment can stimulate the target country's economic development, creating a more conducive environment for you as the investor and benefits for the local industry.
- **Easy International Trade:** Commonly, a country has its own import tariff, and this is one of the reasons why trading with it is quite difficult. Also, there are industries that usually require their presence in the international markets to ensure their sales and goals will be completely met. With FDI, all these will be made easier.

- **Employment and Economic Boost:** Foreign direct investment creates new jobs, as investors build new companies in the target country, create new opportunities. This leads to an increase in income and more buying power to the people, which in turn leads to an economic boost.
- **Development of Human Capital Resources:** One big advantage brought about by FDI is the development of human capital resources, which is also often understated as it is not immediately apparent. Human capital is the competence and knowledge of those able to perform labor, more known to us as the workforce. The attributes gained by training and sharing experience would increase the education and overall human capital of a country. Its resource is not a tangible asset that is owned by companies, but instead something that is on loan. With this in mind, a country with FDI can benefit greatly by developing its human resources while maintaining ownership.
- **Tax Incentives:** Parent enterprises would also provide foreign direct investment to get additional expertise, technology and products. As the foreign investor, you can receive tax incentives that will be highly useful in your selected field of business.
- **Resource Transfer:** Foreign direct investment will allow resource transfer and other exchanges of knowledge, where various countries are given access to new technologies and skills.
- **Reduced Disparity between Revenues and Costs:** Foreign direct investment can reduce the disparity between revenues and costs. With such, countries will be able to make sure that production costs will be the same and can be sold easily.
- **Increased Productivity:** The facilities and equipment provided by foreign investors can increase a workforce's productivity in the target country.
- **Increment in Income:** Another big advantage of foreign direct investment is the increase of the target country's income. With more jobs and higher wages, the national income normally increases. As a result, economic growth is spurred. Take note that larger corporations would usually offer higher salary levels than what you would normally find in the target country, which can lead to increment in income

DRAWBACKS OF FDI

The main drawbacks of FDI (ConnectUS, n.d.) include:

- **Hindrance to Domestic Investment:** As it focuses its resources elsewhere other than the investor's home country, foreign direct investment can sometimes hinder domestic investment.
- **Risk from Political Changes:** Because political issues in other countries can instantly change, foreign direct investment is very risky. Plus, most of the risk factors that you are going to experience are extremely high.
- **Negative Influence on Exchange Rates:** Foreign direct investments can occasionally affect exchange rates to the advantage of one country and the detriment of another.
- **Higher Costs:** If you invest in some foreign countries, you might notice that it is more expensive than when you export goods. So, it is very imperative to prepare sufficient money to set up your operations.
- **Economic Non-Viability:** Considering that foreign direct investments may be capital-intensive from the point of view of the investor, it can sometimes be very risky or economically non-viable.

- **Expropriation:** Remember that political changes can also lead to expropriation, which is a scenario where the government will have control over your property and assets.
- **Negative Impact on the Country's Investment:** The rules that govern foreign exchange rates and direct investments might negatively have an impact on the investing country. Investment may be banned in some foreign markets, which means that it is impossible to pursue an inviting opportunity.
- **Modern-Day Economic Colonialism:** Many third-world countries, or at least those with history of colonialism, worry that foreign direct investment would result in some kind of modern day economic colonialism, which exposes host countries and leave them vulnerable to foreign companies' exploitations.

FDI AND "MAKE IN INDIA"

India has already marked its presence as one of the fastest growing economies of the world. It has been ranked among the top 3 attractive destinations for inbound investments. Since 1991, the regulatory environment in terms of foreign investment has been consistently eased to make it investor-friendly. As per (GOI, 2015) the growth in FDI has been significant after the launch of Make in India initiatives in 2014, with 48 percent increase in FDI equity inflows during 2014-2015. This showcases remarkable pace of approval being accorded by the government and confidence of investors in the resurgent India.

The recent policy measures in FDI (DIPP, n.d.):

- Government have eased FDI norms in 15 major sectors.
- Townships, shopping complexes & business centres – all allow up to 100% FDI under the auto route. Conditions on minimum capitalisation & floor area restrictions have now been removed for the construction development sector.
- India's defence sector now allows consolidated FDI up to 49% under the automatic route. FDI beyond 49% will now be considered by the Foreign Investment Promotion Board. Govt approval route will be required only when FDI results in a change of ownership pattern.
- Private sector banks now allow consolidated FDI up to 74%.
- Up to 100% FDI is now allowed in coffee/rubber/cardamom/palm oil & olive oil plantations via the automatic route.
- 100% FDI is now allowed via the auto route in duty free shops located and operated in the customs bonded areas.
- Manufacturers can now sell their products through wholesale and/or retail, including through e-commerce without Government Approval.
- Foreign Equity caps have now been increased for establishment & operation of satellites, credit information companies, non-scheduled air transport & ground handling services from 74% to 100%.
- 100% FDI allowed in medical devices
- FDI cap increased in insurance & sub-activities from 26% to 49%
- FDI up to 49% has been permitted in the Pension Sector.
- Construction, operation and maintenance of specified activities of Railway sector opened to 100% foreign direct investment under automatic route.

- FDI policy on Construction Development sector has been liberalised by relaxing the norms pertaining to minimum area, minimum capitalisation and repatriation of funds or exit from the project. To encourage investment in affordable housing, projects committing 30 percent of the total project cost for low cost affordable housing have been exempted from minimum area and capitalisation norms.
- Investment by NRIs under Schedule 4 of FEMA (Transfer or Issue of Security by Persons Resident Outside India) Regulations will be deemed to be domestic investment at par with the investment made by residents.
- Composite caps on foreign investments introduced to bring uniformity and simplicity is brought across the sectors in FDI policy.

The Foreign Policy Magazine in its present analysis on a vast number of parameters has rated India as the No.1 destination in the world. Frost & Sullivan, a US based agency has on number of indicators selected the Make in India initiative as the best initiative to drive manufacturing. India stands committed to have a FDI policy and regime which is investor friendly and also promotes investment leading to increased manufacturing, job creation and overall economic growth of the country.

MOTIVATIONS FOR FDI

Motivation is great impetus which drives every object in this world and coming to the various sources of motivation for FDI which must be present in a developing country are: Marketing factors, Cost factors, and Investment factors which form the crux of every country's FDI presence.

Figure 3. Motivations for foreign direct investment

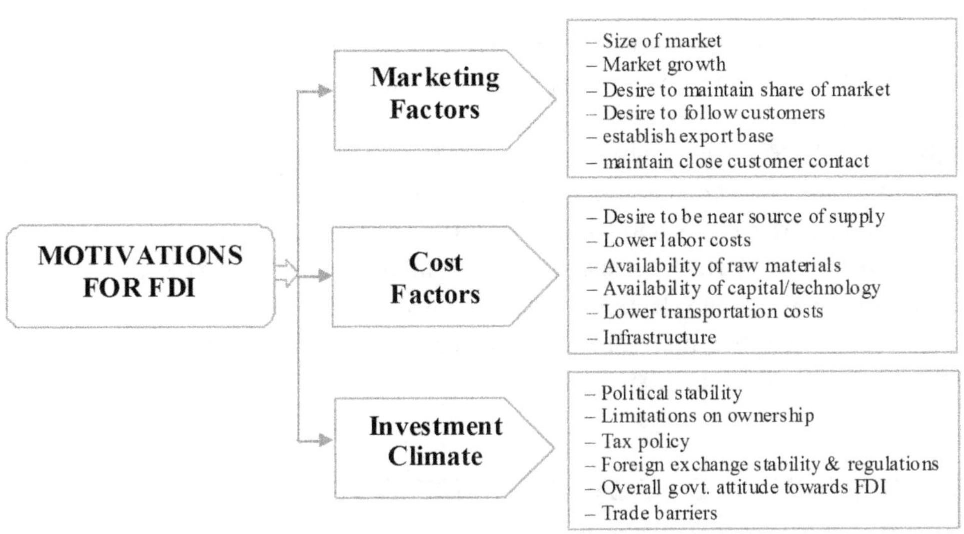

Determinants of Inter-State Variations in FDI In-Flows in India

The following are the factors which differentiate the flow of FDI in different states of India based on the availability are discussed (Sujitha, Mishra, & Chatterjee, 2013).

- **Research and Development Intensity (RDI):** The relationship between R&D efforts and FDI inflows is complex. On the one hand, R&D is expected to raise the quality of human capital and its productivity by improving existing technologies and developing new techniques (Nunnenkamp and Stracke, 2007). In other words, higher R&D is likely to improve technological capabilities, which in turn may result in greater FDI inflows.
- **Implemented Domestic Investment (DI):** Both domestic and foreign investment can add impulse in creation of asset base. In an underdeveloped state, domestic investment may create infrastructure and market opportunities to encourage foreign investors for investing therein (Chatterjee et.al., 2013). Greater domestic investment into a state may also signal better business environment and the thereby attract greater FDI inflows.
- **Transportation and Communication Infrastructure (TCI):** Better transport and communication facilities are expected to provide easy and quick access to input and output markets making the environment largely business conducive (Nunnenkamp and Stracke, 2007). Therefore, the states with better TCI are likely to attract greater FDI inflows.
- **Power Supply (PWR):** Availability of electricity along with other infrastructural parameters is instrumental for bringing in private investment, whereas shortage of it is likely to restrict investment inflows (Archana, 2006). The states with more power shortage are likely to receive less FDI inflows.
- **Educational Infrastructure (EDUI):** Investment requires availability of qualified human capital and, therefore, promoting education is considered as crucial for overall development of an economy (Sen and Pal, 2005). A number of studies observe significant influence of human capital on FDI inflows.
- **Health infrastructure (HI):** Good health facilities have positive impact on labour productivity (Sen and Pal, 2005). Therefore, one may expect a positive relationship between health infrastructure and FDI inflows.
- **Profitability (PROF):** Higher profitability of the existing enterprises in a state indicates better business environment and hence encourages potential investors to invest therein (Chatterjee*et.al.*, 2013). It also raises the ability and willingness of the existing enterprises to expand their business.
- **Risks of Investment (RI):** As many of the potential investors are risk-averse, market risksare likely to play crucial role in selecting investment location. From a firm's perspective, risks and returns are considered as the important performance characteristics that are likely to influence entry decisions (Basant and Saha, 2005).

VARIANTS OF FOREIGN DIRECT INVESTMENT

The way FDI is invested keeps changing according to the need of the hour for every company. On these lines the following are the different ways of pushing in foreign currency in to a nation.

Figure 4. Variants of foreign direct investment

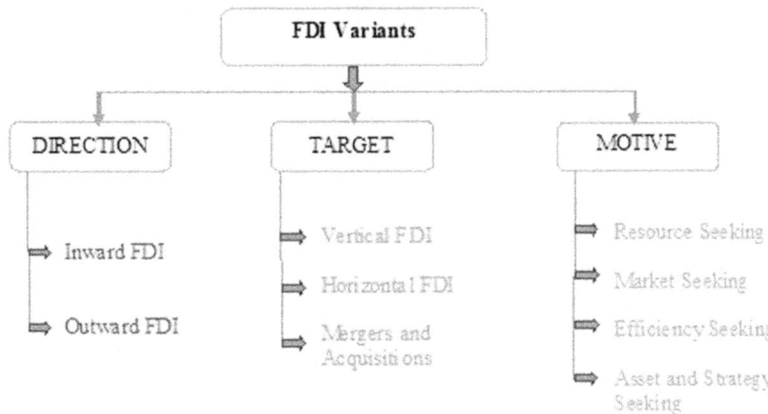

FDI Variations Based on Direction

- **Inward FDI:** Inward investment is the injection of money from an external source into a region, in order to purchase capital goods for a branch of a corporation to locate or develop its presence in the region. Foreign sources, such as transnational corporations or multinational corporations invest money by introducing new industrial sites to an area, in order to produce more of their product, sometimes in response to changes noticed in that area, such as a growing population or enhanced transport network. Inward investment creates jobs in an area and brings wealth into the economy.
- **Outward FDI**: A business strategy where a domestic firm expands its operations to a foreign country either via a Green field investment, merger/acquisition and/or expansion of an existing foreign facility. Employing outward direct investment is a natural progression for firms as better business opportunities will be available in foreign countries when domestic markets become too saturated

FDI Variations Based on Target

- **Vertical FDI:** Vertical FDI, where firms locate different stages of production in different countries foreign direct investment by a firm to establish manufacturing facilities in multiple countries, each producing a different input to, or stage of, the firm's production process.
- **Horizontal FDI:** where multi-plant firms duplicate roughly the same activities in multiple countries, Foreign direct investment by a firm to establish manufacturing facilities in multiple countries, all producing essentially the same thing but for their respective domestic or nearby markets.

FDI Variations Based on Motive

- **Market Seeking:** Firms may go overseas to find new buyers for their goods and services. The top executives or owners of a company may realize that their product is unique or superior to the competition in foreign markets and seek to take advantage of this opportunity. Another motivation for market-seeking occurs when producers have saturated sales in their home market, or when they believe investments overseas will bring higher returns than additional investments at home. This is often the case with high technology goods.

- **Resource Seeking:** Put simply, a company may find it cheaper to produce its product in a foreign subsidiary- for the purpose of selling it either at home or in foreign markets. The foreign facility may be able to obtain superior or less costly access to the inputs of production (land, labor, capital, and natural resources) than at home.
- **Strategic Asset Seeking:** Firms may seek to invest in other companies abroad to help build strategic assets, such as distribution networks or new technology. This may involve the establishment of partnerships with other existing foreign firms that specialize in certain aspects of production.
- **Efficiency Seeking:** Multinational companies may also seek to reorganize their overseas holdings in response to broader economic changes. For example, the creation of a new free trade agreement among a group of countries may suddenly make a facility located in one of those countries more competitive, because of access for the facility to lower tariff rates within the group. Fluctuations in exchange rates may also change the profit calculations of a firm, leading the firm to shift the allocation of its resources.

CSR AND FDI RELATIONSHIP

Speaking of the two variables which are dominating the business environment in every developing country are undeniably Corporate Social Responsibility (CSR) and Foreign Direct Investment (FDI) and speaking of these two factors in combination are very lethal to make a mark in given situation. In terms of internationalization CSR can be viewed as a key component of a program of a corporation creating legitimacy, reputation, and competitive advantage (Fombrun, 1996), in an effort to overcome their "liability of foreignness" (Zaheer, 1995). The relationship between CSR or corporate citizenship and the creation of intangible asset creation is affected by the appropriateness of the activities in which globalizing firms engage (Gardberg and Fombrun, 2006). As globalization increases the reach of corporations and reputationally constricts its degrees of freedom of action in host countries MNEs should be concerned about the development of CSR competitive advantages in the process of internationalization.

The development Corporate Social Responsibility (CSR), Corporate Social Policy, and Socially Responsible Investment (SRI) has taken its own path as various companies have integrated international practices into their long term corporate strategies. There have been great strides in activity related to public relations efforts of various companies with regard to CSR and social policy development (Settles, 2009). While SRI investment funds are rather limited in the many market place bi-lateral and multi-lateral agencies operations have advocated for the inclusion of socially and environmentally responsible requirements when financing or guaranteeing investments. The tangible results in various countries indicate that business has been exposed to CSR concepts, government institutions are interested in social behavior of companies, and major corporations are reporting on their CSR activities.

FDI has been one of the most fascinating and intriguing topics among researchers in international business. Numerous researchers, financial analysts and economists have done remarkable work in the field of FDI. Impact of FDI on host country, and investing country, trends of foreign financial flows and identifying determinants of FDI have been the major areas of past researches undertaken in the context of FDI. In this chapter an endeavour is made to present an overview of some of the more important research studies in the area of FDI. First we have presented a summary of the studies describing role of FDI, its impact on economic development of the host country and trend and progress of financial flows, particularly FDI.

The development impact of foreign investment on host countries has always aroused great deal of controversy. Chenery; Hollis & Montek (2004) stated that external finances could enhance growth prospects of recipient countries by augmenting domestic availability of investable surpluses. In the above framework, external financial inflows are presumed to result in a virtuous circle of growth. who observed that domestic savings in recipient countries could be negative, if capital inflows became large enough, implying thereby that external finance did not necessarily supplement, but might actually replace domestic savings.

John (2003) contends that foreign direct investment creates vertically integrated production units and therefore increases the amount of trade. Numerous factors have compelled many developing economies to change their earlier versions of trade, industrialization and investment policies. For instance India has come out with new policies relating to trade, industrialization and foreign direct investment. This has been because, FDI inflows do not have many of the costs previously associated with it and that many developing countries have managed to industrialize successfully with FDI. The most appropriate examples are of East Asian Economies or newly industrialized economies (NIEs).The benefits of FDI can be maximized only in a relatively free and market oriented environment here private economic decisions don't diverge greatly from the social good (Soon, 2004.A number of studies show the central role played by technology diffusion in the process of economic growth (Grossman and Helpman, 2006; Barro & Sala-I-Martin, 2008).Endogenous growth models look at FDI as an important vehicle for the transfer of technology and knowledge and show that FDI can have long run effects on growth by generating increasing returns in production via externalities and productivity spillovers.

Blomstrom (2007)show the spillover effect of FDI on exports with the example of Bangladesh, where the entry of a single Korean multinational in garment exports led to the establishment of a number of domestic export firms, creating the country's largest export industry. Moreover, FDI can contribute more to growth than domestic investment when there is sufficient absorptive capacity available in the host country.This is because FDI flows today are not confined to the primary sectors of developing countries but to modern manufacturing. To make their operations more productive and efficient, transnationals take with them high levels of technology. Dutt (2007) FDI can lead to higher growth by incorporating new inputs and techniques finds that technology spillovers from FDI in Indian manufacturing have significant benefits, uses urban data to show that FDI produces technological spillovers in China and explains growth differentials among Chinese urban areas. There are good theoretical reasons to show that the growth consequences of FDI depend on what kinds of sectors receive FDI and that the change in sectoral flows strengthens the positive effects and weakens the negative ones.FDI is also an important source of human capital augmentation and provides specific productivity increasing labour training and skill acquisition through knowledge transfers. DeMello and Sinclair (2005) show that FDI can promote knowledge transfers even without significant capital accumulation as in the case of licensing and start-up arrangements, management contracts and joint ventures in general.

The idea of trade-related international knowledge spillovers developed by Grossman and Helpman (2001) is extended by Uwe (2002) to FDI to show that FDI is accompanied by interregional spillovers of knowledge from the more to less advanced countries. Policies leading to an inflow of FDI therefore speed up the growth process and anything from investment controls for TNCs to specific taxes on their repatriation of profits hurts the international growth process and thereby the consumers in the developing country. Thus, theoretically speaking, the main avenues by which FDI can affect growth are productivity spillovers, human capital augmentation and technological change, though it becomes very difficult to incorporate these in empirical studies as these are not easy to measure. The dependency theorists believe that FDI can have a favourable short-term effect on growth. In the long-run, however, as FDI accumulates, it can have a negative effect on the rest of the economy due to the intervening mechanisms of dependency, in particular, "decapitalization" and "disarticulation" Found positive abnormal returns as a result of foreign acquisition in countries in which the firms were not operating before.

Yasheng and Huang (2006) examined the effect of joint venture announcements on stock price with reference to investment in Japan and China respectively. Both studies showed positive abnormal returns about (1 percent in the case of Japan and 52 percent in the case of china) as a result announcements. However, in an examination of 136 foreign investment announcements during the period (1971-86) around the world, He found significant excess negative returns for firms making such decisions. The study by Liu and Wang (2007)in examined the wealth effect for shareholders by classifying foreign investments by geographical boundaries into Asian markets and rest of the world. The results of their study indicate insignificant positive abnormal returns for investments in Asian market, while indicating significant negative abnormal return for rest of the world.

IMPACT OF FDI ON CSR

India being a developing country there are many areas which need to be improved and though efforts are being catered to all those problems by government cum private organization, there is a new ray of hope in the form of FDI which many believe would be impetus to improve societal factors. Though the primary objective of every organization is to earn profit, India has become a hub for business in the last few years where at one stage we can say that foreign countries reap more returns and of course when this part is discussed it is well known fact that FDI is always a Win-Win situation when both host and guest country will have a lot to get benefitted. Time to time this window is widening up positively as world is becoming a global village, countries now are at our door step, this again enhances FDI to great extent.

Well many of the business and software scion are contributing their wealth to needy ones, FDI's on their part have also realized that not just for monetary returns from host country but companies are now putting efforts to be a household name to go with and even companies are leaving no stone unturned to realize this dream. Companies from various sector such as ITC, Wall Mart, Google, Microsoft, Canon, Cisco, Facebook, Infosys, Toshiba, Hewlett Packard, Toyota and many more other companies are constantly contributing s for the betterment of society. The various spheres of society like Education, Environmental Sustainability, Health Care, Governance & Ethics, Literacy Needs, Sanitation Needs, Gender Equality, Protection Of National Heritage, Malnutrition, Eradicating Hunger, Socio-Economic Reports, Tax Contribution, Employment, Knowledge Creation, Local Community And Environmental Development.

When firms are venturing into multiple destinations, sometimes with very different cultures, information imperfections are a major issue. Although countries are now keen to attract FDI, since the entering firm is of unknown type, conflict is possible. This period of high FDI flows has also seen the emergence of a strong focus on corporate social responsibility (CSR). Perhaps this is a lesson learned from the past surge of FDI, which we may see being implemented in the renewed surge. CSR may be a strategy allowing business to adapt to changes in the external environment and opportunities. Does CSR allow firms to do better, earn higher profits yet contribute to the host country? If so, how does it work? What is the quantity required? These are the important question for FDI and for which we seek to address in this chapter. The relationship between foreign direct investment (FDI) and corporate social responsibility (CSR) has recently been made explicit. Many authors claim that there is an evident connection between the rise of CSR and the rise of FDI since the 1990s (Gonzalez-Perez, Riegler, & Riegler, 2011). For instance, CSR could be result of the previous surge of FDI, as a business strategy to adapt to opportunities and challenges in their external environment.

According the a survey by the Political and Economic Link Consulting (PELC) and the Ethical Corporation magazine for the World Bank Group in 2003, it was found that CSR plays a significant role factor in determining the location of multinationals activities (Kolk & Tulder, 2010). Since the mid-1990s, Latin American governments looked forward to increase the FDI especially in telecommunications, health and public services sectors in order to improve the infrastructure and receive new technologies that allow better social conditions for their societies (Tresiman, 2003).

Though FDI has many dimensions to cater for, CSR is one of them which are gaining more priorities. It is clear that both CSR and FDI are expected to be endogenous, because a higher level of FDI can have an increase of responsible business practices, but a higher level of social responsibility within a country can increase its attractiveness for FDI inflows (Gonzalez-Perez, Riegler, & Riegler, 2011).Three factors have facilitated the development of the current era of CSR at the international level:

- The formulation of the field of 'Business Ethics' by academics, policy makers and business firms since the 1960s.
- The perceived decline in state influence in the public sphere and the consequent transposition of governing power to civil society (which has traditionally acted in the private sphere).
- Rapid economic globalization with its effects on societies, the environment, and business strategy.

Since the 1990s the discourse about CSR has become more prominent in managerial, governmental, policy analysis and civil society publications. During the 1990s, some firms began to recognize their role in the social welfare of their stakeholders and assume greater responsibility towards development. The relationship between Foreign Direct Investment (FDI) and CSR is shown in below figure within the framework of analysis of the present research. The relationship between FDI and CSR has been long neglected, although it can have important consequences, as for instance CSR can serve as a signaling device, changing the under-efficient outcome of a Prisoners' dilemma to cooperation as the final equilibrium outcome for companies entering the country (Goyal, 2006).

Foreign Collaborations in India and their CSR

India has been a hub of ubiquitous companies who have invested a lot and have been giving something back for the societal welfare. The below are some of the foreign companies cum Indian companies along with their CSR statements retrieved from their respective websites:

- **CSR at Wallmart:** Creating economic opportunity for our associates, suppliers and people who work in retail and retail supply chains beyond Walmart. Enhancing the sustainability of our operations and product supply chains for people and the planet, and Building strong communities where we operate.

- **CSR at Canon India:** The three core areas that Canon India supports are Eye Care, Education and Environment. The CSR policy aligns with the corporate philosophy 'Kyosei' which means living and working together for the common good. Our employees are encouraged to volunteer their time & skills and enjoy the experience of giving back to the communities in which they work.
- **CSR at Infosys:** Infosys is committed to contributing to the society and established the Infosys Foundation in 1996 as a not-for-profit trust to support our social initiatives. The Foundation supports programs and organizations devoted to the cause of the destitute, the rural poor, the mentally challenged, and the economically disadvantaged sections of the society. The Foundation also helps preserve certain cultural forms and dying arts of India.
- **CSR of Toshiba:** Toshiba Group's Corporate Philosophy emphasizes respect for people, creation of new value, and contribution to society. The Group slogan – "Committed to People, Committed to the Future", expresses the essence of our corporate philosophy. We recognize that it is our corporate social responsibility (CSR) to put our philosophy and slogan into practice in our day-to-day business activities. In doing so, we accord the highest priority to human life and safety and to compliance. The other areas include: Investor relations, Environment, Social contribution activities, and Smart community.
- **CSR of Toyota:** Since its foundation, Toyota has continuously strived to contribute to the sustainable development of society through the manufacture and provision of innovative and quality products and services that lead the times. Motor vehicles greatly expand the freedom of mobility, but are also related to and affect a number of social and environmental issues. Always bearing this in mind, we listen carefully to our customers and neighbors in local communities to pursue our business, seeking harmony with people, society, and the global environment, as well as the sustainable development of society through *monozukuri* (Manufacturing).
- **CSR of Hewlett Packard:** Actions and investments ignite innovation that creates a brighter future for everyone by transforming how people work and live. Strengthening communities and the sustainable development of society at large; improving the environmental performance of our customers, operations, and supply chain; and acting with integrity and respect for human rights around the world.

CONCLUSION AND FUTURE IMPLICATIONS

The chapter provides high-level implications in favour of social responsibility and implementing FDI strategy, and presents the real-world applicability for the conceptual theory. MNEs are full of keenly competition, expediter in tech creativity, more diversified needs from consumers, and uncertainties in circumstances. It also presents are view of selected primary and secondary literature, informed by expert discussions. Interesting information sources may inadvertently have been overlooked, and space limitations have prevented a full exploration of relevant aspects of contemporary business ethics theories and CSR.Developing countries has a key role to play in contributing towards aggregate world cause… considering the depth of the situation and the present scenario which is prevailing in our country is very vital when it comes to FDI and their contribution towards societal growth. The concept of FDI and CSR has always been double edged tools which either make or break. In such a situation Indian representatives have a role to play to decide the extent of FDI inflow with economic development at sight. Currently,

India is at the forefront in attracting and acting as a hub for foreign collaborations, which again makes these foreign companies liable to develop an effective CSR in view of more turnover.

Now it is timely to propose an agenda for further multi-disciplinary research. Concepts FDI and CSR are often addressed by multiple agencies with different goals, cultures and values, working together in networks. Further research into how to lead and manage such networks more effectively could be helpful. More efforts could also be made to integrate management tools into the practice of CSR, Future research could explore the mechanisms linking CSR, ethics, and poverty alleviation. Further attention could be paid to the importance of intercultural factors, leadership and values in institutions, and MNEs when crafting FDI strategies for emerging markets. Topical case studies are needed that integrate issues of CSR, business ethics, and FDI, to help promote understanding of the complexity of the issues in business school programs. It would be interesting to examine the disappointments and failures as well as popular stories of success. This could be a valuable area for student projects and field studies. These are vital challenges to nations and societies. Politicians, scholars, managers, organizations, and communities can all contribute and collaborate in these efforts.

REFERENCES

Archana, V. (2006). *Foreign Direct Investment in India: Industry and State-level Analyses*. (Unpublished Thesis). Indian Institute of Technology, Kharagpur, India.

Archie, B. C. (1991). The Pyramid of Corporate Social Responsibility: Toward the Moral Management of Organizational Stakeholders. *Business Horizons*.

Basant, R., & Saha, S. N. (2005). *Determinants of Entry in the Indian Manufacturing Sector*. Working Paper No.2005-01-01. Indian Institute of Management.

Baskin, J., & Gordon, K. (2005). Corporate Responsibility Practices of Emerging Market Companies. *OECD Publishing*.

Blomstrom, M. (2007). *Transnational corporations and manufacturing exports from developing countries*. New York: United Nations.

Broomhill, R. (2007). *Corporate Social Responsibility: Key Issues and Debates*. Don Dunstan Foundation.

Carroll, A. B. (1999). Corporate social responsibility. Evolution of a definitional construct. *Business & Society*, *38*(3), 268–295. doi:10.1177/000765039903800303

Chatterjee, S., Mishra, P., & Chatterjee, B. (2013). Determinants of Inter-State Variations in FDI Inflows in India. *Eurasian Journal of Business and Economics*, *6*(11), 93–120.

Chenery, H., & Montek, S.A. (2004). Redistribution with growth. London: Oxford University Press.

Connect U. S. (n.d.). *17 Big Advantages and Disadvantages of Foreign Direct Investment*. Retrieved from http://connectusfund.org/17-big-advantages-and-disadvantages-of-foreign-direct-investment

CSR. (n.d.). In *Canon*. Retrieved from http://www.canon.co.in/personal/web/ company/ about/csr

CSR Management. (n.d.). In *Toyota*. Retrieved from http://www.toyota-global.com/sustainability/csr/csr/

CSR Policy. (n.d.). In *Toshiba*. Retrieved from https://www.toshiba.co.jp/ csr/en/policy/aim.htm

DeMello, L. R., & Sinclair, M. T. (2005). *Foreign Direct Investment, Joint Ventures and Endogenous Growth. Department of Economics, University of Kent.*

Devinney, T. M. (2009). Is the socially responsible corporation a myth? The good, the bad, and the ugly of corporate social responsibility. *The Academy of Management Perspectives*, *23*(2), 44–56. doi:10.5465/AMP.2009.39985540

Dunning, J. H. (2006). Upgrading the quality of global capitalism: the moral dimension. In S. C. Jain & S. Vachani (Eds.), Multinational corporations and global poverty reduction (pp. 346-379). Cheltenham, UK: Edward Elgar.

Dunning, J. H. (2009). Location and the multinational enterprise: John Dunning's thoughts on receiving the Journal of International Business Studies 2008 Decade Award. *Journal of International Business Studies*, *40*(1), 20–34. doi:10.1057/jibs.2008.75

Dutt, A. K. (2007). The Pattern of Direct Foreign Investment and Economic Growth. *World Development*, *25*(11), 1925–1936. doi:10.1016/S0305-750X(97)00081-8

EurWORK. (2012). *Corporate Social Responsibility*. Retrieved from http://www.eurofound.europa.eu/observatories/eurwork/industrial-relations-dictionary/corporate-social-responsibility

Fombrun, C. J. (1996). *Reputation: Realizing Value from the Corporate Image*. Boston: Harvard Business School Press.

Font, X., Walmsley, A., Cogotti, S., McCombes, L., & Häusler, N. (2012). Corporate social responsibility: The disclosure–performance gap. *Tourism Management*, *33*(6), 1544–1553. doi:10.1016/j.tourman.2012.02.012

Gardberg, N. A., & Fombrun, C. (2006). Corporate citizenship: Creating intangible assets across institutional environments. *Academy of Management Review*, *31*(2), 329–346. doi:10.5465/AMR.2006.20208684

Gill, A. (2008). Corporate governance as social responsibility: A research agenda. *Berkeley Journal of International Law*, *26*, 452.

Global-responsibility. (n.d.). In *Walmart*. Retrieved from http://corporate.walmart.com/global-responsibility/global-responsibility-report

GOI. (2015). *48% Growth in FDI Equity Inflows after Make in India.* Press Information Bureau, Ministry of Commerce & Industry, Government of India. Retrieved on 14-July-2015 from http://pib.nic.in/newsite/PrintRelease.aspx?relid=123256

Gonzalez-Perez, M. A., Riegler, S., & Riegler, F. X. (2011). Foreign direct investment (FDI) and social responsibility networks (SRN) in Colombia. *GCG: Revista de Globalización. Competitividad y Gobernabilidad*, *5*(1), 42–59.

Gorbunova, Y. (2012). Retrieved from https://ideas.repec.org/a/prg/jnlpep/ v2012y2012i2id415p129-149.htm

Goyal, A. (2006). Corporate Social Responsibility as a Signalling Device for Foreign Direct Investment. *International Journal of the Economics of Business*, *13*(1), 145–163. doi:10.1080/13571510500520077

Greening, D. W., & Turban, D. B. (2000). Corporate social performance as a competitive advantage in attracting a quality workforce. *Business & Society*, *39*(3), 254–280. doi:10.1177/000765030003900302

Grossman, G., & Helpman, E. (2006). *Innovation and Growth in the Global Economy*. Cambridge, MA: MIT Press.

Grossman, G. M., Helpman, E., & Szeidl, A. (2006). Optimal integration strategies for the multinational firm. *Journal of International Economics*, *70*(1), 216–238. doi:10.1016/j.jinteco.2005.07.011

Hopkins, M. (2003). *The Planetary Bargain: Corporate Social Responsibility Matters*. London, UK: Earthscan.

Hopkins, M. (2004). *Corporate social responsibility: an issues paper.* Working Paper No.27. Policy Integration Department. Geneva, Switzerland: International Labour Office.

Hopkins, M. (2007). *Corporate Social Responsibility and International Development: Is Business the Solution?* London, UK: Earthscan.

IndiaBriefing. (2012). *Corporate Social Responsibility in India.* Retrieved from http://www.india-briefing.com/news/corporate-social-responsibility-india-5511.html/

Ioannou, I., & Serafeim, G. (2014). The impact of corporate social responsibility on investment recommendations: Analysts' perceptions and shifting institutional logics. *Strategic Management Journal.*

Isa, S. M. (2012). Corporate Social Responsibility: What can we learn from the Stakeholders? *Procedia: Social and Behavioral Sciences*, *65*, 327–337. doi:10.1016/j.sbspro.2012.11.130

Ismail, M. (2009). Corporate Social Responsibility and Its Role in Community development: An International Perspective. *The Journal of International Social Research*, *2*(9).

John, H. D. (2003a). Multinational enterprises and the global economy. Reading, MA: Addison-Wesley Publishing Company.

Jones, K., & Bartlett, J. L. (2009). The strategic value of corporate social responsibility: A relationship management framework for public relations practice. *Prism, 6*(1).

Kercher, K. (2007). Corporate Social Responsibility: Impact of globalisation and international business. *Corporate Governance eJournal*. Retrieved from http://epublications.bond.edu.au/cgi/viewcontent.cgi?article=1003&amp%3Bcontext=cgej

Khan, M.S., & Khan, A.M. (2015). FDI and Indian Economy: Issues, Challenges and Prospects in India. *PARIPEX - Indian Journal of Research, 4*(12), 44-47.

Kolk, A. (2009). Trajectories of sustainability reporting by MNCs. *Journal of World Business*. doi:10.1016/j.jwb.2009.08.01

Kolk, A., & Lenfant, F. (2009). MNC reporting on CSR and conflict in Central Africa. *Journal of Business Ethics*. doi:10.1007/s10551-009-0271-1

Kolk, A., & Van Tulder, R. (2010). International business, corporate social responsibility and sustainable development. *International Business Review*, *19*(2), 119–125. doi:10.1016/j.ibusrev.2009.12.003

Kotler, P., & Lee, N. (2004a). *Corporate Social Responsibility: Doing the Most Good for Your Company and Your Cause*. Hoboken, NJ: Wiley.

Lall, S., & Narula, R. (2004). Foreign direct investment and its role in economic development: Do we need a new agenda? *European Journal of Development Research*, *16*(3), 447–464. doi:10.1080/0957881042000266589

Lance, M. (2001). What do we mean by corporate social Responsibility? *Corporate Governance*, *1*(2), 16–22. doi:10.1108/EUM0000000005486

Liu, X., & Wang, C. (2007). Does Foreign Direct Investment Facilitate Technological Progress? Evidences from Chinese Industries. *Research Policy*, *32*(6), 945–953. doi:10.1016/S0048-7333(02)00094-X

Make in India. (n.d.). Recent Policy Measures. *Department of Industrial Policy and Promotion, Ministry of Commerce and Industry, Government of India.*

Malhotra, B. (2014). Foreign Direct Investment: Impact on Indian Economy. *Global Journal of Business Management and Information Technology, 4*(1), 17-23.

Mehta, N. (2015). *Corporate Social Responsibility Projects*. Retrieved from http://lionsclubsindia.org/blog/Corporate-Social-Responsibility-Projects-CSR-NGO-In-India-Lions-Clubs-India

Mundra, S., Mundra, M., & Singh, M. (2013). A Review of the Impact of Foreign Direct Investment on Indian Retailing. *International Journal of Science: Basic and Applied Research*, *10*(1), 1–17.

Nunnenkamp, P., & Stracke, R. (2007). *Foreign Direct Investment in Post-Reform India: Likely to work wonders for regional development?* Kiel Working Paper No. 1375.

Reeves, J. E. (2012). *Six Reasons Companies Should Embrace CSR*. Retrieved from http://www.forbes.com/sites/csr/2012/02/21/six-reasons-companies-should-embrace-csr/

Sala-i-Martin, X., & Pinkovskiy, M. (2010). African poverty is falling... much faster than you think! National Bureau of Economic Research.

Satyendra. (2014). *Corporate Social Responsibility*. Retrieved from http://ispatguru.com/corporate-social-responsibility

Sen, J., & Pal, D. P. (2005). On Infrastructure and Economic Development. *Artha Vijnana*, *47*(1-2), 87–98.

Settles, A. M. (2009). Corporate Social Responsibility Impact on Foreign Direct Investment Practices of Russian Multinational Corporations: Do MNCs with Better CSR Practices Have Lower Cost of OFDI? An Examination of Recent Acquisitions. In *Proceedings of the X International Conference on Economic and Social Development*. State University – Higher School of Economics.

Singh, K. (2005). *Foreign direct investment in India: A critical Analysis of FDI from 1991-2005*. Available at SSRN 822584

Social Responsibility. (n.d.). In *Infosys.* Retrieved from https://www.infosys.com/investors/corporate-governance/Pages/social-responsibility.aspx

Soon, L. Y. (2004). *Foreign direct investment in ASEAN.* Malaysian Economic Association.

Stephanie, W. (2015). Corporate social responsibility reporting platforms: Enabling transparency for accountability. *Information Technology Management*, *2*(16), 19–35.

Sustainability. (n.d.). In *Hewlett Packard.* Retrieved from http://www8.hp.com/us/en/hp-information/global-citizenship/index.html

Tawade, P. H. (2013). Corporate social responsibility and FDI in India. *Golden Research Thoughts*, *2*(10), 1–4.

Treisman, D. (2003). Cardoso, Menem, Machiavelli: Political Tactics and Privatisation in Latin America. *Studies in Comparative International Development*, *38*(3), 93–109. doi:10.1007/BF02686201

Uwe, W. (2002). Innovation, Foreign Direct Investment and Growth. *Economica*, *64*, 63–79.

Yasheng, H. (2006). *Foreign Direct Investment (FDI) in China: Why Surging Levels of FDI May Indicate Serious Economic Problems.* Academic Press.

Zaheer, S. (1995). Overcoming the liability of foreignness. *Academy of Management Journal*, *38*(2), 341–363. doi:10.2307/256683

Chapter 15
Foreign Direct Investments, Corporate Social Responsibility, and Economic Development:
Exploring the Relationship and Mitigating the Expectation Gaps

James O. Odia
University of Benin, Nigeria

ABSTRACT

The increase in FDIs to developing countries has also been accompanied with rising societal expectations from the MNCs and TNCs to demonstrate more commitments to CSR. Owing to the natural resources curse, there is increasing expectations by governments, investors, consumers and local communities that businesses, particularly the MNCs and TNCs, should go beyond local regulatory compliance to earn their 'license to operate' by demonstrating that their operations provide a beneficial impact by helping to remedy the societal problems. Although it is doubtful whether businesses will take up such responsibilities, some companies have started to engage in sustainable CSR in area of operations. Therefore, the paper recommends that conscious and sustainable CSR practices of these MNCs/TNCs must be accomplished with corporate accountability in order to have the greatest positive impact on people, environment and foster economic development.

INTRODUCTION

Foreign direct investment (FDI) is an integral part of an open and effective international economic system and a major catalyst to development for developed and developing countries. But the gains accruable from FDI are not automatic and evenly distributed across continents, countries, sectors and local communities. The Organization for Economic Co-operation and Development- OECD (2002) remarked that the flows of FDI to developing countries worldwide currently overshadow official development assistance by a wide margin. Basically, FDI is defined as the investment that is made to acquire a lasting

DOI: 10.4018/978-1-5225-0305-7.ch015

interest by an entity resident in one economy in an enterprise resident in another economy. FDI may be classified as 'greenfield' or 'brownfield' investments, market/resource/efficiency- seeking investments, or mergers and acquisitions. It is a "veritable tool for economic development, employment, technological development, transfer of best practices, innovative industries, a stable source of financing and the spreading of managerial and marketing skills" (OECD, 2000). Beyond the economic benefits, FDI may help improve environmental and social conditions in the host country by, for example, transferring "cleaner" technologies and leading to more socially responsible corporate policies. FDI is regarded as a driver for economic development because it can provide access to new market, cheap capital, technology, management know-how and jobs. Therefore, the benefits that FDI can bring to host economies and the developing countries have often been canvassed by policy-makers. Little wonder many governments have developed enabling policy environment and investment architecture to encourage, attract and reap the full benefits of FDI (OECD, 2008).

However, there are heated debates that the impacts of FDIs and transnational corporations (TNCs) on developing countries have been disadvantageous and resulted in drawbacks such as: deterioration in the balance of payments as profits are repatriated, crowding-out effect in the host economy, dependence on external sources, dilution in control, destructive competition of foreign affiliates with domestic firms and loss of market to foreign firms due to weak competitive capability of the domestic firms (Utting,2003;Shafi,2014). Although FDI to developing African countries has increased, the total contribution to the global value chain is still very small. Nevertheless moving Africa's economies up the global value chain will generate jobs and wealth for a burgeoning population. Africa attracted \$51.98bn in inward capital investment in 2013 compared to the drop of \$46.92bn in 2012.This gives an increase of 10.76% which is a rebound from the inward FDI drop of 2012 from the 2011 level of \$70.92bn. Moreover, FDI flows into Africa and the Middle East increased by 24.27% in 2013.Despite this increase, the number of projects in the region decreased by 8.59% and job creation declined by 12.98%. In the same year, the FDI inflows and outflows for Nigeria was (5.83%) and \$3.06bn (6.37%) respectively. FDI into Africa increased by 64% to \$87bn, while the number of FDI projects declined by 6 percent to 660 in 2014. In 2014, FDI into Africa accounted for 13% of global FDI with the number of projects accounting for 5%.

Although the upsurge in FDIs since the 1980s has been accompanied with increasing corporate social responsibility (CSR) (Jenkins,2005; Goyal,2005), there are debates on the economic development implications of CSR by the TNCs\MNCs in developing countries.CSR refers to the "commitment by business to contribute to sustainable economic development by working with employees, their families, the local community and society at large to improve quality of life, in ways that are both good for business and economic development". Basically, CSR has become a major focus of interest to corporate managers and development practitioners. (Jenkins,2005). It is a signaling for FDI especially for unknown aggressive and accommodating firms (Goyal,2005). CSR can allow firms to do better, earn higher profits while contributing to the host country. Moreover, CSR commitments by multinational companies/enterprises (MNCs/MNEs) can cause important positive changes and economic growth. In fact, CSR initiatives have been found to have positive influence on different aspects of TNCs/MNEs' contributions towards economic development. Therefore, corporations and financial institutions view instrumental CSR and investments as a source of competitive advantage and risk mitigation.

However, it is not just the volume of economic activity that determines development; it is also how business is done which impacts people, the economy and the environment. Although FDI and MNCs/MNEs are believed to promote local and economic development, they have also aroused much controversy as well as social and environmental concerns and benefits. For instance, MNCs/TNCs have often been criticized of: taking undue advantage of poor wages and ineffective labour laws in developing countries; involving in corrupt corporate practices and supporting corrupt government, neo-colonialism, engaging in environmental degradation and pollution, and violating human and labour rights in countries with weak enforcements and where the environmental laws, fiscal regulations, legal regulations are weak (OECD, 2008). For instance, the CSR activities of oil companies and other MNCs in Nigeria are questionable and inadequate despite their claims of doing so much in philanthropies and community developments (Idemudia & Ite, 2006; Idemudia, 2007a &b; Idemudia, 2008; Egbe & Paki, 2011; Alabi & Ntukekpo, 2012; Hashimus & Ango, 2012). According to World Business Council for Sustainable Development, the policies of MNCs have been a major source of prevailing violence in the oil communities of Niger Delta. In fact, the initial hesitations by MNCs to address their social responsibility and contribute to social development enshrined poverty in the Niger-Delta regions (Alabi & Ntukekpo,2012). Jenkins (2005) has argued very strongly and concluded that "CSR as currently practiced is unlikely to play a significant role in poverty reduction in developing countries". He expressed doubts whether reform of CSR can make that objective realizable.

There are 'expectation gaps' between what the MNCs/MNEs are providing in terms of CSR and what the recipient countries expect them to contribute to their socio-economic development (Ojo & Akande, 2014). Businesses are no longer seen as creator of society's problems but they are expected to be part of the solution. There are concerns whether the multinationals are doing enough to help tackle some of the societal challenges and fill 'governance gaps' by contributing to the improvement of the governance, social, ethical, labour and environmental conditions of the developing countries in which they operate. Owing to the natural resources curse, there is increasingly expectations by the various stakeholders including the local communities and governments that businesses should go beyond economic and ethical responsibilities to altruistic and strategic CSR by demonstrating that their operations can a significant impact in helping to address public welfare deficiencies. There are enormous expectations by stakeholders that MNCs should remedy these deficiencies given government failures in most developing countries (Utting, 2000; Bennett, 2002).However, it is doubtful whether MNCs will voluntarily take up these responsibility. Nevertheless, there are renewed increasing calls on business to do more for society (Schrader, 1987; Handy, 2002; Utting & Ives, 2006; Uddin, et al, 2008).Therefore, the challenge is how to forge patterns of businesses or the FDI-CSR model that would benefit the citizens, the local communities, as well as promote the economic development of the host countries and the entire continent.

The chapter considers the relationship between FDI and CSR from the perspective of a developing country like Nigeria. It also examines the various approaches, models and theories of CSR, FDI; the global initiatives on CSR for multinationals and how FDI imparts on CSR and economic development Lastly, the chapter examines the gaps in the FDI-CSR relationship and proffers solutions on how it can be mitigated.

RESEARCH ON FDI, CSR AND ECONOMIC DEVELOPMENT

Background and Literature Review

The various definitions of CSR underscore the impacts that businesses make on society at large and many expectations of society. Although philanthropic responsibilities lie at the root of corporate CSR concerns globally, CSR now encompasses similar terms liketriple bottom line (TPL), corporate citizenship, philanthropy, strategic philanthropy, shared value, corporate sustainability and business responsibility. According to Pirnea, Olaru and Moisa (2011), the evolution of corporate responsibility has been as follows: shareholders (1970s), philanthropy (1980s), corporate governance (early 1990s), stakeholders engagement (late 1990s), corporate accountability (early 2000s) and responsible competitiveness (late 2000s).Garriga and Melé (2004) and Lei (2011) identify four types of CSR theories and related approaches as follows:

1. Instrumental theories where the corporation is seen as an instrument of profit maximization and wealth creation. Examples include: the resource-based, shareholder and strategic CSR approach
2. Political theories which deal with the political power of corporations in society e.g. corporate constitutionalism approach to CSR and corporate citizenship
3. Integrative theories consider how social demands are satisfied. The approaches include: stakeholder, community and social obligations and corporate social performance approach, and
4. Ethical theories highlights the ethical or moral duties of corporations; it comprises CSR paradigms, normative approach and stewardship approaches (Adeyemo, Oyebamiji & Alimi, 2013).

Michael (2003) advances three broad schools of thought on CSR development and practice to include: the neo-liberal, state-led and the third-sector (NGOs); and also highlights the failures and consequences (economic, political and social) of each school. The neo-liberal school focuses on self-regulation by industry based on risks and rewards of CSR activity. Here the CSR decision is more than advantages or benefits from philanthropy but a conscious use of CSR investment and reporting as a market signaling strategic tool (Tirole, 1989). The branding strategy is product certification. However, the neo-liberal school fails to address resource misallocation caused by CSR due to: diversion of managerial time and resources through creation of executive post, distortion in prices, inputs and production because of distorted resources allocation, collective action problem and politicization of organization. The state-led school focuses on national and international regulation and cooperation to enforce CSR obligations on companies. Here, national policy makers and international agencies like the World Bank, UN, OECD are strong advocates of state-led CSR.As against certification, CSR collective action problems is the method for solving collective action problems. Apart from becoming a site of (political) contestations at the company's and international levels, the state-led fails to address the underlying politics behind government- encouraged CSR. The third sector school focuses on the role of profit and not-profit organizations (NGOs, civil societies) as the key motor for CSR (Anheier & Seibels, 1990; Michael,2003). Example of third-sector non-profit NGOs include: World Council for Sustainable Development(WBCSD),Business for Social Responsibility (BSR),Copenhagen Centre; the profit NGOs include: the Coalition for Environmentally Responsible Economies (CERES), SustainAbility and MHC International, CSR Europe. The third sector fails to address issues of self- interest, social contestations in CSR.

The European Commission defines CSR as "the responsibility of enterprises for their impacts on society". On it part, the World Bank on Corporate Sustainability Development (WBCSD) defines CSR as "the continuing commitment by business to contribute to economic development while improving the quality of life of the workforce and their families as well as of the community and society at large". For businesses to meet their CSR obligations, they "should have in place a process to integrate social, environmental, ethical human rights and consumer concerns into their business operations and core strategy in close collaboration with their stakeholders". Generally, CSR refers to the way a business balances its economic, environmental and social concerns (triple-bottom-line approach) and satisfies the expectations of its stakeholders.

Basically, there are two main viewpoints on the roles of business in society: the classical and stakeholder views (Lantos, 2001). The classical view which is based on neo-classical economic theory focuses on making profits for shareholders has two perspectives: the pure profit-making (Friedman,1970; Barry,2000 & 2002) and the constrained profit -making which is aimed at shareholders' value maximization (Friedman,1998; Jensen,2001). The stakeholder view based on stakeholder's theory holds that companies have to consider the interests of all stakeholders (Freeman et al, 2004). Carroll (1979, 1991) argues that CSR is made up of four categories or responsibilities. These are: economic (be profitable), legal (obey the law), ethical (do right) and discretionary or philanthropic (do good) responsibilities. The economic responsibility is the foundation upon which all other responsibilities are predicated and achieved (Carroll,1991).The philanthropic responsibility has been subsumed under ethical and/or economic responsibilities because a firm carries out discretionary for ethical and economic reasons of both (Schwartz &Carroll,2003). Lantos (2002) distinguishes between ethical and philanthropic responsibilities by categorizing CSR into: ethical, altruistic and strategic CSR. According to Lantos (2001), ethical CSR involves morally mandatory fulfillment of economic, legal and ethical responsibilities-by preventing or rectifying harm or social injuries even though the companies do not benefit from such gestures; altruistic CSR is fulfilling the philanthropic responsibilities by going beyond ethical CSR to address or alleviate social problems (the assumption for public welfare deficiencies by companies) regardless of whether or not it benefits the business. Strategic CSR is fulfilling the philanthropic responsibilities which benefit the company through positive publicity and goodwill.

Nevertheless, the CSR debates have centered around ethical (moral) and discretionary (philanthropic) responsibilities of business due to the voluntary corporate behavior and mere compliance by companies (Matten, et al,2003; Branco et al,2007). Visser (2006) argues that CSR responsibilities in Africa is not consistent with Carroll's topology as philanthropic responsibilities come second instead of the fourth position they occupy in developed countries.

Visser (2008) argues that the focus on CSR in developing countries is due to the following reasons: First, developing countries represent the most rapidly expanding economies, and hence the most lucrative growth markets for business. At the present the growth rate of African countries is about 6%.Second, developing countries are where the social and environmental crises are usually most acutely felt in the world. This is owing to the corporate abuses and malpractices by the MNCs and TNCs, government ineffectiveness and weak institutions. Third, developing countries are where globalization, economic growth, investment, and business activity are likely to have the most dramatic social and environmental impacts (both positive and negative)"; and fourth developing countries present a distinctive set of CSR agenda challenges which are collectively quite different to those faced in the developed world. While the issue of poverty, provision of basic infrastructural facilities is peculiar to the developing countries, it is fair business practices that are of concerns in developed concerns. For example, Hashimu and Angus (2012) find weak customers' treatment and poor social obligations of MNCs in Nigeria. The negative impacts of the activities of oil companies' oil spillage, gas flaring, water pollution and environmental degradation in the Niger Delta region of Nigeria and the exploitation of customers by telecommunication companies are also evident.The oil companies and other multinational companies have only given more attention to the affirmative duties in their CSR without addressing the negative injunction duties which have greater implications (Idemudia & Ite, 2006).

Although FDI has been on the increase, the leading destination sectors of foreign investments in Africa have been mining and energy extraction (Coal, Oil & Natural Gas with 38% of total FDI inflows in 2014) the so-called 'resource curse' for countries' economies and its attendant risks given the weak track records of many governments in the region. Resource revenues can be a window of opportunity for economies seeking to diversify and restructure - if managed properly. Again, the history of MNCs / TNCs regarding CSR in these sectors leaves much to be desired as far as sustainable social and economic developments are concerned.

ISSUES, CONTROVERSIES AND PROBLEMS

Approaches to CSR

Visser (2008:473) remarked that "the challenge for CSR in developing countries is framed by a vision that was distilled in 2000 into the Millennium Development Goals - 'a world with less poverty, hunger and disease, greater survival prospects for mothers and their infants, better educated children, equal opportunities for women, and a healthier environment". Unfortunately, these global aspirations are far from being achieved in many developing countries today. The reasons are not far-fetched. The current CSR initiatives emanated from the North in the 1990s following the demand for greater social responsibility from the TNCs when most southern governments were still following the neo-liberal policies of the 1970s.According to Jenkins (2005:528), CSR today has been largely driven by non-governmental organizations (NGOs), trade unions, consumers and shareholders in the North, whose main concerns were environmental impacts, working conditions and human rights. Corporate practices such as transfer pricing, tax avoidance, abuse of market power and poverty reduction or equity are not part of the current CSR mainstream. This re-emphasizes Henderson (2001) position that "today's CSR mark a new departure". Branco and Rodrigues (2007) posit that the present day CSR implies that companies voluntarily integrate social and environmental concerns in their operations and interactions with stakeholders. In stark contrast to many Western CSR priorities of climate change, consumer protection, socially responsible investments and fair trade, Amaeshi et al (2006) argue that CSR in Nigeria is focused on addressing socio-economic development challenges.

Based on the stakeholder theory, there are instrumental and normative approaches to CSR (Donaldson & Preston, 1995). The normative (ethical) approach sees stakeholders as end; whereas the instrumental approach considers stakeholders as a means to an end, that is, its underlying interest is the factors

Table 1. Viewpoints on the roles of business in society

Views	Perspectives	Position on Business Role in Society
Classical	Pure profit making	Business has lower standards of ethics than society and no social responsibility other than obedience to the law
	Constrained profit-making	Business should maximize wealth, obey the law and be ethical
Stakeholder	Socially aware	Business should be sensitive to potential harms of its action on various stakeholders.
	Social activism	Business must use its vast resources for social good, be responsive and embark on programmes to tackle social ills.

Source: Adapted from Lantos (2001)

to take account as well as stakeholders' management to enhance financial performance, profitability, value maximization, survival and growth. CSR motivation is also attributed to the normative and business case or both reasons. While the normative case motivated by the desires to do good depends on religious principles, philosophical references or prevailing social norms, the business case is based on enlightened self- interest.

Although there are arguments on the rightness or wrongness of the actions of corporate leaders on CSR, it is important to distinguish between instrumental or strategic CSR and ethical or philanthropic CSR (Muller & Fahey, 2004; Waldman & Siegel, 2008) as well as voluntary and obligatory CSR. There are arguments that firms should consider CSR as part of their corporate strategy, make it a form of strategic investment (McWilliams, Siegel & Wright, 2006) and use CSR as a source of competitive advantage (Branco & Rodrigues,2006).The strategic use of CSR to seek value maximization in the long-term encompasses the 'enlightened shareholder maximization' by Jensen (2001).Based on the Swanson (1995) economic and duty-aligned approaches in the business-society relation, Maignan and Ralston (2002) outlines three motivations for CSR to include:

1. Economic or utilitarian perspective; CSR is used to achieve corporate objective
2. Negative duty view where CSR is used as legitimacy instrument to show compliance with the norms and expectation of stakeholders and
3. Positive-duty approach where companies embark on CSRs based on self –motivation whether or not they are demanded or expected by the society.

Branco et al (2007) remark that the utilitarian argument is associated with the classical view, negative duty is associated with the instrumental use of stakeholder theory; the positive duty is associated with the normative use of stakeholder theory and activist view of social responsibility.

Bagnoli and Watts (2003), Baron (2001) and McWilliams and Siegel (2001) advocate "profit-maximizing" CSR whereby firms behave in a socially responsible manner because of some anticipated long- run benefits (Porter & Kramer, 2002) such as: a social license to operate, reductions in down-times due to shutdowns, shut-ins and lock-outs, increased corporate reputation, goodwill and customers loyalty. The concerns about strategic CSR include the lack of commitment or collective cooperation for its implementation due to suspicion by lower- level managers and employees that higher-level leaders are not really genuine or authentic in their concerns (Waldman & Siegel, 2008).They may even resort to game practices. Graafland and van de Ven (2006) found a weak correlation between strategic CSR and actual CSR, implying that that strategic CSR view is a necessary but not a sufficient condition for firm's actual CRS involvement. There are arguments that the non-instrumental use of CSR constitutes a waste of organization's resources and firms should not undertake CSR when it is not used instrumentally or when the "return on investment" in CSR is insufficient.

The philanthropic CSR which focuses on education, health and environment is deficient as it does not ensure sustainability of such projects. For instance, a corporation building a classroom or public health centres without considering the provision of teachers or nurses, books or drugs may be counterproductive. Besides, it is prone to corruption. The economic and philanthropic aspects of CSR is mostly common in developing countries of Africa (Visser,2006; Visser, Matten, Pohl & Tolhurst,2007). Amaeshi Adi Ogbechie, and Amao (2006) examine CSR practice in Nigeria whether it was indigenous practice or Western mimicry. Although CSR practice has been influenced by the West, they find that CSR is a localized and socially home-grown. Visser (2008) argues that though many believe that modern CSR is a Western invention, CSRs in developing countries are deep-rooted in indigenous cultural traditions of philanthropy, business ethics and community inclusion.

Mordi, Opeyemi, Tonbara, and Ojo (2012) argue that CSR by Nigerian organizations is mainly philanthropic,economic support and compensatory components. According to them, philanthropic CSR entails donations to community development, cultural practices and celebrations. In economic support, corporate organizations help to provide social infrastructures such as like portable water, schools, parks, health centres and empowerment of the less privileged. Compensatory CSR is where organizations compensate for operational breaches during the production process to individuals or institution affected. A major challenge to CSR in Nigeria is the ineffectiveness of the legal provisions (Mordi et al,2014). Nevertheless the factors influencing the CSR initiatives by companies in Nigeria include: competition, employees demand and pressure groups (Adeyemo et al, 2013), activities of civics societies (Adegboyega & Taiwo, 2011),profitability (Osemene, 2012),community pressures, legal requirements, competitors and firm's ethical values (Onwuegbuchi, 2009).According to the CSR-in-Action report for 2013, most of the CSR activities by national and multinational companies in Nigeria are philanthropic in nature. Ojo and Akande (2014) argue that where a society craves for basic amenities like portable water, medical facilities, good roads and electricity to mention few, and MNCs offer scholarship awards to gifted and perhaps indigent students might be too individualistic, cosmetic, non-utilitarian and not altruistic enough. The voluntary initiative by MNCs to CSR is found to be completely inadequate response to the devastating impacts of MNCs (Christian Aid, 2004).

Visser (2008) refers to the CSR that is philanthropic, risked-based, image and publicity driven, specialized, standardized, marginal and western as CSR1.0.It is argued that as the world becomes more connected and global challenges like poverty and climate change loom larger, businesses that still practice CSR1.0 will be left behind and gives way for companies that embrace CSR2.0. According to Visser (2010a & 2010b), CSR 2.0 is referred to as "corporate responsibility and sustainability".Unlike CSR1.0, the CSR2.0 is collative, reward-based, performance - driven, integrated, diversified scalable and global. The DNA strands of CSR 2.0 is conceived as a spiral, interconnected and non-hierarchical levels representing economic, human, social and environmental responsibility and sustainability systems (Pirnea, Olaru & Moisa,2011).

Models of CSR

The different foreign investors in the African continent include the Western (US, UK etc) and the BRICS countries. Among the BRICS, China has the highest FDIs and she has continued to increase her investments in Africa following the "go-global" strategy in 1996 (Olga, 2014). Each of the investor like China seems to have their own designed CSR. Despite the late coming of the Chinese companies to the African scene, the Corporation law of China in 2006 provides the legal foundation for their CSR while the Guidelines for Central State-Owned Enterprises regarding the implementation of CSR of 2008 require them to establish necessary mechanisms to fulfill CSR so as to be " human-oriented, stick to scientific development, responsible to stakeholders and environment" so as to achieve the harmony between enterprises' growth, society and environment. Guoqiang, Zadek and Wickerham (2009) argue that more Chinese companies and industrial sectors are complying with international standards and they have started to use the UN Global Compact, GRI and ISO standards.

It has been argued that the international standards on CSR might act as barriers to new Chinese businesses coming to Africa because the CSR standards set to guide the practice of Western companies could limit the Chinese business strategies and CSR practice (Forstater, Zadek, Guang, Yu, Hong & George, 2010).A major difference in CSR conception between Chinese and Western model relates to the degree their business practices reinforce or undermine local legal and political institutions, particularly in institutionally weak countries. Essentially the Western model encourages compliance with international best practices, transparency and accountability in the managing of natural resource revenue and overcoming corruption. This is not completely the same with the Chinese business model with access to their government's low-cost and long-term capital to directly provide public infrastructure which do not meet local needs and unsupported with maintenance (Forstater et al, 2010). Olga (2014) argues that CSR is not among core corporate strategic management of many Chinese; CSR is marginalized and there is less incentives for absolute commitment by frontline managers and the local staff. Chinese enterprises in their quest to conquer natural resources from the developing countries of Africa need to improve and take seriously the issue of sustainable management of natural resources in order to add values to the local economies.

Theories Underpinning CSR

Within social and environmental reporting (SER) and embedded notions of CSR, various theoretical frameworks have been used to examine the issue of CSR practice. According to Spence, Husillos and Correa-Ruiz (2010), "the theoretical frameworks on SER have been essentially but not exclusively limited to stakeholder, legitimacy and marxist political economy". Others are shareholder theory (Friedman,1970), institutional (Campbell, 2007) and resources dependence theories. Drawing support for stakeholder theory for CSR debates (Matten,Crane & Chapple,2003; Garriga & Mele,2004), Branco and Rodrigues (2007) argue that the notions of CSR should be situated on stakeholder theory because it addresses both normative and instrumental aspects of CSR. Moreover, stakeholders theory is more encompassing than the shareholder theory with the social and economic goals integrally connected and considers the long-term value maximization of the firm (Porter & Kramer, 2002; Freeman, Wicks & Parmer,2004). Although the stakeholder theory suggest that strategic CSR could lead to better corporate performance and reputation (Fombrun,2005, Freeman, Harrison, Wicks, Parmar & Colle, 2007), Michael (2003) argue that the stakeholder model can politicize the organization at the governance and operational levels; it can make CSR a political system of lobbying for budgetary resources and senior managerial attention (Barry,2000& 2002). Spence, Husillos and Correa-Ruiz (2010) criticize the erstwhile theories on CSR and advocate the role of accounting in bringing about social change than the self-referential-and perhaps self-serving-pragmatism characteristic of extant SER researches. Their suggestion for corporate accountability and response to democratic and/or popular demands by the diverse groups might involve actual social struggle.

According to Utting (2005), corporate accountability suggests that the TNCs/MNCs should be made to account to the stakeholders through appropriate punishments or sanctions. CSR has been conceived as a means of legitimacy management that a company can showcase prove their engagement to their stakeholders of the rightness of their actions and activities. But corporate accountability is complaints-based system of regulation which is meant to identify, investigate, publicize and seek redress for corporate malpractices as a support to regulation.

Basically, disclosures or communication about CSR activities help companies to address legitimacy threats (Gray, Owen & Adams 1996; Dowling & Pfeffer,1975). However, there is a danger if a company's CSR activities are detached from the actual problems in the host country. The CSR activities of most

MNCs/TNCs follows a similar trends aim at scoring positive media publicity and reputation building rather deliberate prioritization of CSR projects to address critical society's problems (Frynas,2005:585). This eventually leads to green washing (Greer & Bruno, 1996). Apart from using CSR for altruistic intentions and good global citizen, Sprinkle and Maines (2010) argue that organizations may engage in CSR activities as "window dressing" to appease various stakeholder groups such as non-governmental organizations (NGOs) and avoid negative publicity and other actions from other stakeholders. Little wonder, some observers have stated that "CSR is a con job...a neat trick used by NGOs as old-fashioned blackmail" (Albrechtsen, 2006, p. 12). Porter and Kramer (2006:80) argue that "heightened corporate attention to CSR has not been entirely voluntary... the most common corporate response has been neither strategic nor operational but cosmetic". Consequently, Frynas (2008) expressed doubts whether the complex development problems of society might 'easily' be solved by corporate involvement given lack of support for such a claim. Again, Egbe and Paki (2011) argue that because of the inability of TNCs\ MNCs to look beyond profit in rendering CSR services, and their complicity in corruption issues like the case of Siemens and Halliburton, human right abuses, environmental disregards, social and economic dislocation, voluntary principles/guidelines are being put in place to checkmate the activities of MNCs in the developing countries.

Global Initiatives: Principles and Guidelines on CSR

Some of the global initiatives on CSR include: the UN Global Compact, UN Guiding Principles on Business and Human Rights, International Labour Organization's (ILO) tripartite declaration of principles on multinational enterprises and social policy, OECD guidelines for multinational enterprises, Institute of Social and Ethical Accountability: AccountAbility's AA1000 series of standards, Social Accountability International (SAI): SA 8000 Standard, ISO 26000 on Social responsibility, OECD CSR policy tool, Global Compact Self-Assessment Tool, the SROI Network, the LBG model. There are evidences that CSR codes, standards and initiatives are key drivers for CSR in developing countries and help to ensure best and transparent business practices by MNCs. Although, there are arguments whether these initiatives have failed to completely address the core problems of developing countries, the lack of specificity and strict enforcement coupled with the non-domestication of these standards still create avenues for poor CSR practices by multinational companies.

The UN Global Compact (UNGC) has ten broad principles dwelling on environment, human rights, labor, and anti-corruption. It also provides guidance, tools and collaboration networks to assist companies to meet and communicate these principles. The UN Global Compact's ten principles are backed by universal declarations such as the UN Declaration of Human Rights or ILO Labour principles referred to as "global values". The OECD Guidelines for Multinational Enterprises (MNEs) establish the standard behavioural norms for the MNEs by ensuring that their activities are in harmony with national policies in the countries of operation in order to strengthen the mutual confidence between them. This is to ensure that MNEs make positive contributions to the socio-economic development and minimize the challenges and difficulties in their countries of operations. The Guideline covers a broad range of MNE operations from: employment and industrial relations, environmental protection, information disclosure, competition, financing, taxation to science and technology. Since the design of the Guideline is not country or company specific, that it is, supra-national and supra-corporate, there may be challenge for MNES especially in countries where it is not domesticated.

A number of these standards relevant to natural resources exploration and business development in African countries include the Extractive Industry Transparency Initiative (EITI) which is being domesticated by the countries, Kimberley Process, Equator Principles, Voluntary Principles on Security and Human Rights, the, the Forest Stewardship Council Principles, and the World Bank environmental and social standards. In Nigeria, the debates on whether CSR should be catered for by law or left to individuals and organizations morality has long been debated (Mordi, Opeyemi, Tonbara & Ojo, 2012). Although Section 279(4) of the Companies and Allied Matters Acts (CAMA) of 1990 deals on employees, National Environmental Standards and Regulations Enforcement Agency (Establishment) NESRA Act of 2007 on environmental protection, Harmful Waste (Special Criminal Provisions Act) relates to CSR issues. The Nigeria Extractive Industry Transparency Initiative (NEITI) is expected foster transparency, accountability and corruption-free in the operations and payments processes in Nigerian extractive industry. Currently, there is no specific law in Nigeria that makes it mandatory for companies to either incorporate environmental preservation into their company policies or enforce the compliance thereto. The bill on CSR seeking to establish the Corporate Social Responsibility Commission ("CSR Commission") before the Nigerian national assembly since 2012 is yet to be passed into law. Ayorinde (2007) argues that CAMA requires companies to pay taxes, rates and levies but it does not include the provision of social infrastructures or amenities its immediate environment. Nevertheless, companies are expected to make positive impacts as responsible citizens on their environments in order to enjoy peaceful, positive relationship and performance. But there is no legal provision companies can be held accountable for environmental protection, then no offence can arise and there can never be any sanction.

Again Ijaiya (nd) observed that CSR practice by companies in Nigeria is discretionary as there is no specific legislation on CSR. Besides, none of the international CSR Instruments such as the OECD Guidelines for MNEs, the UN Global Compact and the 1998 ILO Declaration on Fundamental Principles and Rights at Works has been domesticated in Nigeria. Besides, the Nigerian Stock Exchange does not yet require companies to comply with the principles of the UN global compact, Global Reporting Initiatives (GRI), and the Dow Jones Sustainability Index (DJSI) before listing into the stock exchange like some other emerging economies. (Odia,2009).

Adegboyega and Taiwo (2011), and Davenport (2000) argue that CSR gained prominence in Nigeria in the 1990s following the internationalization of the conflicts between oil/ gas companies and their host communities. In fact, the conflicts between Ogoni people and Shell Petroleum Development Company (SPDC) in1992 (Kretzman,1995) resulted in a shift in companies' attitude towards CSR and from internal to external delivery of CSR following their realization of the impact of CSR on corporate image or reputation, safety of corporate assets and improvement in corporate performances (Lewis, 2003). These developments have led to various CSR interventions such as agriculture development, capacity building, economic empowerment and provision of rural infrastructure in health, education and potable water (See Table 2).Some of the business entities in Nigeria have foundations for delivering their CSR. For example, Leventis Foundation, MTN Foundation, Shell Foundation and British-American Tobacco, Nigeria (BATN) Foundation

According to Idemudia (nd), the gravitation from the provision of social infrastructures to capacity building and economic empowerment through the provision of micro-credits schemes, skills acquisition and investment in small and medium enterprises by oil companies was due to:

Table 2. Selected CSR interventions in Nigeria by sectors

Sectors	CSR Intervention	Key Contributors
Agriculture	Provision of extension services	Oil & Gas, FBOs, Manufacturing companies
	Input supply	Oil & Gas, FBOs, NGOs,
	Capacity building	Oil & Gas companies, NGOs, FBOs
Water and sanitation	Provision of potable water	Oil & Gas companies, WaterAid, Food and Beverages
	Provision of sanitation facilities	Oil & Gas companies
Health	Provision of infrastructure and equipment	Oil & Gas companies, Banks, Telecoms companies
	Delivery of services	FBOs
	Supply of drugs/consumables	Oil & Gas companies, international NGOs
	Advocacy and sensitization	International NGOs, local NGOs
Education	Provision of infrastructure	Oil & Gas, Banks, Food & Beverages companies, FBOs.
	Provision of supplies & consumables	Oil & Gas companies, Banks, Food & Beverages companies.
	Provision of scholarships	Oil & Gas companies, Banks
	Endowment of academic chairs	Banks, Oil & Gas companies
	Sponsorship of academic conferences	Oil & Gas companies
	Provision of educational services	FBOs
	Sponsorship of scholarly competitions	Telecoms companies, Food & Beverages companies
Capacity building and economic empowerment	Apprenticeship and economic empowerment programmes	Oil & Gas companies
	Vocational training	FBOs, Oil & Gas companies
Credits	Micro-credit	Oil & Gas companies
	ACGSF	Oil & Gas companies
	SMEEIS	Banks
Others (infrastructure)	Roads	Oil & Gas companies
	Electricity	Oil & Gas companies
	Markets	Oil & Gas companies

Source: Adegboyega and Taiwo (2011)

1. True sustainable community development is based on the wealth creation within communities rather than the redistribution of income, assets or gifts,
2. Need to incorporate other NGOs to assist the oil companies and
3. Government had enormous resources from the creation of Niger-Delta Development Commission (NDDC) to build infrastructure.

Again the oil companies-community development partnership initiatives through strategic alliance (SA), programme partnership (PP) and programme implementation partnership (PIP) have not yield the expected results of making significant impacts on host communities because of the failure to integrate the negative injunction duties into such partnerships and projects.

FDI and Economic Growth

In recent years FDIs have attracted renewed interest both in the underdeveloped and developed countries even though there are growing suspicious about foreign direct investments at the World Trade Organization (WTO) (Anyanwu, 1998). Aremu (1997) categorizes the various types of foreign investment in Nigeria into five as: wholly foreign owned; joint ventures; special contract arrangements; technology management and marketing arrangements; and subcontract co-production and specialization. According to Kumar (2007), FDI could include: a parent enterprise injecting equity capital by acquiring shares in a foreign, reinvesting the affiliate's earnings and short-or foreign investment as a percentage of the Gross Domestic Product (GDP).

Unlike CSR and economic development many researchers have examined the relationship between FDI and economic growth in Nigeria with mixed findings. For example while Aluko (1961), Ariyo (1998), Otepola (2002), Mojekwu and Ogege (2012) reports positive linkage between FDI and economic growth in Nigeria whereas Endozien (1968), Adelegan (2000), Bashir (2013) find negative and non-significant relationship. Ekpo (2003) finds that various government policies on private sector development including its foreign component appear not to have significant impact on Nigeria's economic development. Akinlo (2004) found that foreign capital has a small and not statistically significant effect on economic growth in Nigeria. Ayanwale and Bamire (2001) assess the influence of FDI on firm's level productivity in Nigeria and report a positive spillover of foreign firms on domestic firm's productivity. Using the two-gap model and various econometric techniques, Bashir (2013) found a negative relationship between FDI and real growth. Odozi (1995) notes that foreign investment in Nigeria was made up of mostly "Greenfield" investment, that is, it is mostly utilized for the establishment of new enterprises and some through the existing enterprises in the early 1960s. Aremu (1997) noted that while the FDI regime in Nigeria was generally improving, some serious deficiencies remain in the area of the corporate environment (such as corporate law, bankruptcy, labour law, etc.) and institutional uncertainty, as well as the rule of law. Alfaro (2003) affirms that the contribution of DFI to economic growth is dependent on the sectors of the economy. For example, he finds that DFI in-flows to the primary sector record a negative effect on growth whereas the effect on service sector is not so clear.

Agrawal (2000) examines the economic impact of FDI in five South Asia countries:India, Pakistan, Bangladesh, Sri Lanka and Nepal. The results reveal negative impact prior to 1980, mildly positive for early 1980s and strongly positive impact over the late 1980s and early 1990s.Schoors and Van der Tol, Batoldus (2002) argue that at early developmental stages and/or transition to the market economies, FDI may have a negative impact on growth of the recipient economy, or the" market stealing" effect, because domestic firms are less productive than their foreign counterparts and hence they are driven out of market. Schoors et al (2002) find however that the positive effect is the negative one. They also find that cross-sectional, intersectional spillover effects are more important than the spillover effects diffused within the sector into which FDI was injected.

Issues and Challenges of FDI and Economic Growth

Among the potential drawbacks of FDI include: a decrease in the balance of payments because profits are repatriated and offset by incoming FDIs, no direct linkage with local communities, potential harmful environmental impact in sensitive industries, social disruptions of accelerated commercialization, and the effects on competition in national markets. Some host countries see over dependence on foreign enterprises as a threat or loss of political sovereignty. They are also afraid of losing control to outsiders. Moreover, the positive effects of FDI are mitigated by a partial "crowding out" of domestic investments. Even some expected benefits may prove elusive if, for example, the host economy, in its current state of economic development, is not able to take advantage of the technologies or know-how transferred through FDI. Therefore, some countries restrict FDIs due to opposition from (or on behalf of) domestic competitors fear of foreign dominance, nationalistic interests such as acquisition of national brands, exploitation of resources and pursuit of policies such as restrictions on foreign equity ownership, technology transfer, forced domestication/minimum local content or value-added restrictions. The critical issues relating to national security, critical infrastructure, sensitive technologies and balance of trade imbalance have also been advanced for FDI restrictions (OECD,2000,2002; Schwab,2013; World Economic Forum,2013).

The rise of emerging economies and power rivalries between the US and China have limited MNCs and SOEs' investments in both territories; unfortunately this has been justified as protection of national security and indigenous innovation (Wang,2013). FDI is also limited by the fragmented governance and lack of comprehensive multilateral treaty or institution to oversee investment activity. Stephenson and Dadush (2013) argue that the complex and overlay disciplines at different levels, overlapping obligations and divergent interpretations can generate costs in the form of time and inefficiencies. This can make investors to engage in "forum shopping".

The somewhat FDI's 'smaller effect on growth' has been linked to the presence of "threshold externalities". Therefore, developing economies need to reach a certain level of infrastructural development, education, technology and health to benefit from FDI flows into their markets. Financial markets that are underdeveloped, weak and inefficient can prevent a country from harnessing full benefits of FDIs. Moreover, weak financial intermediation affects more adversely the domestic enterprises than their foreign counterparts. Mooran (2000) posits that FDI is most likely to be harmful, in fact actually damaging to the growth and welfare of the developing countries and the economies-in-transition when the investor is sheltered from competition in the domestic market and burdened with high domestic content, a strong push for mandatory joint venture and technology-sharing requirements. FDI typically originates in international industries where there are high barriers to entry and deploys itself in domestic markets of developing countries where there are high degrees of concentration. Besides the potential harmful activities like pollution, inadequate health and safety standards or abusive subcontractor's behavior which could be corrected by "good citizenship" behaviour, the possibility of foreign investment causing fundamental economic distortions and pervasive damage to a country's developmental prospects is also present.

CSR and Socio-Economic Development in Nigeria

One contending issue has been the lack of accurate, reliable and up-to-date data relating to CSR. CSR remains mainly within the philanthropic space from donation institutional building to community development through various projects in Nigeria. While some companies have gone beyond philanthropic CSR to sustainable development there is less reporting on social and environmental issues, and codes of conduct on bribery and corruption (Adeolu & Afolabi,2010). The efforts of the multinationals have not contributed immensely to socio-economic development. This supports the findings of Ite (2004) that the absence of nation-wide macro-economic planning and management, equitable resource allocation and enabling environment have significant impact on the overall CSR performance of MNCs in developing countries. Therefore, where there are poor macroeconomic indices, bad governance and government failure, the contributions of MNCs to poverty alleviation and CSR will also be affected

(Ite,2004; Obi,2015).Oko and Agbonifoh (2014) find that the Niger Delta area of Nigeria is poorly developed because the government is unwilling to sacrifice the high returns from oil earnings for the region's development, and the lack of will power to regulate the activities of MNCs. They advocate a collaborative action and implementation plan among the stakeholders in the oil industry as well as the setting up of CSR committee by TNCs to foster economic development of the area. This might address the accusations and counter-accusations by the oil MNCs and host communities. For instance, while the MNCs/TNCs argue there is no legal obligation binding them to construct expensive road or any other project (Ogbuma,1987), the host communities respond that oil TNCs owe them a 'pay back development and alternative means of livelihood', having destroyed and turned their wetlands into wastelands (Zabbey,2009).The TNCs had also erroneously assumed that as long as they meet the conditions for license to operate and pay correct taxes to the Federal Government of Nigeria, they have no extra obligation to the oil-producing communities. These issues probably account for low corporate responsiveness and apathy by the MNCs/TNCs to CSR projects. The need to reverse these trends is the root-cause of restiveness, agitations and conflicts in the Niger-Delta.

Blowfield (2005) argues that despite the overlap between development and business goals, companies engage with developing economies for commercial reasons, not developmental ones. Moreover, Blowfield and Frynas (2005) fault the claims that CSR should contribute to alleviate poverty and achieve other developmental goals as unwarranted. Boyle and Boguslaw (2007) call for more active acknowledgement of poverty and the MNCs\TNCs to frame their corporate leadership to address its reduction. According to Frynas (2005), the failure of business to take up CSR is due to: "the primacy of the business case. incompatibility of corporate objectives with developmental objectives, country and context-specific issues, failure to involve the beneficiaries of CSR, lack of human resources, social attitudes of oil company staff, a focus on technical and managerial solutions, and failure to integrate CSR initiatives into a larger development plan". The author concludes that CSR practice by the oil industry presently limited potentials to foster sincere development of the local communities. Utting (2005) advocates corporate accountability for MNCs/TNCs because their CSR agenda exclude key political and economic mechanisms through which they undermine the development prospects of their countries. Unlike, the Nigerian CSR bill which is yet to be passed into law, the India's Companies Act of 2013 took CSR to the front burner through its disclose-or-explain mandate in order to promote greater transparency and disclosure of CSR by Indian companies. Basically, CSR in India focuses on what is done with profits after they are made.

SOLUTIONS AND RECOMMENDATIONS ON BRIDGING THE EXPECTATION GAPS

The governments in developing countries must become responsive in her roles to their citizens' needs. It is also the responsibility of government to ensure that adequate regulatory and enforcement frameworks exist which would ensure that companies carry out their operations in an environmentally responsible manner and in the event of non-compliance, that the laws are appropriately enforced. According to the World Bank Economic Commission for Africa (2015), countries should continue to build robust institutions that maintain and improve the business environment, economic governance and macroeconomic management in order to benefit from the increasing FDI flows. They should establish productive market-state relations that harmonize the economic, social and environmental goals to reap the benefits of FDI.

Countries engage in a global competition, establish investment promotion agencies and enact policies to incentivize FDI in order to attract the "right" kind of FDI.

In setting a new agenda for MNCs and TNCs. Hatcher (2002) argues that as the roles and responsibilities of government are being redefined and the boundaries between business and government become less clear, business leaders are facing a daunting array of challenges. There is a need for businesses to speak up for themselves for greater transparency, venture beyond mere compliance with national regulatory systems, fashion the new regulatory and trading environments of the future, and shoulder the burdens of shaping the business agenda. Responsible firms are clear about environmental laws, regulations and policies, and they comply with them. They also strengthen the social and environmental integrity of their investment and supply chain strategies, upgrade to higher-value activities as well as transcend towards corporate responsibility and sustainability.

Best CSR practices by the MNCs for developing countries should involve the following broad strategies. First, effective community development partnership should be cross-sector partnership with government, civil society, labour unions rather than voluntary philanthropy CSR by the MNCs, which only creates dependence and open to gross corruption. The partnership must also involve the local communities in the bottom-up approach for optimum results. The second strategy entails investment in improving governance, capacity building and efficiency of local and regional government through shared training. Third, there should be active engagement with social entrepreneurs and also supporting them financially in cash and kind. This would create the possibility for scalable solutions to sustainable development challenges. Fourth, there is the need for accountability reports. The misuse of CSR funds can be prevented if accounts for such activities are transparent fully audited and reported in the balance sheet. This would also aid public awareness and critique of CSR activities by the TNCs and MNCs.

Moreover, investors need to know the global initiatives and best practices on CSR including labour employment and environmental standards they are supposed to respect and comply with in developing countries of operations. There is also need for the re-negotiation and harmonization of the rules governing investment flows for foster integration, cooperation and global economic development. The North-South divide on the issue of CSR agenda and investment flows must be addressed to pave way for sustainable CSR practices and FDI flows to the benefits of all. To ensure that the increasing investment into the resource curse sector benefits the host countries, there should determined effort to address corrupt practices - bribery and payments in these countries. The group of international arbitration must refuse to enforce contracts obtained by corrupt means by any foreign investors and TNC/MNC.The loopholes in the Foreign Corrupt Practices Act and OECD Anti-Bribery Convention must be blocked to stop the corruption by local and international investors' collaboration.

CONCLUSION AND FURTHER RESEARCH

The chapter examines the role of FDI and CSR in the economic development of developing countries. Amidst the rising expectations of society and other stakeholders, businesses are enjoined go beyond compliance to be part of the solution of society since they are part of the creator of the society's problems. Corporate leaders of the MNCs and TNCs must understand their commitment to corporate responsibility and sustainability and expressed their genuine attempts to solve society's problem by investing in projects or progammes with positive and value-added impact on the people, environment and the economy as well as trying to remedy some of the fundamental imbalances such as oil spillage, gas flaring, water and land pollution, environmental degradation created by their activities by deliberate commitment to altruist and strategic CSR. The government of developing countries must make genuine commitments to close up the governance gaps and put in place effective laws and institutions which will enable them not only to attract, retain and reap the full benefits of FDI but also boost responsible behavior by businesses to CSR and ultimately leads to economic development It is through collaborative, win-win approach by all stakeholders-government, businesses, local communities- that developing economies can achieve the greatest good from the FDI- CSR relations.For further research the paper suggests investigation into the impact of laws on CSR in enhancing commitment to CSR by multinational companies.

REFERENCES

Adegboyega, O., & Taiwo, M. (2011). Contribution of corporate social responsibility to agriculture and rural development in Nigeria. *Journal of Sustainable Development in Africa*, *13*(4), 110–129.

Adelegan, J.O. (2000). Foreign direct investment and economic growth in Nigeria: A seemingly unrelated model. *African Review of Money, Finance and Banking*, 5–25.

Adeyemo, S. A., Oyebamiji, F. F., & Alimi, K. (2013). An valuation of factors influencing corporate social responsibility in Nigerian manufacturing companies. *International Journal of Academic Research in Economics and Management Sciences*, *2*(6), 54–63.

Akinlo, A. E. (2004). *Foreign direct investment and growth in Nigeria*: An empirical investigation. *Journal of Policy Modeling*, *26*(5), 627–639. doi:10.1016/j.jpolmod.2004.04.011

Alabi, O. F., & Ntukekpo, S. S. (2012). Oil companies and corporate social responsibility in Nigeria: An empirical assessment of Chevron's community development projects in the Niger Delta. *British Journal of Arts and Social Sciences*, *4*(2), 361–374.

Aluko, S. A. (1961). Financing economic development in Nigeria. *The Nigerian Journal of Economic and Social Studies*, *3*(1), 39–67.

Anheier, H., & Seibels, W. (1980). The third sector, comparative studies of non-profit organizations. de Gruyter.

Anyanwu, J. C. (1998). An econometric investigation of determinants of foreign direct investment in Nigeria in the Growth Process. *Proceedings of the Nigerian Economic Society Conference.*

Aremu, J.A. (1997). *Foreign direct investment and performance*. Paper delivered at a workshop on Foreign Investment Policy and Practice organized by the Nigerian Institute of Advanced Legal Studies, Lagos, Nigeria.

Ariyo, A. (1998). Investment and Nigeria's economic growth in Investment in the Growth Process. *Proceedings of Nigerian Economic Society Annual Conference 1998.*

Adeolu, O. A., & Afolabi, E. O. (2010). Corporate social responsibility and sustainable community development in Nigeria: WAPCO, a case from the cement industry. *Social Responsibility Journal*, *6*(4), 522–535. doi:10.1108/17471111011083419

Agrawal, P. (2000). *Economic impact of foreign direct investment in South Asia*. Bombay, India: Indira Gandhi Institute of Development Research.

Akinlo, A. E. (2004). Foreign direct investment and growth in Nigeria: An empirical investigation. *Journal of Policy Modeling*, *26*(5), 627–639. doi:10.1016/j.jpolmod.2004.04.011

Alabi, O. F., & Ntukekpo, S. S. (2012). Oil companies and corporate social responsibility in Nigeria: An empirical assessment of Chevron's community development projects in the Niger Delta. *British Journal of Arts and Social Sciences*, *4*(2), 361–374.

Albrechtsen, J. (2006, March 29). This business of moral coercion is just a hoax. *The Australia*.

Amaeshi, K., Adi, B., Ogbechie, C., & Amao, O. (2006). *Corporate social responsibility in Nigeria: Western mimicry or indigenous practices?* Research Paper Series, International Centre for Corporate Social Responsibility, Nottingham University.

Ayanwale, A.B. &, Bamire, A.S. (2001). *The influence of FDI on firm level productivity of Nigeria's Agro/Agro-Allied Sector.* Final Report presented to the African Economic Research Consortium, Nairobi, Kenya.

Ayorinde, B. (2007). *The challenges of corporate social irresponsibility in the Niger Delta regions of Nigeria – The imperative of legislative reform*. Paper presented at the 5th International Conference on International Environmental Law, New Delhi, India.

Bagnoli, M., & Watts, S. (2003). Selling to socially responsible consumers: Competition and the private provision of public goods. *Journal of Economics & Management Strategy*, *12*(3), 419–445. doi:10.1162/105864003322309536

Baron, D. (2001). Private politics, corporate social responsibility and integrated strategy. *Journal of Economics & Management Strategy*, *10*(1), 7–45. doi:10.1162/105864001300122548

Barry, N. P. (2000). Controversy:Do corporations have any responsibility beyond making a profit? *Journal of Markets and Morality*, *3*(1), 100–107.

Barry, N. P. (2002). The stakeholder concept of corporate control is illogical and impractical. *The Independent Review*, *6*(4), 541–554.

Bashir, O. K. (2013). Foreign assistance and economic growth in Nigeria: The two-gap model framework. *American International Journal of Contemporary Research*, *3*(10), 153–160.

Bennett, J. (2002). Multinational corporations, social responsibility and conflict. *Journal of International Affairs*, *55*(2).

Brautigam, D. (2008). Chinese business and African development: Flying geese or hidden dragon? In C. Alden, D. Large, & R. M. S. Soares de Oliveira (Eds.), *China returns to Africa: A rising power and a continent embrace*.

Blowfield, M. (2005). Corporate social responsibility: Reinventing the meaning of development. *International Affairs*, *81*(3), 515–524. doi:10.1111/j.1468-2346.2005.00466.x

Blowfield, M., & Frynas, J. G. (2005). Setting new agendas: Critical perspectives on corporate social responsibility in the developing world. *International Affairs, 81*(3), 499–513. doi:10.1111/j.1468-2346.2005.00465.x

Boyle, M., & Boguslaw, J. (2007). Business, poverty and corporate citizenship: Naming the issues and framing solutions. *Journal of Corporate Citizenship, 26*(26), 101–120. doi:10.9774/GLEAF.4700.2007.su.00013

Campbell, J. L. (2007). Why would corporations behave in socially responsible ways? An institutional theory of corporate social responsibility. *Academy of Management Review, 32*(3), 946–967. doi:10.5465/AMR.2007.25275684

Carkovic, M., & Levine, R. (2002). *Does foreign direct investment accelerate economic growth?* University of Minnesota Working paper.

Carroll, A. B. (1979). A three-dimensional conceptual model of corporate social performance. *Academy of Management Review, 4*(4), 497–505.

Carroll, A. B. (1991). The pyramid of corporate social responsibility: Toward the moral management of organizational stakeholders. *Business Horizons, 34*(4), 39–48. doi:10.1016/0007-6813(91)90005-G

Christian Aid. (2004). *Behind the mask: The real face of corporate social responsibility*. London: Christian Aid.

CSR-in Action. (2013). *The collective social investment report*. Nigeria.

Davenport, K. (2000). Corporate citizenship: A stakeholder approach for defining corporate social performance and identifying measures for assessing It. *Business & Society, 39*(2), 210–219. doi:10.1177/000765030003900205

Donaldson, T., & Preston, L. E. (1995). The stakeholder theory of the corporation: Concepts, evidence and implication. *Academy of Management Review, 20*(1), 65–91.

Egbo, O.P. (2011). Bivariate causality analysis on the impact of FDI inflows and economic growth in Nigeria. *Journal of Internet Banking and Commerce, 16*(3), 1-16.

Egbe, O. D., & Paki, F. A. E. (2011). The rhetoric of corporate social responsibility (CSR) in the Niger Delta. *American International Journal of Contemporary Research, 1*(3), 123–133.

Ekpo, A. H. (2003). The relative contribution of public sector and private sector investment to Nigeria's economic development since 1960. In Nigerian economy: Structure, growth and development. Benin City: Mindex Publishers.

Endozien, E. G. (1968). Linkages, direct foreign investment and Nigeria's economic development. *The Nigerian Journal of Economic and Social Studies, 10*(2), 119–213.

Friedman, M. (1998). The social responsibility of business is to increase its profit. In Perspectives in business ethics. Singapore: McGraw Hill.

Friedman, M. (1970). The social responsibility of business to increase its profits. *New York Times, 13*, 122–126.

Forstater, M., Zadek, S., Guang, Y., Yu, K., Hong, X. C., & George, M. (2010). *Corporate responsibility in African development: Insights from an emerging dialogue*. The Institute of West-Asian and African Studies of the Chinese Academy of Social Sciences, October Working Paper No. 60.

Fombrun, C. (2005). Building corporate reputation through CSR initiatives: Evolving standards. *Corporate Reputation Review*, *8*(1), 7–11. doi:10.1057/palgrave.crr.1540235

Freeman, R. E., Wicks, A. C., & Parmar, B. (2004). Stakeholder theory and the corporate objective revisited. *Organization Science*, *15*(3), 364–369. doi:10.1287/orsc.1040.0066

Freeman, R. E., Harrison, J. S., Wicks, A. C., Parmar, B. L., & de Colle, S. (2007). Stakeholder theory: The state of the art. Cambridge University Press

Frynas, J. G. (2005). The false developmental promise of corporate social responsibility: Evidence from multinational oil companies. *International Affairs*, *81*(3), 581–598. doi:10.1111/j.1468-2346.2005.00470.x

Frynas, J. G. (2008). Corporate social responsibility and international development: Critical assessment. *Corporate Governance*, *16*(4), 274–281. doi:10.1111/j.1467-8683.2008.00691.x

Garriga, E., & Melé, D. (2004). Corporate social responsibility theories: Mapping the territory. *Journal of Business Ethics*, *53*(1–2), 51–71. doi:10.1023/B:BUSI.0000039399.90587.34

Goyal, A. (2005). *Corporate social responsibility as a signaling of FDI*. Indira Gandhi Institute of Development Research.

Graafland, J., & van de Ven, B. (2006). Strategic and moral motivation for corporate social responsibility. *Journal of Corporate Citizenship*, *22*, 111–123.

Greer, J., & Bruno, K. (1996). *Greenwash: the reality behind corporate environmentalism*. New York: Apex Press.

Guoqiang, L., Zadek, S., & Wickerham, J. (2009). *Advancing sustainable competitiveness of China"s transnational corporations*. AccountAbility/ Development Research Center of the State Council of the People's Republic of China.

Handy, C. (2002). What is a business for? *Harvard Business Review*, *80*(12). PMID:12510537

Hashimus, B., & Ango, N. A. (2012). Multinational companies corporate social responsibility performance in Lagos State, Nigeria: A quantitative analysis. *European Journal of Globalization and Development Research*, *5*(1), 247–264.

Henderson, D. (2001). *Misguided virtue: False notions of corporate social responsibility*. London: Institute of Economic Affairs.

Idemudia, U., & Ite, U. E. (2006). Corporate-community relations in Nigeria's oil: Challenges and imperatives. *Corporate Social Responsibility and Environmental Management Journal*, *13*(4), 194–206. doi:10.1002/csr.101

Idemudia, U. (2007a). Community perceptions and expectations: Reinventing the wheels of corporate social responsibility practices in the Nigerian oil Industry. *Business and Society Review*, *112*(3), 369–405. doi:10.1111/j.1467-8594.2007.00301.x

Idemudia, U. (2007b). *Corporate partnership and community development in Nigerian oil industry: Strength and limitations*. Geneva: United Nations Research Institute for Social Development.

Idemudia, U. (2008). Conceptualising the CSR and development debate: Bridging existing analytical gaps. *Journal of Corporate Citizenship*.

Idemudia, U. (n.d.). *Corporate partnerships and community development in the Nigerian oil industry: Strengths and limitations*. Lancaster University.

Ijiaya, H. (n.d.). Challenges of corporate social responsibility in the Niger Delta region of Nigeria. *Journal of Sustainable Development Law and Policy, 3*(1).

Ite, U. E. (2004). Multinationals and corporate social responsibility in developing countries: A case study of Nigeria. *Corporate Social Responsibility and Environmental Management, 11*(1), 1–11. doi:10.1002/csr.49

Kretzman, S. (1995). Nigeria's drilling fields': Shell oil's role in repression. *Multinational Monitor, 16*, 1–2.

Lantos, G. P. (2001). The boundaries of strategic corporate social responsibility. *Journal of Consumer Marketing, 18*(7), 595–630. doi:10.1108/07363760110410281

Lantos, G. P. (2002). The ethnicity of altruistic corporate social responsibility. *Journal of Consumer Marketing, 19*(3), 205–230. doi:10.1108/07363760210426049

Lewis, S. (2003). Reputation and corporate responsibility. *Journal of Communication Management, 7*(4), 356–364. doi:10.1108/13632540310807494

Jenkins, R. (2005). Globalization, corporate social responsibility and poverty. *International Affairs, 3*(3), 525–540. doi:10.1111/j.1468-2346.2005.00467.x

Jensen, M. C. (2001). Value maximization, stakeholder theory and the corporate objective function. *Journal of Applied Corporate Finance, 14*(3), 8–21. doi:10.1111/j.1745-6622.2001.tb00434.x

Maignan, I., & Ralston, D. A. (2002). Corporate social responsibility in Europe and the US: Insights from businesses self presentations. *Journal of International Business Studies, 33*(3), 497–514. doi:10.1057/palgrave.jibs.8491028

Matten, D., Crane, A., & Chapple, W. (2003). Behind the mask: Revealing the true face of corporate citizenship. *Journal of Business Ethics, 45*(1/2), 109–120. doi:10.1023/A:1024128730308

McWilliams, A., & Siegel, D. (2001). Corporate social responsibility: A theory of the firm perspective. *Academy of Management Review, 26*(1), 117–127.

McWilliams, A., Siegel, D., & Wright, P. M. (2006). Corporate social responsibility: Strategic implications. *Journal of Management Studies, 43*(1), 1–18. doi:10.1111/j.1467-6486.2006.00580.x

Michael, B. (2003). Corporate social responsibility in international development: An overview and critique. *Corporate Social Responsibility and Environmental Management, 10*(3), 115–128. doi:10.1002/csr.41

Mojekwu, J. N., & Samson Ogege, S. (2012). Foreign direct investment and the challenges of sustainable development in Nigeria. *Journal of Research in International Business and Management*, *2*(7), 190–198.

Mordi, C., Opeyemi, S. I., Tonbara, M., & Ojo, S. (2012). Corporate social responsibility and the legal regulation in Nigeria. *Economic Insights-Trends and Challenges*, *LXIV*(1), 1–8.

Muller, J., & Fahey, J. (2004). Hydrogen man. *Forbes*, (Dec): 27.

Obi, A. E. (2015). Corporate social responsibility, oil exploration and the Niger Delta question. *Arabian Journal of Business and Management Review*, *4*(11), 23–34.

Odozi, V. A. (1995). *An overview of foreign investment in Nigeria 1960 – 1965*. Central Bank of Nigeria, Research Department Occasional Paper No. 11.

OECD. (2000). *Foreign direct investment, development and corporate responsibility*. Paris: OECD.

OECD. (2002). *Foreign direct investment for development, maximising benefits, minimizing costs*. Paris: OECD.

OECD. (2008). *The impact of foreign direct investment on wages and working conditions*. OECD-ILO conference on corporate social responsibility, Paris, France.

Oghuma, A. (1987, December 28). Oil producing areas have turned oasis of poverty amidst sprawling wealth. *Newswatch Magazine*, 22-21.

Ojo, O., & Akande, O. (2014). Societal perception of the corporate social responsibility of Lafarge Cement Nigeria Plc. *Research Journal of Business Management and Accounting*, *3*(2), 13–20.

Oko, A. E. N., & Agbonifoh, B. A. (2014). Corporate social responsibility in Nigeria: A study of the petroleum industry and the Niger Delta area. *International Review of Social Sciences and Humanities*, *6*(2), 214–238.

Olga, T. (2014). *Chinese foreign direct investment in Africa in corporate social responsibility context*. Working paper No.29. Maastricht School of Management.

Onwuegbuchi, C. (2009). *Telecom operators as socially responsible organisations*. Communication Week Media Ltd.

Osemene, O. F. (2012). Corporate social responsibility practices in mobile telecommunications industry in Nigeria. *European Journal of Business and Management*, *4*(8), 149–157.

Otepola, A. (2002). *Foreign direct investment as a factor of economic growth in Nigeria*. Dakar, Senegal: IDEP.

Sprinkle, G. B., & Maines, L. A. (2010). The benefits and costs of corporate social responsibility. *Business Horizons*, *53*(5), 445–453.

Pirnea, I. C., Olaru, M., & Moisa, C. (2011). Relationship between corporate social responsibility and social sustainability. *Economy Transdisciplinary Cognition*, *14*(1), 36–43.

Porter, M. E., & Kramer, M. R. (2002). The competitive advantages of corporate philanthropy. *Harvard Business Review*, *80*(12), 56–68. PMID:12510538

Porter, M. E., & Kramer, M. R. (2006). Strategy and society:The link between competitive advantage and corporate social responsibility. *Harvard Business Review, 84*(12), 78–92. PMID:17183795

Rosenzweig, P. M., & Singh, J. V. (1991). Organizational environments and the multinational enterprise. *Academy of Management Review, 16*(2), 340.

Schoors, K. & Van der Tol, B. (2002). *The productivity effect of foreign ownership on domestic firms in Hungary*. EEA Venice Conference Paper.

Schrader, D. E. (1987). The corporation and profits. *Journal of Business Ethics, 6*(8), 589–601. doi:10.1007/BF00705775

Schwab, S. (2013). *Why countries say they impose barriers to FDI in foreign direct investment as a key driver for trade, growth and prosperity: The case for a multilateral agreement on investment.* World Economic Forum, Geneva, Switzerland.

Schwartz, M. S., & Carroll, A. B. (2003). Corporate social responsibility: A three-domain approach. *Business Ethics Quarterly, 13*(4), 503–530. doi:10.5840/beq200313435

Shafi, M. (2014). Relationship between FDI inflows and economic growth: A review. *Singaporean Journal of Business Economics and Management Studies, 2*(9), 67–77. doi:10.12816/0003906

Spence, C., Husillos, J., & Correa-Ruiz, C. (2010). Cargo cult science and the death of politics: A critical review of social and environmental accounting research. *Critical Perspectives on Accounting, 21*(1), 76–89. doi:10.1016/j.cpa.2008.09.008

Stephenson, S., & Dadush, U. (2013). *The current (fragmented) governance of FDI in foreign direct investment as a key driver for trade, growth and prosperity: The case for a multilateral agreement on investment.* World Economic Forum, Geneva, Switzerland.

Swanson, D. L. (1995). Addressing a theoretical problem by reorienting the corporate social performance model. *Academy of Management Review, 20*(1), 43–63.

Tirole, J. (1989). Network externalities, standardization and compatibility. In *The theory of industrial organization*. MIT Press.

Uddin, M. B., Hassan, M. R., & Tarique, K. M. (2008). *Three dimensional aspects of corporate social responsibility*. Daffodil International University. *Journal of Business and Economics, 3*(1).

UNCTAD. (2005). *Economic development in Africa: Rethinking the role of foreign direct investment.* Geneva: United Nations Conference on Trade and Development.

Utting, P. (2000). *Business Responsibility for Sustainable Development*. Geneva 2000 Occasional Paper No. 2. United Nations Research Institute for Social Development (UNRISD).

Utting, P. (2003). Promoting Development through corporate social responsibility – Prospects and limitations. *Global Future*, 11-13.

Utting, P. (2005). Corporate responsibility and the movement of business. *Development in Practice, 14*(3&4), 375–388. doi:10.1080/09614520500075797

Visser, W. (2006). Revisiting Carroll's CSR pyramid: An African perspective. In E. R. Pedersen & M. Hunicke (Eds.), *Corporate citizenship in developing countries: New partnership perspectives* (pp. 29–56). Copenhagen: Copenhagen Business School Press.

Visser, W., Matten, D., Pohl, M., & Tolhurst, N. (2007). *The A to Z of corporate social responsibility*. London: Wiley.

Visser, W. (2008). Corporate social responsibility in developing countries. In The Oxford handbook of corporate social responsibility. Oxford, UK: Oxford University Press.

Visser, W. (2008). *CSR 2.0 – the new era of Corporate Sustainability and Responsibility*. CSR Inspiration Series, No.1.

Visser, W. (2010a). *CSR 2.0: The future of corporate social responsibility*. Retrieved from www.csrinternational.org

Visser, W. (2010b). The evolution and revolution of corporate social responsibility. In Responsible business: How to manage a CSR strategy successfully. CSR 2.0.

Waldman, D. A., & Siegel, D. (2008). Defining the socially responsible leader. *The Leadership Quarterly*, *19*(1), 117–131.

Wang, Y. (2013). *Why countries constrain FDI: The political economy of asymmetry in foreign direct investment as a key driver for trade, growth and prosperity: The case for a multilateral agreement on investment*. World Economic Forum, Geneva, Switzerland.

World Economic Forum. (2013). *Foreign direct investment as a key driver for trade, growth and prosperity: The case for a multilateral agreement on investment*. World Economic Forum, Geneva, Switzerland.

Zabbey, N. (2009). *Pollution and poverty in the Niger Delta region-What is the responsibility of oil companies in Nigeria*. Paper Presented at the University of Stavenger.

Zhang, K.H. (2001). Does foreign direct investment promote economic growth? Evidence from East Asia and Latin America. *Contemporary Economic Policy*, *19* (2), 175 – 185.

Section 7

Recommendations and Conclusion:

Incorporating the Role of Economic and Legal Actors in the Legislative Process as a Means of Addressing Current Imbalances of Corporate Social Responsibility in the Prevailing Foreign Direct Investment Climate

Chapter 16
Recommendations:
Addressing the Imbalances of Corporate Social Responsibility in Developed and Developing Countries

Marianne Ojo
North-West University, South Africa

ABSTRACT

As well as contributing to a deeper insight of why focus of Corporate Social Responsibility varies between developed and developing countries, this chapter is aimed at contributing to knowledge and providing a better understanding of institutional and corporate structures operating in developed and developing countries. Such institutional and corporate structures constituting some of the factors which may impact a firm's responsibilities to much wider stakeholders, and particularly its commitment to ensuring that its activities do not adversely impact the ecosystem in which it operates. By incorporating the role of corporate governance, importance and significance of innovation and entrepreneurship, the chapter not only aims to recommend means whereby Corporate Social Responsibility can serve as a more effective tool for promoting worthy causes, and ensuring that obligations to the ecosystem and wider stakeholders are facilitated, but also highlight why a redress in the focus of Corporate Social Responsibility, as regards developing countries particularly, needs to be re-evaluated.

INTRODUCTION

Whilst Corporate Social Responsibility is considered to be generally used as "an umbrella term to describe the complex and multifaceted relationships between business and society and to account for the economic, social and environmental impacts of business activity", another definition which incorporates the role of corporate governance, regards corporate social responsibility as:

DOI: 10.4018/978-1-5225-0305-7.ch016

a model of extended corporate governance whereby those in control of the firm have responsibilities that range from the fulfillment of their fiduciary duties owed towards the owners (principal), to the fulfillment of analogous fiduciary duties owed towards all the firm's stakeholders (Sacconi, 2004:6).

In this sense, a distinction is drawn between the traditional principal agent theory which involves a narrower range of stakeholders and the stakeholder theory which embraces, not just those stakeholders with direct stakes, but also those whose lives are likely to be impacted by the firm's activities - particularly with respect to social, economic and environmental consequences. Given the uncertainty and unpredictability of such consequences, the topic of incomplete contracts and their role in the stakeholder theory model becomes apparent. It is precisely because of the uncertainties concerning who is likely to be affected as a result of the firm or enterprise's actions, particularly in unforeseen circumstances based on longer term future occurrences that contingencies need to be provided for in such contracts.

Even though it may not be obvious or initially apparent, the most unlikely of all locals residing within the locality of the operation of a firm's activities, may eventually be entitled to a stake of the firm's revenues, in the form of compensation, where such an individual is affected in any adverse way, as a result of activities - and particularly environmentally damaging activities, which not only impact the social or financial means of likelihood of such an individual, but which could also have life threatening or health related repercussions.

In line with the requirements and demand for a comparative based research on the topic, as well as one that investigates the roots, distinguishing features, and institutional structures that may impact Corporate Social Responsibility (hereinafter referred to as CSR), at varying degrees, this chapter will focus on investigations and objectives which are aimed at providing explanations or justifications for differences in the way CSR is perceived in developed and developing countries. It will also seek to justify the jurisdictional focus attributed to CSR in developing and developed countries.

AIMS AND OBJECTIVES OF THE CHAPTER

In line with the main objective of this chapter, namely highlighting differences in the way CSR is portrayed in developing and developed countries, as well as variables which are in operation, the first objective of the chapter will be to:

1. Investigate the reasons for differences in the way CSR is regarded and approached between developed and developing countries, as well as justifying or providing grounds for non justification of such differences.
    a. As well as analyzing and investigating whether and why CSR focuses on attributes such as ethical, legal responsibilities and corporate governance mechanisms - with respect to developed countries, the causes attributed to a focus on variables and factors such as economic, political, social and environmental considerations - with respect to developing countries, will also be investigated.
2. To investigate whether CSR does indeed play a more pivotal role or focus as regards philanthropic or charitable projects in developing countries and whether this applies to certain countries than others.

3. In line with the above objective, this chapter will also seek to explore how CSR can benefit locals in developing countries.

Further, as highlighted under the second investigational aim, this objective will seek to consolidate on environmental considerations by highlighting how economic, social, political and technological attributes can ultimately impact environmental goals of enterprises or outcomes of their operations.

In so doing, it will seek to illustrate that institutional and corporate structures within these systems do indeed impact CSR behavior or the way CSR is portrayed across several jurisdictions - whether these are developed or developing countries.

In facilitating this aim, the chapter, through the first objective, will seek to investigate why firm profits or revenues, which are intended towards charitable projects in developing countries, are diverted from their intended destinations. Whilst charitable objectives may constitute the firm's goal, other factors: namely, political influences or inadequate corporate governance structures or mechanisms, may hinder the fulfillment of enterprise's corporate goal of charitable donation.

Further, incidences of misappropriation of intended charitable donations within firm's management are frequently known to occur or have been reported - hence resulting in intended charitable donations either being diverted from their objective, or targeted goal or funds being substantially reduced, as a result of such misappropriation.

Given these considerations, as well as profound evidence of lack of operation of effective corporate governance mechanisms and structures in developing countries, should there not be a re-think in the role and focus of CSR in developing countries?

Whilst charitable projects could still feature prominently as goals, such goals require a vehicle whereby their realization could be facilitated and achieved - such a vehicle assuming the form of effective corporate governance mechanisms and structures.

Hence whilst charitable projects may still constitute the ultimate goal, greater focus, than is presently the case, should be accorded to the role which CSR can assume in facilitating the operation of more effective corporate governance mechanisms, which in turn, will facilitate the goal of charitable donations and ensuring that intended targets receive such donations.

Research Questions

In line with the research objectives, research questions to be addressed follow thus:

1. Why are there differences in the way CSR is regarded and approached between developed and developing countries? Further, how can such differences be justified or how are these not justified?
2. Does CSR play a more pivotal role or focus as regards philanthropic or charitable projects in developing countries and does this apply to certain countries than others?
3. How can CSR benefit locals in developing countries, as well as the goals of charitable donations and projects more effectively?
4. How can CSR be effectively enhanced to, better serve the needs of developing countries, as well as developed countries?

Research Methodology

Adopting a pre dominant qualitative based research approach, this research will involve a critical analysis, from a comparative perspective, as well as theoretical considerations, opinions, arguments and authorities on the topic - with particular reference to views expressed as being contributory to differences in CSR focus and portrayals in developed and developing countries. As well as providing further recommendations for future research, the chapter will also seek to recommend and propose new approaches through the incorporation of previous and current literature as a way of addressing and mitigating imbalances in the focus accorded by developing and developed countries to CSR. Further, it will also incorporate results of case studies and empirical evidence in arriving at its conclusions.

BACKGROUND TO THE TOPIC AND LITERATURE REVIEW

Reasons for differences in the way CSR is regarded and approached between developed and developing countries, as well as the justification and non justification of such differences.

Table 1 illustrates the differences in priorities between developed and developing countries, as highlighted by Jamali.

As clearly stated by Jenkins (2005:540):

given the lack of an explicit focus on poverty reduction, the first question that needs to be addressed is whether or not CSR as it is currently practised helps indirectly reduce poverty.

In this respect, a distinction needs to be drawn between the role which philanthropic responsibilities can assume in facilitating poverty reduction – as well as environmental initiatives, and an express designation of poverty reduction as an objective – within the sphere of Carroll's pyramid of Corporate Social Responsibility.

Table 1.

Developed Countries	Developing Countries
Cultural Factors: • Religion is separated from business practices	Cultural Factors: • Religious beliefs • Personal beliefs
Political Factors: • Absence of corruption • Powerful government	Political Factors: • Corruption • Poor governance • Political instability • Lack of accountability
Economic Factors: • High Income • High GDP	Economic Factors: • Low Income • Low GDP • High Inflation
CSR Priorities: • Consumer Protection • Fair trade	CSR Priorities: • Poverty Alleviation (amongst others)

Source: Jamali, 2014

Figure 1. Concept and definition of corporate social responsibility
Source: (Google, n.d.)

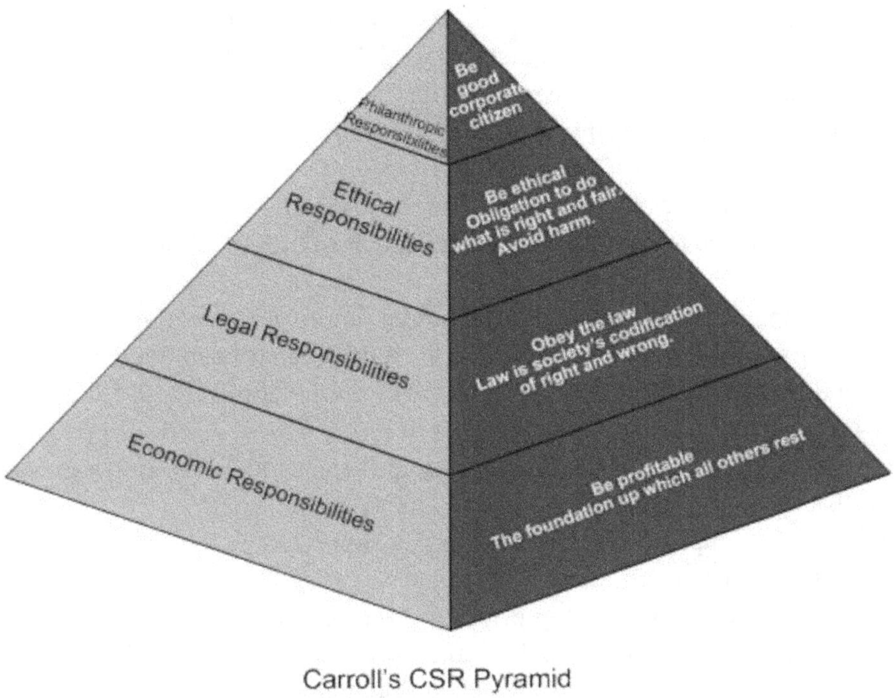

Carroll (1979:499) initially designated the fourth level of responsibility as the discretionary category – rather than the level of philanthropic responsibility.

Various views regarding the meaning of social responsibility, as highlighted by Carroll (1979:499), are as follows:

- Profit making only (Friedman)
- Giving beyond profit making (Davis, Backman)
- Going beyond economic and legal requirements (McGuire)
- Voluntary activities (Manne)
- Economic, legal, voluntary activities (Steiner)
- Concentric circles, ever widening (CED, Davis and Blomstrom)
- Concern for the broader social system (Eells and Walton)
- Responsibility in a number of social problem areas (Hay, Gray and Gates)
- Giving way to social responsiveness (Ackerman and Bauer, Sethi)

Carroll added that, "in order for a definition of social responsibility to fully address the entire range of obligations business has to society, it must embody:

- The economic,
- Legal;
- Ethical; and

- Discretionary categories of business performance.

In "challenging the accuracy and relevance Carroll's CSR Pyramid" and in arguing that the model does not represent the optimal model for understanding CSR in general, and CSR in Africa in particular, Visser (2006:36,37) adds that: "Most of the research on Carroll's CSR Pyramid has been in an American context. Nevertheless, several of the empirical studies already discussed suggest that culture may have an important influence on perceived CSR priorities."

Despite criticisms of Carroll's pyramid, as presented by Visser, he acknowledges that Carroll's pyramid of CSR is widely referred to in various literature and attributes the following reasons (Visser:33):

1. The model is simple, easy to understand and has an intuitively appealing logic;
2. Over the 25 years since Carroll first proposed the model, it has been frequently reproduced in top management and CSR journals, mostly by Carroll himself (Carroll, 1979, 1983, 1991, 1994, 1998, 2000, 2004);
3. Carroll has sought to assimilate various competing themes into his model, e.g. corporate citizenship (Carroll, 1998) and stakeholders (Carroll, 2004);
4. The model has been empirically tested and largely supported by the findings (Aupperle, Carroll, & Hatfield, 1985; Pinkston & Carroll, 1994); and
5. The model incorporates and gives top priority to the economic dimension as an aspect of CSR, which may endear business scholars and practitioners. In fact, Carroll (1991) goes so far as to point out how little his definition of CSR differs from Friedman's (1970) view of the responsibilities of the firm.

Issues, Controversies, Problems

Empirical Studies on Corporate Social Responsibility

In following up Visser's argument that Carroll's model of CSR does not represent the optimal model for understanding CSR in general, and CSR in Africa in particular, we will now consider the empirical studies which Visser referred to.

Visser cites Crane & Matten (2004) by accentuating the fact that they address CSR in a European context using Carroll's CSR Pyramid. Furthermore, in trying to emulate the way that Crane and Matten (2004) incorporated Carroll's pyramid to describe CSR in Europe, a four-part construction is used by Visser to investigate how CSR can be reflected from an African perspective (see Visser:36,37).

SOLUTIONS AND RECOMMENDATIONS

Whilst Visser's representation of Carroll's pyramid, from an African context, may more accurately reflect what Corporate Social Responsibility should be, given the level of corruption, lack of adequate and effective corporate governance mechanisms – when compared to its European and Western counterparts, this should also not exclude the fact that philanthropic responsibilities have been as equally ineffective in achieving their desires aims and objectives.

Figure 2. Africa's corporate social responsibility pyramid
(Source: Visser, 2006:37)
According to Visser (2006), Ethical Responsibilities should correspond and align with the:
Adoption of voluntary codes of governance and ethics
Legal Responsibilities: *Ensure good relations with government officials*
Philanthropic Responsibilities: *Set aside funds for corporate social/community projects; and*
Economic Responsibilities: *provide investment, create jobs and pay taxes.*

Whilst philanthropic responsibilities may be regarded with greater respect and executed on a greater priority, the level and volumes of charitable donations, does not necessarily equate to the belief and demonstration that such funds are necessarily being transformed for the intended targets and benefits.

In this respect, and in the same vein, philanthropic and legal/ethical responsibilities share a common denominator in Africa: all require effective and reliable channels of enforcement, distribution and compliance mechanisms.

Whilst supporting both models, it should also be re-iterated that ideally, no level of responsibility should be treated with lesser respect than the other. Just as legal and ethical responsibilities can be regarded as being more important than mere profitable maximization objectives, philanthropic responsibilities can also serve as a valuable means and channel of charitable donations and initiatives which whilst facilitating goal and poverty alleviation, also serve to further environmental initiatives. Environmental and poverty alleviation, as previously argued in the chapter are areas in need of greater focus and attention. Hence whilst it is generally acknowledged by both models that economic responsibilities are accorded greater priorities – both from a European and African perspective, the actual fact remains as concerning the need to accord greater focus and priority to goals aimed at poverty alleviation and environmental issues.

As illustrated by recent global developments, falling oil and gas prices, whilst inflicting damaging and lower revenues for the energy industry, resulting in loss of jobs, is also: Compelling wider repercussions of attracting greater focus on environmental issues and more cost effective, environmental friendly ways of generating energy – namely, through renewable and other alternative sources of energy.

Further, as regards legal responsibilities, as commented on by Visser, it is to be added that, ensuring good relations with government officials does not necessarily facilitate compliance with law and

Figure 3. Proposed model: Overlapping layers and strata denote interdependence of responsibilities in their ability to function effectively
The lines denote the strata. Unlike the proposed model whose strata and lines separate (and lie between) economic, legal, ethical and philanthropic responsibilities, the dividing lines/strata are more clear cut under Carroll's CSR pyramid: economic, legal, ethical and philanthropic responsibilities are above their dividing lines and strata (and do not fall in between the lines as depicted under the proposed model). Under this proposed model, the responsibilities bounce between the lines/strata rather than a clear cut distinction above the lines – as presented in Carroll's CSR pyramid.

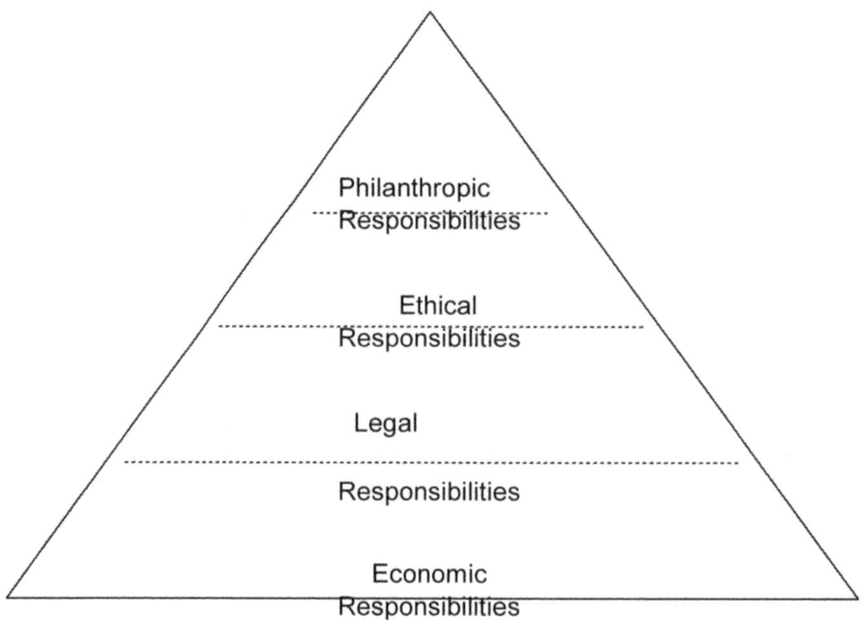

regulations. Rather, some may argue that it serves as an avenue for the promotion of bribery and corruption. Hence the importance of safeguards and ensuring that effective corporate mechanisms are in place – particularly where whistle blowers are likely to be intimidated or where there is evidence that cosy and undue proximity in relationships between corporate managers and government officials has resulted in the compromise and override of the observance of rules, codes of conduct, necessarily controls and regulations.

FUTURE RESEARCH DIRECTIONS

As already highlighted in the chapter, more research aimed at encouraging greater focus on goals aimed at poverty alleviation, as well as environmental initiatives are encouraged. Hence whilst to an extent, supporting Carroll and Visser's models of CSR, the main issue, as highlighted by Jenkins, needs to be "whether or not CSR as it is currently practiced, helps indirectly reduce poverty." Compliance with corporate governance mechanisms, bribery and corruption remains a huge challenge for many jurisdictions – particularly developing countries.

As also illustrated with corporate collapses like Enron, the observance of international accounting standards, as well as creative accounting practices aimed at overriding and manipulating accounting policies remains a huge concern. With the global adoption of International Financial Reporting Standards

(IFRS), it is hoped that some degree of consistency, comparability and harmonization will be achieved as a means of addressing inconsistencies and discrepancies which arise as a result of different treatments of accounting policies and accounting standards in various jurisdictions. Where a degree of comparability and consistency can be achieved, such likelihood or tendencies for creative accounting practices could be better controlled and minimized. Further, greater transparency and disclosure would be achieved with the mitigation of inconsistent treatments and application of accounting standards. Huge progress is being made with the global adoption of IFRS.

CONCLUSION

It has been highlighted in the chapter, that regardless of the stratus or level of the pyramid, be it the least prioritized, be it legal, ethical or philanthropic responsibilities, as long as such a level could be harnessed towards poverty alleviation initiatives – as well as environmental initiatives, then the degree of importance within the pyramid is irrelevant – given the interdependency of individual layers or strata.

Without effective corporate governance mechanisms which facilitate compliance and enforcement – which are ultimately fostered through rules, regulations, legal codes, ethical codes and norms, such vital and crucial goals and objectives of Corporate Social Responsibility would not be realized. Without effective corporate governance mechanisms, millions of stakeholders – and particularly broader stakeholders – such as local communities and the environment, would be the greatest victims of corporate collapses. As evidenced by corporate collapses such as Enron, it can be seen that even the economic responsibility and objective of profit maximization was ultimately, not realized – where ethical codes, legal and accounting responsibilities, were not complied with.

In this sense, rather than visualize the responsibilities (responsibilities denoted within the sphere of Carroll's pyramid of CSR) from a stratified perspective, it would be more helpful to visualize these responsibilities from a circular, or rather dependent, perspective – in the sense that one responsibility and objective is defeated where the other suffers. Where corporate governance mechanisms do not operate as effectively as they should, by reason of inadequate enforcement and compliance with rules, regulations, codes and ethics, then corporate goals of profit maximization, as well as those aimed at furthering philanthropic and charitable goals aimed at poverty alleviation and environmental initiatives may fail – owing to lack of resources or owing to a diversion of the funds into the wrong channels through bribery and corruption.

REFERENCES

Aupperle, K. E., Carroll, A. B., & Hatfield, J. D. (1985). An Empirical Examination of the Relationship Between Corporate Social Responsibility and Profitability. *Academy of Management Journal*, *28*(2), 446–463.

Aupperle, K. E., Hatfield, J. D., & Carroll, A. B. (1983). *Instrument Development and Application in Corporate Social Responsibility*. Academy of Management Proceedings.

Carroll, A. B. (1979). A Three-Dimensional Model of Corporate Performance. *Academy of Management Review*, *4*(4), 497–505. Retrieved from http://www.jstor.org/stable/257850?seq=1#page_scan_tab_contents

Carroll, A. B. (1983). Corporate social responsibility: Will industry respond to cut-backs in social program funding? *Vital Speeches of the Day*, *49*, 604–608.

Carroll, A. B. (1991). The Pyramid of Corporate Social Responsibility: Toward the Moral Management of Organizational Stakeholders. *Business Horizons*, *34*, 39–48.

Cole, M. A., Elliott, R. J. R., & Zhang, J. (2009). Corruption, good governance and FDI location in China: A province-level analysis. *The Journal of Development Studies*, *45*(9), 1494–1512.

Crane, A., & Matten, D. (2004). *Business Ethics*. Oxford, UK: Oxford University Press.

D'Amato, A., Henderson, S., & Florence, S. (2009). Corporate Social Responsibility and Sustainable Business A Guide to Leadership Tasks and Functions. Retrieved from http://www.ccl.org/leadership/pdf/research/corporatesocialresponsibility.pdf

Davis, K., & Blomstrom, R. L. (1966). *Business and its Environment*. New York: McGraw Hill.

Eweje, G. (2006). The Role of MNEs in Community Development Initiatives in Developing Countries: Corporate Social Responsibility at Work in Nigeria and South Africa. *Business & Society*, *45*(2), 93–129.

Eweje, G. (2014). Corporate Social Responsibility and Sustainability: Emerging Trends in Developing Economies Critical Studies on Corporate Responsibility. *Governance and Sustainability*, *8*, 45–77.

Fitch, G. (1976). Achieving Corporate Social Responsibility. *Academy of Management Review*, *1*(1), 38–46.

Friedman, M. (1970). The Social Responsibility of Business Is to Increase its Profits. *New York Times*, pp. 122-126.

Google. (n.d.). Retrieved from: https://www.google.co.uk/search?q=carroll's+pyramid+of+csr&biw=1366&bih=578&tbm=isch&imgil=HGdTbntI6FbdFM%253A%253BES0dR2Kp9tyZHM%253Bhttp%25253A%25252F%25252Fresearch-methodology.net%25252Fcarrolls-csr-pyramid-and-its-applications-to-small-and-medium-sized-businesses%25252F&source=iu&pf=m&fir=HGdTbntI6FbdFM%253A%252CES0dR2Kp9tyZHM%252C_&usg=__WrVlfmZZMbth79ZDuCBj_Zq1Z5-4%3D&ved=0ahUKEwjTuaC8wfzKAhUEthQKHfbYAxwQyjcIMw&ei=ejTDVtOUNoTsUvaxj-AB#imgrc=HGdTbntI6FbdFM%3A

Goyal, A. (2006). Corporate Social Responsibility as a Signalling Device for Foreign Direct Investment. *International Journal of the Economics of Business*, *13*(1), 145–163.

Jamali, D. (2010). The CSR of MNC Subsidiaries in Developing countries: Global, Local, Substantive or Diluted? *Journal of Business Ethics*, *93*, 181–200.

Jamali, D. (2014). CSR in Developing Countries Through An Institutional Lens. In G. Eweje (Ed.), *Corporate Social Responsibility and Sustainability: Emerging Trends in Developing Economies Critical Studies on Corporate Responsibility, Governance and Sustainability* (Vol. 8, pp. 45–77). Emerald Group Publishing Ltd.

Jamali, D., & Mirshak, R. (2007). Corporate Social Responsibility: Theory and Practice in a Developing Country Context. *Journal of Business Ethics*, *72*(1), 243–262.

Jamali, D., & Neville, B. (2011). Convergence versus Divergence of CSR in Developing Countries: An Embedded Multi-layered Institutional Lens. *Journal of Business Ethics*, *102*(4), 599–621.

Jenkins, R. (2005). Globalization, Corporate Social Responsibility and poverty. *International Affairs*, *81*(3), 525–540.

Jenkins, R., Pearson, R., & Seyfang, G. (2002). *Corporate Responsibility & Labour Rights: Codes of Conduct in the Global Economy*. Londres: Earthscan.

Manne, H., & Wallich, H. C. (1972). *The Modern Corporation and Social Responsibility*. Washington D.C American Enterprise Institute for Public Policy Research.

Ojo, M. (2013). Audits, Audit Quality and Signalling Mechanisms: Concentrated Ownership Structures. *American Research Journal of Humanities and Social Sciences, 1*(2).

Ordonez-Ponce, E. (2014). The Challenges from Economic to Sustainable Development: The Chilean Perspective. In G. Eweje (Ed.), *Corporate Social Responsibility and Sustainability: Emerging Trends in Developing Economies Critical Studies on Corporate Responsibility, Governance and Sustainability* (Vol. 8, pp. 45–77). Emerald Group Publishing Ltd.

PCAOB. (2013). *Proposed 2014 Budget and Strategic Plan: Expansion of Consulting Practice and Other Non Audit Businesses*. PCAOB.

Pinkston, T. S., & Carroll, A. B. (1996). A Retrospective Examination of CSR Orientations: Have They Changed? *Journal of Business Ethics*, *15*(2), 199–206.

Prieto-Carron, M., Lund-Thomsen, P., Chan, A., & Bhushan, C. (2006). Critical Perspectives on CSR and Development: What We Know, What We Don't Know and What We Need to Know. *International Affairs*, *82*(5), 977–987.

Sacconi, L. (2004). *Corporate Social Responsibility (CSR) as a Model of 'Extended' Corporate Governance: An Explanation Based on the Economic Theories of Social Contract*. Reputation and Reciprocal Conformism.

Spulber, D. (2014). *The Innovative Entrepreneur New York and Cambridge*. Cambridge University Press.

Toppinen, A., Zhang, Y., Hansen, E., Kurki, K., & Li, N. (2014). Role of Corporate Responsibility: Insights From Three Forest Industry Multinationals Investing in China. *Journal of Small Business Management*.

Visser, W. (2006). *Revisiting Carroll's CSR Pyramid An African Perspective*. Academic Press.

Visser, W. (2008). Corporate Social responsibility in Developing Countries. In A. Crane, A. McWilliams, D. Matten, J. Moon, & D. Siegel (Eds.), *The Oxford Handbook of Corporate Social Responsibility* (pp. 473–479). Oxford, UK: Oxford University Press.

World Bank. (2002). *Engaging the Private Sector in Forest Sector Development*. Retrieved from http://siteresources.worldbank.org/EXTFORSOUBOOK/Resources/02-FSB-Ch02.pdf

World Bank. (2013). *How We Classify Countries*. Retrieved from http://data.worldbank.org/about/country-and-lending-groups

Chapter 17
Parliamentary Sovereignty, the Rule of Law, and the Separation of Powers:
Involving Other Actors in the Legislative and Judiciary Process

Marianne Ojo
North-West University, South Africa

ABSTRACT

This chapter is aimed at highlighting how common law has evolved over the centuries, namely through the flexibility accorded to judicial precedents, as well as through the evolutionary nature evidenced in the processes and rules applied in statutory interpretation. In addition to illustrating how informational asymmetries can be mitigated through de centralization, facilitated with courts employing the use of non-legal agents such as expert witnesses - as evidenced in the Daubert case, Pepper v Hart also illustrates how common law has evolved through the scope and permissibility of aids to statutory interpretation. Whilst financial markets and changes in the environment impact legislators, and whilst it is widely accepted that legislation constitutes the supreme form of law, the necessity for judges to introduce a certain level of flexibility will also contribute towards ensuring that legitimate expectations of involved parties are achieved - particularly where the construction of the words within a statute gives rise to considerable ambiguity. By way of reference to landmark rulings in the United States, cases such as Daubert and The Estate of Edgar A. Berg v. Commissioner, this paper also aims to illustrate the vital role increasingly assumed by non-legal actors, and why this approach should constitute a trend to be adopted in European common and civil law jurisdictions. This being the case given the failures and flaws of references to Parliamentary material and whether these should be permitted as an aid to the construction of legislation which is ambiguous or obscure, as illustrated in the case of Pepper v Hart.

DOI: 10.4018/978-1-5225-0305-7.ch017

INTRODUCTION

To Be or Not to Be Regulated: Purposive Rules and the Centralization of Information

The de-centralization of the judicial and legislative process has advanced over the years – as evidenced by the engagement of legal, non-legal and economic actors in the judicial and rule making process. This serves as testimony to the fact that judges may not be fully equipped to allocate resources in such a way that maximal efficiency or the best outcome is derived for involved parties. Other non-legal actors such as financial experts are now being engaged as expert witnesses by judges in deciding landmark judgments.

Decentralization denotes the involvement of and delegation of roles to various actors other than judges. These actors, and more specifically non legal actors, are not responsible for creating the law or making ultimate decisions but their involvement helps shape the processes of judicial decision making. In this sense, decentralization does not imply a delegation of decision making by judges to such actors, but is used with particular reference to the process of delegation and involvement of processes – not delegation or decentralization of decisions. The involvement of non-legal actors is not intended to serve as a means of transferring the judge's role to such actors in matters of judicial decisions – even though their involvement influences such decisions. The involvement of non-legal actors and also economic agents helps facilitate accountability into the processes – they are not there to make decisions but to facilitate a more accountable framework in which decisions are made. Judges are still expect to assume some form of responsibility and the involvement of other non-legal and particularly economic actors, serves as a reminder that whilst such actors cannot replace the role assigned to judges, there are also limits whereby a judge can exercise the required competence in arriving at decisions which confer maximum economic efficiency to those parties involved.

As well as a tool which serves to facilitate greater checks and accountability in the judicial and law making process, de centralization is also accentuating its role as a mechanism whereby the efficient allocation of resources can be realized. In addition to highlighting the consensus on the views of Posner and Hayek, in respect of de centralization of information within the judicial process, this chapter aims to address why de centralization serves as a vital tool in facilitating the objective of common law as an efficiency allocation mechanism. The central recurring theme of this chapter, however, is the illustration of the evolution of common law – as reflected through the decentralization of information resource and the engagement of non-legal actors in the judicial process, as well as the rules of statutory interpretation and extrinsic aids of interpretation that have been admitted into the judicial process over the years.

Cooter and Rubinfeld have been selected to corroborate the theoretical framework and element of my literature review – namely the common law efficiency theory. According to Cooter and Rubinfeld (1994: 437), fair and accurate outcomes requires courts to resolve cases by applying the law and courts have complete information when full knowledge of the law and all the facts that are relevant to the case, are available and are at disposal to deciding matters at hand. Further they are of the opinion that complete information at trial results in a judgment that is accurate relative to existing law; and that to the extent that liability law is designed to internalize costs, accurate results will generate efficient incentives. In the same manner, they further argue, that complete information in bargaining before trial promotes settlement on terms approximating the complete information judgment.

The importance of measures aimed at ensuring that the court receives complete information, prior to the case or trial – as a means of generating efficient outcomes in the delivery of judgments, is hereby emphasized. However current issues revolving around procedures aimed at obtaining complete information is also highlighted. Such problems in their opinion, could be mitigated where the court is able to ascertain the value of information to the requesting party – hence ensuring that such a party fully pays the associated costs of complying with rules (Cooter & Rubinfeld, 1994: 437).

The importance of ascertaining the stakes involved for the involved parties is not only vital from the perspective of delivering efficient outcomes – which would re inforce the role of common law as a tool for promoting the efficient allocation of resources, but also highlight why the determination of such stakes constitutes an influential factor in the evolution of common law. Section II of the Literature Review further corroborates and consolidates on this point.

As well as introducing the central issue surrounding the efficient allocation of resources, namely, informational asymmetries – and how these can be mitigated through decentralization, the literature review section also highlights the central issue surrounding the efficient allocation of resources, namely, informational asymmetries – and how these can be mitigated through decentralization. In so doing, it will incorporate discussions on the theory of Efficiency of the Common Law Hypothesis, as well as evaluate claims that support the view that the evolution of common is influenced by the litigants and not judges.

As well as elaborating on how the chapter and topic "revisits Posner, Hayek and the Economic Analysis of Law", the third section also consolidates on the de centralization of information retained by judges in the judicial process by way of reference to Posner's views on Hayek and Kelsen's concepts of law. This section highlights Posner and Hayek's consensus on the importance of decentralization, as well as the incorporation of non-legal actors as tools for facilitating the efficient allocation of resources in common law. This section also attempts to harmonize any conflicting views that may appear to arise between Posner and Hayek's views on the role of non-legal actors in the judicial process. Whilst reflecting support for de centralization, as well as the consensus of the evolution of the law, the section also contrasts and seeks to harmonize Posner and Hayek's views of what roles should be assumed by economic actors and judges in the judicial process.

In arriving at a conclusion that many factors determine and have influenced the evolution of common law over the years, the concluding section also highlights why it is necessary to engage non legal actors in the judicial process and why European courts and jurisdictions should embrace this trend which is prominent in Forensic Accounting, as adopted in courts in the United States.

Role Assumed by Judges and Growing Involvement of Non Legal Actors in Judicial Process

The development of judicial precedents and the role of judges in the interpretation of statutes and legislation - to better align with the original intent of the legislator, has been evidenced over the past centuries. Certain cases, however, have reflected possibilities whereby judicial development may generate outcomes which are contrary to legislative intent. This can be illustrated by section 10(b) and Rule 10b-5 of the Securities Exchange Act of 1934, which has been highlighted as having been interpreted "to require corporate insiders and tippees to either disclose material inside information or refrain from trading." (see SEC v Texas Gulf Sulphur Co).

Carlton and Fischel (1983:884) argue that such judicial development is contrary to legislative intent and that no evidence exists to support the fact that Congress intended to prohibit insider trading. (see also SEC v Texas Gulf Sulphur Co).

Further, whereas Hayek is considered to view the common law as a "spontaneous order which regulates society better than a person could" (Hayek, 1960, 1973). Posner (2005) is considered to view the law as "an order consciously made through the efforts of judges and legislators" (Zywicki & Sanders, 2008) Such differing views about levels of control of the law and perceptions of being regulated and the ability to regulate, can be regarded as influential factors governing the opinions also shared by Posner and Hayek on the roles of judges – one which Posner considers to be more active than passive, based on his conception of law as "an order consciously made through the efforts of judges and legislators."

However Posner's conception of the law as an "an order consciously made through the efforts of judges and legislators," appears to exclude his acknowledgement of the engagement of non-legal actors as instruments or means of attaining legal goals. This will be now be discussed in greater detail, as well as under section C of this chapter.

The evolutionary nature of common law and the more passive role assumed by judges is highlighted in the landmark case of The Estate of Edgar A. Berg v. Commissioner (T. C. Memo 1991- 279).

According to DiGabriele (2007), the discipline of valuing closely held companies further evolved with each organization's development and issuance of competing business valuation standards creating dissimilarity among the discipline (Cercone, 2002). He contrasts this with reference to the difference of opinion by Beatty, Riffe, and Thompson (1999), who contend that the court expects an expert's valuation to be biased toward the benefit of the party compensating them. Accordingly, he adds that this produces subjective valuation estimates that are consistent with the underlying incentives of the expert and that the Courts are then left to rely on these subjective and imperfect valuations in deriving the final estimated value.

In highlighting how the Tax Court responded to the above fragmentation, DiGabriele (2007, 2009) makes the following observations:

- In rejecting the Estate's experts, the Tax Court accepted the IRS's expert because he had the background and training desired by the court and developed discounts by referring to specific studies of comparable properties and demonstrating how they applied to the asset being examined.
- This case marked the beginning of the Tax Court leaning toward the side with the valuation perceived as the most comprehensive and logical (Wietzke, 2002).

The above case not only illustrates the more passive role assumed by judges in relying on expert opinions which may influence courts' decisions, but also acknowledgement on the part of judges, that they may not be well equipped with the necessary competence, expertise and knowledge in arriving at decisions which can be considered maximally efficient. The allocation, delegation or decentralization of information resource, as well as the involvement of other actors in the judicial process, also serves as a means of ensuring that greater accountability, supervision and more efficient outcomes are achieved. The value attributed to expertise and the need to engage experts in achieving more efficient outcomes, also extends to the principal agent and stakeholder theory.

The question revolving around why firms might want to allocate "property rights in valuable information (Carlton & Fischel, 1983)" to managers, rather than to shareholders, is not merely based on the premises that managers may value such information more than shareholders, but also attributed to the ability of such agents to better monitor, supervise and account for the distribution and dissipation of such information in a manner and timing (which shareholders are less better equipped and specialized to handle).

Why firms might want to allocate "property rights in valuable information" to managers, rather than to shareholders? Even though certain shareholders may value information more than others and qualify to assume the role of residual holders of property rights, such shareholders may not be well equipped with the necessary expertise to undertake the required levels of monitoring activities – hence resulting in greater inefficiency or costs than would be the case where monitoring responsibilities are undertaken by the agents or managers.

From this perspective, it could be argued that whilst information may overwhelm and control those who are less specialized and equipped to handle such information – by virtue of inadequate accountability mechanisms, the delegation and de centralization of such information to those who are better specialized and equipped to handle such priceless resources and privileged public utilities, generates an outcome whereby such information is better regulated, as well as delegated, to achieve maximal efficiency and optimal outcomes. Even in cases where regulation is undertaken by adequately equipped regulators, lack of adequate accountability mechanisms may result in incidents involving regulatory capture.

In their article, Carlton and Fischel (1983:895), also argue that "even if Federal regulation is justified on the basis of law enforcement cost, firms should have the opportunity to opt out of the regulation in the absence of any showing of third party effects, and that such firms are best judges of how to structure the terms of their employment contracts." In this sense, self-regulation is justified on the basis of flexibility and the potential to minimize unwarranted regulatory costs and burdens.

The argument for enforced self-regulation relates to the fact that whilst individual firms may be the best judges to decide on the design of their contracts, in order for those contracts to be tailor made to adjust better to their firm's needs, self-regulation through these firms, may be better enforced by the State and through the courts. Furthermore, even with its advantages, certain disadvantages can also be attributed to self-regulation.[1] As well as being consequential of a lack of transparency in a regulatory and supervisory regime, regulatory capture is also more likely to occur where a system of self-regulation operates.

Posner's contribution to Law – particularly in the fields of regulation and regulatory capture, as well as Economics, will now be discussed briefly.

Accountability in Regulation: Posner and the Theory of Regulatory Capture

The theory of regulatory capture was introduced by Richard Posner (1974) who argued that „regulation is not about the public interest at all, but is a process, by which interest groups seek to promote their private interest."

Posner (1974:356) also provides criticisms of both the traditional public interest theory of regulation and "the newer economic theory" which regards regulation as "a service supplied to effective political interest groups."

The independence of the regulator from the industry which is being regulated is vital to ensuring that regulatory capture does not occur. Regulatory capture is less likely to occur where more actors are involved in the regulatory process and is more likely to occur where there is regular contact between the regulator and the regulated (firms). Whilst these actors may have their interests, and whilst despite such interests, it may be optimal allocating these resources to certain agents, the engagement of courts serves in many respects, as a means of efficiently allocating available resources – in such a way whereby a greater level of maximization of utilities is achieved.

As well as the attribute of efficient allocation of resources, flexibility is also certainly a crucial and vital element in all evolutionary processes, and has been a feature of common law- within the context of judicial precedents- particularly when contrasted with the principle of *stare decisis*.

As highlighted by Zywicki and Sanders (2008: 577):

Preservation of legitimate expectations often will be best furthered, not by adherence to precedence, but by a prudent and thoughtful updating of rules to adapt to changing needs and expectations. In particular, because legal rules are just one element of the set of rules and practices that guide individual behavior in society, changes in non-legal rules may also affect legal rules such that in order to best preserve expectations and predictability about others' actions, it will become necessary to amend some legal rules to better cohere with changing legal and non-legal rules. The objective is to increase social coordination such that individuals will have maximum freedom to act on local information as it arises. Interpersonal coordination, not aggregate economic efficiency, should be the overarching goal of the legal system.

Hence the need for a reasonable balance between certainty and flexibility in the judicial process is also evident. To what extent should certainty and rigidity in the process be sustained in order to preserve the legitimate expectations of those parties involved? Moreover, it is also reflected that "the thoughtful updating of rules" as a means of adapting to changing needs and expectations is necessary in the goals of preserving legitimate expectations.

The aim of the ensuing section is to highlight the importance of the purposive application of rules in the "updating" process. Such a goal will be facilitated by way of reference to the rules of statutory interpretation. The section also aims to highlight why the engagement of non-legal actors in the judicial process serves as a tool for bolstering claims relating to the efficiency of common law as a resource allocation mechanism.

BACKGROUND AND LITERATURE REVIEW: THE EVOLUTION OF COMMON LAW

Theories and Analyses on the Efficiency of Common Law

Rubin (1977: 61) argues that the efficiency of common law, to the extent that such exists, can be explained by the evolutionary model whereby it is more likely that parties will litigate inefficient rules than efficient rules. As well as his opinion, that, if decisions are made randomly, that there will be a movement in the direction of efficient laws, he is of the view that,

Evolutionary pressure arises from the behavior of the litigants – rather than the judges. In so doing he bolsters this by stating that where neither party is interested in precedent, there is no incentive to litigate and hence no pressure on the law to change.

However such "evolutionary pressure" can also arise from the stakes involved – independent of the precedents. Where such stakes are high, particular in terms of reputation and benefits to be accrued (which may not even necessarily be immediate), then regardless of costs involved, or the precedent which currently governs such a case, the parties, depending on their bargaining powers, will be induced to pursue the case.

Further, even where such parties, are induced or propelled to contest current judicial precedents, the ultimate outcome, as regards whether such law will be altered or whether a new judicial precedent will be established – overriding or reversing the previous ones, lies with the judge or the court – who may reverse existing precedents or in the case of an appeal, decline such appeal – based on prevailing social attitudes, as well as rules of evidence which may be admissible or in admissible in such cases.

What is admissible in certain cases, can be illustrated with the *Daubert* Case[2] whereby the criteria of relevance and reliability were highlighted as being crucial factors in the admissibility of evidence. Such factors also having being tried and tested in order to facilitate admissibility. The Daubert case is also reflective of decisions not being ultimately influenced by the judge's opinion – but by way of reference to an expert opinion – in cases where the judge is not adequately equipped with the required expertise or knowledge of the field involved – for example, in cases which relate to Accounting, Finance and Business matters.

The Daubert standard of evidentiary reliability, according to DiGabriele (2011), is codified in Federal Rule of Evidence 702 which he further adds, defines the admissibility of expert testimony based on the following:

1. If scientific, technical, or other specialized knowledge will assist the trier of fact to understand the evidence or to determine a fact in issue, a witness qualified as an expert by knowledge, skill, experience, training, or education, may testify thereto in the form of an opinion or otherwise, if:
    a. The testimony is based upon sufficient facts or data,
    b. The testimony is the product of reliable principles and methods, and
    c. The witness has applied the principles and methods reliably to the facts of the case.

He also highlights the fact that whilst Daubert is the law in federal courts and more than fifty percent of the states, the Frye standard still remains the general acceptance test for the determination of the admissibility of scientific evidence in the remaining venues.[3]

Where the financial environment has evolved to such an extent that calls for a change in the law, such a change may be instigated by legislators, rather than through the courts. In exceptional circumstances, however, courts may be induced to alter or amend the law – depending on the level of determination of the parties involved in pursuing such cases further – which arises from the stakes involved. As evidenced, through the hierarchical structure of the judicial system in the UK, (as well as the US), relatively few cases progress to the Courts of Appeals and even fewer to the House of Lords – in proportion to those which initially advance to district or high courts.

In the UK, Parliament (Acts of Parliament, statutes and legislation) remains supreme and it is more frequently the case that judges are trying to overturn previous court decisions than the law lords trying to interfere with judge made law. Legislation cannot be changed – till a new one is passed by legislature to update a current or previously existing one. Till this is done and till a Bill becomes a Statute/Legislation/Act of Parliament, it must only be interpreted by judges (according to the intent of Parliament). The form of law which is more subject to manipulation and which also subject to being overridden, overturned or reversed in subsequent cases is judge made law which is being interpreted on the basis of a legislation – hence the rules of statutory interpretation which are aimed at aiding judges to interpret legislation. The legislation remains the same till superseded by new legislation which comes into being as a result of an introduced and approved Bill – the interpretation of the legislation also constitutes the basis for overturning or reversing previous or current judicial precedents.

In concluding that "courts should decide only the questions presented, and to leave the further development of this important area of the law to future cases", the Daubert case also highlighted the fact that even though judges were expected to assume a degree of gate keeping role in deciding on matters involving admissibility of "proffered" (pages 600 and 601) DAUBERT v. MERRELL DOW PHARMACEUTICALS, INC 509U.S.579, 1993) expert opinion, that this did not impose on them the responsibility to become amateur scientists in assuming such a role.

Efficiency of The Common Law Hypothesis: Addressing Information Asymmetries

Parisi (2004: 195) states, that, according to the efficiency of the common law hypothesis, first introduced by Coase (1960), and then extended by Posner in 1994, common law rules attempt to allocate resources efficiently in a typically Pareto or Kaldor Hicks efficient manner.

Further, he makes reference to Priest's analysis that "inefficient rules impose greater costs on the parties who are governed by such rules than is the case with efficient rules – thus making the stakes in the dispute greater", and that where such stakes are greater, litigation is more evident than settlement (Parisi, 2004: 196).

Such emphasis on the stakes – rather than the litigants, as being influential in the evolution of common law constitutes a focal point of discussion. Stakes, in this regards, is considered to embrace all driving factors which govern and impact the current judicial environment - as well as a consideration of repercussions (present and future) which could arise from a failure to address such conditions. It is precisely because of those stakes which could be involved, that the availability of relevant and complete information – at the court's disposal, as well as mechanisms and tools which aid in facilitating the collection of such information, hence avoiding unnecessary information asymmetries which could affect the efficiency of the Common Law Hypothesis, need to be secured and deployed.

Parisi's reference to Cooter and Rubinfeld (1989) also highlights the application and importance of ascertaining property rights in valuable information:

That "an efficient resolution occurs when (see Parisi, 2004: 196; Cooter & Rubinfield, 1989):

- Legal entitlements are assigned to the parties who value them the most
- Where legal liabilities are allocated to those parties who can bear them at the lowest cost
- When transaction costs are minimized

As already highlighted under the introductory section, it is vital to ascertain the parties who value the information most, as well as recover the full compliance costs for the request of such information. Such a stance, in Cooter and Rubinfeld's opinion (1989:437), would not only mitigate incidences whereby misuse and abuse by externalizing costs, occurs but also facilitate a process whereby discovery misuse and abuse can be eliminated by shifting the reasonable cost of compliance to the requesting party.

Whilst Whitman's model (2000:781) emphasizes the role of judicial opinion in shaping the evolution of the system, and whilst he affirms that judges' opinions and beliefs affect the development of law might seem obvious, he also re iterates the importance of recognizing that such ''demand-side'' approaches can only explain so much - in light of models of the evolution of law that emphasize the capacity of law to develop independently of or even in spite of judges' opinions. He adds that the model confirms the intuition that trends in judicial thinking do indeed strongly influence the direction of legal change, though not so strongly that current legal doctrine can be explained exclusively in terms of the opinions of the present pool of judges (see Whitman, 2000:781). Further, he lists history, expectations, and judicial preferences as factors which interact to determine the course of legal change.

The following section is aimed at illustrating how common law has evolved over the centuries, namely through the flexibility accorded to judicial precedents, as well as through the evolutionary nature evidenced in the processes and rules applied in statutory interpretation and the role of judges in such interpretation.

The Evolution of Common Law: Rules of Statutory Interpretation

The purposive intent of rules and the legislator constitutes a fundamental characteristic of the common law system. In illustrating the increased role of judges, by not only adhering to the legislator or legislation, and the growing importance of interpreting rules with intent, the application of rules of statutory interpretation and the evolution of such rules will be elaborated on:

The Literal Rule of Statutory Interpretation

This usually constitutes the basic, starting point in construing a piece of legislation. Under this rule, judges are required to interpret statutes and legislation according to their ordinary, natural and dictionary meaning even if the outcome of such an interpretation may generate absurd or ridiculous results. Judges' roles are considerably limited and restricted under this rule and may be regarded as being more passive when compared to their roles under the other methods of statutory interpretation. Whilst certainty appears to be an advantage of complying with this rule, such advantageous attributes must be weighed against the results which are obtained where absurd outcomes are generated and the legitimate expectations of parties involved are effectively not met.

For this purpose, the golden rule constitutes the next resort where absurd results need to be mitigated.

The Golden Rule of Statutory Interpretation

Under this rule, judges are not only required to give effect to the literal meaning and application of the rule, but should also do so with the aim and purpose of avoiding an absurd result. The golden rule is namely, thus:

The golden rule is that the words of a statute must prima facie be given their ordinary meaning. - Viscount Simon (Nokes v Doncaster Amalgamated Collieries, 1940)

The Mischief Rule of Statutory Interpretation

The mischief rule represents a much narrower application of the golden rule - narrower in the sense of its greater focus on the intent of the legislator. Its application is considered necessary where a statute is considered to have been introduced as a means of remedying or rectifying a defect or problem (the mischief) in the common law.

An extension of the application of the mischief rule is embodied in the fourth and final rule of statutory interpretation being considered under this heading: namely, the purposive rule or the Rule in Heydon's Case.

The Purposive Rule or The Rule in Heydon's Case

The purposive rule or the rule in Heydon's case, has at its core purpose, the discovery of the intent of Parliament or the legislator, namely, What purpose was the statute enacted to rectify- for which the common law had a defect or needed to be rectified?

From the above-mentioned rules an evolvement of the role of judges is demonstrated – both in respect of a greater role given to judges to interpret according to the intent of the legislator, and also in respect of analytic reasoning and balancing.

It is quite understandable as regards why Hayek and Posner's backgrounds have considerably impacted their perspectives of the role of judges.

As will be illustrated under section C, the de centralization of the judicial process, through the participation of economic and non legal actors, as means of achieving judicial goals in the efficient allocation of resources, is acknowledged by Posner. Hence to the extent that both Posner and Hayek share the view that the decentralization of law respectively facilitates the attainment of goal of efficient resource allocation and promotes the rule of law, a consensus for the de centralization of rules is shared by Hayek and Posner.

According to Zywicki and Sanders (2008:559),

Posner conceives law to be a series of disparate rules and as purposive. He believes that a judge should examine an individual rule and come to a conclusion about whether the rule is the most efficient available," whilst Hayek is considered to "conceive law as a purpose independent set of legal rules bound within a large social order.

These views will now be examined to a broader context under a landmark ruling which has not only contributed to judges' abilities to introduce aids as a means of interpreting statutes to a more effective extent, but also demonstrates the interdependency of rules - from one social order to the next.

Pepper v Hart: The Mischief Rule and the Inclusion of Aids (Parliamentary Privileged Information) as a Means to Statutory Interpretation

Pepper v Hart (1992) represented a landmark ruling in the sense that it was the first time whereby the use of privileged parliamentary debates, information and records (Hansard) were permitted as admissible aids to statutory interpretation. The case involved the valuation of employee benefits for income tax purposes - given the ambiguous wordings of the statute involved. The following issues were raised in the case (1992):

1. Should existing rule prohibiting any reference to Parliamentary material (Hansard) in construing legislation be relaxed, and if so, to what extent?
2. If so, does the case fall within the category of cases where reference to Parliamentary proceedings should be permitted?
3. If reference to Parliamentary proceedings is permissible, what is the true construction of the statutory provisions?
4. If reference to Parliamentary proceedings is not permissible, what is the true construction of the statutory provisions?

As per Lord Browne-Wilkinson:

Reference to Parliamentary material should be permitted as an aid to the construction of legislation which is ambiguous or obscure, or the literal meaning of which leads to an absurdity. Even in such cases, references in court to Parliamentary material should only be permitted where such material clearly discloses the mischief aimed at or the legislative intention lying behind the ambiguous or obscure words (See Pepper v Hart; Styles, 1994).

Section 63 of the 1976 Finance Act constituted the central piece of legislation in the case. It is obvious that in such cases – not just those cases involving contentious attributions to the construction of the piece of legislation, but those whose scope may lie beyond the scope and principal expertise of the judge, aids to statutory interpretation may be justified where such aids are vital to efficient allocation of resources, as well as generating outcomes which could be considered to be reasonably efficient within the ambit of legitimate expectations of the parties involved.

Should judicial decisions be criticized for generating more efficient and purposive outcomes particularly where the legislative source being referred to (regardless of whether such a source is privileged information), has not been altered in any sense, but has simply served as a means of shedding more light, providing more information, and giving purpose and meaning (or more meaning) to the legislation at hand?

The decision has been criticized from the perspective that it leads to rigidity in the application of of its judgment rather than the flexibility intended under the 1976 Legislation by Parliament. The ratio decidendi or principle decided, namely that "that the 'proper' proportion must always be the marginal cost", in Bennion's view, results in rigidity which could not have been intended by the legislators.

As concluded by Bennion (1995; Hansard, 1995):

- Parliament, in adopting the wording of clause (6), must have contemplated not only that the conferred power of judgment would exercized by officials rather than Ministers (and on appeal or review the courts), but that it would produce answers that would be different in different cases and might, in the light of experience or changing circumstances, be varied over time.

NON LEGAL FACTORS WHICH HAVE IMPACTED AN EVOLUTION IN COMMON LAW: ECONOMIC ANALYSES OF THE LAW

Decentralization through Non Legal Agents: A Trend for European Common and Civil Law Systems to Adopt?

Given the failures and flaws of references to Parliamentary material and whether these should be permitted as an aid to the construction of legislation which is ambiguous or obscure, as illustrated in the case of Pepper v Hart, should greater involvement of non-legal actors in European jurisdictions, civil and common law systems, not be encouraged?

As highlighted in the Daubert case, and The Estate of Edgar A. Berg v. Commissioner the de centralization of information resource, has been increasingly taking place over the years – as evidenced by the engagement of legal, non-legal and economic actors in the rule making process and judicial process. This serves as testimony to the fact that judges may not be fully equipped to allocate information in such a way that maximal efficiency or the best outcome is derived for involved parties. As already highlighted under the introductory section, other non-legal actors such as financial experts are now being in engaged as expert witnesses whose expertise are incorporated by judges in deciding landmark judgments. The use of legal actors to fill in gaps which are aimed at ensuring that judges acquire complete information which is fundamental to the efficient allocation of resources, is illustrated by the following extract from Posner's statement (2001:20):

The point I want to emphasize here is that the content of the legal norms that judges create by their decisions is not given by Kelsen's concept of law. As one of his natural-law critics puts it, "How the judge arrives at his decision is [for Kelsen] a 'meta-legal' question without interest for the jurist." Kelsen's rejection of natural law, his emphasis on jurisdictional at the expense of substantive norms, his repeated references to judicial discretion, his claim that application of law is not mechanical but often involves "the creation of a lower norm on the basis of a higher norm," his acknowledgment that sometimes the only preexisting law that a court can apply to decide a case is the law that confers the power of decision on the court, and his concept of interpretation as a frame rather than an algorithm, delimit a broad range of judicial action that is free (in the sense of "free range" chicken) yet lawful. The judges have to fill it with something, but while that something is lawful, it is not the law.

The role of judges, hence has evolved to the extent whereby the expertise of non-legal actors, as well as the incorporation of non-legal medium, through decentralization, whether these constitute non-governmental organizations, or financial experts, are required to be engaged in the legislating and interpretation of the law, in order for such judicial capacities to attain their maximal potential.

Reasons in favor of decentralization are as follows:

1. The need to mitigate incidences related to regulatory capture and the abuse of concentrated powers and information in the hands of centralized system – as well as facilitating separation of powers between the executive, legislature and judiciary.
2. The need to facilitate the goal of efficient allocation of resources
3. Mitigating inefficiencies attributed to increased costs arising from poor allocation of resources and unfavorable outcomes – which result in re- litigation.

As already highlighted under the literature review, the efficiency of common law, to the extent that such exists, can be explained by the evolutionary model whereby it is more likely that parties will litigate inefficient rules than efficient rules (see Rubin, 1977:6). Further, as highlighted by Parisi (2004:196), "inefficient rules impose greater costs on the parties who are governed by such rules than is the case with efficient rules – thus making the stakes in the dispute greater, and that where such stakes are greater, litigation is more evident than settlement."

The efficiency of common law as a mechanism for the efficient allocation of resources, and particularly information resources, would also be enhanced through the engagement of other actors in the legislative and judicial process.

Disadvantages of Centralization and Concentration of Information: The Need for Engagement of Other Actors in the Legislative and Judicial Process

Maintaining the Rule of Law and Avoiding the Abuse of Powers

Disadvantages associated with the centralization and concentration of information in the hands of a powerful actor usually revolve around insufficient checks and balances which could result in abuse of powers and lack of adequate mechanisms of accountability.

As illustrated with the need to ascertain those litigants who value information most – hence conferring not only the rights of property information to such litigants, but also ensuring that adequate funds are collected from such litigants to facilitate efficient allocation of resources and adequately cover compliance costs – it is necessary to ensure that discovery abuse does not take place. The access to, and availability of information in the judicial process is increasingly assuming fundamental importance. Of vital significance are also those channels through which such vital information is dissipated. As previously highlighted (Rubin, 1977:437), discovery misuse and abuse can be eliminated by shifting the reasonable cost of compliance to the requesting party.

The following section is aimed at highlighting Posner and Hayek's consensus on the importance of decentralization, as well as the incorporation of non-legal actors as tools for facilitating the efficient allocation of resources in common law.

As illustrated previously, decentralization and the involvement of non-legal medium also serve to illustrate the evolution of common law from the more centralized role previously assumed by judges (now devolved through other non-legal actors) as well as the increased role being assumed by litigants through the need to ascertain those who value information rights the most. Whilst it is argued that litigants influence the evolution of common law (Priest, 1977), the role of judicial opinion in shaping the evolution of the system, is also emphasized (see Whitman, 2000:781).

The effectiveness of de centralization as an information gathering mechanism, employed in the judicial process is illustrated in the following statement by Posner (2001:30):

There are two ways of establishing norms to guide human behavior. In one, which Hayek calls "constructivist rationalism," they are prescribed from the top down by a legislature, a bureaucracy, or a judiciary—in other words by experts who gather the information necessary to formulate by the method of reason the best possible set of norms. This method, as we might guess from Hayek's aversion to central planning, he rejects as requiring too much information to be feasible; in addition, it endangers liberty by enlarging the administrative powers of government and thus weakening the rule of law."

Posner (2001:31) further adds:

The alternative method of creating norms is that of custom, and is based on the superiority of what Hayek calls "spontaneous order" over order brought about by plan or design. The word "spontaneous," with its connotation of suddenness, is not the best term for what he has in mind; "unplanned" or "undesigned" would be better and "evolved" would be best, given his emphasis on the analogy of natural selection.

The above statements, whilst reflecting support for de centralization, as well as the consensus of the evolution of the law, is to be contrasted with Posner and Hayek's view of what roles should be assumed by economic actors and judges in the judicial process:

Whilst Posner (2001:37) highlights his support for Hayek's view that law owes much to custom and that custom is a reliable guide to efficient methods of cooperation, he considers Hayek's idea, "that the only thing a judge should do is enforce custom, without any consideration of its consequences, because custom is the only legitimate law and so a legal judgment not founded on it is not true law",[4] as being too narrow – adding that it "extinguishes any explicit role for economic analysis in adjudication." Posner herein underlines his support for a more active (rather than passive role) to be assumed by judges.

He also distinguishes Hayek and Kelsen by adding that whilst Hayek, excludes the possibilities and position that economic analysis might occupy in adjudication, Kelsen, opens that space wide.

However, it appears that Hayek is also in favor of the engagement of non-legal actors in the judicial process. This is reflected where he states that "the ultimate decisions must be left to the people who know directly of the relevant changes and of the resources immediately available to meet them" – as well as his affirmation of the need of decentralization as a means of ensuring that "the knowledge of the particular circumstances of time and place will be promptly used."

"Ultimate decisions" should still be left to judges – however this is not to preclude the fact that judges will be able to facilitate better ultimate decisions through the involvement of non-legal and/or economic actors who will not only assist judiciary in informing them of "relevant changes and immediate resources to meet them", but also inform them in acquiring vital knowledge of circumstances which would not have been otherwise gained if the recruitment of such actors had not been possible.

COMPARISONS BETWEEN THE EXECUTIVE, JUDICIARY AND LEGISLATIVE BRANCHES IN THE UNITED KINGDOM AND THE UNITED STATES

Whilst some authorities consider the House of Lords to be the lower house, its position as the Upper Chamber/House of the legislature can be justified, and is synonymous to the role assumed by the United States House of Representatives. This is all the more particularly evident given its prominent roles in both legislative and judiciary functions – as opposed to the House of Common's role in principally related legislative functions.

CONCLUSION

If we can agree that the economic problem of society is mainly one of rapid adaptation to changes in the particular circumstances of time and place, it would seem to follow that the ultimate decisions must be left to the people who are familiar with these circumstances, who know directly of the relevant changes and of the resources immediately available to meet them.

We need decentralization because only thus can we ensure that the knowledge of the particular circumstances of time and place will be promptly used (Hayek, 1945: 519-530).

Table 1. Parliamentary sovereignty, the rule of law and separation of powers: administrative accountability

	The United Kingdom	The United States
The Executive	This is synonymous with the Government and also assumes the form and authority of the Prime Minister who presides over the Government	This is also affiliated with the Government and also assumes the role and position of the President who is presides over the Government (Cabinet) and is also Commander in Chief of the Armed Forces
The Judiciary	The judiciary in the United Kingdom is comprised of court system which differs between Scotland and the legal system that operates in England and Wales. Whilst the county courts, magistrates and crown courts (representing civil and criminal cases respectively), constitute the lower courts, the hierarchy is followed by high courts, the Courts of Appeal (civil and criminal divisions), and then the House of Lords (which assumes the highest hierarchy).	The United States Supreme Court is synonymous with the House of Lords as assuming the highest judicial level in terms of judicial hierarchy. Unlike the House of Lords, its functions are solely confined to judicial roles and it is not involved in legislative functions which are primarily executed by Congress.
The Legislature	The legislature in the United Kingdom is fused – with the legislative arm (Parliament) comprising of the Crown (the Queen), as well the House of Commons (lower court) and the House of Lords. From this sense the term "Parliamentary Sovereignty or Parliamentary Supremacy" is coined since legislation approved or passed as a Bill (which later becomes legislation or Acts of Parliament) is supreme and cannot be overridden by other forms of regulations unless they are repealed.	The legislative arm in the United States, namely, Congress, is comprised of the Senate, and the House of Representatives. The immense influence and powers granted to both chambers in the United States in preventing the passing of legislation – as well as powers to prevent the executive from executing legal related functions can be contrasted to the position in the United Kingdom where most Bills which are passed usually become law – with the Crown approving most of these Bills (Royal Assent) in order for them to become legislation. The last recorded event was in 1707 where a Bill was not granted Royal Assent during the time of Queen Anne (in relation to the "settling of militia in Scotland")

Table 2. Comparison between the British House of Commons and the United States' House of Representatives

	House of Commons	House of Representatives
Basic functions	The forum for the formation and maintenance of the Government	A legislative and oversight forum whose policy preferences may or may not coincide with those of the separately elected government, that is, the presidency and the rest of the executive branch.
Sizes of Constituencies and Membership	Various statutes have often altered the size of the House of Commons	The size of the House of Representatives has been fixed by law at 435 since 1910, although a temporary increase to 437 was permitted to provide seats for Representatives from Alaska and Hawaii from 1959 to 1961
Roles and Responsibilities of Governmental and Legislative Representatives	The Prime Minister, although head of the Government and an MP, is not the Leader of the House of Commons	Sitting Members of the U.S. Congress cannot simultaneously serve in the President's Cabinet, because such service is an "incompatible office" under the Constitution.

Source: R.E. Petersen, Parliament and Congress: A Brief Comparison of the British House of Commons and the U.S. House of Representatives May 19, 2005

In relating the above statement to the previous section and the need for the involvement of non-legal actors as a means of attaining common law attributes of economic efficiency in efficient allocation of resources, fostering greater accountability in the judicial process, and an avenue which would better serve as aids to statutory interpretation, the vital role served by the decentralization of information as resource, can be re iterated. Ultimate decisions must be left to judges – however, judges require the involvement of non-legal actors in certain instances which may be necessary to facilitate the efficient allocation of resources. The efficient allocation of resources may still be achieved without the involvement of non-legal actors – however, maximal efficiency may also be derived where such non legal actors are involved. In certain cases, it may well be that non legal actors play such a fundamental role that their exclusion in the judicial process would only generate inefficient results and outcomes for parties involved.

In very interesting fashion, decentralization is also essential towards ensuring that possibilities for regulatory capture are minimized.

Why might firms want to allocate "property rights invaluable information" to managers, rather than to shareholders? Because centralization of information in the ambit of those better equipped and specialized to handle such information warrants such a move.

Centralization and decentralization should thus be viewed from relative (as opposed to absolute) perspectives. Support for centralization of information is justified where such information resides within capable and more equipped ambits who will transform such information for the purposes of maximization of wealth or utilities. Given such merits, there still exists the need for checks and balance to ensure that such powers are not abused. In like manner, decentralization of information may still be facilitated optimally taking into account timing, manner of the dissipation, and agents involved in the distribution of such information.

Judges should certainly not make and unmake the law in certain cases - the supremacy of Parliament should be adhered to. Judge made law, namely common law, however constitutes an exception where the principle of *stare decisis* cannot hold in a world which is constantly changing and where those changes need to be incorporated into decisions if such decisions are to generate meaningful results. The evolutionary nature of common law and the flexibility it confers in introducing greater relevance, by virtue of passage of time or other environmental factors, serves as a vital attribute in its ability to facilitate efficiency in the allocation of resources – and particularly, information resource.

Prices, for example, constitute examples of vital information which need to be updated constantly if wages which were earned centuries ago, are to have meaningful and reasonable importance and values in modern day valuation and measurements. Markets will definitely evolve and adequate rules are needed to regulate the markets. This is very evident given the fact that market failures, namely information asymmetries exist, and also the fact that the Efficient Markets Hypothesis does not hold in its entirety. Decentralization, hence constitutes a means of not only mitigating information asymmetries, but also ensuring that efficient maximization of resource utilization and allocation, takes place.

Hence the decentralization of powers and information, in this case, from the executive and legislature to the judiciary, should be viewed positively as a means of addressing and mitigating informational asymmetries resulting from ambiguous, confusing and misleading words within a statute and also resulting in more efficient allocation of resources, and awarding of damages to the parties involved.

Given the possible failures and flaws of references to Parliamentary material and whether these should be permitted as an aid to the construction of legislation which is ambiguous or obscure, as illustrated in the case of Pepper v Hart, greater involvement of non-legal actors in European jurisdictions, civil and common law systems, should definitely be encouraged.

REFERENCES

Aldashev, G. (2009). Legal Institutions, Political Economy, and Development. *Oxford Review of Economic Policy*, *25*(2), 257–270. doi:10.1093/oxrep/grp016

Ayres, I., & Braithwaite, J., (1992). *Responsive Regulation: Transcending the Deregulation Debate*. Oxford University Press.

Bennion, F. (1995). *How they all got it wrong in Pepper v. Hart*. Academic Press.

Boettke, P. (2010). *Information and Knowledge: Austrian Economics in Search of its Uniqueness*. Retrieved from http://papers.ssrn.com/sol3/papers.cfm?abstract_id=1537989

Brudney, J. (2010). *The Story of Pepper v Hart: Examining Legislative History Across the Pond*. Public Law and Legal Theory Working Paper Series No 124. Retrieved from http://papers.ssrn.com/sol3/papers.cfm?abstract_id=1601291

Carlton, D., & Fischel, D. (1983, May). The Regulation of Insider Trading. *Stanford Law Review*, *35*(5), 857–895. doi:10.2307/1228706

Cooter, R. D., & Rubinfeld, D. L. (1994). An Economic Model of Legal Discovery. *The Journal of Legal Studies, 23*(1), 435-463. Retrieved from http://www.jstor.org/stable/724329

Cooter, R.D., & Rubinfeld, D.L. (1989). *Economic Analysis of Legal Disputes and Their Resolution*. Retrieved from http://works.bepress.com/robert_cooter/30

Daubert v. Merrell. (1993). Dow Pharmaceutical, Inc 509 U.S.579

DiGabriele, J.A. (2007). To Have and to Hold: An Empirical Investigation of Preferences for Valuation Methods of Closely Held Companies in the Matrimonial Court. *Journal of Forensic Accounting, 8*(1-2).

DiGabriele, J.A. (2008). Forensic Accounting and The Marital Life Style Analysis. *The Journal of Forensic Accounting, 9*(1).

DiGabriele, J.A. (2009). Gender, Valuation of Private Companies, and State Specific Variables in the Division of Marital Assets. *Journal of Legal Economics, 15*(2).

DiGabriele, J. A. (2009). Matrimonial Business Valuations and the AICPA Statement on Standards for Valuations Services No. 1. *American Journal of Family Law*, *23*(2).

DiGabriele, J. A. (2011). Evidentiary Reliability, Valuation Standards, and Rules of Thumb. *American Journal of Family Law. Volume*, *25*(1), 16–22.

Fon, V., & Parisi, F. (2006). Judicial Precedents in Civil Law Systems: A Dynamic Analysis, 26. *International Review of Law and Economics*, *26*(4), 519–535. doi:10.1016/j.irle.2007.01.005

Garoupa, N., & Liguerre, C. G. (2011). The Syndrome of the Efficiency of Common Law. *Boston University Journal of Internal Law*. Retrieved from http://papers.ssrn.com/pape.tar?abstract_id=1674170

Gennaioli, N., & Shleifer, A. (2007). The Evolution of Common Law. *Journal of Political Economy*, *115*(1), 43–68. doi:10.1086/511996

Grabosky, P., & Braithwaite, J. (1986). *Of Manners Gentle: Enforcement Strategies of Australian Business Regulatory Agencies*. Melbourne: Oxford University Press.

Hayek, F. A. (1945). The Use of Knowledge in Society. *The American Economic Review, 35*(4), 519-530. Retrieved from http://www.jstor.org/discover/10.2307/1809376?uid=3739920&uid=2&uid=4&uid=3739256&sid=21104299293711

Hayek, F. A. (1960). *The Constitution of Liberty*. Chicago: University of Chicago Press.

Hayek, F. A. (1973). *Law, Legislation and Liberty: Rules and Order* (Vol. 1). Chicago: University of Chicago Press.

Hayek, F. A. (1976). *Law, Legislation and Liberty: The Mirage of Social Justice* (Vol. 2). Chicago: University of Chicago Press.

Jha, K. (2012). *Examining the Current Importance of Pepper v Hart*. Retrieved from http://papers.ssrn.com/sol3/papers.cfm?abstract_id=2149694

La Porta, R., de Silanes, F. L., & Shleifer, A. (2008). The Economic Consequences of Legal Origins, 46. *Journal of Economic Literature*, *46*(2), 285–332. doi:10.1257/jel.46.2.285

Mahoney, P. (2001). The Common Law and Economic Growth: Hayek Might Be Right, 30. *The Journal of Legal Studies*, *30*(2), 503–525. doi:10.1086/322053

Ojo, M. (2011). *Co-operative and Competitive Enforced Self-Regulation: The Role of Governments, Private Actors and Banks in Corporate Responsibility*. Retrieved from http://mpra.ub.uni-muenchen.de/27850/1/MPRA_paper_27850.pdf

Parisi, F. (2004). The Efficiency of the Common Law Hypothesis. In The Encyclopedia of Public Choice (pp. 519-522). Academic Press.

Pepper v Hart [1992] 3 WLR 1032, [1993] 1 All ER 42, HL (E)

Posner, R. A. (1974, Autumn). Theories of Economic Regulation. *The Bell Journal of Economics and Management Science*, *5*(2), 335–358. doi:10.2307/3003113

Posner, R. A. (2001). *Kelsen*. Hayek, and the Economic Analysis of Law.

Posner, R. A. (2003). *Kelsen versus Hayek: Pragmatism, Economics and Democracy. In Law, Pragmatism, and Democracy*. Cambridge, MA: Harvard University Press.

Posner, R. A. (2005). Hayek, Law, and Cognition. *New York University Journal of Law and Liberty, 147*.

Posner, R. A. (2013). *Reflections on Judging*. Cambridge, MA: Harvard University Press.

Priest, G. L. (1977). The Common Law Process and the Selection for Efficient Rules. *The Journal of Legal Studies*, *6*(1), 65–82. doi:10.1086/467563

Rubin, P. H. (1977). Why is Common Law Efficient? *The Journal of Legal Studies, 6*(1), 51-63. Retrieved from http://www.jstor.org/stable/724189

SEC v Texas Gulf Sulphur Co, 401 F.2d 833 (2d Cir 1968) (en banc), cert denied, 404 U.S 1005 (1971).

Stringham, E. (2001). Kaldor-Hicks Efficiency and the Problem of Central Planning. *Quarterly Journal of Austrian Economics*, *4*(2).

Styles, S. C. (1994, Spring). The Rule of Parliament: Statutory Interpretation After Pepper v Hart. *Oxford Journal of Legal Studies*, *14*(1), 151–158. doi:10.1093/ojls/14.1.151

The Estate of Edgar A. Berg v. Commissioner (T. C. Memo 1991279).

Whitman, D. G. (2000, June). Evolution of the Common Law and the Emergence of Compromise. *The Journal of Legal Studies*, *29*.

Zywicki, T. J., & Sanders, A. B. (2008, February). Posner, Hayek & the Economic Analysis of Law. *Iowa Law Review*, *93*(2), 559–603.

ENDNOTES

1 For further information on the advantages and disadvantages of Self-Regulation, Enforced Self-Regulation see M Ojo, "Co-operative and Competitive Enforced Self-Regulation: The Role of Governments, Private Actors and Banks in Corporate Responsibility http://mpra.ub.uni-muenchen.de/27850/1/MPRA_paper_27850.pdf; also see I Ayres and J Braithwaite, Responsive Regulation: Transcending the Deregulation Debate Oxford University Press at page 102

2 In distinguishing this statement between previous decisions, it was added that "General acceptance is not a necessary precondition to the admissibility of scientific evidence under the Federal Rules of Evidence, but the Rules of Evidence— especially Rule 702—do assign to the trial judge the task of ensuring that an expert's testimony both rests on a reliable foundation and is relevant to the task at hand" see page 597 "Finally, "general acceptance" can yet have a bearing on the inquiry. A "reliability assessment does not require, although it does permit, explicit identification of a relevant scientific community and an express determination of a particular degree of acceptance within that community." See opinion of court at page 594

3 In this respect he adds that Frye does require expert testimony to be founded in generally accepted scientific principles that are recognized in the particular field; and there must be evidence that the technique has been used.

4 Which he regards as a slight exaggeration of his position

Compilation of References

Abu-Hassan, K. (1986). *Public Accounting and the Accounting Profession in Malaysia*. Paper presented at the Universiti Utara Malaysia's Professional Lecture Series, October, Universiti Utara Malaysia, Jitra.

ADBI. (2009). *Demand for Infrastructure Financing in Asia 2010–2020. ADBI Internal Report*. Tokyo: ADBI.

Adegboyega, O., & Taiwo, M. (2011). Contribution of corporate social responsibility to agriculture and rural development in Nigeria. *Journal of Sustainable Development in Africa, 13*(4), 110–129.

Adelegan, J.O. (2000). Foreign direct investment and economic growth in Nigeria: A seemingly unrelated model. *African Review of Money, Finance and Banking*, 5–25.

Adeolu, O. A., & Afolabi, E. O. (2010). Corporate social responsibility and sustainable community development in Nigeria: WAPCO, a case from the cement industry. *Social Responsibility Journal*, *6*(4), 522–535. doi:10.1108/17471111011083419

Adeyemo, S. A., Oyebamiji, F. F., & Alimi, K. (2013). An valuation of factors influencing corporate social responsibility in Nigerian manufacturing companies. *International Journal of Academic Research in Economics and Management Sciences*, *2*(6), 54–63.

Adi, A. A., & Ogbole, F. O. (2013). *Foreign Direct Investment in China: Its Sectoral and Aggregate Impact on Economic Growth*. MPRA Paper No. 62166. Retrieved from http://mpra.ub.uni-muenchen.de/62166/

Agosin, M. R., & Machado, R. (2007). Openness and the international allocation of foreign direct investment. *The Journal of Development Studies*, *43*(7), 1234–1247. doi:10.1080/00220380701526410

Agrawal, G., & Khan, M. (2011). Impact of FDI on GDP: A Comparative Study of China and India. *International Journal of Business and Management, 6*(10). doi:10.5539/ijbm.v6n10p71

Agrawal, P. (2000). *Economic impact of foreign direct investment in South Asia*. Bombay, India: Indira Gandhi Institute of Development Research.

Ahmad-Noordin, Z. (1981). Proposal for the Establishment of A National Institute of Public Finance and Accountancy. *The Malaysian Accountant*, *2*(1), 25–28.

Ahmad-Noordin, Z. (1986). Value for Money Audits - The Practical Aspect. In *Proceedings for the MIA and MACPA jointly organised 5th ASEAN Federation of Accountants Conference*.

Akinlo, A. E. (2004). Foreign direct investment and growth in Nigeria: An empirical investigation. *Journal of Policy Modeling*, *26*(5), 627–639. doi:10.1016/j.jpolmod.2004.04.011

Al Nasser, O. M. (2010). How does foreign direct investment affect economic growth? The role of local conditions. *Latin American Business Review*, *11*(2), 111–139. doi:10.1080/10978526.2010.486715

Alabi, O. F., & Ntukekpo, S. S. (2012). Oil companies and corporate social responsibility in Nigeria: An empirical assessment of Chevron's community development projects in the Niger Delta. *British Journal of Arts and Social Sciences, 4*(2), 361–374.

Albrechtsen, J. (2006, March 29). This business of moral coercion is just a hoax. *The Australia.*

Aldashev, G. (2009). Legal Institutions, Political Economy, and Development. *Oxford Review of Economic Policy, 25*(2), 257–270. doi:10.1093/oxrep/grp016

Aliran (1981b). *Corruption.* Aliran.

Aliran. (1981a). *Aliran Speaks: Being a Collection of Aliran's Views on Various Social Issues From August 1977 to September 1981.* Aliran.

Aliran. (1988). *Issues of the Mahathir Years.* Aliran.

Aluko, S. A. (1961). Financing economic development in Nigeria. *The Nigerian Journal of Economic and Social Studies, 3*(1), 39–67.

Amaeshi, K., Adi, B., Ogbechie, C., & Amao, O. (2006). *Corporate social responsibility in Nigeria: Western mimicry or indigenous practices?* Research Paper Series, International Centre for Corporate Social Responsibility, Nottingham University.

Anheier, H., & Seibels, W. (1980). The third sector, comparative studies of non-profit organizations. de Gruyter.

Annual Report on the OECD Guidelines for Multinational Enterprises 2010 Corporate Responsibility: Reinforcing a Unique Instrument. (2010). OECD Publishing.

Annual Report on the OECD Guidelines for Multinational Enterprises 2014 Responsible Business Conduct by Sector. (2015). OECD Publishing.

Annual Report on the OECD Guidelines for Multinational Enterprises. (2010). *Corporate Responsibility: Reinforcing a Unique Instrument.* OECD Publishing.

Annual Report on the OECD Guidelines for Multinational Enterprises. (2014). Responsible Business Conduct by Sector. OECD Publishing.

Anyanwu, J. C. (1998). An econometric investigation of determinants of foreign direct investment in Nigeria in the Growth Process. *Proceedings of the Nigerian Economic Society Conference.*

Archana, V. (2006). *Foreign Direct Investment in India: Industry and State-level Analyses.* (Unpublished Thesis). Indian Institute of Technology, Kharagpur, India.

Archie, B. C. (1991). The Pyramid of Corporate Social Responsibility: Toward the Moral Management of Organizational Stakeholders. *Business Horizons.*

Aremu, J.A. (1997). *Foreign direct investment and performance.* Paper delivered at a workshop on Foreign Investment Policy and Practice organized by the Nigerian Institute of Advanced Legal Studies, Lagos, Nigeria.

Ariyo, A. (1998). Investment and Nigeria's economic growth in Investment in the Growth Process.*Proceedings of Nigerian Economic Society Annual Conference 1998.*

Armstrong, P. (1985). Changing Management Control Strategies: The Role of Competition Between Accountancy and Other Organizational Professions. *Accounting, Organizations and Society, 10*(2), 129–148. doi:10.1016/0361-3682(85)90012-1

Armstrong, P. (1987). The Rise of Accounting Controls in British Capitalist Enterprises. *Accounting, Organizations and Society*, *12*(5), 415–436.

ASEAN Accounting Research Unit. (1992). The Auditing Framework in ASEAN. School of Accounting and Business Research Centre, Nanyang Technological University, Singapore.

Atkinson, A., Waterhouse, & Wells. (1997). A Stakeholder Approach to Strategic Performance Measurement. *Sloan Management Review*.

Aupperle, K. E., Carroll, A. B., & Hatfield, J. D. (1985). An Empirical Examination of the Relationship Between Corporate Social Responsibility and Profitability. *Academy of Management Journal*, *28*(2), 446–463.

Aupperle, K. E., Hatfield, J. D., & Carroll, A. B. (1983). *Instrument Development and Application in Corporate Social Responsibility*. Academy of Management Proceedings.

Ayanwale, A.B. &, Bamire, A.S. (2001). *The influence of FDI on firm level productivity of Nigeria's Agro/Agro-Allied Sector.* Final Report presented to the African Economic Research Consortium, Nairobi, Kenya.

Ayorinde, B. (2007). *The challenges of corporate social irresponsibility in the Niger Delta regions of Nigeria – The imperative of legislative reform*. Paper presented at the 5th International Conference on International Environmental Law, New Delhi, India.

Ayres, I., & Braithwaite, J., (1992). *Responsive Regulation: Transcending the Deregulation Debate*. Oxford University Press.

Ayres, I., & Braithwaite, J. (1995). *Responsive Regulation: Transcending the Deregulation Debate*. Oxford, UK: Social Legal Studies.

Azham, M. A. (2002). *Ethnicity, Foreign Investments and Strong Pragmatic Government: Towards Interpreting Accounting Progress in Malaysia*. Paper presented at the Universiti Teknologi MARA organised Conference on Financial Reporting: Issues in the 21st Century, Shah Alam.

Azham, M. A. (1994). *Accountability in the Audit Profession in Malaysia*. Kuala Lumpur: University of Malaya Press.

Bagnoli, M., & Watts, S. (2003). Selling to socially responsible consumers: Competition and the private provision of public goods. *Journal of Economics & Management Strategy*, *12*(3), 419–445. doi:10.1162/105864003322309536

Baron, D. (2001). Private politics, corporate social responsibility and integrated strategy. *Journal of Economics & Management Strategy*, *10*(1), 7–45. doi:10.1162/105864001300122548

Barro, R. J., & Gordon, D. B. (1983). Rules, discretion and reputation in a model of monetary policy. *Journal of Monetary Economics*, *12*(1), 123–125. doi:10.1016/0304-3932(83)90051-X

Barry, N. P. (2000). Controversy:Do corporations have any responsibility beyond making a profit? *Journal of Markets and Morality*, *3*(1), 100–107.

Barry, N. P. (2002). The stakeholder concept of corporate control is illogical and impractical. *The Independent Review*, *6*(4), 541–554.

Basant, R., & Saha, S. N. (2005). *Determinants of Entry in the Indian Manufacturing Sector*. Working Paper No.2005-01-01. Indian Institute of Management.

Bashir, O. K. (2013). Foreign assistance and economic growth in Nigeria: The two-gap model framework. *American International Journal of Contemporary Research*, *3*(10), 153–160.

Baskin, J., & Gordon, K. (2005). Corporate Responsibility Practices of Emerging Market Companies. *OECD Publishing*.

Bass, J. R. (1973). *Malaysian Politics, 1968-1970: Crisis and Response*. (Unpublished PhD Thesis). University of California, Berkeley, CA.

BBC. (2016a). Tata: Government considers 'all options' for Port Talbot. *BBC news*. Retrieved from: http://www.bbc.co.uk/news/business-35923626

BBC. (2016b). Britain's steel industry: What's going wrong? by Tim Bowler Business reporter. *BBC News*. Retrieved from: http://www.bbc.co.uk/news/business-34581945

BBC. (2016c). *Port Talbot Tata Steel: Assembly set for crisis recall*. Retrieved from: http://www.bbc.co.uk/news/uk-wales-politics-35923463

BBC. (2016d). *Tata Steel plans to sell loss-making UK plants*. Retrieved from: http://www.bbc.co.uk/news/business-35922046

Beck, T., Demirgüç-Kunt, A., & Levine, R. (2000). A New Database on Financial Development and Structure. *World Bank Economic Review, 14*, 597-605.

Beck, T., Demirgüç-Kunt, A., & Levine, R. (2009). *Financial Institutions and Markets across Countries and over Time: Data and Analysis*. Policy Research Working Paper 4943. World Bank.

Beck, G. W. (1974). *Public Accountants in Australia – Their Social Role*. Melbourne: Australian Accounting Research Foundation.

Beck, T., Demirgüç-Kunt, A., & Levine, R. (2010). Financial Institutions and Markets across Countries and over Time: The Updated Financial Development and Structure Database. *The World Bank Economic Review*, *24*(1), 77–92. doi:10.1093/wber/lhp016

Benau, M. A. G., Humphrey, C., Moizer, P., & Turley, S. (1993). Auditing Expectations and Performance in Spain and Britain: A Comparative Analysis. *The International Journal of Accounting*, *28*, 281–307.

Bennett, J. (2002). Multinational corporations, social responsibility and conflict. *Journal of International Affairs*, *55*(2).

Bennion, F. (1995). *How they all got it wrong in Pepper v. Hart*. Academic Press.

Berger, H., de Haan, J., & Eijffinger, S. (2001). Central Bank Independence: An Update of Theory and Evidence. *Journal of Economic Surveys*, *15*, 3–40.

Best, P. J., Buckby, S., & Tan, C. (2001). Evidence of the Audit Expectation Gap in Singapore. *Managerial Auditing Journal*, *16*(3), 134–144. doi:10.1108/02686900110385579

Blomstrom, M. (2007). *Transnational corporations and manufacturing exports from developing countries*. New York: United Nations.

Blonigen, B. A., Davies, R. B., Waddell, G. R., & Naughton, H. T. (2007). FDI in space: Spatial autoregressive relationships in foreign direct investment. *European Economic Review*, *51*(5), 1303–1325. doi:10.1016/j.euroecorev.2006.08.006

Blowfield, M. (2005). Corporate Social Responsibility: Reinventing the Meaning of Development? *International Affairs*, *81*(3), 515–524. doi:10.1111/j.1468-2346.2005.00466.x

Blowfield, M., & Frynas, J. G. (2005). Setting new agendas: Critical perspectives on corporate social responsibility in the developing world. *International Affairs*, *81*(3), 499–513. doi:10.1111/j.1468-2346.2005.00465.x

Boettke, P. (2010). *Information and Knowledge: Austrian Economics in Search of its Uniqueness*. Retrieved from http://papers.ssrn.com/sol3/papers.cfm?abstract_id=1537989

Bowe, H., Miletkov, M., & Wintoki, B. M. (2013). *When does the adoption and use of IFRS increase foreign investment?* University of Virginia Working Paper.

Boyle, M., & Boguslaw, J. (2007). Business, poverty and corporate citizenship: Naming the issues and framing solutions. *Journal of Corporate Citizenship*, *26*(26), 101–120. doi:10.9774/GLEAF.4700.2007.su.00013

Brautigam, D. (2008). Chinese business and African development: Flying geese or hidden dragon? In C. Alden, D. Large, & R. M. S. Soares de Oliveira (Eds.), *China returns to Africa: A rising power and a continent embrace*.

Brennan, M. (1985). Class, Politics and Race in Modern Malaysia. In R. Higgott & R. Robison (Eds.), *Southeast Asia: Essays in the Political Economy of Structural Change* (pp. 93–127). London: Routledge and Kegan Paul.

Briston, R. J. (1978). The Evolution of Accounting in Developing Countries. *The International Journal of Accounting*, *14*(1), 105–120.

Broomhill, R. (2007). *Corporate Social Responsibility: Key Issues and Debates*. Don Dunstan Foundation.

Brown, D. K., Deardorff, A. V., & Stern, R. M. (1998). Trade and labour standards. *Open Economies Review*, *9*(2), 179–194. doi:10.1023/A:1008268419257

Brown, R. E. (1962). Changing Audit Objectives and Techniques. *Accounting Review*, *37*, 696–703.

Bruce, S. W. (1988). *Certified Public Accountants: A Profession in Crisis*. (Unpublished PhD Thesis). Claremont Graduate School.

Brudney, J. (2010). *The Story of Pepper v Hart: Examining Legislative History Across the Pond*. Public Law and Legal Theory Working Paper Series No 124. Retrieved from http://papers.ssrn.com/sol3/papers.cfm?abstract_id=1601291

Burchell, S., Clubb, C., & Hopwood, A. G. (1985). Accounting in its Social Context: Towards a History of Value Added in the United Kingdom. *Accounting, Organizations and Society*, *10*(4), 381–413. doi:10.1016/0361-3682(85)90002-9

Burchell, S., Clubb, C., Hopwood, A. G., Hughes, J., & Nahapiet, J. (1980). The Roles of Accounting in Organizations and Society. *Accounting, Organizations and Society*, *5*(1), 5–27. doi:10.1016/0361-3682(80)90017-3

Calvo, G. A. (1978). On the Time Consistency of Optimal Policy in a Monetary Economy. *Econometrica*, *46*(6), 1411-1428. Retrieved from http://www.jstor.org/stable/1913836

Campbell, J. L. (2007). Why would corporations behave in socially responsible ways? An institutional theory of corporate social responsibility. *Academy of Management Review*, *32*(3), 946–967. doi:10.5465/AMR.2007.25275684

Carkovic, M., & Levine, R. (2002). *Does foreign direct investment accelerate economic growth?* University of Minnesota Working paper.

Carlton, D., & Fischel, D. (1983, May). The Regulation of Insider Trading. *Stanford Law Review*, *35*(5), 857–895. doi:10.2307/1228706

Carmona, S., & Trombetta, M. (2008). On the global acceptance of the IAS/IFRS accounting standards: The logic and implications of the principle-based system. *Journal of Accounting and Public Policy*, *27*(6), 455–461. doi:10.1016/j.jaccpubpol.2008.09.003

Carnegie, G. D., & Napier, C. J. (1996). Critical and Interpretive Histories: Insights into Accounting's Present and Future Through Its Past. *Accounting, Auditing & Accountability Journal*, *9*(3), 7–39. doi:10.1108/09513579610121956

Carney, M. (2016). The Turn of the Year. Text of the Peston Lecture by Mr Mark Carney, Governor of the Bank of England and Chairman of the Financial Stability Board, at the Queen Mary University of London, London, UK.

Carroll, A. B. (1979). A three-dimensional conceptual model of corporate social performance. *Academy of Management Review*, *4*(4), 497–505.

Carroll, A. B. (1979). A Three-Dimensional Model of Corporate Performance. *Academy of Management Review*, *4*(4), 497–505. Retrieved from http://www.jstor.org/stable/257850?seq=1#page_scan_tab_contents

Carroll, A. B. (1983). Corporate social responsibility: Will industry respond to cut-backs in social program funding? *Vital Speeches of the Day*, *49*, 604–608.

Carroll, A. B. (1991). The pyramid of corporate social responsibility: Toward the moral management of organizational stakeholders. *Business Horizons*, *34*(4), 39–48. doi:10.1016/0007-6813(91)90005-G

Carroll, A. B. (1991, July-August). The Pyramid of Corporate Social Responsibility: Toward the Moral Management of Organizational Stakeholders. *Business Horizons*.

Carroll, A. B. (1999). Corporate social responsibility. Evolution of a definitional construct. *Business & Society*, *38*(3), 268–295. doi:10.1177/000765039903800303

Carter, C. R. (2005). Purchasing corporate responsibility and firm performance: The key mediating roles of organisational learning and supplier performance. *International Journal of Physical Distribution & Logistics Management*, *35*, 177–194. doi:10.1108/09600030510594567

Castellano, J. G. (2002). *Chair's Corner*. AICPA. Available at http://www.aicpa.org/pubs/cpaltr/sept2002/chair.htm

Central Bank. (1987). *The Role of External Auditors in the Supervision of Financial Institutions in Malaysia*. Kuala Lumpur: SEACEN.

Chandana, C., & Peter, N. (2006). *Economic Reforms, Foreign Direct Investment and its Economic Effects in India*. Kiel Working Paper No. 1272.

Chandler, R. A., Edwards, J. R., & Anderson, M. (1993). Changing perceptions of the role of the company auditor: 1840 – 1940. *Accounting and Business Review*, *23*(Autumn), 443–459. doi:10.1080/00014788.1993.9729890

Chandra, M. (1989). *Challenges and Choices in Malaysian Politics and Society*. Penang: Aliran.

Chan, P., & Horii, K. (1986). *Impact of the New Economic Policy on the Malaysian Economy: With Special Reference to Ownership and Control*. Tokyo: Institute of Developing Economies.

Chatterjee, S., Mishra, P., & Chatterjee, B. (2013). Determinants of Inter-State Variations in FDI Inflows in India. *Eurasian Journal of Business and Economics*, *6*(11), 93–120.

Chee, S. H. (1971). *Sociocultural Pluralism and Political Change: The Dilemmas of the Bimodal Society in Malaya*. (Unpublished PhD Thesis). University of Pittsburgh.

Chen, et al.. (1999). *Is Accounting Information Value Relevant in the Emerging Chinese Stock Market?* Academic Press.

Chen, , Chen, S., & Su, X. (2001). Is Accounting Information Value-Relevant in the Emerging Chinese Stock Market? *Journal of International Accounting, Auditing & Taxation*, *10*(1), 1–22. doi:10.1016/S1061-9518(01)00033-7

Chenery, H., & Montek, S.A. (2004). Redistribution with growth. London: Oxford University Press.

Choo, K. E. (1991). *'Trust Me' Approach of Professional Accountants vs 'Show Me' Attitude of the Public Towards Professional Ethics*. Paper presented at the MIA and MACPA jointly organised 7th National Accountants Conference, Kuala Lumpur.

Christian Aid. (2004). *Behind the mask: The real face of corporate social responsibility*. London: Christian Aid.

Christopher E. (2007). The FDI – Employment Link in a Globalizing World: The Case of Argentina, Brazil and Mexico. Employment Analysis Unit, Employment Strategy Department, Employment Strategy Papers.

Clark, C. (1940). *The Conditions of Economics Press*. London: Macmillian.

Coady, D., Gillingham, R., Ossowski, R., Piotrowski, J., Tareq, S., & Tyson, J. (2010). *Petroleum product subsidies: Costly, inequitable, and rising*. IMF Staff Position Note No. 10/05. Washington, DC: International Monetary Fund. Available at http://www.imf.org/external/pubs/ft/spn/2010/spn1005.pdf

Coady, D., Gillingham, R., Ossowski, R., Piotrowski, J., Tareq, S., & Tyson, J. (2010). *Petroleum Product Subsidies: Costly, Inequitable, and Rising*. IMF Staff Position Note No. 10/05. Washington, DC: International Monetary Fund. Available at http://www.imf.org/external/pubs/ft/spn/2010/spn1005.pdf

Cohen Commission : Commission on Auditors' Responsibilities. (1978). AICPA.

Cole, M. A., Elliott, R. J. R., & Zhang, J. (2009). Corruption, good governance and FDI location in China: A province-level analysis. *The Journal of Development Studies*, *45*(9), 1494–1512.

Committee on International Accounting Operation and Education. 1976-78, of the American Accounting Association. (1978). Accounting Education and the Third World. American Accounting Association.

Connect U. S. (n.d.). *17 Big Advantages and Disadvantages of Foreign Direct Investment*. Retrieved from http://connectusfund.org/17-big-advantages-and-disadvantages-of-foreign-direct-investment

Cooper, D., & Sherer, M. J. (1984). The Value of Corporate Accounting Reports: Arguments for a Political Economy of Accounting. *Accounting, Organizations and Society*, *9*(3/4), 207–232. doi:10.1016/0361-3682(84)90008-4

Cooter, R. D., & Rubinfeld, D. L. (1994). An Economic Model of Legal Discovery. *The Journal of Legal Studies*, *23*(1), 435-463. Retrieved from http://www.jstor.org/stable/724329

Cooter, R.D., & Rubinfeld, D.L. (1989). *Economic Analysis of Legal Disputes and Their Resolution*. Retrieved from http://works.bepress.com/robert_cooter/30

Crane, A., & Matten, D. (2004). *Business Ethics*. Oxford, UK: Oxford University Press.

CSR Management. (n.d.). In *Toyota*. Retrieved from http://www.toyota-global.com/sustainability/csr/csr/

CSR Policy. (n.d.). In *Toshiba*. Retrieved from https://www.toshiba.co.jp/ csr/en/policy/aim.htm

CSR. (n.d.). In *Canon*. Retrieved from http://www.canon.co.in/personal/web/ company/ about/csr

CSR-in Action. (2013). *The collective social investment report*. Nigeria.

Cukierman, A. (1992). *Central Bank Strategy, Credibility, and Independence*. Cambridge, MA: MIT Press.

D'Amato, A., Henderson, S., & Florence, S. (2009). Corporate Social Responsibility and Sustainable Business A Guide to Leadership Tasks and Functions. Retrieved from http://www.ccl.org/leadership/pdf/research/corporatesocialresponsibility.pdf

Dahl, R. A. (1967). *Pluralist Economy in the United States*. Rand McNally.

Daily Telegraph. (2016). *Steel industry dealt hammer blow as Tata withdraws from UK*. Retrieved from: http://www.telegraph.co.uk/business/2016/03/29/port-talbot-steels-itself-for-tata-decision/

Daily Telegraph. (n.d.). *Arthur Andersen Returns Twelve Years After Enron Scandal*. Retrieved from http://www.telegraph.co.uk/finance/newsbysector/banksandfinance/11069713/Arthur-Andersen-r eturns-12-years-after-Enron-scandal.html

Danjsmee. (2012). Retrieved from: https://danjsmee.wordpress.com/2012/12/10/the-approach-to-csr-more-important-than-csr-itself/

Darnill, A. (1992, March). The Profession and the Public. Singapore Accountant, 23-25.

Daubert v. Merrell Dow Pharmaceuticals, Inc., 509 U.S. 579 (1993)

Daubert v. Merrell. (1993). Dow Pharmaceutical, Inc 509 U.S.579

Davenport, K. (2000). Corporate citizenship: A stakeholder approach for defining corporate social performance and identifying measures for assessing It. *Business & Society*, *39*(2), 210–219. doi:10.1177/000765030003900205

Davis, K., & Blomstrom, R. L. (1966). *Business and its Environment*. New York: McGraw Hill.

De Beelde, I., Cooreman, S., & Leydens, H. (n.d.). *Expectation of Users of Financial Information with Regard to the Tasks Carried Out by Auditors*. University of Ghent. Available at: www.fetew.ugent.be/fac/research/WP/Papers/wp_99_75.pdf

DeFond, M., Hu, X., Hung, M., & Li, S. (2010). *The impact of mandatory IFRS adoption on foreign mutual fund ownership: The role of compatibility*. IAS Working Paper.

DeMello, L. R., & Sinclair, M. T. (2005). *Foreign Direct Investment, Joint Ventures and Endogenous Growth. Department of Economics, University of Kent.*

Devinney, T. M. (2009). Is the socially responsible corporation a myth? The good, the bad, and the ugly of corporate social responsibility. *The Academy of Management Perspectives*, *23*(2), 44–56. doi:10.5465/AMP.2009.39985540

Diawara, K., & Lavallée, S. (2014). Corporate Social Responsibility (CSR) in the Ohada Law. *Journal of Business Law and Ethics*, *2*(2), 39-62.

Dicksee, L. (1892). *Auditing: A Practical Manual for Auditors*. Academic Press.

DiGabriele, J. A., & Ojo, M. (2013). Objectivity and Independence: The Dual Roles of External Auditors and Forensic Accountants. *Journal of Forensic and Investigative Accounting*, *6*(2). Retrieved from http://papers.ssrn.com/sol3/papers.cfm?abstract_id=2231524

DiGabriele, J., & Ojo, M. (2013). Objectivity and independence: The Dual Roles of External Auditors and Forensic Accountants. *Journal of Forensic and Investigative Accounting*, *6*(2).

DiGabriele, J.A. (2007). To Have and to Hold: An Empirical Investigation of Preferences for Valuation Methods of Closely Held Companies in the Matrimonial Court. *Journal of Forensic Accounting*, *8*(1-2).

DiGabriele, J.A. (2008). Forensic Accounting and The Marital Life Style Analysis. *The Journal of Forensic Accounting*, *9*(1).

DiGabriele, J.A. (2009). Gender, Valuation of Private Companies, and State Specific Variables in the Division of Marital Assets. *Journal of Legal Economics*, *15*(2).

DiGabriele, J. A. (2009). Matrimonial Business Valuations and the AICPA Statement on Standards for Valuations Services No. 1. *American Journal of Family Law*, *23*(2).

DiGabriele, J. A. (2011). Evidentiary Reliability, Valuation Standards, and Rules of Thumb. *American Journal of Family Law*, *25*(1), 16–22.

DiGabriele, J. A. (2011). Evidentiary Reliability, Valuation Standards, and Rules of Thumb. *American Journal of Family Law. Volume*, *25*(1), 16–22.

DiGabriele, J. A., & Ojo, M. (2016). *Corporate Social Responsibility and Foreign Direct Investment: Engaging Innovation.* Auditors and Stakeholders in Corporate Social Responsibility.

Dimos, A. (2011). *IFRS and European commercial banks: Value relevance and economic consequences.* (Doctoral thesis), University of Birmingham, Birmingham, UK.

Djojohadikusomo, S. (1968/69). Trade and Aid in South-East Asia, Vol. 1: Malaysia and Singapore. University of Malaya Co-op, Kuala Lumpur.

Donaldson, T., & Preston, L. E. (1995). The stakeholder theory of the corporation: Concepts, evidence and implication. *Academy of Management Review*, *20*(1), 65–91.

Draghi, M. (2016). *How Domestic Economic Strength Can Prevail over Global Weakness.* Keynote speech by Mr Mario Draghi, President of the European Central Bank, at the Deutsche Börse Group New Year's reception 2016, Eschborn.

Dunning, J. H. (2006). Upgrading the quality of global capitalism: the moral dimension. In S. C. Jain & S. Vachani (Eds.), Multinational corporations and global poverty reduction (pp. 346-379). Cheltenham, UK: Edward Elgar.

Dunning, J. H. (2009). Location and the multinational enterprise: John Dunning's thoughts on receiving the Journal of International Business Studies 2008 Decade Award. *Journal of International Business Studies*, *40*(1), 20–34. doi:10.1057/jibs.2008.75

Dutt, A. K. (2007). The Pattern of Direct Foreign Investment and Economic Growth. *World Development*, *25*(11), 1925–1936. doi:10.1016/S0305-750X(97)00081-8

Dyball, M. C., & Valcarcel, L. J. (1999). The "Rational" and "Traditional": The Regulation of Accounting in the Philippines. *Accounting, Auditing & Accountability Journal*, *12*(3), 303–327. doi:10.1108/09513579910277384

Dye, T. R. (1986). *Who's Running America?* (4th ed.). Prentice-Hall.

Ebert, S., Metschies, G. P., Schmid, D., & Wagner, A. (2009). International Fuel Prices 2009 (6th ed.). Eschborn: Deutsche Gesellschaft für Technische Zusammenarbeit.

Eden, Y., Ovadia, A., & Zuckerman, B. A. (2003, May). Rethinking Sarbanes-Oxley: Why the Act Doesn't Serve the Interests of the Industry or the Markets. CMA Management, 32-35.

Edward, M. G., & Erika, W. (2001), Foreign Direct Investment in China: Effects on Growth and Economic Performance. In Achieving High Growth: Experience of Transitional Economies in East Asia. Oxford University Press.

Edwards, C. B. (1975). *Protection, Profits and Policy: An Analysis of Industrialization in Malaysia.* (Unpublished PhD Thesis). University of East Anglia.

Edwards, M. (2004). *Future positive: International co-operation in the 21st century.* London: Earthscan.

Egbe, O. D., & Paki, F. A. E. (2011). The rhetoric of corporate social responsibility (CSR) in the Niger Delta. *American International Journal of Contemporary Research*, *1*(3), 123–133.

Egbo, O.P. (2011). Bivariate causality analysis on the impact of FDI inflows and economic growth in Nigeria. *Journal of Internet Banking and Commerce, 16*(3), 1-16.

Ekpo, A. H. (2003). The relative contribution of public sector and private sector investment to Nigeria's economic development since 1960. In Nigerian economy: Structure, growth and development. Benin City: Mindex Publishers.

Emerging Market Economics. (2002). *Pro-poor Investment: Maximizing the Contribution of Investment and Business to Poverty Reduction, Report to the Department for International Development.* London: DFID.

Endozien, E. G. (1968). Linkages, direct foreign investment and Nigeria's economic development. *The Nigerian Journal of Economic and Social Studies*, *10*(2), 119–213.

Enthoven, A. J. H. (1973). *Accountancy and Economic Development Policy*. Amsterdam: North-Holland Publishing Company.

Enthoven, A. J. H. (1977). *Accountancy Systems in Third World Economies*. Amsterdam: North-Holland Publishing Company.

Epstein, M., & Geiger, M. (1994). Investor Views of Audit Assurance: Recent Evidence of the Expectation Gap. *Journal of Accountancy*, *177*(1), 60–66.

Esty, D. C., & Geradin, D. (2001). *Regulatory Competition and Economic Integration: Comparative Perspectives*. Oxford University Press.

Eu-Jin, T., & Cobbin, P. (2005). *A Re Visitation of the 'Audit Expectations Gap': Judicial and Practitioner Views on the Role of the Auditor in late-Victorian England.* Academic Press.

EurWORK. (2012). *Corporate Social Responsibility*. Retrieved from http://www.eurofound.europa.eu/observatories/eurwork/industrial-relations-dictionary/corporate-social-responsibility

Eweje, G. (2006). The Role of MNEs in Community Development Initiatives in Developing Countries: Corporate Social Responsibility at Work in Nigeria and South Africa. *Business & Society*, *45*(2), 93–129.

Eweje, G. (2014). Corporate Social Responsibility and Sustainability: Emerging Trends in Developing Economies Critical Studies on Corporate Responsibility. *Governance and Sustainability*, *8*, 45–77.

Fadzly, A. N., & Ahmad, Z. (2004). Audit Expectation Gap – The Case of Malaysia. *Managerial Auditing Journal*, *19*(7), 897–915. doi:10.1108/02686900410549420

FEE. (2012). *The Functioning of Audit Committees*. Discussion Paper June 2012. Retrieved from http://www.fee.be/index.php?option=com_content&view=article&id=519&Itemid=106&lang=n

Ferguson, C. B., Richardson, G. D., & Wines, G. (2000). Audit Education and Training: The Effect of Formal Studies and Work Experience. *Accounting Horizons*, *14*(2), 137–167. doi:10.2308/acch.2000.14.2.137

Fetscherin, M., Voss, H., & Gugler, P. (2010). 30 Years of foreign direct investment to China: An interdisciplinary literature review. *International Business Review*, *19*(3), 235–246. doi:10.1016/j.ibusrev.2009.12.002

Findlay, R. (1978). Relative Backwardness, Direct Foreign Investment and the Transfer of Technology: A Simple Dynamic Model. *The Quarterly Journal of Economics*, *92*(1), 1–13. doi:10.2307/1885996

Fisher, A. G. B. (1939). Production, Primary, Secondary and Tertiary. *The Economic Record*, *15*(1), 24–38. doi:10.1111/j.1475-4932.1939.tb01015.x

Fitch, G. (1976). Achieving Corporate Social Responsibility. *Academy of Management Review*, *1*(1), 38–46.

Flint, D. (1983). The Scope for Auditing Research. In *Discussion Papers of Symposium on Auditing Research*. The University of Glasgow Press.

Fofana, I., Chitiga, M., & Mabugu, R. (2009). Oil Prices and the South African Economy: A Macro-Meso-Micro Analysis. *Energy Policy*, *37*(December), 5509–5518. doi:10.1016/j.enpol.2009.08.030

Fombrun, C. (2005). Building corporate reputation through CSR initiatives: Evolving standards. *Corporate Reputation Review*, *8*(1), 7–11. doi:10.1057/palgrave.crr.1540235

Fombrun, C. J. (1996). *Reputation: Realizing Value from the Corporate Image*. Boston: Harvard Business School Press.

Font, X., Walmsley, A., Cogotti, S., McCombes, L., & Häusler, N. (2012). Corporate social responsibility: The disclosure–performance gap. *Tourism Management*, *33*(6), 1544–1553. doi:10.1016/j.tourman.2012.02.012

Fon, V., & Parisi, F. (2006). Judicial Precedents in Civil Law Systems: A Dynamic Analysis, 26. *International Review of Law and Economics*, *26*(4), 519–535. doi:10.1016/j.irle.2007.01.005

Forstater, M., Zadek, S., Guang, Y., Yu, K., Hong, X. C., & George, M. (2010). *Corporate responsibility in African development: Insights from an emerging dialogue*. The Institute of West-Asian and African Studies of the Chinese Academy of Social Sciences, October Working Paper No. 60.

Fortanier, F., & Van Wijk, J. (2010). Sustainable tourism industry development in sub Saharan Africa: Consequences of foreign hotels for local employment. *International Business Review*.

Frank, E. K., Lowe, D. J., & Smith, J. K. (2001). The Expectation Gap: Perceptual Differences between Auditors, Jurors and Students. *Managerial Auditing Journal*, *16*(3), 145149. doi:10.1108/02686900110385588

Freeman, R. E., Harrison, J. S., Wicks, A. C., Parmar, B. L., & de Colle, S. (2007). Stakeholder theory: The state of the art. Cambridge University Press

Freeman, R. E., Wicks, A. C., & Parmar, B. (2004). Stakeholder theory and the corporate objective revisited. *Organization Science*, *15*(3), 364–369. doi:10.1287/orsc.1040.0066

Friedland, J. (1989, November 9). A Call to Account. *Far Eastern Economic Review*, 70-5.

Friedman, M. (1970). The Social Responsibility of Business Is to Increase its Profits. *New York Times*, pp. 122-126.

Friedman, M. (1970). The social responsibility of business to increase its profits. *New York Times*, *13*, 122–126.

Friedman, M. (1998). The social responsibility of business is to increase its profit. In Perspectives in business ethics. Singapore: McGraw Hill.

Fritz, S., & Lammle, C. (2003). *The international harmonization process of accounting standards*. (Master's thesis), Linkoping University, Linkoping, Sweden.

Frontline: Bigger than Enron: Accounting Lesson. (n.d.). Available at http://www.pbs.org/wgbh/pages/frontline/shows/regulation/lessons/

Frost, S., & Ho, M. (2005). Going out: The growth of Chinese foreign direct investment in Southeast Asia and its implications for corporate social responsibility. *Corporate Social Responsibility and Environmental Management*, *12*(3), 157–167. doi:10.1002/csr.98

Frye v. United States, 293 F. 1013 (D.C. Cir.1923)

Frynas, J. G. (2005). The false developmental promise of corporate social responsibility: Evidence from multinational oil companies. *International Affairs*, *81*(3), 581–598. doi:10.1111/j.1468-2346.2005.00470.x

Frynas, J. G. (2008). Corporate social responsibility and international development: Critical assessment. *Corporate Governance*, *16*(4), 274–281. doi:10.1111/j.1467-8683.2008.00691.x

FSB (Financial Stability Board). (2008). *Enhancing Market and Institutional Resilience*. Retrieved from www.financialstability-board.org

Gale, B. (1985). *Politics and Business: A Study of Multi-Purpose Holdings Berhad*. Petaling Jaya: Eastern Universities Press.

Gardberg, N. A., & Fombrun, C. (2006). Corporate citizenship: Creating intangible assets across institutional environments. *Academy of Management Review*, *31*(2), 329–346. doi:10.5465/AMR.2006.20208684

Garoupa, N., & Liguerre, C. G. (2011). The Syndrome of the Efficiency of Common Law. *Boston University Journal of Internal Law*. Retrieved from http://papers.ssrn.com/pape.tar?abstract_id=1674170

Garriga, E., & Melé, D. (2004). Corporate social responsibility theories: Mapping the territory. *Journal of Business Ethics*, *53*(1–2), 51–71. doi:10.1023/B:BUSI.0000039399.90587.34

Gennaioli, N., & Shleifer, A. (2007). The Evolution of Common Law. *Journal of Political Economy*, *115*(1), 43–68. doi:10.1086/511996

Gill, A. (2008). Corporate governance as social responsibility: A research agenda. *Berkeley Journal of International Law*, *26*, 452.

Global-responsibility. (n.d.). In *Walmart*. Retrieved from http://corporate.walmart.com/global-responsibility/global-responsibility-report

GOI. (2015). *48% Growth in FDI Equity Inflows after Make in India*. Press Information Bureau, Ministry of Commerce & Industry, Government of India. Retrieved on 14-July-2015 from http://pib.nic.in/newsite/PrintRelease.aspx?relid=123256

Gomez, E. T. (1990). *Politics in Business: UMNO's Corporate Investments*. Petaling Jaya: Forum Enterprise.

Gomez, E. T. (1994). *Political Business: Corporate Involvement of Malaysian Political Parties*. Townsville, Queensland: Centre for South East Asian Studies, James Cook University.

Gomez, E. T. (1997). The Economics and Politics of Privatization in Malaysia. *Journal of the Asia Pacific Economy*, *2*(2), 178–200. doi:10.1080/13547869708724616

Gonzalez Perez, M., Riegler, S., & Riegler, F. (2011). *Foreign Direct Investment (FDI) and Social Responsibility Networks (SRN) in Colombia*. Academic Press.

Gonzalez-Perez, M. A., Riegler, S., & Riegler, F. X. (2011). Foreign direct investment (FDI) and social responsibility networks (SRN) in Colombia. *GCG: Revista de Globalización. Competitividad y Gobernabilidad*, *5*(1), 42–59.

Google. (n.d.). Retrieved from: https://www.google.co.uk/search?q=carroll's+pyramid+of+csr&biw=1366&bih=578&tbm=isch&imgil=HGdTbntI6FbdFM%253A%253BES0dR2Kp9tyZHM%253Bhttp%25253A%25252F%25252Fresearch-methodology.net%25252Fcarrolls-csr-pyramid-and-its-applications-to-small-and-medium-sized-businesses%25252F&source=iu&pf=m&fir=HGdTbntI6FbdFM%253A%252CES0dR2Kp9tyZHM%252C_&usg=__WrVlfmZZMb-th79ZDuCBj_Zq1Z54%3D&ved=0ahUKEwjTuaC8wfzKAhUEthQKHfbYAxwQyjcIMw&ei=ejTDVtOUNoTsUvaxj-AB#imgrc=HGdTbntI6FbdFM%3A

Gorbunova, Y. (2012). Retrieved from https://ideas.repec.org/a/prg/jnlpep/ v2012y2012i2id415p129-149.htm

Gore, C. (2000). The Rise and Fall of the Washington Consensus as a Paradigm for Developing Countries. *World Development*, *28*(5), 789–804.

Goyal, A. (2005). *Corporate social responsibility as a signaling of FDI*. Indira Gandhi Institute of Development Research.

Goyal, A. (2006). Corporate Social Responsibility as a Signalling Device for Foreign Direct Investment. *International Journal of the Economics of Business*, *13*(1), 145–163. doi:10.1080/13571510500520077

Graafland, J., & van de Ven, B. (2006). Strategic and moral motivation for corporate social responsibility. *Journal of Corporate Citizenship*, *22*, 111–123.

Grabosky, P., & Braithwaite, J. (1986). *Of Manners Gentle: Enforcement Strategies of Australian Business Regulatory Agencies*. Melbourne: Oxford University Press.

Gramling, A., Schatxberg, J., & Wallace, A. (1996, Spring). The Role of Undergraduate Auditing Coursework in Reducing Audit Expectation Gap. *Issues in Accounting Education*, 131–146.

Greenaway, D., Sapsford, D., & Pfaffenzeller, S. (2007). Foreign direct investment, economic performance and trade liberalisation. *World Economy*, *30*(2), 197–210. doi:10.1111/j.1467-9701.2007.00887.x

Greening, D. W., & Turban, D. B. (2000). Corporate social performance as a competitive advantage in attracting a quality workforce. *Business & Society*, *39*(3), 254–280. doi:10.1177/000765030003900302

Greer, J., & Bruno, K. (1996). *Greenwash: the reality behind corporate environmentalism*. New York: Apex Press.

Grossman, G. M., Helpman, E., & Szeidl, A. (2006). Optimal integration strategies for the multinational firm. *Journal of International Economics*, *70*(1), 216–238. doi:10.1016/j.jinteco.2005.07.011

Grossman, G., & Helpman, E. (2006). *Innovation and Growth in the Global Economy*. Cambridge, MA: MIT Press.

Gul, F. (1983). *History and Development of Accounting Education in Malaysia*. Singapore: The Regional Institute of Higher Education and Development.

Guoqiang, L., Zadek, S., & Wickerham, J. (2009). *Advancing sustainable competitiveness of China"s transnational corporations*. AccountAbility/ Development Research Center of the State Council of the People's Republic of China.

Gupta, S., Verhoeven, M., Gillingham, R., Schiller, C., Mansoor, A., & Cordoba, J. P. (2000). *Equity and Efficiency in the Reform of Price Subsidies: A Guide for Policymakers*. Washington, DC: International Monetary Fund.

Guy, D. M., & Sullivan, J. D. (1988, April). The Expectation Gap Auditing Standards. *Journal of Accountancy*, 36–44.

Hagiwara, Y. (1972). Political Culture and Communalism in West Malaysia. *The Developing Economies*, *10*(3), 250–266. doi:10.1111/j.1746-1049.1972.tb00281.x

Hai, G. J. (1970/71). Recent Legislation on the Profession of Accountancy in Malaysia and Singapore. *The Accounting Journal*, *1*(1), 25–36.

Hanafiah, N. (1990). *Ethical Standards in the Accounting Profession*. Paper presented at the Universiti Utara Malaysia and Petronas jointly organised Seminar on Management Ethics, Kuala Lumpur.

Handy, C. (2002). What is a business for? *Harvard Business Review*, *80*(12). PMID:12510537

Hara, F. (1991). Malaysia's New Economic Policy and The Chinese Business Community. *The Developing Economies*, *29*(4), 350–370. doi:10.1111/j.1746-1049.1991.tb01040.x

Hashimus, B., & Ango, N. A. (2012). Multinational companies corporate social responsibility performance in Lagos State, Nigeria: A quantitative analysis. *European Journal of Globalization and Development Research*, *5*(1), 247–264.

Hayden, J. (2015, September). Under Pressure. *Finance & Development*.

Hayek, F. A. (1945). The Use of Knowledge in Society. *The American Economic Review*, *35*(4), 519-530. Retrieved from http://www.jstor.org/discover/10.2307/1809376?uid=3739920&uid=2&uid=4&uid=3739256&sid=21104299293711

Hayek, F. A. (1960). *The Constitution of Liberty*. Chicago: University of Chicago Press.

Hayek, F. A. (1973). *Law, Legislation and Liberty: Rules and Order* (Vol. 1). Chicago: University of Chicago Press.

Hayek, F. A. (1976). *Law, Legislation and Liberty: The Mirage of Social Justice* (Vol. 2). Chicago: University of Chicago Press.

Hayo, B., & Hefeker, C. (2002). Reconsidering Central Bank Independence. *European Journal of Political Economy, Elsevier*, *18*(4), 653–674. doi:10.1016/S0176-2680(02)00113-1

Henderson, D. (2001). *Misguided virtue: False notions of corporate social responsibility*. London: Institute of Economic Affairs.

Henock, L., & Oktay, U. (2015). *The effect of IFRS on foreign direct investments: Evidence from cross-border acquisitions.* SSRN Working Paper.

Higgins, R. (1963). The development of international law through the political organs of the United Nations. Oxford Univ. Press.

High Level Task Force on Innovative International Financing for Health Systems. (2009). More *Money for Health, and More Health for the Money*. Author.

Hirschman, A. (1958). *The Strategy of Economic Development*. New Haven, CT: Yale University Press.

Hirschman, C. (1971). Ownership and Control in the Manufacturing Sector of West Malaysia. *UMBC Economic Review*, *7*(1), 20–39.

Hirschman, C. (1983). Ownership and Control in the Manufacturing Sector of West Malaysia. In D. Lim (Ed.), *Further Readings on Malaysian Economic Development* (pp. 209–220). Kuala Lumpur: Oxford University Press.

Hopkins, M. (2004). *Corporate Social Responsibility: An Issues Paper*. Working Paper No. 27. Policy Integration Department World Commission on the Social Dimension of Globalization International Labor Office Geneva.

Hopkins, M. (2004). *Corporate social responsibility: an issues paper.* Working Paper No.27. Policy Integration Department. Geneva, Switzerland: International Labour Office.

Hopkins, M. (2003). *The Planetary Bargain: Corporate Social Responsibility Matters*. London, UK: Earthscan.

Hopkins, M. (2007). *Corporate Social Responsibility and International Development: Is Business the Solution?* London, UK: Earthscan.

Hopper, T. M., Storey, J., & Willmott, H. (1987). Accounting for Accounting Towards the Development of a Dialectical View. *Accounting, Organizations and Society*, *12*(5), 437–456. doi:10.1016/0361-3682(87)90030-4

Hopper, T., & Powell, A. (1985). Making Sense of Research into the Organizational and Social Aspects of Management Accounting: A Review of its Underlying Assumptions. *Journal of Management Studies*, *22*(5), 429–465. doi:10.1111/j.1467-6486.1985.tb00007.x

Hopwood, A. G. (1987). The Archeology of Accounting Systems. *Accounting, Organizations and Society*, *12*(3), 207–234. doi:10.1016/0361-3682(87)90038-9

Horii, K. (1991). Disintegration of the Colonial Economic Legacies and Social Restructuring in Malaysia. *The Developing Economies*, *24*(4), 281–313.

Hui, L. M. (1983). The Ownership and Control of Large Corporations in Malaysia: The Role of Chinese Businessmen. In L. Y. C. Lim & L. A. P. Gosling (Eds.), *The Chinese in Southeast Asia: Ethnicity and Economic Activity* (Vol. I, pp. 275–315). Maruzen Asia, Singapore.

Hui, L. M. (1988). Contradictions in the Development of Malay Capital: State, Accumulation and Legitimation. In J. G. Taylor & A. Turton (Eds.), *Sociology of 'Developing Societies' Southeast Asia* (pp. 19–32). London: Macmillan Education Ltd. doi:10.1007/978-1-349-19568-8_2

Humphrey, C., Moizer, P., & Turley, S. (1992). The Audit Expectations Gap - Plus Ca Change, Plus C'est La Meme Chose? *Critical Perspectives on Accounting*, *3*(2), 137–161. doi:10.1016/1045-2354(92)90008-F

Humphrey, C., Moizer, P., & Turley, S. (1993). The Audit Expectations Gap in Britain: An Empirical Investigation. *Accounting and Business Review*, *23*(sup1), 395–411. doi:10.1080/00014788.1993.9729907

Iamsiraroj, S., & Doucouliagos, H. (2015). *Does Growth Attract FDI?* Discussion Paper No. 2015-18. Retrieved from http://www.economics-ejournal.org/economics/discussionpapers/2015-18http://www.economics-ejournal.org/economics/journalarticles/2015-19

ICAEW (2015). *The effects of mandatory IFRS adoption in the EU: A review of empirical research.* ICAEW's Financial Reporting Faculty.

Idemudia, U. (2008). Conceptualising the CSR and development debate: Bridging existing analytical gaps. *Journal of Corporate Citizenship.*

Idemudia, U. (n.d.). *Corporate partnerships and community development in the Nigerian oil industry: Strengths and limitations.* Lancaster University.

Idemudia, U. (2007a). Community perceptions and expectations: Reinventing the wheels of corporate social responsibility practices in the Nigerian oil Industry. *Business and Society Review*, *112*(3), 369–405. doi:10.1111/j.1467-8594.2007.00301.x

Idemudia, U. (2007b). *Corporate partnership and community development in Nigerian oil industry: Strength and limitations.* Geneva: United Nations Research Institute for Social Development.

Idemudia, U., & Ite, U. E. (2006). Corporate-community relations in Nigeria's oil: Challenges and imperatives. *Corporate Social Responsibility and Environmental Management Journal*, *13*(4), 194–206. doi:10.1002/csr.101

IFRS. (2013). *IASB issues Discussion Paper on Conceptual Framework.* IFRS.

IFRS. (2013). IFRS News: IASB issues Discussion Paper on Conceptual Framework July/Aug 2013 IFRS 3. *Business Combinations.* Retrieved from http://www.iasplus.com/en/standards/ifrs/ifrs3

IFRS. (2014). *Fairness of Reporting, Acceptable Accounting Risk and the IASB's Conceptual Framework Review: Insights from the Enron Trial.* IFRS.

IFRS. (2016). *IFRS 16 Leases, Project Summary and Feedback Statement January 2016.* IFRS.

Ijiaya, H. (n.d.). Challenges of corporate social responsibility in the Niger Delta region of Nigeria. *Journal of Sustainable Development Law and Policy, 3*(1).

IMF. (2013). *Energy Subsidy Reform: Lessons and Implications.* IMF.

IndiaBriefing. (2012). *Corporate Social Responsibility in India.* Retrieved from http://www.india-briefing.com/news/corporate-social-responsibility-india-5511.html/

Institute for Fiscal Studies (IFS). (2012). *Tax and Benefit Tables.* Available at www.ifs.org.uk/fiscalFacts/taxTables

International Monetary Fund. (2013). *Energy Subsidy Reform: Lessons and Implications.* Author.

International Monetary Fund. (2015). World Economic Outlook "Uncertainty, Complex Forces Weigh on Global Growth. *IMF Survey. International Monetary Fund, 6*(October). Retrieved from http://www.imf.org/external/pubs/ft/survey/so/2015/res100615a.htm

Ioannou, I., & Serafeim, G. (2014). The impact of corporate social responsibility on investment recommendations: Analysts' perceptions and shifting institutional logics. *Strategic Management Journal.*

Iršová, Z., & Havránek, T. (2013). Determinants of horizontal spillovers from FDI: Evidence from a large meta-analysis. *World Development, 42*, 1–15. doi:10.1016/j.worlddev.2012.07.001

Isa, S. M. (2012). Corporate Social Responsibility: What can we learn from the Stakeholders? *Procedia: Social and Behavioral Sciences, 65*, 327–337. doi:10.1016/j.sbspro.2012.11.130

Ismail, M. S. (1994). The Role of Public Sector in the Malaysian Economy. In National Institute of Public Administration Malaysia (Ed.), Malaysian Development Experience: Changes and Challenges. INTAN.

Ismail, M. (2009). Corporate Social Responsibility and Its Role in Community development: An International Perspective. *The Journal of International Social Research, 2*(9).

Ite, U. E. (2004). Multinationals and corporate social responsibility in developing countries: A case study of Nigeria. *Corporate Social Responsibility and Environmental Management, 11*(1), 1–11. doi:10.1002/csr.49

Jacob, R. (1992). Can You Trust That Audit? *Fortune, 18*(November), 91–94.

Jamali, D. (2010). The CSR of MNC Subsidiaries in Developing countries: Global, Local, Substantive or Diluted? *Journal of Business Ethics, 93*(S2), 181–200. doi:10.1007/s10551-010-0560-8

Jamali, D. (2014). CSR in Developing Countries Through An Institutional Lens. In G. Eweje (Ed.), *Corporate Social Responsibility and Sustainability: Emerging Trends in Developing Economies Critical Studies on Corporate Responsibility, Governance and Sustainability* (Vol. 8, pp. 45–77). Emerald Group Publishing Ltd.

Jamali, D., & Mirshak, R. (2007). Corporate Social Responsibility: Theory and Practice in a Developing Country Context. *Journal of Business Ethics, 72*(1), 243–262.

Jamali, D., & Mirshak, R. (2007). Corporate social responsibility: Theory and practice in a developing country context. *Journal of Business Ethics, 72*(1), 243–262. doi:10.1007/s10551-006-9168-4

Jamali, D., & Neville, B. (2011). Convergence versus Divergence of CSR in Developing Countries: An Embedded Multi-layered Institutional Lens. *Journal of Business Ethics, 102*(4), 599–621. doi:10.1007/s10551-011-0830-0

James, L., & Kam, K. (2006). China's FDI-income growth nexus. *The 17th Annual Conference of the Association for Chinese Economic Studies.* Victoria University.

Jenkins, R. (2005). Globalization, Corporate Social Responsibility and poverty. *International Affairs, 81*(3), 525–540.

Jenkins, R. (2005). Globalization, Corporate Social Responsibility and Poverty. *International Affairs, 81*(3), 525–540. doi:10.1111/j.1468-2346.2005.00467.x

Jenkins, R., Pearson, R., & Seyfang, G. (2002). *Corporate Responsibility & Labour Rights: Codes of Conduct in the Global Economy.* Londres: Earthscan.

Jensen, M. (2001). Value Maximization, Stakeholder Theory, and the Corporate Objective Function. *Journal of Applied Corporate Finance*, (Fall), 821.

Jensen, M. C. (2001). Value maximization, stakeholder theory and the corporate objective function. *Journal of Applied Corporate Finance*, *14*(3), 8–21. doi:10.1111/j.1745-6622.2001.tb00434.x

Jensen, N. M. (2003). Democratic governance and multinational corporations: Political regimes and inflows of foreign direct investment. *International Organization*, *57*(3), 587–616. doi:10.1017/S0020818303573040

Jesudason, J. V. (1989). Ethnicity and the Economy: The State, Chinese Business, and Multinationals in Malaysia. Oxford University Press.

Jha, K. (2012). *Examining the Current Importance of Pepper v Hart*. Retrieved from http://papers.ssrn.com/sol3/papers.cfm?abstract_id=2149694

Jiang, J., & Masaru, L. (2010). *How does FDI Affect the Regional Economic Growth in China? Evidence from Sub-regions and Industries of the Jiangxi Province, P.R. China*. IDEC, Hiroshima University Discussion Paper.

Jiménez, A. (2011). Political risk as a determinant of Southern European FDI in neighboring developing countries. *Emerging Markets Finance and Trade*, *47*(4), 59–74. doi:10.2753/REE1540-496X470404

John, H. D. (2003a). Multinational enterprises and the global economy. Reading, MA: Addison-Wesley Publishing Company.

Johnson, T. J., & Caygill, M. (1971). The Development of Accounting Links in the Commonwealth. *Accounting and Business Review*, *1*(2), 155–173. doi:10.1080/00014788.1971.9728562

Jomo, K. S. (1986). *A Question of Class: Capital, the State, and Uneven Development in Malaya*. Singapore: Oxford University Press.

Jomo, K. S. (Ed.). (1995). *Privatizing Malaysia: Rents, Rhetoric, Realities*. Oxford, UK: Westview Press.

Jones, K., & Bartlett, J. L. (2009). The strategic value of corporate social responsibility: A relationship management framework for public relations practice. *Prism, 6*(1).

Junid, S. (1980). *British Industrial Investments in Malaysia, 1963-1971*. Kuala Lumpur: Oxford University Press.

Kandil, M. (2011). Financial flows to developing and advanced countries: Determinants and implications. *International Journal of Development Issues*, *10*(1), 60–91. doi:10.1108/14468951111123337

Kaplan, R. S., & Norton, D. P. (2008a). Mastering the Management System. *Harvard Business Review*, (January), 6257. PMID:18271319

Kaplan, R. S., & Norton, D. P. (2008b). *The Execution Premium: Linking Strategy to Operations for Competitive Advantage*. Boston: HBS Press.

Kasim, M. A., & Mohd-Hanafi, S. R. (2005). *An Empirical Study on the Effect of Undergraduate Auditing Course in Reducing Audit Expectation Gap at Universiti Tenaga Nasional (UNITEN)*. Paper presented at the AAAA Conference, Kuala Lumpur, Malaysia

Kaufman, M. S. (2006). *The Status of Daubert in State Court*. Atlantic Legal Foundation. Retrieved from http://www.atlanticlegal.org/daubertreport.pdf

Kennedy, J. (1993). *A History of Malaya* (3rd ed.). Kuala Lumpur: S. Abdul Majeed and Co.

Kercher, K. (2007). Corporate Social Responsibility: Impact of globalisation and international business. *Corporate Governance eJournal*. Retrieved from http://epublications.bond.edu.au/cgi/viewcontent.cgi?article=1003&amp%3Bcontext=cgej

Khan, M. H. (2000). Rural Poverty in Developing Countries. *Finance & Development, 37*. Retrieved from http://www.imf.org/external/pubs/ft/fandd/2000/12/khan.htm

Khan, M.S., & Khan, A.M. (2015). FDI and Indian Economy: Issues, Challenges and Prospects in India. *PARIPEX - Indian Journal of Research, 4*(12), 44-47.

Koh, H., & Woo, W. (1998). The Expectation Gap in Auditing. *Managerial Auditing Journal, 13*(3), 147–154. doi:10.1108/02686909810208038

Kolins, W. (1988). *The New Auditing Standards*. The Financial Manager.

Kolk, A. & Van Tulder, R. (2010). International Business, Corporate Social Responsibility and Sustainable Development. *International Business Review, 19*(1).

Kolk, A. (2009). Trajectories of sustainability reporting by MNCs. *Journal of World Business*. doi:10.1016/j.jwb.2009.08.01

Kolk, A., & Lenfant, F. (2009). MNC reporting on CSR and conflict in Central Africa. *Journal of Business Ethics*. doi:10.1007/s10551-009-0271-1

Kolk, A., & van Tulder, R. (2010). International Business, Corporate Social Responsibility and Sustainable Development. *International Business Review, 19*(2), 119–125.

Kolk, A., & Van Tulder, R. (2010). International business, corporate social responsibility and sustainable development. *International Business Review, 19*(2), 119–125. doi:10.1016/j.ibusrev.2009.12.003

Koon, T. Y. (1994). *Employee Fraud in Malaysia: A Case Study*. (Unpublished PhD Thesis). University of London.

Kotler, P., & Lee, N. (2004a). *Corporate Social Responsibility: Doing the Most Good for Your Company and Your Cause*. Hoboken, NJ: Wiley.

KPMG. (2010). *Briefing Sheet Conceptual Framework for Financial Reporting Chapters 1 and 3, October 2010 Issue 213 NACVA, Standard 3.8*. Retrieved from http://www.nacva.com/PDF/NACVA_Standards.pdf

Kranacher, M.-J. (2006, April). Regulating the Accounting Profession: What Distinguishes a CPA from an Accountant? *The CPA Journal*. Available online at http://www.cpajournal.com/

Kretzman, S. (1995). Nigeria's drilling fields': Shell oil's role in repression. *Multinational Monitor, 16*, 1–2.

Kuala Lumpur Stock Exchange and Malaysian Strategic Consultancy Sdn. Bhd. (Eds.). (1992). Malaysia The Rising Star: Business and Investment Opportunities and Challenges Towards 2020. KLSE and MSC Sdn. Bhd.

Kunio, Y. (1988). *The Rise of Ersatz Capitalism in South-East Asia*. Oxford University Press.

Kydland, F., & Prescott, E. (1977). Rules Rather than Discretion: The Inconsistency of Optimal Plans. *Journal of Political Economy, 85*(3), 473–490. doi:10.1086/260580

La Porta, R., de Silanes, F. L., & Shleifer, A. (2008). The Economic Consequences of Legal Origins, 46. *Journal of Economic Literature, 46*(2), 285–332. doi:10.1257/jel.46.2.285

Lall, S., & Narula, R. (2004). Foreign direct investment and its role in economic development: Do we need a new agenda? *European Journal of Development Research, 16*(3), 447–464. doi:10.1080/0957881042000266589

Lance, M. (2001). What do we mean by corporate social Responsibility*? Corporate Governance, 1*(2), 16–22. doi:10.1108/EUM0000000005486

Lantos, G. P. (2001). The boundaries of strategic corporate social responsibility. *Journal of Consumer Marketing*, *18*(7), 595–630. doi:10.1108/07363760110410281

Lantos, G. P. (2002). The ethnicity of altruistic corporate social responsibility. *Journal of Consumer Marketing*, *19*(3), 205–230. doi:10.1108/07363760210426049

Lasmin. (2012). The unwanted effects of international financial reporting standards (IFRS) adoption on international trade and investments in developing countries. *Journal of Economics and Economic Education Research, 13*(1).

Laura, A. (2003). Foreign Direct Investment and Growth: Does the Sector Matter. Harvard Business School.

Lee, T., & Palaniappan, A. (2006). *Audit Expectation Gap: An Empirical Study in Malaysia*. Paper presented in The Malaysian Finance Association's 8th Annual Conference at University Malaysia Sabah, Kota Kinabalu.

Lehman, C., & Tinker, A. (1987). The 'Real' Cultural Significance of Accounts. *Accounting, Organizations and Society*, *12*(5), 503–522.

Leigh, M. (1992). Politics, Bureaucracy, and Business in Malaysia: Realigning the Eternal Triangle. In A. J. MacIntyre & K. Jayasuriya (Eds.), *The Dynamics of Economic Policy Reform in South-East Asia and the South-West Pacific* (pp. 115–123). Singapore: Oxford University Press.

Leong, H. K. (1988). *Indegenizing the State: The New Economic Policy and the Bumiputera State in Peninsular Malaysia*. (Unpublished PhD Thesis). Ohio State University.

Levine, R. (2005). Finance and Growth: Theory and Evidence. In P. Aghion & S. Durlauf (Eds.), *Handbook of Economic Growth*. Amsterdam: North Holland.

Lewis, S. (2003). Reputation and corporate responsibility. *Journal of Communication Management*, *7*(4), 356–364. doi:10.1108/13632540310807494

Liang, F. S. (1989). How Old is the Auditing Profession in Singapore? *Singapore Accountant*, *5*(7), 9–10.

Liggio, C. (1974). The Expectation Gap: The Accountant's Waterloo. *Journal of Contemporary Business*, *3*, 27–44.

Lim, J. (2006, April 9). When Practical Training Falls Short. New Strait Times.

Lim, D. (1973). *Economic Growth and Development in West Malaysia*. Oxford University Press.

Lim, H. (1993). Address by the ICPAS President, Mr Lim Hock San, at the ICPAS' 30th Anniversary Dinner held at the Neptune Theatre Restaurant on 6 March 1993. *Singapore Accountant*, *9*, 9.

Limlingan, V. S. (1986). *The Overseas Chinese in ASEAN: Business Strategies and Management Practices*. Manila: Vita Development Corporation.

Limlingan, V. S. (1994). *The Visible Hand and the Developing Economy: Essays on Management in Southeast Asia* (2nd ed.). Manila: De La Salle University Press.

Linderberg, M. M. (1973). *Foreign and Domestic Investment in the Pioneer Industry Program, Malaysia 19651970, Political, Economic, and Social Impacts*. (Unpublished PhD Thesis). University of Southern California.

Lipsey, R. E. (2002). *Home and Host Country Effects of FDI*. National Bureau for Economic Research, Working Paper No. 92939.

Liu, X., & Wang, C. (2007). Does Foreign Direct Investment Facilitate Technological Progress? Evidences from Chinese Industries. *Research Policy*, *32*(6), 945–953. doi:10.1016/S0048-7333(02)00094-X

Loayza, N., & Ranciere, R. (2006). Financial Development, Financial Fragility, and Growth. *Journal of Money, Credit and Banking*, *38*(4), 1051–1076. doi:10.1353/mcb.2006.0060

Loft, A. (1986). Towards a Critical Understanding of Accounting: The Case of Cost Accounting in the U.K., 1914-1925. *Accounting, Organizations and Society*, *11*(2), 137–169. doi:10.1016/0361-3682(86)90028-0

Lowe, D. J. (1994). The Expectation Gap in the Legal System: Perception Differences between Auditors and Judges. *Journal of Applied Business Research*, *10*(Summer), 39–44.

Low, L. (2005). *Foreign Investment in Guangdong: Effects on Economic, Growth and Regional Distribution Determinants*. Hong Kong Baptist University.

Lucas, R. E., & Sargent, T. J. (1981). Rational Expectations and Econometric Practice. University of Minnesota Press.

Mahoney, P. (2001). The Common Law and Economic Growth: Hayek Might Be Right, 30. *The Journal of Legal Studies*, *30*(2), 503–525. doi:10.1086/322053

Maignan, I., & Ralston, D. A. (2002). Corporate social responsibility in Europe and the US: Insights from businesses self presentations. *Journal of International Business Studies*, *33*(3), 497–514. doi:10.1057/palgrave.jibs.8491028

Make in India. (n.d.). Recent Policy Measures. *Department of Industrial Policy and Promotion, Ministry of Commerce and Industry, Government of India.*

Malhotra, B. (2014). Foreign Direct Investment: Impact on Indian Economy. *Global Journal of Business Management and Information Technology, 4*(1), 17-23.

Management Accounting. (1985). Accountants Must Clean Up Their Act – Rep. John Dingell Speaks Out. Author.

Manne, H., & Wallich, H. C. (1972). *The Modern Corporation and Social Responsibility*. Washington D.C American Enterprise Institute for Public Policy Research.

Martens, S. C., & McEnroe, J. E. (1991). Inter-professional Struggles over Definition: Lawyers, Accountants and Illegal Acts. *Critical Perspectives on Accounting*, *2*(4), 375–384. doi:10.1016/1045-2354(91)90009-3

Matten, D., Crane, A., & Chapple, W. (2003). Behind the mask: Revealing the true face of corporate citizenship. *Journal of Business Ethics*, *45*(1/2), 109–120. doi:10.1023/A:1024128730308

McWilliams, A., & Siegel, D. (2000). Research notes and communications: Corporate social responsibility and financial performance: Correlation or Misspecification? *Strategic Management Journal*, *21*(5), 603–609. doi:10.1002/(SICI)1097-0266(200005)21:5<603::AID-SMJ101>3.0.CO;2-3

McWilliams, A., & Siegel, D. (2001). Corporate social responsibility: A theory of the firm perspective. *Academy of Management Review*, *26*(1), 117–127.

McWilliams, A., Siegel, D., & Wright, P. M. (2006). Corporate social responsibility: Strategic implications. *Journal of Management Studies*, *43*(1), 1–18. doi:10.1111/j.1467-6486.2006.00580.x

Means, G. P. (1986). Ethnic Preference Policies in Malaysia. In N. Nevitte & C. H. Kennedy (Eds.), *Ethnic Preference and Public Policy in Developing Societies* (pp. 95–118). Boulder, CO: Lynne Reinner Publishers, Inc.

Megat, A. R. (1979). *Future of the Accountancy Profession in Malaysia*. Paper presented at the MACPA 21st Anniversary Seminar, Kuala Lumpur.

Mehta, N. (2015). *Corporate Social Responsibility Projects*. Retrieved from http://lionsclubsindia.org/blog/Corporate-Social-Responsibility-Projects-CSR-NGO-In-India-Lions-Clubs-India

Michael, B. (2003). Corporate social responsibility in international development: An overview and critique. *Corporate Social Responsibility and Environmental Management*, *10*(3), 115–128. doi:10.1002/csr.41

Miller, P., & O'Leary, T. (1987). Accounting and the Construction of the Governable Person. *Accounting, Organizations and Society*, *12*(3), 235–265. doi:10.1016/0361-3682(87)90039-0

Minai, B., Mustapha, M., & Saleh, A. (2005). *An Empirical Investigation of Perceived Benefits of Practical Training Using Factor Analysis*. Paper presented at the 6th Asian Academy of Management Conference, Perak, Malaysia.

Mohamed, S., & Muhamad Sori, Z. (2002, January). Audit Expectation Gap – The Malaysian Experience. *The Chartered Secretary*, 12-15.

Mohd.-Ariff, Y. (1993). *Securities Commission: Regulator of the Capital Market*. Paper presented at the 9th National Accountants' Conference, Kuala Lumpur.

Mohd.-Salleh, M. (1989). *The Equity Structure of Listed Companies*. Paper presented at the Persatuan Sains Sosial Malaysia and Institut Pengajian Tinggi, Universiti Malaya jointly organised New Economic Policy and Its Future conference, Universiti Malaya.

Mohd.-Salleh, M. (1993). The Malaysian Capital Market: New Rules of the Game. *Capital Markets Review*, *1*(1), 1–21.

Mohd.-Sheriff, M.-K. (1992). Economic Outlook and Privatization Trends Towards 2020. In Kuala Lumpur Stock Exchange and Malaysian Strategic Consultancy Sdn. Bhd. (Eds.), Malaysia The Rising Star: Business and Investment Opportunities and Challenges Towards 2020. KLSE and MSC Sdn. Bhd.

Mojekwu, J. N., & Samson Ogege, S. (2012). Foreign direct investment and the challenges of sustainable development in Nigeria. *Journal of Research in International Business and Management*, *2*(7), 190–198.

Monroe, G. S., & Woodliff, D. R. (1993). The Effect of Education on the Audit Expectation Gap. *Accounting and Finance*, *33*(May), 61–78. doi:10.1111/j.1467-629X.1993.tb00195.x

Mordi, C., Opeyemi, S. I., Tonbara, M., & Ojo, S. (2012). Corporate social responsibility and the legal regulation in Nigeria. *Economic Insights-Trends and Challenges*, *LXIV*(1), 1–8.

Moussalli, S. (2005). Accounting for the Journal's First 100 Years: A Timeline From 1905 to 2005. *Journal of Accountancy*. Available at: http://www.aicpa.org/pubs/jofa/oct2005/index.htm

Muller, J., & Fahey, J. (2004). Hydrogen man. *Forbes*, (Dec): 27.

Mundra, S., Mundra, M., & Singh, M. (2013). A Review of the Impact of Foreign Direct Investment on Indian Retailing. *International Journal of Science: Basic and Applied Research*, *10*(1), 1–17.

Nadia, D. (2006). *Does the Worldwide Shift of FDI from Manufacturing to Services Accelerate Economic Growth - a GMM estimation study*. The Graduate Center, CUNY.

National Operations Council. (1969). *The May 13 Tragedy: A Report*. National Operation Council.

Nawaz, M. K. (1965). The meaning and range of the principle of self-determination. *Duke Law Journal*, *1965*(1), 82–101. doi:10.2307/1371019

Needles, B. E. Jr. (1976). Implementing a Framework for the International Transfer of Accounting Technology. *The International Journal of Accounting*, *12*(1), 45–62.

Neely, A., & Adams, C. (2002). *Performance Prism: The Scorecard for Measuring and Managing Stakeholder Relationships*. Financial Times/Prentice Hall

Nestle. (2014). *Nestle in Society: Creating Shared Value (and Meeting Our Commitments) Summary Report 2013*. Author.

Nestle. (2014). *Nestle in Society: Creating Shared Value (and Meeting Our Commitments) Summary Report 2013*. Nestle.

Nicole, M., & Sandra, P. (2005). *FDI Impact on Growth: Spatial Evidence from China*. Academic Press.

Nicole, M., & Sandra, P. (2007). FDI in Chinese Cities: Spillovers and Impact on Growth. The World Economy Journal Compilation, 837-862.

Nielsen, L. (2009). *Global Relative Poverty*. IMF Working Paper. Office of Internal Audit and Inspection, IMF.

Nunnenkamp, P., & Stracke, R. (2007). *Foreign Direct Investment in Post-Reform India: Likely to work wonders for regional development?* Kiel Working Paper No. 1375.

Obi, A. E. (2015). Corporate social responsibility, oil exploration and the Niger Delta question. *Arabian Journal of Business and Management Review*, *4*(11), 23–34.

Odozi, V. A. (1995). *An overview of foreign investment in Nigeria 1960 – 1965*. Central Bank of Nigeria, Research Department Occasional Paper No. 11.

OECD. (2000). *Foreign direct investment, development and corporate responsibility*. Paris: OECD.

OECD. (2000). *Main determinants and impacts of foreign direct investment on China's economy*. Working papers on international investment Number 2000/4. OECD.

OECD. (2002). *Foreign direct investment for development, maximising benefits, minimizing costs*. Paris: OECD.

OECD. (2005). Guidelines on Corporate Governance of State Owned Enterprises 2005. OECD.

OECD. (2007). *Methodology For Assessing the Implementation of the OECD Principles of Corporate Governance*. OECD.

OECD. (2008). *OECD Guidelines for Multinational Enterprises*. OECD Publishing.

OECD. (2008). *The impact of foreign direct investment on wages and working conditions*. OECD-ILO conference on corporate social responsibility, Paris, France.

OECD. (2009a). *Private Sector Participation in Water Infrastructure*. Paris: OECD.

OECD. (2009b). *The Financial Crisis: Reform and Exit Strategies*. Retrieved from http://www.oecd.org/daf/ca/corporategovernanceandthefinancialcrisis.htm

OECD. (2009c). *Business Ethics and OECD Principles: What Can Be Done to Avoid Another Crisis*. OECD.

OECD. (2011). *Enhancing the Role of the Boards of Directors of State Owned Enterprises*. Retrieved from http://www.oecd.org/daf/ca/boardpracticesincentivesandgoverningrisks.htm

OECD. (2011). *OECD Guidelines for Multinational Enterprises*. OECD Publishing. 10.1787/9789264115415-en

OECD. (2012). *Strategic Transport Infrastructure Needs to 2030*. Paris: OECD.

OECD. (2014). *Guidelines On Corporate Governance Of State-Owned Enterprises*. OECD.

OECD. (2015). *Guidelines On Corporate Governance Of State-Owned Enterprises*. OECD.

OECD-ILO. (2008). *The impact of Foreign Direct Investment on Wages and Working Conditions Conference On Corporate Social Responsibility Employment and Industrial Relations: Promoting Responsible Business Conduct in a Globalizing Economy*. OECD.

Oghuma, A. (1987, December 28). Oil producing areas have turned oasis of poverty amidst sprawling wealth. *Newswatch Magazine*, 22-21.

Ojo, M. (2005). *The External Auditor's Role in Bank Regulation and Supervision: Helping the Regulator Avoid Regulatory Capture*. Paper presented at the 2006 Institute for Business and Finance Research Conference, Costa Rica.

Ojo, M. (2006). *Audit Independence: Its Importance to the External Auditor's Role in Banking Regulation and Supervision*. Paper presented at the 2006 Institute for Business and Finance Research Conference, Costa Rica.

Ojo, M. (2006). Avoiding Another Enron: The Role of the External Auditor in Financial Regulation and Supervision. In Global Auditing: Concepts and Concerns. ICFAI University Press.

Ojo, M. (2006). *The Role of External Auditors and International Accounting Bodies in Financial Regulation and Supervision*. Paper presented at the 2006 SASE (Society for the Advancement of Socio Economics) Conference in Trier.

Ojo, M. (2008). *The Role of the External Auditor in Bank and Supervision: A Comparative Analysis Between the UK, Germany, Italy and the USA* (PhD Thesis). Oxford Brookes University.

Ojo, M. (2010). The Role of the IASB and Auditing Standards in the Aftermath of the 2008/2009 Financial Crisis. European Law Journal, 16(5).

Ojo, M. (2011). *Co-operative and Competitive Enforced Self-Regulation: The Role of Governments, Private Actors and Banks in Corporate Responsibility*. Retrieved from http://mpra.ub.uni-muenchen.de/27850/1/MPRA_paper_27850.pdf

Ojo, M. (2011a). Cooperative and Competitive Enforced Self-Regulation: The Role of Governments, Private Actors and Banks in Corporate Responsibility. *Journal of Financial Regulation and Compliance, 19*(2).

Ojo, M. (2011b). Building on the trust of management: overcoming the paradoxes of principles based regulation. Law and Prosociality, 30(7).

Ojo, M. (2013). Audits, Audit Quality and Signalling Mechanisms: Concentrated Ownership Structures. *American Research Journal of Humanities and Social Sciences, 1*(2).

Ojo, M. (2013). Recovering from the Global Financial Crisis: Achieving Financial Stability in Times of Uncertainty. Business Experts Press.

Ojo, M. (2014). *Credit Risk Measurement, Leverage Ratios and Basel III*. Paper presented at the Third International Conference on Credit Analysis and Risk Management.

Ojo, M. (2014). *Why the Traditional Principal Agent Theory May No Longer Apply to Concentrated Ownership Systems and Structures*. Paper presented at the Third International Conference on Humanities, Economics and Geography, Abu Dhabi. doi:10.15208/beh.2013.16

Ojo, M. (2014b). *The Adoption of International Financial Reporting Standards and Basel III Requirements: A Justification for the Role of Audits?*. Paper presented at the International Conference on New Trends in Business, Management, and Social Sciences, Marina Bay Sands, Singapore

Ojo, M. (2014c). *Role of External Auditors in Corporate Governance and Financial Reporting: Capital and Liquidity Requirements, and the Finance Theory*. Academic Press.

Ojo, M. (2015). Audits, Audit Quality and Signaling Mechanisms: Concentrated Ownership Structures. *American Research Journal of Humanities and Social Sciences, 1*(2). Retrieved from www.arjonline.org

Ojo, M. (2015). *Regulating Self-Regulation: Audits and Accounting Mechanisms*. Science Publishing Group. Retrieved from: http://www.sciencepublishinggroup.com/book/B-978-1-940366-52-4.aspx

Ojo, M. (2015a). Implementing Basel III Through the Capital Requirements Directive (CRD) IV: Leverage Ratios and Capital Adequacy Requirements. *Journal of Business Law and Ethics, 3*(1).

Ojo, M. (2015b). *The Unintended Consequences and Challenges of the Basel III Leverage Ratio: Supplementary Leverage Ratios*. Academic Press.

Ojo, M. (2016b). *Regulating Stock Market Crashes and Information Uncertainty: A Matter of Regulatory Style and Structure?*. Forthcoming.

Ojo, M. (Forthcoming). *E Commerce As a Tool For Resource Expansion: Postal Partnerships, Data Protection Legislation and the Mitigation of Implementation Gaps*. IGI Global Publications.

Ojo, M. (2006). Avoiding Another Enron: The Role of the External Auditor in Financial Regulation and Supervision. In *Global Auditing: Concepts and Concerns*. ICFAI University Press.

Ojo, M. (2011). Cooperative and Competitive Enforced Self Regulation: The Role of Governments, Private Actors and Banks in Corporate Responsibility. *Journal of Financial Regulation and Compliance, 19*(2).

Ojo, M. (2014a). *Role of External Auditors in Corporate Governance and Financial Reporting*. Kindle Books and Amazon Publications.

Ojo, M. (2015). *Regulating Self-Regulation: Audits and Accounting Mechanisms*. Amazon Publishing.

Ojo, M. (2016a). E Commerce As a Tool For Resource Expansion: Postal Partnerships. *Data Protection Legislation and the Mitigation of Implementation Gaps. IGI Global Publications.*

Ojo, M. (forthcoming). E Commerce As a Tool For Resource Expansion: Postal Partnerships, Data Protection Legislation and the Mitigation of Implementation Gaps. *IGI Global Publications*.

Ojo, O., & Akande, O. (2014). Societal perception of the corporate social responsibility of Lafarge Cement Nigeria Plc. *Research Journal of Business Management and Accounting*, *3*(2), 13–20.

Oko, A. E. N., & Agbonifoh, B. A. (2014). Corporate social responsibility in Nigeria: A study of the petroleum industry and the Niger Delta area. *International Review of Social Sciences and Humanities*, *6*(2), 214–238.

Okpala, K. E. (2012). Adoption of the IFRS and financial statements effects: The perceived implications on FDI and global economy. *Australian Journal of Business and Management Research*, *2*(5), 76–83.

Olga, T. (2014). *Chinese foreign direct investment in Africa in corporate social responsibility context*. Working paper No.29. Maastricht School of Management.

Ong, B. K. (1987). Market Manipulation and the Securities Industry Act 1983. *The Malaysian Accountant*, *2*(4), 25–31.

Onn, F. C. (1989). *Malaysian Corporate Economy Restructuring: Progress Since 1970*. Paper presented at the Persatuan Sains Sosial Malaysia and Institut Pengajian Tinggi, Universiti Malaya jointly organized New Economic Policy and Its Future Conference, Universiti Malaya.

Onwuegbuchi, C. (2009). *Telecom operators as socially responsible organisations*. Communication Week Media Ltd.

Ordonez-Ponce, E. (2014). The Challenges from Economic to Sustainable Development: The Chilean Perspective. In G. Eweje (Ed.), *Corporate Social Responsibility and Sustainability: Emerging Trends in Developing Economies Critical Studies on Corporate Responsibility, Governance and Sustainability* (Vol. 8, pp. 45–77). Emerald Group Publishing Ltd.

Osemene, O. F. (2012). Corporate social responsibility practices in mobile telecommunications industry in Nigeria. *European Journal of Business and Management*, *4*(8), 149–157.

Otepola, A. (2002). *Foreign direct investment as a factor of economic growth in Nigeria.* Dakar, Senegal: IDEP.

Otero, J., & Manuel, R. (2006). Inflation Before and After Central Bank Independence: The Case of Colombia. *Journal of Development Economics, Elsevier, 79*(1), 168–182. doi:10.1016/j.jdeveco.2004.12.005

Parisi, F. (2004). The Efficiency of the Common Law Hypothesis. In The Encyclopedia of Public Choice (pp. 519-522). Academic Press.

Parker, W. C. Jr. (1973). *Communications and the May 13th Crisis: A Psychocultural Interpretation.* Kuala Lumpur: University Malaya Press.

Parry, I. W. H. (2011). How Much Should Highway Fuels Be Taxed? In U.S. Energy Tax Policy. Cambridge, UK: Cambridge University Press.

Parry, I. W. H., & Strand, J. (2011). *International Fuel Tax Assessment: An Application to Chile.* IMF Working Paper No. 11/168. Washington, DC: International Monetary Fund. Available at http://www.imf.org/external/pubs/ft/wp/2011/wp11168.pdf

Parry, I. W. H., & Small, K. A. (2005). Does Britain or the United States Have the Right Gasoline Tax? *The American Economic Review, 95*(4), 1276–1289. doi:10.1257/0002828054825510

PCAOB. (2013). *Proposed 2014 Budget and Strategic Plan: Expansion of Consulting Practice and Other Non Audit Businesses.* PCAOB.

Peng, K. K. (1979). *Dependence and the Malaysian Economy.* (Unpublished Master Thesis). Universiti Sains Malaysia.

Peng, O. C. (1989). *Auditor's Report - Where Lies its Values?* Paper presented at the MIA and MACPA jointly organised 5th National Accountants Conference, Kuala Lumpur.

Peng, K. K. (1983). *The Malaysian Economy.* Kuala Lumpur: Sdn. Bhd.

Pepper v Hart [1992] 3 WLR 1032, [1993] 1 All ER 42, HL (E)

Phenix, P. (1986, April). Directors, Shareholders and Auditors Under the Companies Act 1965 - As Amended. The Malaysian Accountant, 7-16.

Pierce, B., & Kilcommins, M. (1996). *The Audit Expectation Gap: The Role of Auditing Education.* DCUBS Research Paper Series, No. 13. DCUBS Dublin. Available at: http://www.dcu.ie/dcubs/research_papers/index.shtml

Pillai, P. N. (1984). *Companies and Securities Handbook - Singapore & Malaysia.* Singapore: Butterworths.

Pinkston, T. S., & Carroll, A. B. (1996). A Retrospective Examination of CSR Orientations: Have They Changed? *Journal of Business Ethics, 15*(2), 199–206.

Pirnea, I. C., Olaru, M., & Moisa, C. (2011). Relationship between corporate social responsibility and social sustainability. *Economy Transdisciplinary Cognition, 14*(1), 36–43.

Porter, B., & Gowthorpe, C. (2001). *The Audit Expectation-Performance Gap: Some New Evidence from the United Kingdom.* Paper presented at the National Auditing Conference, Leicester, UK.

Porter, B. (1993). An Empirical Study of the Audit Expectation-Performance Gap. *Accounting and Business Review, 24*(93), 49–68. doi:10.1080/00014788.1993.9729463

Porter, B., Simon, J., & Hatherly, D. (2005). *Principles of External Auditing.* John Wiley & Sons, Ltd.

Porter, M. E., & Kramer, M. R. (2002). The competitive advantages of corporate philanthropy. *Harvard Business Review*, *80*(12), 56–68. PMID:12510538

Porter, M. E., & Kramer, M. R. (2006). Strategy and society:The link between competitive advantage and corporate social responsibility. *Harvard Business Review*, *84*(12), 78–92. PMID:17183795

Posner, R. A. (2005). Hayek, Law, and Cognition. *New York University Journal of Law and Liberty, 147.*

Posner, R. A. (1974, Autumn). Theories of Economic Regulation. *The Bell Journal of Economics and Management Science*, *5*(2), 335–358. doi:10.2307/3003113

Posner, R. A. (2001). *Kelsen*. Hayek, and the Economic Analysis of Law.

Posner, R. A. (2003). *Kelsen versus Hayek: Pragmatism, Economics and Democracy. In Law, Pragmatism, and Democracy*. Cambridge, MA: Harvard University Press.

Posner, R. A. (2013). *Reflections on Judging*. Cambridge, MA: Harvard University Press.

Power, M. (1993). *The Politics of Financial Auditing*. Oxford, UK: The Political Quarterly Publishing Co. Ltd.

Power, M. (1997). *The Audit Society*. Oxford, UK: University Press.

Prahalad, C. K. (2002). Serving the world's poor profitably. *Harvard Business Review*, *9*(48). PMID:12227146

Priest, G. L. (1977). The Common Law Process and the Selection for Efficient Rules. *The Journal of Legal Studies*, *6*(1), 65–82. doi:10.1086/467563

Prieto-Carron, M., Lund-Thomsen, P., Chan, A., & Bhushan, C. (2006). Critical Perspectives on CSR and Development: What We Know, What We Don't Know and What We Need to Know. *International Affairs*, *82*(5), 977–987.

Puthucheary, J. (1960). *Ownership and Control in the Malayan Economy*. Eastern Universities Press Ltd.

Ram, G. S. (1985). *Criminal Law and Commercial Crimes*. Paper presented at the HRM Fighting Financial Fraud, Kuala Lumpur.

Redha, A. (1985). *Capital Accumulation and the State in Malaysia. Ilmu Masyarakat, 8,*1–27.

Reeves, J. E. (2012). *Six Reasons Companies Should Embrace CSR.* Retrieved from http://www.forbes.com/sites/csr/2012/02/21/six-reasons-companies-should-embrace-csr/

Report by the Secretary-General in Pursuance of the Resolution Adopted by the Security Council at its 1049th Meeting on 31 July 1963 (S15380), U.N. Doc. No. S/5448, at 4 (1963).

Reputation and Reciprocal Conformism Securities and Exchange Commission. (2002). *Study Pursuant to Section 108(d) of the Sarbanes-Oxley Act of 2002 on the Adoption by the United States Financial Reporting System of a Principles-Based Accounting System.* SEC.

Restoy, F. (2016). The Organisation of Financial Supervision. Speech by Mr Fernando Restoy, Deputy Governor of the Bank of Spain, participating in the presentation of the "Guide to the Spanish Financial System" (Guía del Sistema Financiero Español), compiled by AFI (Analistas Financieros Internacionales) and sponsored by Funcas (Fundación de las Cajas de Ahorros), Madrid, Spain.

Rodriguez, P., Siegel, Hillman, & Eden. (2006). *Three Lenses on the Multinational Enterprise: Politics, Corruption, and Corporate Social Responsibility*. Number 0608.

Rohwer, J. (1995). *Asia Rising: How History's Biggest Middle Class Will Change the World.* Singapore: Butterworth Heinemann Asia.

Rosenzweig, P. M., & Singh, J. V. (1991). Organizational environments and the multinational enterprise. *Academy of Management Review*, *16*(2), 340.

Rubin, P. H. (1977). Why is Common Law Efficient? *The Journal of Legal Studies, 6*(1), 51-63. Retrieved from http://www.jstor.org/stable/724189

Russell, G. (1986). All Eyes on Accountants. *Time*, *21*(April), 58.

Sacconi, L. (2004). *Corporate Social Responsibility (CSR) as a Model of 'Extended' Corporate Governance: An Explanation Based on the Economic Theories of Social Contract*. Reputation and Reciprocal Conformism.

Sacconi. (2004). *Corporate Social Responsibility (CSR) as a Model of 'Extended' Corporate Governance: An Explanation Based on the Economic Theories of Social Contract, Reputation and Reciprocal Conformism.* Author.

Sacconi, L. (2004). *Corporate Social Responsibility (CSR) as a Model of 'Extended' Corporate Governance: An Explanation Based on the Economic Theories of Social Contract*. Academic Press.

Sakagami, M., Yoshimi, H., & Okano, H. (1999). Japanese Accounting Profession in Transition. *Accounting, Auditing & Accountability Journal*, *12*(3), 340–357. doi:10.1108/09513579910277401

Sala-i-Martin, X., & Pinkovskiy, M. (2010). African poverty is falling... much faster than you think! National Bureau of Economic Research.

Samuels, J. M., & Piper, A. G. (1985). *International Accounting: A Survey*. London: Croom Helm.

Sarbanes-Oxley Act of 2002

Saruwatari, K. (1991). Malaysia's Localization Policy and its Impact on British-Owned Enterprises. *The Developing Economies*, *24*(4), 371–386.

Satyendra. (2014). *Corporate Social Responsibility*. Retrieved from http://ispatguru.com/corporate-social-responsibility

Schlossstein, S. (1991). *Asia's New Little Dragons: The Dynamic Emergence of Indonesia, Thailand and Malaysia.* Chicago: Contemporary Books.

Schoors, K. & Van der Tol, B. (2002). *The productivity effect of foreign ownership on domestic firms in Hungary.* EEA Venice Conference Paper.

Schrader, D. E. (1987). The corporation and profits. *Journal of Business Ethics*, *6*(8), 589–601. doi:10.1007/BF00705775

Schwab, S. (2013). *Why countries say they impose barriers to FDI in foreign direct investment as a key driver for trade, growth and prosperity: The case for a multilateral agreement on investment.* World Economic Forum, Geneva, Switzerland.

Schwartz, M. S., & Carroll, A. B. (2003). Corporate social responsibility: A three-domain approach. *Business Ethics Quarterly*, *13*(4), 503–530. doi:10.5840/beq200313435

SEC v Texas Gulf Sulphur Co, 401 F.2d 833 (2d Cir 1968) (en banc), cert denied, 404 U.S 1005 (1971).

Seidler, L. J. (1967). *The Function of Accounting in Economic Development - Turkey as a Case Study.* London: Frederick and Prager Publishers.

Sen, J., & Pal, D. P. (2005). On Infrastructure and Economic Development. *Artha Vijnana*, *47*(1-2), 87–98.

Settles, A. M. (2009). Corporate Social Responsibility Impact on Foreign Direct Investment Practices of Russian Multinational Corporations: Do MNCs with Better CSR Practices Have Lower Cost of OFDI? An Examination of Recent Acquisitions. In *Proceedings of the X International Conference on Economic and Social Development*. State University – Higher School of Economics.

Shafi, M. (2014). Relationship between FDI inflows and economic growth: A review. *Singaporean Journal of Business Economics and Management Studies*, *2*(9), 67–77. doi:10.12816/0003906

Shearman & Sterling LLP. (2014). *Enhanced Leverage Ratios for UK Financial Institutions*. Author.

Shing, G. Y. Y. (1981). The Audit License. *The Malaysian Accountant*, *2*(2), 32–33.

Siang, L. K. (1982). *Malaysia in the Dangerous 80s*. Petaling Jaya: Democratic Action Party.

Siang, L. K. (1986). *Malaysia: The Crisis of Identity*. Petaling Jaya: Democratic Action Party.

Sikka, P., Puxty, A., Willmott, H., & Cooper, C. (1998). The Impossibility of Eliminating the Expectation Gap: Some Theory and Evidence. *Critical Perspectives on Accounting*, *9*(3), 299330. doi:10.1006/cpac.1997.0159

Sikka, P., Willmott, H. C., & Lowe, T. (1989). Guardians of Knowledge and Public Interest: Evidence and Issues of Accountability in the UK Accountancy Profession. *Accounting, Auditing & Accountability Journal*, *2*(2), 47–71. doi:10.1108/09513578910132286

Singh, K. (2005). *Foreign direct investment in India: A critical Analysis of FDI from 1991-2005*. Available at SSRN 822584

Social Responsibility. (n.d.). In *Infosys*. Retrieved from https://www.infosys.com/investors/corporate-governance/Pages/social-responsibility.aspx

Soon, L. Y. (2004). *Foreign direct investment in ASEAN*. Malaysian Economic Association.

Spence, C., Husillos, J., & Correa-Ruiz, C. (2010). Cargo cult science and the death of politics: A critical review of social and environmental accounting research. *Critical Perspectives on Accounting*, *21*(1), 76–89. doi:10.1016/j.cpa.2008.09.008

Sprinkle, G. B., & Maines, L. A. (2010). The benefits and costs of corporate social responsibility. *Business Horizons*, *53*(5), 445–453.

Spulber, D. (2014). *The Innovative Entrepreneur New York and Cambridge*. Cambridge University Press.

Spulber, D. (2014). *The Innovative Entrepreneur*. New York: Cambridge University Press. doi:10.1017/CBO9781107239012

Steinberg, R. B., & Walker, D. E. (1997). The AICPA National Conference on SEC Developments. *The CPA Journal, 47*.

Stephanie, W. (2015). Corporate social responsibility reporting platforms: Enabling transparency for accountability. *Information Technology Management*, *2*(16), 19–35.

Stephenson, S., & Dadush, U. (2013). *The current (fragmented) governance of FDI in foreign direct investment as a key driver for trade, growth and prosperity: The case for a multilateral agreement on investment.* World Economic Forum, Geneva, Switzerland.

Stringham, E. (2001). Kaldor-Hicks Efficiency and the Problem of Central Planning. *Quarterly Journal of Austrian Economics*, *4*(2).

Styles, S. C. (1994, Spring). The Rule of Parliament: Statutory Interpretation After Pepper v Hart. *Oxford Journal of Legal Studies*, *14*(1), 151–158. doi:10.1093/ojls/14.1.151

Sum, H. L. C., & Wishart, D. A. (1989). Commercial Law. In A. Krishnan (Ed.), *Survey of Malaysian Law* (pp. 113–124). Kuala Lumpur: Malayan Law Journal Sdn. Bhd.

Susela, S. D. (1999). 'Interests' and Accounting Standard Setting in Malaysia. *Accounting, Auditing & Accountability Journal, 12*(3), 357–387. doi:10.1108/09513579910277410

Sustainability. (n.d.). In *Hewlett Packard*. Retrieved from http://www8.hp.com/us/en/hp-information/global-citizenship/index.html

Swanson, D. L. (1995). Addressing a theoretical problem by reorienting the corporate social performance model. *Academy of Management Review, 20*(1), 43–63.

Syed, H. A. (1984). Social Relations: The Ethnic and Class Factors. In H. A. Syed (Ed.), *Ethnicity, Class and Development in Malaysia* (pp. 13–31). Kuala Lumpur: Malaysian Science Social Association.

Tawade, P. H. (2013). Corporate social responsibility and FDI in India. *Golden Research Thoughts, 2*(10), 1–4.

Tay, J. S. W. (1994). Malaysia. In T. E. Cooke & R. H. Parker (Eds.), *Financial Reporting in the West Pacific Rim* (pp. 231–264). London: Routledge.

Teik, G. C. (1971). The May Thirteenth Incident and Democracy in Malaysia. Oxford University Press.

The Estate of Edgar A. Berg v. Commissioner (T. C. Memo 1991279).

Timokhina, O. (2014). *Chinese Foreign Direct Investment in Africa in Corporate Social Responsibility Context.* Maastricht School of Management Working Paper No. 2014/29.

Tinker, A. M. (1980). Towards a Political Economy of Accounting: An Empirical Illustration of the Cambridge Controversies. *Accounting, Organizations and Society, 5*(1), 147–160. doi:10.1016/0361-3682(80)90031-8

Tirole, J. (1989). Network externalities, standardization and compatibility. In *The theory of industrial organization.* MIT Press.

Tong, T. L., & Ann, C. T. (1996, April). Non-Disclosure in the Abridged Profit and Loss Accounts of Malaysian Listed Corporations. The Malaysian Accountant, 2-5.

Tong, T. L., Zainal, A. K., & Wah, C. P. (1989). *Information Needs of Users and Voluntary Disclosure Practices of Malaysian Listed Corporations*. Paper presented at the International Accounting Seminar on Accounting Trends, Issues and Challenges, Universiti Pertanian Malaysia.

Toppinen, A., Zhang, Y., Hansen, E., Kurki, K. & Li, N. (2014). Role of Corporate Responsibility: Insights From Three Forest Industry Multinationals Investing in China. *Journal of Small Business Management.*

Toppinen, A., Zhang, Y., Hansen, E., Kurki, K., & Li, N. (2014). Role of Corporate Responsibility: Insights From Three Forest Industry Multinationals Investing in China. *Journal of Small Business Management.*

Treisman, D. (2003). Cardoso, Menem, Machiavelli: Political Tactics and Privatisation in Latin America. *Studies in Comparative International Development, 38*(3), 93–109. doi:10.1007/BF02686201

Tsamenyi, M., & Uddin, S. (2008). *Corporate governance in less developed and emerging economies*. Bingley: JAI Press. doi:10.1016/S1479-3563(08)08018-3

Turner, L. (2006, March). In the Public Interest: Regulating with a Customer Focus. *The CPA Journal*. Available online at http://www.cpajournal.com/

Uddin, M. B., Hassan, M. R., & Tarique, K. M. (2008). *Three dimensional aspects of corporate social responsibility.* Daffodil International University. *Journal of Business and Economics*, *3*(1).

UNCTAD. (1999). *Trends in international investment agreements: An Overview*. UNCTAD.

UNCTAD. (2003). *Dispute Settlement: World Trade Organization, Anti-Dumping Measures*. New York: United Nations Publications.

UNCTAD. (2005). *Economic development in Africa: Rethinking the role of foreign direct investment*. Geneva: United Nations Conference on Trade and Development.

UNCTAD. (2009). *The Role of International Investment Agreements in Attracting Foreign Direct Investment to Developing Countries*. New York: United Nations.

UNCTAD. (2010). *Most-Favoured-Nation Treatment*. New York: United Nations.

UNCTAD. (2011a). *Local Production of Pharmaceuticals and Related Technology Transfer: A Series of Case Studies by the UNCTAD Secretariat*. New York: United Nations.

UNCTAD. (2011b). *Foreign Direct Investment in LDCs: Lessons Learned from the Decade 2001–2010 and the Way Forward*. New York: United Nations.

UNCTAD. (2011c). *Investment and Enterprise Responsibility Review*. New York: United Nations.

UNCTAD. (2011d). *Development-led globalization: Towards sustainable and inclusive development paths. Report of the Secretary-General of UNCTAD to UNCTAD XIII*. United Nations.

UNCTAD. (2012). *Investment Policy Framework for Sustainable Development: Towards a New Generation of Investment Policies (IPFSD)*. New York: United Nations.

UNCTAD. (2012). *World Investment Report 2012: Towards a new generation of investment policies*. Geneva: United Nations.

UNCTAD. (2013a). *Investment Policy Review: Bangladesh*. New York: United Nations.

UNCTAD. (2013b). *Economic Development in Africa Report 2013: Intra-African Trade – Unlocking Private Sector Dynamism*. New York: United Nations.

UNCTAD. (2013c). *The Least Development Countries Report 2013: Growth with Employment for Inclusive and Sustainable Development*. New York: United Nations.

UNCTAD. (2014). *Investing in the SDGs: An Action Plan*. UNCTAD.

UNCTAD. (2014). *Investing in the SDGs: An action plan*. United Nations.

UNCTAD. (2014). *Skill Development in the Bangladesh Garments Industry: the Role of TNCs*. New York: United Nations.

UNCTAD. (2014). *World Investment Report 2014: Investing in the SDGs, An Action Plan*. UNCTAD.

UNCTAD. (2014). World Investment Report 2014: Investing in the SDGs: An Action Plan. United Nations.

Utting, P. (2000). *Business Responsibility for Sustainable Development*. Geneva 2000 Occasional Paper No. 2. United Nations Research Institute for Social Development (UNRISD).

Utting, P. (2003). Promoting Development through corporate social responsibility – Prospects and limitations. *Global Future*, 11-13.

Utting, P. (2005). Corporate responsibility and the movement of business. *Development in Practice, 14*(3&4), 375–388. doi:10.1080/09614520500075797

Utusan Malaysia. (2004, September 9). *MEF: Sistem Pendidikan Negara Gagal*. Author.

Uwe, W. (2002). Innovation, Foreign Direct Investment and Growth. *Economica, 64*, 63–79.

Vincent, P., & Andrea, A. (2004). *Private sector development*. World Bank Group Vice President note 273.

Visser, W. (2008). Corporate social responsibility in developing countries. In The Oxford handbook of corporate social responsibility. Oxford, UK: Oxford University Press.

Visser, W. (2008). *CSR 2.0 – the new era of Corporate Sustainability and Responsibility*. CSR Inspiration Series, No.1.

Visser, W. (2010a). *CSR 2.0: The future of corporate social responsibility*. Retrieved from www.csrinternational.org

Visser, W. (2010b). The evolution and revolution of corporate social responsibility. In Responsible business: How to manage a CSR strategy successfully. CSR 2.0.

Visser, W. (2006). *Revisiting Carroll's CSR Pyramid An African Perspective*. Academic Press.

Visser, W. (2006). Revisiting Carroll's CSR pyramid: An African perspective. In E. R. Pedersen & M. Hunicke (Eds.), *Corporate citizenship in developing countries: New partnership perspectives* (pp. 29–56). Copenhagen: Copenhagen Business School Press.

Visser, W. (2008). Corporate Social responsibility in Developing Countries. In A. Crane, A. McWilliams, D. Matten, J. Moon, & D. Siegel (Eds.), *The Oxford Handbook of Corporate Social Responsibility* (pp. 473–479). Oxford, UK: Oxford University Press.

Visser, W., Matten, D., Pohl, M., & Tolhurst, N. (2007). *The A to Z of corporate social responsibility*. London: Wiley.

Vreeland, N., Dana, G. B., Hurwitz, G. B., Just, P., Moeller, P. V., & Shinn, R. S. (1976). *Area Handbook for Malaysia* (3rd ed.). Washington, DC: U.S. Government Printing Office.

Wa, J., & Selva, M. (1993). *The Audit Expectation Gap in Hong Kong*. Paper presented to Fifth Annual Conference of Accounting Academics, Hong Kong.

Wai, T. T. (1982). *Income Distribution and Determination in West Malaysia*. Oxford University Press.

Waldman, D. A., & Siegel, D. (2008). Defining the socially responsible leader. *The Leadership Quarterly, 19*(1), 117–131.

Walton, P. (1986). The Export of British Accounting Legislation to Commonwealth Countries. *Accounting and Business Review, 16*(64), 353–357.

Wan, X. (2010). A Literature Review on the Relationship between Foreign Direct Investment and Economic Growth. *International Business Research, 3*(1).

Wang, Y. (2013). *Why countries constrain FDI: The political economy of asymmetry in foreign direct investment as a key driver for trade, growth and prosperity: The case for a multilateral agreement on investment*. World Economic Forum, Geneva, Switzerland.

Wang, J. Y., & Blomstrom, M. (1992). Foreign Investment and Technology Transfer: A Simple Model. *European Economic Review*, 36.

Wei, Y. (2013). *The effect of FDI on employment in China*. Graduate Theses and Dissertations. Paper 13379.

Wen, M. (2003). FDI, Regional Geographical and Market Conditions, and Regional Development: A Panel Study on China. Division of Economics. *RSPAS, ANU, 15*(7), 1–28.

Whalley, J., & Xian, X. (2006). *China's FDI and Non-FDI Economies and the Sustainability of Future High Chinese Growth*. National Bureau Economics Research Working Papers.

Whitman, D. G. (2000, June). Evolution of the Common Law and the Emergence of Compromise. *The Journal of Legal Studies, 29*.

Willmott, H. C. (1985). Setting Accounting Standards in the UK: The Emergence of Private Accounting Bodies and Their Role in the Regulation of Public Accounting Practice. In W. Streeck & P. Schmitter (Eds.), *Private Interest Government: Beyond Market and State*. London: Sage.

Willmott, H. C. (1991). The Auditing Game: A Question of Ownership and Control. *Critical Perspectives on Accounting, 2*(1), 109–121. doi:10.1016/1045-2354(91)90021-5

Woolf, E. (1985, April). We Must Stern the Tide of Litigation. The Accountant, 1819.

Woon, T. K. (1982). The Role of the Malaysian State in the Restructuring of Employment. Jurnal Ekonomi Malaysia, 6, 32-62.

Woon, T. K., & Kam, W. P. (1989). *Restructuring of Employment*. Paper presented at the Persatuan Sains Sosial Malaysia organised National Economic Policy and Its Future seminar, Kuala Lumpur.

Wooster, R. B., & Diebel, D. S. (2010). Productivity spillovers from foreign direct investment in developing countries: A meta-regression analysis. *Review of Development Economics, 14*(3), 640–655. doi:10.1111/j.1467-9361.2010.00579.x

World Bank. (2002). *Engaging the Private Sector in Forest Sector Development*. Retrieved from http://siteresources.worldbank.org/EXTFORSOUBOOK/Resources/02-FSB-Ch02.pdf

World Bank. (2013). *How We Classify Countries*. Retrieved from http://data.worldbank.org/about/country-and-lending-groups

World Economic Forum. (2013). *Foreign direct investment as a key driver for trade, growth and prosperity: The case for a multilateral agreement on investment*. World Economic Forum, Geneva, Switzerland.

Yan, L. S. (1994). The Malaysian Economy, 1957-91: An Overview. In National Institute of Public Administration Malaysia (Ed.), Malaysian Development Experience: Changes and Challenges. INTAN.

Yasheng, H. (2006). *Foreign Direct Investment (FDI) in China: Why Surging Levels of FDI May Indicate Serious Economic Problems*. Academic Press.

Yoshimi, H. (n.d.). *Audit Expectation Gap in Japan: A Comparative Analysis with Britain*. Discussion Paper Series A, No.28. Faculty of Economics, Hokkaido University.

Yun, H. A. (1984). Capitalist Development, Class and Race. In H. A. Syed (Ed.), *Ethnicity, Class and Development in Malaysia* (pp. 296–328). Kuala Lumpur: Malaysian Science Social Association.

Zabbey, N. (2009). *Pollution and poverty in the Niger Delta region-What is the responsibility of oil companies in Nigeria*. Paper Presented at the University of Stavenger.

Zaheer, S. (1995). Overcoming the liability of foreignness. *Academy of Management Journal, 38*(2), 341–363. doi:10.2307/256683

Zainal-Aznam, Y. (1994). Growth and Equity in Malaysia. In National Institute of Public Administration Malaysia (Ed.), Malaysian Development Experience: Changes and Challenges. INTAN.

Zainal-Aznam, Y. (1991). Distributional Policies and Programmes: The Malaysian Experience. In L. K. Hock & S. Nagaraj (Eds.), *The Malaysian Economy Beyond 1990: International and Domestic Perspectives* (pp. 343–379). Persatuan Ekonomi Malaysia, Kuala Lumpur.

Zhang, K. (2001). How Does FDI Affect Economic Growth in China? *Economics of Transition*, 1-23.

Zhang, K. (n.d.). *Foreign Direct Investment and Economic Growth in China: A Panel Data Study For 1992 -2004.* Academic Press.

Zhang, K.H. (2001). Does foreign direct investment promote economic growth? Evidence from East Asia and Latin America. *Contemporary Economic Policy*, *19* (2), 175 – 185.

Zhang. (2006). *Foreign Direct Investment and Economic Growth in China.* WTO China and Asian Economics held at International University of Business and Economics (UIBC), Beijing, China.

Zywicki, T. J., & Sanders, A. B. (2008, February). Posner, Hayek & the Economic Analysis of Law. *Iowa Law Review*, *93*(2), 559–603.

About the Contributors

Marianne Ojo has published a total of more than 80 internationally peer-reviewed books, ISI accredited journal articles, book chapters and conference proceedings papers. She currently works as Visiting Professor, post-doctoral researcher as well as university lecturer and Visiting Scholar at North West University. She is currently also engaged in several projects at affiliated universities in the United States as well as supervision of graduate and non-graduate students. Furthermore, she serves as a reviewer for various scientific and academic journals which have been accredited with highest credentials at international level. Her previous academic commitments include Insolvency and Research work at LTB, Frankfurt, Research Fellow at the Center for European Law, University of Bremen (2007 – 2010), Teaching Associate and Graduate Teaching Assistant at Oxford Brookes University (2004 – 2007). She has also collaborated with several other authors as well as contributed in several consultation and academic exercises with the Bank for International Settlements.

* * *

Azham Md Ali is a Professor of Accounting and Finance, currently at the Universiti Pendidikan Sultan Idris. His main areas of specialization include accounting, auditing, governance and political economy. Amongst his collaborative publications are: Audit Challenges in Malaysia Today, The Audit Expectations Gap in Malaysia: An Investigation into Causes and Remedies.

Olusegun Felix Ayadi received the Doctor of Philosophy (PhD) degree in Finance from The University of Mississippi. He is currently the J.P. Morgan Chase Endowed Chair and Professor of Finance, at the Jesse H. Jones School of Business, Texas Southern University, Houston, Texas, USA. He teaches finance courses to both graduate and undergraduate students. He was a Fulbright Scholar in the College of Business and Social Sciences at Covenant University in Nigeria from January 2012 through August 2012. Professor Ayadi has published over sixty-five refereed articles in several academic journals including: Journal of Banking and Finance; Global Finance Journal; Journal of Multinational Financial Management; The International Journal of Finance; International Review of Financial Analysis; Journal of Emerging Markets; Journal of Asian and African Studies; and OPEC Review.dit

Jose DeLarosiere, studied Economics as a major for his undergraduate studies – as well as completed his postgraduate universities in Brazil. Having worked as a lecturer for several years in the Faculty of Social Sciences in Rio de Janeiro, he decided to further his career in the area of Financial Economics – with a focus on the stock markets and government regulation and policies. He is also particularly interested in research related to the BRICS economies – as well as the impact of regulatory and economic reforms and policies on emerging economies.

Maria DiGabriele currently works as an Associate Professor at the New York University. Having published various articles in Financial and Legal related disciplines, she hopes to consolidate on previous and current publications.

Genevieve Dupont is currently working as a lecturer and hopes to consolidate on her teaching with research publications in internationally accredited and peer reviewed journals. She is involved in several charity and humanitarian projects which are dedicated towards causes of alleviating poverty – in collaboration with organizations such as UNICEF and the International Monetary Fund (IMF). She is also involved in economic and environmental awareness programs which are targeted towards the reduction of carbon emissions, greater use of renewable energy resources and investigating the impact of fossil fuels and energy generating resources on the environment – in addition to their financial and economic influences. She is a huge fan of American literature – in particular, Harper Lee and was inspired to work on her current projects after having visited magnificent wildlife and safari reserves in which she experienced life enduring memories of wonderful sunsets and the nature and wildlife in places such as Kenya, South Africa and Costa Rica. Her future projects, collaborations and forthcoming publications include: "To Whom Much is Given: Environmental and Economic Impacts of Nuclear Energy Projects", "Cost Effectiveness and Cost Cutting Policies: Dealing with Financial Consequences of Declining Global Oil prices". Naturally her favorite Quote: "With Great Power Comes Great Responsibility."

Jon Edwards is currently working as a Visiting Scholar at Goethe University, Frankfurt am Main, 60323, Frankfurt. He also hopes to consolidate on his publications - particularly in relation to global and financial markets.

Teck Heang Lee is a senior lecturer at the Faculty of Accountancy and Management, Tunku Abdul Rahman University (UTAR). His notable collaborations with Azham Ali include: Quality in Qualitative Studies: The Case of Validity, Reliability and Generalizability, The Evolution of Auditing: An Analysis of the Historical Development, Towards an Understanding of the Audit Expectation Gap, The Audit Expectation Gap: A Review of the Contributing Factors, The Evolving Role of Auditors: Where Do We Go From Here?, Towards Reducing Audit Expectations Gap: Possible Mission, A Study of Auditors' Responsibility for Fraud Detection in Malaysia. His areas of specialization focus on audit expectations gap, internal audit and history of auditing.

Rosli Mohamad is an accountancy lecturer at the Universiti Utara Malaysia, College of Business. His areas of specialization include Accounting Information Systems, E Commerce, E Business, Information Technology in Small Medium Enterprises. Publications include: Electronic Commerce Adoption in SMEs: The Trend of Prior Studies, Malaysian Corporate Website: A Survey of Web Characteristics, A Comparative Study of E Commerce Degree Programs in the US, UK, Australia and Selected Asian Countries.

Sarah Newton graduated with a BSc in Accounting and a Master's degree in Economics, and wishes to consolidate on her PhD, with legal - as well as financial related research. She has worked as a lecturer and Visiting Scholar at several universities in the United Kingdom and hopes that greater focus on the research aspect of her work will broaden horizons and career possibilities globally.

James O. Odia (PhD) is a Senior Lecturer in the Department of Accounting in the University of Benin, Benin City where he lectures both undergraduate and post - graduate students. His current research interests include: Corporate Sustainability Practices and Strategy Management by firms.

Chandra Sekhar Patro is currently pursuing his Ph.D in Commerce and Management Studies from Andhra University. He has post-graduate degree in Master of Commerce (M.Com.) from Andhra University, Master in Financial Management (MFM) from Pondicherry University, and also MBA (HR & Finance) from JNT University. Mr. Patro has over 9 years of teaching experience in higher education. Mr. Patro has gained very good knowledge in Human Resource Management and Accountancy/Finance subjects. He has published number of research papers in reputed National and International Journals and also presented papers in National and International Conferences.

Kamakula Madhu Kishore Raghunath is presently working as Assistant Professor in the Department of Management Studies at GVP College of Engineering (Autonomous). He has a Post-graduate degree in Management with Finance and Marketing specializations from Jawaharlal Nehru Technological University. Mr. Madhu is a SET qualified faculty with over four years of teaching experience in higher education. Mr. Madhu has good knowledge in Finance and Marketing subjects. His research interests include Supply Chain Management, Marketing, and Finance topics.

James Rossi is a Senior Lecturer at University of Greenwich. Having studied economics - with a focus on lecturing and teaching, the author would like to consolidate on publications relating to the field of law and economics - as well as legal related research. Further, as evidenced through this contribution, the important links between accounting, economics, and law - as illustrated by the impact of IFRS adoption globally, and their relevance in financial capital markets, it is hoped, will be emphasized. His forthcoming publications include: "Taxes, Consumer Spending, Manufacturing and Infrastructure: The Real Price of Investment", "Preserving Natural Habitats and Heritages: Economic Rewards in Investments", "Matters of National Interest and Security: Trade and Foreign Direct Investment", and "Powerful Trade Partners and the Economics of Poverty: Investing in the Future". His principal interests and hobbies includes listening to classical music, playing the piano – as well as other instruments.

Marta Vidal, BSc and MBA from ESADE Business School, is a PhD student in Management at Complutense University and Assistant Professor of Management at European University of Madrid.

Javier Vidal-García is Assistant Professor of Finance at University of Valladolid, Spain. He has a BSc in Management from Queen´s University Belfast, MSc in Finance from Aston Business School, MA in Economics from Autonomous University of Madrid, Phd in Financial Economics from Complutense University of Madrid and has been postdoctoral fellow at the Harvard Business School.

Nor Zalina Mohamad Yusof is also a lecturer at the Universiti Utara Malaysia School of Accountancy Malaysia. Her publications include: Corporate Governance and Audit Report Lag in Malaysia, The Malaysian Market for Audit Services: Ethnicity, Multinational Companies and Auditor Choices, Financial Restatements and Corporate Governance among Malaysian Listed Companies, The Provision of Non Audit Services, Audit Fees and Auditor Independence.

Index

F

G

H

I

J

L

M

N

P

R

S

T

U

V

W

www.ingramcontent.com/pod-product-compliance
Lightning Source LLC
LaVergne TN
LVHW060420300926
849162LV00006B/1476